The
Indian
Rights
Association

THE
INDIAN
RIGHTS
ASSOCIATION

The Herbert Welsh Years
1882–1904

WILLIAM T. HAGAN

The University of Arizona Press
Tucson, Arizona

About the Author

WILLIAM T. HAGAN has studied and written about Indian history and federal Indian policy for more than thirty years. Since 1969 he has been Distinguished Professor of History at the State University of New York, College at Fredonia. Among his many books and articles are *Indian Police and Judges* and *United States-Comanche Relations*. Hagan has held numerous academic consulting and editorial positions, including membership since 1972 on the Advisory Committee for the Newberry Library's Center for the History of the American Indian.

Publication of this book is made possible in part by a grant from the Publications Program of the National Endowment for the Humanities.

THE UNIVERSITY OF ARIZONA PRESS

The book was set in 10/12 VIP Baskerville.
Manufactured in the U.S.A.

Library of Congress Cataloging in Publication Data

Hagan, William Thomas.
    The Indian Rights Association.

    Bibliography: p.
    Includes index.
    1. Indian Rights Association—History—19th century.
2. Welsh, Herbert, 1851-1941.   3. Indians of North
America—Government relations—1869-1934.   4. Indians of
America—Land tenure.   I. Title.
E93.H224   1985   322.1'197'073   84-22774

ISBN 0-8165-0879-8

To John P. Saulitis
and the staff of Daniel Reed Library,
whose cooperation made this book possible

Contents

ILLUSTRATIONS

❖ ❖ ❖

Preface

In December 1983 the Indian Rights Association celebrated a centennial of service to Native Americans. In that century its perceptions of
Indian needs underwent inevitable changes. In 1882 the founders of
the IRA, together with other friends of the Indian, had no doubt that
total assimilation was the prescription for Native American survival
and happiness. In contrast, a hundred years later the association has as
one of its major projects the support of Indian groups seeking federal
recognition and resumption —or for many eastern tribes acquisition
for the first time —of the status of wards of the federal government.
This position constitutes a one-hundred-and-eighty-degree change of
course. However, the record of the IRA simply reflects the rethinking
that has taken place not only among the freinds of the Indian but in the
ranks of members of the executive and legislative branches of government. Instead of preaching assimilation, federal officials today pay lip
service to self-determination: the right of the Indian to live as a
member of a tribe, free of federal control, yet continuing to enjoy
federal financial support. What has not changed is the IRA's devotion
to what it considers the Indian's best interest. And, unlike the pater-
nalism of the early years of the association, today IRA policy is set by
Native Americans working easily with the descendants of Philadelphia's founders of the organization.

   This study is restricted to the early years of the IRA, 1882 to 1904.
That period saw it founded and reach its period of greatest influence
under the leadership of Herbert Welsh. I have attempted to reveal the
circumstances of the association's origin, its mode of operation, and its

impact on the implementation of goverment Indian policy and the Indians themselves. The range of the IRA's activities was remarkable, and it would be impossible in a single volume to cover all of its operations even for this limited period. Inevitably, it was necessary to make choices, and no one else covering the same period would be likely to make precisely the same selections as I have made to illustrate the history of such an active group.

Aside from the broad scope of its operations, the major problem for the historian of the IRA is the wealth of materials available. Matthew Sniffen, who began as a clerk with the association in 1884 and over the next two years presided over the introduction of its filing system, estimated in 1903 that the IRA received and responded to about 3,000 letters a year. Sniffen's system preserved almost all of the association's correspondence and publications. It is unusual to see a reference to any letters for this period which cannot be located. In addition, letters by Herbert Welsh for the period prior to 1886, and an occasional one after that written during summer vacations or while on the road on association business, have been located. They appear in collections of papers of his correspondents in the formative period, such men as General S. C. Armstrong, Dr. James E. Rhoads, Captain Richard H. Pratt, and Senator H. L. Dawes. The result is an unusually full documentary record, which is both a blessing and a burden to the researcher. Anyone working on an Indian topic for this period would do well to check the collection. This task, however, is not easy. At the beginning of each letterbook is an alphabetized list of addressees, but no subject categories. Incoming correspondence is arranged strictly by date. Jack T. Ericson, who edited the Microfilming Corporation of America's edition of the association's papers, included in his *Guide* a useful overview by year and an index of "important" correspondence. For the serious researcher these items are helpful although no substitute for the painful task of a frame-by-frame examination of what comes to seem an endless series of documents.

In the several years I have devoted to this project I have been aided by many people whose help it is my pleasure to acknowledge. They include Robert Kvasnicka and Richard Crawford of the National Archives, and the staffs of the Haverford College Library, the Yale University Library, the Hampton Institute Library, the Harvard Law School Library, and the Historical Society of Pennsylvania. I owe a special debt of gratitude to John P. Saulitis, Director of Fredonia's Daniel Reed Library, and his fine staff. Other individuals who have aided me in this long quest include Adam Simms, Donald L. Parman, John Shapard, Elizabeth Blaisdell, Gary D. Barber, Andrew Welsh,

Andrew D. Imbrie, Douglas Shepard, Laurence M. Hauptman, and Floyd O'Neil. Sandra L. Cadwalader, the Executive Secretary of the Indian Rights Association, has been most helpful in responding to a number of inquiries. Mary Notaro did her usual excellent job of typing, and my wife, Charlotte N. Hagan, aided me at all stages in the preparation of the manuscript.

W. T. H.

CHAPTER ONE

Two Proper Philadelphians
Meet the Indians

On May 17, 1882, the town of Chamberlain, Dakota Territory, received two visitors from the East, Herbert Welsh and Henry S. Pancoast. Within the next four weeks the two young Philadelphians would first cross the Missouri to the Lower Brulé Indian Agency and subsequently visit three other Sioux agencies—Santee, Yankton, and Rosebud. Much of this time they were guided by the Protestant Episcopal Church's Bishop of Niobrara, William Hobart Hare, and it was at his invitation that Welsh and Pancoast were visiting the Sioux. As a result of their experience in May and June of 1882, the young men developed an interest in the Native Americans that they would carry with them the rest of their lives. The principal result of this interest would be the founding of the Indian Rights Association. Henry Pancoast would be a leading member of the IRA in the first two decades of the association. His friend Herbert Welsh, however, clearly would have the leading role in founding the IRA and would dominate it during the association's formative first twenty years.

Like his friend Henry Pancoast, Welsh was what one student of Philadelphia society has referred to as a Proper Philadelphian.[1] Born in 1851, he was the eighth and last child of John and Mary Lowber Welsh. His mother died when Herbert was still an infant, but his father lived until 1888, and he and Herbert had a warm relationship. John Welsh was the son of a successful Philadelphia merchant and also had prospered in business. Herbert Welsh declined to follow in the footsteps of his father and grandfather. He had inherited sufficient property from his father and maternal grandfather to enable him to live comfortably

[1]

Herbert Welsh, circa 1883
Courtesy Indian Rights Association

by the standards of upper-middle-class Philadelphia and to pursue his avocations. In contrast, his brother John Lowber Welsh continued the family's business tradition and was one of the richest men in Pennsylvania when he died in 1904. Indeed, the older brother was closely identified with railroad, steel, banking, and urban traction interests at a time when Herbert was publishing and editing a journal highly critical of the Philadelphia traction systems with which brother John was associated.

While John was establishing himself in the business world, the young Herbert Welsh was being educated at Philadelphia's Episcopal Academy. It was an exclusive private school of which William Hobart Hare's father had been headmaster and which the future bishop also had attended. The academy's graduates usually enrolled at the University of Pennsylvania, as did Herbert Welsh in 1867.[2]

At the university Welsh refined the writing style which would stand him in good stead in his long career as a publicist. He also gained experience in public speaking and shared the Prize in Declamation with Hampton Carson, later a prominent member of the Philadelphia bar and an attorney representing the Indian Rights Association in a celebrated case. Phi Beta Kappa was another honor Welsh accumulated while at Penn. That he did not neglect the social side of university life, however, is evidenced by his selection by his classmates as the recipient of the Wooden Spoon, each graduating class's award to its best-liked member.

Upon graduation Welsh embarked upon the serious study of art, intending to make painting his career. He also found time to court and marry Fanny Frazer, daughter of a leading Philadelphia family. Their marriage of sixty-six years was noted more for longevity than for happiness. Fanny frequently complained of ill health, which was at least one factor in preventing her from accompanying her active husband in his frequent travels in behalf of Indians and other causes. Late in their marriage he described their nearly half a century together as a "tragedy." At one point even Fanny's own brother advised Herbert to consider a divorce.

Shortly after their marriage in 1873, the Welshes departed for Paris, where they lived for a year in a pension near the Arc de Triomphe. Herbert pursued his education as an artist, studying for a time with Léon Joseph Florentin Bonnat, noted for his portraits and his renditions of religious scenes.

The Welshes returned to Philadelphia in the spring of 1874, and in 1882 were residing in Germantown, a suburb with a pronounced Quaker flavor. Herbert led a quiet life punctuated by travel abroad, including a visit to England while his father was United States Minister to the Court of Saint James. As his family grew—the Welshes had four children—he devoted himself to them, to his painting, and to his church. His father was a vestryman in St. Peter's for forty-two years, and Herbert served St. Michael's in the same capacity and as superintendent of its Sunday school. Religion was a very real force in his life and in that of his few close friends. A letter to him while he was in Dakota, written by perhaps his closest friend, J. Rodman Paul, reflected this emphasis. Paul's six-page letter contained but one reference to Indians, a sophomoric injunction to Welsh to "beware of the subtleties of the red-men and to bring a whole scalp to your admiring friends." Most of the letter was devoted to a discourse on Episcopal theological trends and to a ceremony Paul had attended, a mutual friend's ordination as a deacon. Paul regretted, and he clearly thought he had a sympathetic ear in Welsh, that their church was becoming too intellectualized, with too little concern for the "preaching of Christ as the Redeemer of sinful men."[3]

Welsh's motivation for devoting most of his time and energy to reform movements was his concept of Christian responsibility. As he phrased it after his return from Dakota Territory, the question of Christ's church's response to the plight of the Indian had but one answer, "so long as she shall pretend to follow in the footsteps of her Master."[4]

Once embarked upon a career as a reformer, Welsh exhibited all the optimism and commitment associated with the breed. The seed had been planted early. When his father died in 1886, the son recalled a fragment of a sermon he had heard as a small boy in John Welsh's company: "good men looked each other in the face and said what is now to be done?" From 1882 on, rarely did Herbert Welsh fail to respond in such a situation.[5] Indeed, it was Bishop Hare's search for help for his missions that led Welsh and Henry Pancoast to visit Dakota in 1882.

Herbert was not the first Welsh to become involved in Indian affairs. William Welsh, Herbert's uncle, had been the first chairman of the Board of Indian Commissioners, the group of philanthropists appointed by President Grant in 1869 to exercise some oversight of the purchase of supplies for Indian reservations. William's wife, Mary, was the founder of the Indian's Hope Association, an organization of Episcopal women devoted to support of their church's Native American missions. Until her death of 1898, Mary Welsh encouraged her nephew's Indian work. John Welsh, Herbert's father, while not particularly interested in the Native American, is best remembered in Philadelphia for his public service and philanthropy. His was the leading role in organizing Philadelphia's Centennial Exhibition in 1876, and his grateful fellow citizens presented him with $50,000, which he used to endow a chair in literature at the University of Pennsylvania.

Given the environment in which Welsh and his friend Pancoast had been reared, their reactions to their western experience might have been anticipated. They found the Dakota landscape harshly beautiful, with a clarity and brilliancy novel to easterners. But they regarded the newly incorporated Chamberlain, with its single street of unpainted frame buildings straggling up a hill from the railroad depot, as a blot on the landscape. What attracted Pancoast was the tableau, the "wonderful patch of moving color against the vivid green," formed by a herd of cattle grazing on a hill near the town.[6]

Neither were they favorably impressed by the border whites, treating them with the scornful condescension typical of upper-class easterners. Pancoast, who was more inclined than Welsh to record his impressions of the general setting, saw nothing glamorous or redeeming in the frontier population. He described his fellow passengers on the Chamberlain-bound train as "the Falstaff's army of discontented, unsuccessful men—the gamblers, emigrants, and convicts—that go out as representatives of our dominant race to conquer the wilderness."[7] These were the "scum of many nations, complacently taking claims on land wrested" from the Native Americans.[8] He mocked their accents—"Yes, we're a-gittin along pooty well"[9]—and even dismissed a flaxen-haired young immigrant girl who had caught his attention as having "meaningless blue eyes."[10]

The first Indians they saw, "dressed in an unromantically civilized manner" and regarding the train "with a dignified solidity," were a disappointment.[11] But before the month was up Welsh and Pancoast would see tribesmen who better accorded with their expectations: "on ponies, dashing and wheeling over the hills with a peculiarly Indian recklessness and grace," while "brilliant costumes and strange ornaments sparkled in the sunshine."[12] Welsh, the artist, saw in them "a touch of the Orient . . . which might have inspired the genius of Delacroix or Décamp."[13]

Compared with the white borderers, the Indians in their narrative emerge as imposing, handsome people. Welsh described the first chief he saw as "a tall, well-built man, whose cleanly dress and dignity of bearing would, doubtless, have surprised those among my readers who imagine all Indians to be filthy and degraded."[14] Similarly, Henry Pancoast described the Sioux as "tall, fine looking men, the faces of many showing great character and intelligence"—a marked contrast to the "Falstaff's army" of whites he saw migrating to the frontier.[15]

Their visit to four agencies, although all were on the Great Sioux Reservation, did give them a glimpse of the great differences in Indian conditions that perplexed and confused the members of Congress who tried to shape United States Indian policy, as well as the Indian service personnel who were responsible for its implementation. The Sioux of the Santee Reservation, in northeastern Nebraska about a hundred miles down the Missouri from Chamberlain, impressed Welsh as having made the most progress in civilization of any of the tribes he visited. They wore what was referred to as citizen's dress, had exchanged their tepees for frame houses or log cabins, no longer wore paint or danced, and many of them had selected land in severalty and were opening their own farms. The Episcopal Church and the American Board of Foreign Missions operated five missions there, some of them manned by Indian ministers. Five boarding schools, one of them across the Missouri River at Springfield, provided relatively good educational facilities.

At the other extreme was Rosebud Agency. Rumor of an outbreak there had been a factor in Bishop Hare's altering the route they took to Rosebud. There proved to be no substance to the report, but the young Philadelphians realized they were meeting a different type of Sioux. These carried rifles, painted their faces, and wore feathers. Welsh and Pancoast found no fields cultivated by Indians at Rosebud, nor was there a government school. The church at the agency headquarters was attended principally by whites and mixed-bloods, and Welsh and Pancoast observed at Rosebud the distribution of rations "on the hoof."

As at many agencies of the Plains Indians, beef cattle were issued every ten days or two weeks. The Indians turned the event into a modified buffalo hunt by chasing the cattle down and finishing them off with their bows, rifles, and pistols. The downed animals were then butchered on the spot. Frontier whites looked forward to the excitement and color of issue days, although visitors from the East frequently were shocked by the noise, violence, and bloodshed. A young woman at the Sioux agency once considered asking the SPCA to intervene! Welsh observed the cattle issue from a distance and congratulated himself that "no ill-directed bullet or stray steer came towards us."[16]

The Philadelphians had arrived at Rosebud only a few days after the celebration of the annual Sun Dance. Although quite religious themselves, Welsh and Pancoast showed little empathy for the ceremonies of the tribesmen. Thirty to forty Sioux had demonstrated their spiritual commitment by undergoing the grueling experience, and they and their relatives had distributed gifts freely to celebrate the occasion. Welsh acknowledged that the Sun Dance, by attracting large numbers of Indians, had a beneficial social function. However, he deplored the "barbarous tortures," which he said tended "to keep alive old and savage customs." Nor did he approve of the celebrants distributing gifts to those "less fortunate or more lazy than themselves." Unable to comprehend the depth of the Native American's devotion to his religious practices, Welsh actually asked if it were not possible to

> turn this heathen festival into a Fourth of July picnic, offer some servicable reward to those who had proved themselves industrious during the year past, discourage a baneful generosity on the part of those whose labors had won success, and entirely prohibit the degrading spectacle of self-torture.[17]

Clearly his month among the Sioux had only begun his education.

The specific purpose of the Welsh-Pancoast visit had been to acquaint the two men with the activities and needs of the Episcopal mission under Bishop Hare. As a result they spent what would otherwise have been a disproportionate share of their time visiting missions and schools. Three important Sioux agencies similar to Rosebud—Pine Ridge, Cheyenne River, and Standing Rock—they did not even glimpse. If they had, possibly they would have been less sanguine about the rapidity with which Indians could be stripped of their culture and have another imposed upon them.

Their Sioux itinerary had the effect of bringing Welsh and Pancoast most often into contact with "progressive" Sioux, those associated with the schools and missions of the agencies. At Lower Brulé they attended church services on the only two full days they were there, never leaving the agency headquarters. Then followed a week at Hope School at Springfield, hardly a typical Sioux environment. Their stay at Springfield was interrupted only by a visit to schools on the Santee Reservation, across the Missouri from Springfield. It was St. Paul's School at Yankton which drew them to that agency, and, as usual, what they saw of the rest of the area was incidental to the progress from one church or school to another.

En route from Yankton to Rosebud the party passed the night at Fort Niobrara. It was Welsh's first visit to a military post, and he was pleasantly surprised at the warmth and cordiality of their reception. Although they remained only overnight, he obviously was favorably impressed by his first contact with army officers.[18]

One of the most important results of the trip to Dakota Territory was the contacts Welsh made. Throughout the month he met people with whom he would maintain relations for years to come. They would constitute for him a valuable network of informants, responding to his requests for unofficial versions of reservation happenings, or volunteering information as they sought his help for concerns of their own. Generally they were missionaries and teachers, particularly Episcopalians, but Welsh also established relationships with reservation employees and even some Indians, usually mixed-bloods.

The two men who guided Welsh and Pancoast from Chamberlain to Lower Brulé were typical of the contacts Welsh had made. Reverend Luke Walker was a full-blood Sioux, though hardly a typical one, being an Episcopal presbyter and married to a white woman. Welsh's other guide was the Reverend H. Burt, who ten years earlier had been in seminary when he heard Welsh's uncle, William, make a plea for people to undertake missionary work. Crow Creek Agency, adjoining Lower Brulé, was Reverend Burt's home, and he had become fluent in Lakota. Fifteen years later Welsh was still depending upon him for inside information on Crow Creek.

Another contact Welsh made which he would exploit on several occasions over the years was Reverend William J. Cleveland, Episcopal missionary at Rosebud. Also proficient in Lakota, Reverend Cleveland acted as interpreter for Welsh and Pancoast and profited from his knowledge of the Sioux and reservation conditions. Following the Ghost Dance uprising in 1890, the IRA employed the missionary to provide the association with an account of the origins of the difficulty. Several years later the IRA again drew upon Cleveland's expertise, this time for an investigation of problems at Fort Berthold Agency.

All of the men he became acquainted with played a role in shaping Welsh's views of the problems of Indian-white relations in 1882 and for many years thereafter. But beyond a doubt the individual who had the most influence on Welsh was Bishop William Hobart Hare. Thirteen years older than Welsh, Hare came from the same Philadelphia social stratum. Welsh had known the Episcopal clergyman during his years in the city, and, when Hare became involved in expensive litigation as a defendant in a libel suit, Welsh helped raise defense funds for him. By his willingness to dedicate himself to a lifetime of ministering to the Sioux, the bishop exemplified the values that were so important to his fellow Episcopalian. During the two decades under discussion Bishop Hare was the most important single force in shaping Welsh's views on Indian affairs in the Dakotas and Nebraska, and on Indian-white relations generally.

The pamphlet that resulted from Welsh's Dakota experience in 1882 clearly indicated his assessment of the Native American and his future. Published before the organization of the IRA, it forecast the assocation's objectives and techniques. In it Welsh took a clear stand on the power of nurture over nature, declaring that "the Indian, like most men, brings forth good or evil fruit according to the treatment he receives or the circumstances with which he is surrounded."[19] Indians, like whites, were "God's children upon the earth," and "the best and deepest instincts of human hearts belong not to one race, nor to one color."[20] The only difference Welsh was willing to admit to was the failure of the Indian to measure up to the Anglo-Saxon's "capability for sustained effort."[21] However, he found Reverend Luke Walker, the full-blood Sioux, living proof of an Indian's ability to close the gap.

Welsh was convinced that a Christian education, land in severalty, a legal system, competent agents, and a gradual reduction of government rations constituted a formula that could elevate the Indian to the point that he could be fully assimilated into American society. The Christian education would teach him "to be cleanly, honest, industrious, as well as to attend the services and sacraments of the Church."[22] Boarding schools were preferable to day schools, as they separated the child from the ignorance and filth of savage camps, from the closest contact with the barbarity of a nomadic and warlike people.

The shift from holding land in common to holding it in severalty was essential, in Welsh's judgment, to wean the Indians from nomadism. Severalty also would enable the tribesman to enjoy the rewards of his labor. Without it the Indian farmer could know no security—"the greedy eye of some white neighbor spies his success, and Congress knows no peace until he is driven westward."[23]

The third ingredient, the extension to the Indian population of a law code comparable to the one their white neighbors lived under, Welsh did not expand upon. His lawyer companion did. Henry Pancoast argued that if the Indians' tribal organization was destroyed, and he believed that destruction must occur, there had to be some replacement for "their own primitive regulations for the repression and punishment of crime."[24]

Both men had been impressed by the seemingly unlimited control of the Indian agent and his resulting tremendous capacity for good or ill. They came back from Dakota Territory convinced that the quality of the agents was a big factor in any program of Indian civilization. Welsh said the agent could encourage and reward the progressive tribesman, and by his religious and home life set a valuable example. Or he could be "devoid of dignity, capacity, sympathy, puffed up with a sense of his own importance . . . violent in his exercise of authority, petty in his jealousy . . . insolent, and frequently unjust . . . indiscreet, or as is but too often the case, immoral in the conduct of his private life."[25] Obviously Welsh had observed or heard of some of the less effective agents. Curiously, the only one he singled out for praise was one he had not personally observed, Dr. V. T. McGillycuddy of Pine Ridge, whom he lauded for having accomplished much with Indians as "savage" as those at Rosebud.[26]

A final necessity, as seen by the young Philadelphian, was a gradual reduction in the rations the government issued the Indians. Not only did the rations remove the incentive to self-support, by being issued at ten-day intervals at a central location they disrupted any efforts at self-support. Indians were encouraged to locate not where the land was best for farming, but near the ration issue point. Those families who did settle twenty or thirty miles away spent much of their time on the road, making adequate care of livestock and crops impossible.

Above all Welsh stressed that his proposals were practical and not tinged with sentimentality. Already he was reacting to the charge that eastern reformers were sentimental do-gooders. Nevertheless, the young Philadelphian returned to his native city intending to publicize the accomplishments and needs of the missions of his friend and mentor in Indian affairs, Bishop William Hobart Hare. It would be the first step in a chain of events leading to the emergence of the IRA as the most active and influential Indian reform group in the late nineteenth century.

CHAPTER TWO

The Birth of the
Indian Rights Association

Although his *Four Weeks Among Some of the Sioux Tribes* showed no sign
of it, Herbert Welsh did not return from Dakota Territory to an area
oblivious to the Indian issue or lacking in proposed remedies. To some
extent he was preaching to the converted. In addition to the already
mentioned activity of the Episcopalians in behalf of Bishop Hare's
missions, Quaker societies in Philadelphia had been active in Indian
affairs for more than a century, especially in those years when President Grant had involved them in the Indian Service. This participation
had tapered off in the next administration, although Quakers continued to maintain a lively interest in the welfare of the Native American.[1]

Other individuals and groups had entered the Indian field in a
burst of activity in the late 1870s. A. B. Meacham, whom Modoc
Indians had nearly killed, founded in Philadelphia in 1878 *The Council
Fire,* a monthly dedicated to the American Indian.[2] Philadelphians who
would take up the Indian cause in this period were Mary L. Bonney and
Amelia Stone Quinton. Both were active Baptists with backgrounds in
teaching and reform work before their involvement in Indian affairs.
Miss Bonney was moved to action in the spring of 1879 on learning of
the pressure being exerted by the railroads to open up Indian Territory
(Oklahoma), if necessary by violating treaties. She drafted a petition
supporting the tribal position and hoped to have it taken up by her
church's Women's Home Mission Society. Lost in the flurry of other
business, the petition languished until Miss Bonney, who was busy with
her duties as head of a Philadelphia girls' school, brought it to the

attention of her friend Mrs. Amelia S. Quinton. Mrs. Quinton, recently returned from England, plunged into the work and helped to revise the original document and to obtain more signatures. Early in 1880 the petition, grown to a roll 300 feet long, was presented to President Hayes and subsequently to Congress. Before Welsh and Pancoast set off for Dakota Territory, Bonney and Stone had presented two more petitions, the third one bearing more than 100,000 signatures, and had formalized their organization. Called earlier the Indian Treaty-keeping and Protective Association, this cumbersome title was exchanged in 1882 for the National Indian Association. The following year it would become the Women's National Indian Association. Organized around a central executive committee, the association's rapid expansion into other cities and states was facilitated by a constitution permitting the establishment of semi-autonomous associate committees, eighty-three of them emerging by 1886.[3]

Boston was the other center for friends of the Indian in 1882. Public meetings in 1879 inspired by the tribulations of the small Ponca tribe had led to the creation of the Boston Indian Citizenship Committee. Its organizing session featured the governor of Massachusetts and the mayor of Boston. Among its more active members were *Atlantic Monthly* publisher H. O. Houghton, Harvard law professor James B. Thayer, and businessmen Frank Wood and Joshua W. Davis. The committee also welcomed ladies into membership, and two of prominence were Mrs. Stephen H. Bullard, sister of President Eliot of Harvard, and Mrs. Augustus Hemenway, a generous contributor to many good causes. The most celebrated member of the Boston committee by 1882 was Helen Hunt Jackson, who the previous year had published her scathing study of United States Indian policy, *A Century of Dishonor*. The Boston committee also claimed credit for having enlisted the help of Massachusetts Senator H. L. Dawes, who would be the author of the important severalty law in 1887 and the principal Senate spokesman of friends of the Indian until his retirement from Congress in 1893.

Welsh's advocacy of severalty, education, and a system of laws to prepare the Indian for assimilation clearly represented nothing new as to either objective or means. All had been urged for many years. The Board of Indian Commissioners recommended them in its first annual report in 1869, and continued to do so. A. B. Meacham's *Council Fire,* in its first issue, proposed "Bibles, Books, and Ballots" as the motto for United States Indian policy.[4] Title in fee simple to at least 160 acres, expanded educational opportunities, and legal protection were urged by the Women's National Indian Association in its third petition, presented to Congress in 1881.

Nor did government officials lag behind public sentiment. Early in its career the Indian Rights Association could claim that it was "in hearty sympathy with the general policy advanced by the Indian Bureau."[5] Since 1850 virtually every treaty establishing a reservation had either mandated severalty or offered it as an option. An examination of the annual reports of the commissioners of Indian affairs and the secretaries of the interior, and of presidential papers, reveals at least a verbal commitment to education and security of land title for the Native American.

Government officials also shared Welsh's concern that issuing rations to reservation inhabitants was depriving them of incentive. Even as Welsh was preparing for his trip to Dakota Territory, Congress had required that the Indians be informed that in the future they would have to provide more of their own support. A circular authorized by Secretary of the Interior H. M. Teller, and issued over the signature of the commissioner of Indian affairs, ordered agents to inform their Indian charges that "labor is not degrading, but on the contrary is ennobling, and that if they ever expect to become rich and powerful as the white races, they must learn the lessons of industry and economy."[6]

Secretary Teller, like Welsh, was disturbed at the persistence of the Sun Dance and comparable "heathenish" ceremonies. Shortly after Welsh registered his disapproval of the Plains Indian ritual, the secretary took the steps that led to the appearance on most reservations of Courts of Indian Offenses, courts designed specifically to discourage such activities.[7]

If Welsh would make a contribution to solving what was referred to as the "Indian problem," it would not be because he had come up with any new ideas as a result of his Dakota experience. For that matter, it is not clear that he returned to Philadelphia intending to do more than publicize Bishop Hare's missions. A local paper had printed one letter that Welsh had written to the editor while in Dakota.[8] In that, he had done little more than record his initial impressions of Lower Brulé, impressions repeated almost verbatim in his *Four Weeks Among Some of the Sioux Tribes*, published in the autumn of 1882.

Back in Philadelphia, Welsh did move closer to involving himself in Indian affairs. He wrote to people whom he had met in Dakota and offered his services. In the case of the Santees he volunteered to do what he could to relieve their anxiety about titles to their land. Many had taken allotments as provided under the Sioux Treaty of 1868 but had not received their patents. Welsh checked with the General Land Office and was informed that the treaty provision was insufficient and that only Congress could authorize the patents.[9]

Welsh's offer of help to Bishop Hare elicited a suggestion that he might undertake to publicize the success the Episcopal missions had enjoyed and raise funds for their support. Welsh did embark upon a series of speaking engagements in Philadelphia and elsewhere in the

East, usually to church groups. He also published and distributed the pamphlet *Four Weeks Among Some of the Sioux Tribes*. What he must have been saying in his lectures can be deduced from a manuscript dated November 15, 1882, and entitled, "A Practical View of the Indian Question." As in his pamphlet Welsh expressed full confidence in the ability of the Native American to survive and even flourish if exposed to the beneficent influences of Christianity, education, allotment in severalty, and a system of laws. The present policy, he claimed, might "feed the contractor, gratify the cupidity of frontier land speculators, or stimulate railway enterprise," but at the cost of a "frightful incubus of hate and crime . . . upon the shoulders of the nation."[10]

The response to Welsh's efforts was gratifying. One member of his audience at an Episcopal mission conference held in Brooklyn spoke of it as a "wonderful meeting" and acclaimed Welsh as "a messenger from God."[11] A gentleman who heard Welsh speak at Germantown's Christ Church was similarly moved, writing him: "Your telling oratory upon the 'Indian Question' . . . haunts me continually, and I now feel that I must do something to the furtherance of the cause."[12] Although Welsh sought outlets for his views in the local press and spoke to organizations like the Philadelphia Social Science Association, the burden of his work was with Episcopal Church groups. As he remembered it over a decade later, "we determined to do all in our power to make the situation known to the public, especially to the Christian public which is at all times anxious to carry out the ideals of Christianity into public as well as private life."[13]

Meanwhile, Welsh began to contact people in the East with some role or interest in Indian affairs, including his fellow Philadelphian Dr. James E. Rhoads. Dr. Rhoads had been a practicing physician before turning to the philanthropy which was a natural outgrowth of his Quaker training. A leader of the Associated Executive Committee of Friends (Orthodox) on Indian Affairs, he had represented that organization at the joint meetings of the Board of Indian Commissioners and representatives of missionary boards which took place every January in Washington. He also was editor of the *Friends Review* and in a few months would become the first president of Bryn Mawr College.

Captain Richard H. Pratt and Mrs. Amelia S. Quinton were two others Welsh approached. Captain Pratt already had established himself as a strong voice on Indian matters.[14] A career army officer, he had commanded Indians enlisted to serve as army scouts before he was detached to take charge of Plains Indian prisoners accused of hostilities in 1874–1875. While acting as their jailor at Fort Marion, Florida, the captain became convinced of their potential as peaceful and industri-

Captain Richard H. Pratt, founder of Carlisle Institute
Courtesy National Archives

ous members of American society. Pratt arranged to enroll some of his younger charges at Hampton Institute, where he and they came under the influence of General S. C. Armstrong, founder of that celebrated school for blacks. When Pratt went on in 1879 to launch Carlisle Institute, the new school clearly reflected the example of Hampton. However, the captain was not content to remain in the shadow of anyone. Under his vigorous and imaginative leadership Carlisle had emerged by 1882 as the model for a new system of government-run off-reservation boarding schools for Indians. At Carlisle, Pratt preached complete assimilation of the Native American and opposed anything that would block, or even delay, the process. The reservations, which nearly all reformers regarded as necessary way stations for the Indians in preparation for assimilation and citizenship, he abominated. As he put it to Welsh, with his usual force, in December of 1882: "If we want success we must tear down reservation prison bars, allow freedom of growth by contact with civilization and its fullest experience to the largest number possible."[15]

Mrs. Quinton was more of the conventional reformer. She and her organization, the Women's National Indian Association, favored a more gradual approach employing the same techniques Welsh and other reformers advocated. They valued the reservation as a setting from which undesirable whites could be excluded while the Native American was prepared for the new responsibilities he would assume, it was hoped, in about a generation. Mrs. Quinton was delighted to see Welsh preparing to take an active role in Indian affairs. "Thank God for your advent into this so needy work," was her response to the founding of the Indian Rights Association.[16]

Such an organization had not been Welsh's intention when he returned from Dakota Territory in the summer of 1882. The idea seems to have gradually emerged as he made his rounds lecturing on the Indian problem and talking and corresponding with people like Mrs. Quinton and Dr. Rhoads. Initially he considered a strictly Episcopal organization; however, he finally opted for an association open to people of all religious faiths. Perhaps Rhoads's insistence that the new organization should be substantial enough to maintain a lobbyist in Washington helped Welsh make up his mind.[17] The Episcopalians were pressed to support Bishop Hare's missionary diocese without taking on other responsibilities.

To launch a major organization like the one he had in mind, Herbert Welsh lacked the prestige and stature which would attract the right people. His father, John Welsh, former ambassador to England as well as a leading Philadelphia philanthropist and businessman, did have the necessary standing and was prepared to put it at his son's disposal. As a result it was John Welsh who issued the invitations to a meeting at his home to consider "organizing an association for the protection of the rights of Indians."[18]

It was indeed a distinguished gathering of about forty Proper Philadelphians. Mayor Samuel G. King presided, and a cross-section of prominent men were in attendance, plus younger men of Herbert Welsh's age group, some of them friends like J. Rodman Paul, N. Dubois Miller, and Hampton L. Carson.

The older group which supplied the distinction needed to give the new organization validity was impressive. It included John Wanamaker, wealthy merchant and philanthropist and later Postmaster General in the Harrison administration. H. H. Houston had large holdings in shipping, railroad, and oil, and W. W. Harding was the publisher of the Philadelphia *Inquirer*. A local steel magnate who accepted John Welsh's invitation was William Sellers, president of the Midvale Steel Company and the Edgemoor Iron Company.

Although Episcopalians were most numerous, the presence of Dr. George Dana Boardman, pastor of the First Baptist Church, and Quakers James E. Rhoads and Philip C. Garrett gave the organization the necessary ecumenical quality. Like many other Philadelphia Quakers of his class, Garrett was a graduate of Haverford College. He was no stranger to good causes, having worked for prison reform and for the improvement of the administration of public charity. When invited to John Welsh's home in December 1882, Garrett also was the head of Philadelphia's Committee of One Hundred, a group of the city's most distinguished citizens, who had banded together to try to do something about its corrupt government. It was hoped he would enjoy more success in dealing with the Indian question.

The Philadelphia *Inquirer* gave good coverage of the meeting at John Welsh's home, editors rarely ignoring gatherings attended by their publishers. "Mr. Herbert Welsh's interesting lectures and address in behalf of the Indians," the story began, "seem to have borne good fruit."[19] It also noted that others had spoken, including Henry Pancoast and Eli K. Price.

Eli Price was one of Philadelphia's distinguished elder statesmen, a man in his eighties who was a trustee of the University of Pennsylvania and vice president of the American Philosophical Society. He expressed his approval of land in severalty, although Price was concerned that the Native American not be rushed into it before he could defend himself from people who would take advantage of his ignorance and gullibility to steal his land. In conclusion, Price indicated his "willingness to co-operate with the young men who were pressing forward so noble a movement as the rescue of the aboriginal races."[20]

Henry Pancoast, one of those young men, drew on his recollections of his trip to Dakota and argued for a legal system which would protect the individual property rights the reformers hoped to see the Indians acquire. As the keynote speaker, Herbert Welsh stressed themes from his pamphlet, *Four Weeks Among Some of the Sioux Tribes.* He told his audience that Indians were capable of civilization and enlivened his argument with personal observations from his western trip. One episode which he must have related many times to audiences since his return from Dakota Territory involved a Lower Brulé named Useful Heart and his favorite daughter, a convert to Christianity. Despite his name, Useful Heart was pictured by Welsh as an incorrigible warrior and hunter—that is, until his daughter on her deathbed convinced him to go to the "foot of the Cross."[21]

After the last speaker had been recognized and had had his say, the vital business of organizing the Indian Rights Association was accomplished expeditiously. During a recess a committee of three— Welsh, Pancoast, and N. Dubois Miller, a young attorney and personal friend of Welsh—quickly produced a constitution, probably from Welsh's pocket. After the group voted to accept the document, the chairman then appointed a committee, undoubtedly also selected in advance, to choose officers and make other necessary arrangements. This committee consisted of five men, including again Welsh, Pancoast, and Miller.

In the next two weeks the committee, chaired by Miller, selected a panel of officers. For president they nominated Wayne MacVeagh, a choice calculated to inspire confidence in the new association. A distinguished member of the Philadelphia bar, MacVeagh was appointed United States minister to Turkey by President Grant and served as attorney general under President Garfield. When approached by John Welsh to accept the presidency of the IRA, he quickly consented.[22]

The constitution also called for a board of counselors, elder statesmen, and for these posts the committee nominated five men, including John Welsh and Eli K. Price. This position would be dropped several years later, after it had served its purpose of associating with the infant organization the names of prominent Philadelphians.

The key position of corresponding secretary was reserved by Welsh for himself. He and the other officers also would serve on an executive committee along with eight elected members, including Philip Garrett, Henry Pancoast, and Dr. Rhoads. The committee was expected to be the real driving force in the organization. It would pass on membership applications and in general "carry out the objects of the Association."[23]

At a second general meeting December 29, this time at the Board of Trade, forty-eight people appeared to approve the slate of officers and sign the constitution. The IRA was organized and ready for action. However, its objectives and the tactics to achieve them still remained broad generalities. Clause II of the constitution stated:

> The object of this Association shall be to secure to the Indians of the United States the political and civil rights already guaranteed to them by treaty and statutes of the United States and such as their civilization and circumstances may justify.

Clause IV spoke to the question of tactics:

> For the purpose of carrying out its object the Association shall endeavor in every proper way to influence public opinion and the legislation of Congress, and assist the executive officers of the Government in the enforcement of the laws passed for the protection and education of the Indians.

This description was somewhat expanded by the charge to the executive committee in Clause VI:

> to carry out the objects of the Association by the diffusion of knowledge on the subject through means of public meetings, publications, and the formation of similar associations throughout the country. . . .[24]

In the less than six months since his return from Dakota Territory, Herbert Welsh had moved from a position of advocacy of Episcopal missions for the Indians to playing the leading role in the creation of the IRA, an association whose membership was open to all and which was dedicated to improving the lot of the entire Indian population, not just those served by Episcopal missionaries. Welsh had deliberately involved prestigious Philadelphians in the founding of the IRA, but its success or failure would largely depend upon his willingness to devote to it his full time and energy, neglecting his art and, on occasion, his family. Equally indispensable to the success of the IRA would be the support and counsel Welsh was to receive from young friends like Henry Pancoast, Rodman Paul, and Dubois Miller, and the older and more experienced hands like the Quakers Dr. Rhoads and Philip Garrett.

CHAPTER THREE

The IRA Establishes
Its Role

In the two years and a half following the initial meeting in John Welsh's parlor in December 1882, the IRA went through a difficult period. Despite its impressive launching it had to establish itself as a functioning organization. This task had been accomplished by the spring of 1885, when the IRA had a permanent office in Philadelphia, a resident lobbyist in Washington, and was in a relatively sound financial situation. It no longer needed to seek issues to contest; its reputation was such that friends of the Indian, and occasionally Indians themselves, came to the IRA for help. It also had established a working relationship with the Board of Indian Commissioners, the Women's National Indian Association, and the newly emerged Lake Mohonk Conference. The mainspring of the young IRA, as he would be for the next twenty years, was Herbert Welsh.

As the IRA's constitution indicated, its framers intended that the executive committee, meeting monthly, should wield the real power. All association policy decisions were to emanate from it. The president's role could be an influential one, although apparently Wayne MacVeagh was willing to do little more than lend his name and prestige to the infant organization. With the exception of a few people like Henry Pancoast and his brother Charles, and J. Rodman Paul, the executive committee members were hardly more dedicated. Some meetings failed to attract a quorum, and the four committees to which the members were assigned functioned only sporadically. The Finance Committee, as Welsh once remarked bitterly, had informed him that he "was better fitted than any one else to raise the necessary funds for carrying on the work," and he therefore felt he "must go into the streets and beg."[1]

As the one member with the needed talents and the willingness to invest them fulltime in the organization, Welsh inevitably became more than just the corresponding secretary. He played the principal role in setting the IRA's course and dominated its activities. For advice and counsel in this early period he drew heavily on Dr. Rhoads and Hampton's General S. C. Armstrong.

Even before the IRA was organized, Dr. Rhoads had urged Welsh to confer with General Armstrong.[2] Mrs. John Jacob Astor, who invited Welsh to speak in New York City, also asked the general to meet with the young Philadelphian.[3] By means of a series of letters and one visit to Hampton, Welsh did get the benefit of Armstrong's advice, which the general was happy to offer as he and Dr. Rhoads were interested in seeing the new organization succeed. As Rhoads confided to Armstrong: "We can use H. Welsh, and uphold him in awakening interest in the general subject. He will *grow* and become well informed and practically useful as he goes on."[4]

Even before the organizational meeting at John Welsh's home, Rhoads had broached with Welsh the possibility of having an agent in Washington to maintain liaison with Congress and the Indian Office.[5] During the Grant administration the Quakers had done so and found it useful. At General Armstrong's suggestion, the American Missionary Society had employed Charles C. Painter to represent it in connection with its activities in the Negro and Indian mission fields. As corresponding secretary of something called the National Education Committee, Painter lobbied for these good causes in Washington. Armstrong and Rhoads thought Painter might perform the same service for the IRA, and at their suggestion Welsh got in touch with Painter in January 1883.[6]

It would be more than two years, however, before Painter's relationship with the association finally was defined. Meanwhile, he would be considered for the editorship of *Council Fire*, if the IRA took it over from the Blands. Washington physician Thomas A. Bland and his wife, Cora, had helped Alfred Meacham launch the journal and then assumed editorial responsibilities when Meacham died early in 1882. Apparently Dr. Rhoads first raised the question of the IRA's obtaining *Council Fire* and installing Painter as editor. Armstong liked the idea, and Painter was receptive if he could get it "away from the Cora Bland atmosphere and surroundings."[7] The executive committee approved the acquisition of the paper, but the deal fell through when the association discovered that it would have to assume liabilities the paper had incurred under the Blands and Meacham.[8]

General S. C. Armstrong, founder of Hampton Institute
Courtesy Historical Society of Pennsylvania

Although the editorship failed to materialize, Painter did go to work for the IRA in the summer of 1883. It was during the period of growing pains for the new organization, and initially the relationship was not a very satisfying one for Painter. The Boston Branch of the IRA pledged to raise a portion of his salary, and Painter sometimes identified himself as an employee of that branch. However, the Boston people were unable to meet their full commitment, and the central office in Philadelphia had to assume the full obligation in April 1884. This arrangement was formalized the following year, when the executive committee authorized employing Painter at a salary of $2,200 per year.[9]

In Charles Painter the IRA acquired the services of an experienced lobbyist with excellent credentials among reformers. A Virginian by birth, he was an 1858 graduate of Williams College. The son of a planter who emancipated his slaves before the Civil War, Painter had demonstrated his own commitment to the cause by serving on the faculty of Fisk University, established after the war to provide higher education for blacks. Although a Congregationalist minister, he was commonly addressed as "Professor" because of the Fisk faculty experience. Until his death in 1895 Painter represented the IRA in Washington and also traveled widely, investigating reservation conditions in the West and engaging in fund-raising and general public relations work in the East. Welsh regarded him as "discreet, wholly honest, unselfish and devoted.[10] There were those, however, who found him prickly. Professor Painter was not the smooth, ingratiating figure usually associated with the term "lobbyist."

At the same time that the relationship of Painter with the association was being solidified, another key figure in the organization was being recruited, Matthew K. Sniffen. As the scope of the IRA activity grew, it became readily apparent that the organization could not be run out of Welsh's hip pocket. He first sought and received authorization from the executive committee to rent office space and then in March 1884 was permitted to employ Sniffen as a clerk at a modest five dollars a week.[11] Only seventeen when hired, Sniffen, like Painter, proved to be a real asset. As Welsh was on the road much of the time, the youth was left in charge of the Philadelphia office. He began to maintain files, preserving virtually all the correspondence of the association, files which have been both a joy and a heavy burden to those interested in the IRA's history. For at least a decade Sniffen labored in relative obscurity. However, in the early 1890s, when Welsh's expanding commitments led him to delegate more responsibility to Sniffen, the young man came into his own. Long-lived like Welsh, Sniffen was in the employ of the association until his retirement in 1939, for thirty of those years acting as executive secretary.

Charles C. Painter
Courtesy Historical Society of Pennsylvania

Before an office could be opened and a clerk employed, the IRA needed to recruit members, establish the branch associations expected to be a vital part of its organization, and raise funds. These burdens fell almost completely on Herbert Welsh. Without his intense activity in the early years the IRA could never have become more than a loose local organization along the lines of the Boston Indian Citizenship Committee.

During the first two years Welsh made ninety-nine public addresses, nearly all of them in the East. The audiences were usually church-related groups, most frequently Episcopal, or friends of the Indian meeting in private homes. On his first extended tour, in February 1883, Welsh spoke fourteen times in communities from New York City to Portland, Maine, to audiences numbering as few as twenty-five and as many as eight hundred.[12] At a Boston club he addressed nearly fifty individuals whom he described as "gentlemen of distinction, literary and medical men."[13] It was not his usual audience, and he confided to his wife, Fanny, his misgivings about appearing before "men whom I knew were not favorable to such religious views as I professed." In the same letter to Fanny, Welsh expressed disappointment at not having heard from her, "but I suppose the children have kept you busy." She seems to have had no interest in her husband's Indian work, and his preoccupation with it must have further damaged an already fragile relationship.

In his public addresses on his February swing through the East, Welsh hoped to excite interest in the Indian cause and win friends and support for the IRA. In Boston he helped found the first branch of the association, a branch whose membership overlapped that of the Boston Indian Citizenship Committee. Apparently Welsh hoped the IRA could emulate the Women's National Indian Association and acquire branches all over the United States. Twenty-three were established in the first two years, but three of them quickly became inactive, and the remainder had difficulty finding a role.[14] The central office in Philadelphia used the branches only to raise funds, distribute literature, and inspire letters and petitions in behalf of causes identified by the Philadelphia leadership.

Some branches, nevertheless, were launched with enthusiasm. Frederic Gardiner, Jr., the leader of the one in Middletown, Connecticut, wrote the commissioner of Indian affairs to brag of the appearance of that branch with its one hundred members, and the formation of other units in that state.[15] Unfortunately, such enthusiasm was usually shortlived. Excluded from the executive committee in this early period, and limited to sending a few delegates to the annual meeting in Philadelphia, local branches usually lost interest rather quickly.

Half of the annual $2 dues for local branches, with a minimum assessment of $25 per branch, was to go to the Philadelphia office. Nevertheless, in actual fact the branches provided disappointingly little financial support. And the $2 dues charged the Philadelphia association's membership, 180 in 1883 and almost 250 in 1884, could hardly have covered the cost of printing and mailing the copies of IRA publications that each member received. Welsh quickly learned that he would have to seek contributions from sympathetic individuals, and this task became one of his most onerous responsibilities. However, it was these large contributors who kept the IRA afloat. Of the nearly $4,000 it raised in 1884, more than half of it came from donors of $50 or more, a single contributor being responsible for $1,000 of the total.[16]

Besides the cost of printing 37,000 copies of fourteen different publications and distributing them to members and interested parties in 1883 and 1884, the IRA also had to raise the money for office expenses and salaries for Sniffen and Painter. Welsh accepted no compensation for his fulltime devotion to the cause, but he did bill the IRA for actual travel expenses.

This travel by Welsh and others, and particularly their extended investigations of conditions on western reservations, was a considerable financial burden to the organization. However, Welsh considered it of utmost importance. "As you well know," he wrote General Armstrong, "it is only from the personal knowledge that such journeys afford that one's opinions and utterances gather force."[17] In the first two years Welsh made an extended trip to the Sioux agencies and another to the Southwest.

Welsh's return to the Sioux agencies in the spring of 1883 was motivated principally by the association's concern over the government's efforts to further reduce Sioux landholdings. Painter also would be there. Not yet an employee of the IRA, his expenses were being paid from funds raised in Boston with the help of General Armstrong.[18] Besides Painter, Welsh expected to see other eastern friends of the Indian who planned to rendezvous at Santee.

In the five weeks Welsh spent among the Sioux in May and June, he visited most of their agencies, including two he had missed on his first trip, Cheyenne River and Pine Ridge.[19] He spent ten days at the latter, the home of the Oglala Sioux. In the process Welsh confirmed some of his earlier impressions, renewed earlier contracts, and made some new ones. Once again Bishop Hare was a traveling companion during most of the trip. And again they spent what appeared to be a disproportionate amount of time at schools and churches. Nevertheless, particularly at Pine Ridge, Herbert Welsh had an opportunity to see the Indians at

Matthew K. Sniffen
Courtesy Historical Society of Pennsylvania

their camps remote from the agency. Everywhere he sought opportunities to quiz individual Indians about the work of the Sioux Commission, which had negotiated with them for a land cession a few
months earlier. Among those with whom he talked were Spotted
Thunder, the Upper Brulé chief, and American Horse and George
Sword, both Oglalas. The last was a well-known captain of Indian
police at Pine Ridge. Welsh also exploited his contacts among the
Indians associated with the Episcopal Church, including Reverend
Amos Ross, a native missionary, and Philip Deloria, an Episcopal deacon with whom Welsh was to have a long acquaintance.

Welsh clearly was most impressed by what he saw at Pine Ridge.
The home of 8,000 Oglalas, it demonstrated to him both the mag-
nitude of the problem and the possibility of its solution. Visiting the
camps away from the agency, sleeping in a buffalo robe on the ground,
and eating by a campfire, Welsh felt he was experiencing the Indians as
they really were. Despite their "very wild appearance," he felt no
apprehension. He assured Fanny of the "extraordinary fact . . . that one
is more secure as to property and life in travelling among the wildest of
these Indians than in many of the border white settlements."[20] The
artist in him was inspired by what he saw at one service Bishop Hare
held:

> the wildest and most picturesque of congregations . . . that I
> have yet seen . . . adorned with costumes which could hardly
> be surpassed by a fancy ball—blue and scarlet yellow and white
> green and black—all were represented. You can hardly imag-
> ine any thing more extraordinary than the appearance of these
> men women and children by the flickering light of some dozen can-
> dles. . . .[21]

While at Pine Ridge, Welsh was a guest in the home of the agent,
Dr. Valentine T. McGillycuddy. The agent had been in office since
1879. A former army surgeon, he had been acquainted with the Sioux
before coming to Pine Ridge. A strong-willed man, Dr. McGillycuddy
had asserted his control over the entire agency, something many agents
never succeeded in doing for agencies smaller and less turbulent than
Pine Ridge. Welsh was very impressed by McGillycuddy and the "perfect order and cleanliness" around the agency headquarters.[22] The
visitor praised the agent for reducing rations, thus realizing a saving to
the government of nearly $200,000 without seriously depriving the
Indians. This reduction was important to Welsh, who still felt that
the ration system was "simply a premium offered to idleness and
pauperism."[23]

The Philadelphian lauded Dr. McGillycuddy's Indian police force, which gave the agent the necessary leverage in dealing with chiefs like Red Cloud, the famed Oglala who had played a leading role in the fighting of the 1860s and still had well-armed followers. Welsh had arrived in Sioux country shortly after the secretary of the interior had issued orders to replace the rifles of the police with revolvers. Like Agent James G. Wright of Rosebud, another official of whom he formed a good opinion, Welsh felt the secretary's order would put the police at the mercy of their rifle-bearing fellow tribesmen.

On this visit Welsh witnessed an Indian dance at Pine Ridge, which McGillycuddy permitted the Oglalas to perform around the flagpole in the midst of the agency headquarters. Painted and decorated with feathers and animal skins, they moved to the rhythm of a large drum, their heads shaking and bodies quivering. Welsh took comfort in the thought that the "frequency of these dances is greatly decreasing, and the growth of industry among the people will doubtless soon do away with them altogether."[24] Ever the optimist, Welsh concluded from what he had seen on his trip that "there is no reason why this large and important body of Indians should not, within a comparatively short period of time, become a civilized and self-supporting people."[25]

A year later Welsh made his first visit to the Southwest.[26] This travel was inspired by his recognition of the need to broaden his acquaintance with Native Americans. He also must have been swayed by Navajo Agent D. M. Riordan, whom he met when the agent and an Indian delegation visited Philadelphia in the winter of 1883–1884. Riordan advised Welsh on his itinerary and assured the Philadelphian a warm reception in the Southwest.

Accompanied by Frederic Gardiner, Jr., the dynamic corresponding secretary of the Middletown, Connecticut, branch, Welsh left Philadelphia at the end of April 1884. They spent the first week on the upper Río Grande in Pueblo country. Like other visitors to what Welsh called the "land of sunlight," he was struck by the "extraordinary brillancy of sky and atmosphere which hangs over and surrounds all."[27] He found little here to relate to his Dakota Territory experience. In contrast with the Sioux the Pueblos were farmers who received very little government aid. In Welsh's judgment they had "but small claim to physical beauty."[28] He observed that the children were neither "so attractive, or in appearance so intelligent, as the Sioux children of the North."[29] Visiting the pueblo of San Ildefonso, the Philadelphian felt as if he had "stepped from the life of to-day . . . into some remote and unknown period."[30] The spectacle of the low-lying adobe buildings framed against the distant snow-clad mountains challenged the artist in Welsh, and he made a hasty pencil sketch to the amusement of a curious audience of women and children. Gardiner had brought a camera and took many snapshots.

After a week in the upper Río Grande Valley, Welsh and Gardiner took a train to within twenty-five miles of the Navajo Agency. At the station they were met by Agent Riordan, who was in the process of leaving government employment. He turned them over to Chee Dodge, a mixed-blood Navajo who was the agent's interpreter and would play a prominent role in Navajo affairs for the next half century.

On the twenty-five-mile wagon ride to Fort Defiance, the site of the agency, the occasional red sandstone cliffs along the way assumed shapes that reminded Welsh of towering fortresses or oriental cities complete with "domes of mosques and slender minarets."[31] Equally colorful were the Navajos themselves, with their silver and turquoise jewelry and hair tied up in red handkerchiefs. Welsh was confident that, with their intelligence and industry, they had a bright future if handled properly. A conversation with Manuelito, the current head chief and a former warrior of renown, further convinced him of Navajo potential.[32]

As usual the Episcopalian was unimpressed by the spiritual side of Indian life, dismissing the Navajo medicine dance he witnessed as "neither a very interesting, nor edifying performance." The "demonical shoutings and howlings," Welsh concluded, would do little for the sick man whose condition elicited them.[33] The following day being Sunday, and no clergyman within a hundred miles, it was Welsh's turn to mystify the Navajos. He conducted church services at the local school and reported that the children in his audience "looked and listened in wondering silence."[34]

Welsh was complimentary of Navajo crafts. Among the tribesmen he met an outstanding silversmith. The Philadelphia artist admired his work, as he did the Navajo blankets seen at the trading posts. Welsh discussed the eastern market potential for the durable and handsome blankets in his pamphlet summarizing the trip.

In their travels on the reservation Welsh and Gardiner met several traders, among them the celebrated Lorenzo Hubbell, who did so much to further the Navajo blanket trade, and the equally well known Thomas V. Keam. An Englishman, Keam had come to the United States as a young man and enlisted in the cavalry. After military service he found employment as first an interpreter, then a clerk, and finally a special agent for the Navajos. By 1875 he had secured a license to trade with the Hopis, whose small reservation was an enclave in the heart of the larger Navajo domain. When Welsh met him, Keam was operating from a post he had built in a canyon that bore his name. He was trying to dispose of his property to the government as the site for an Indian school. However, the validity of his land title was in question, and he was happy to meet someone from the East who might help him with his campaign. Welsh thought the location a good one for a school and was anxious to do anything which would increase Indian educational facilities.

While at Keam's Canyon, Welsh and Gardiner took an overnight side trip to two of the Hopi villages on nearby First Mesa. Welsh compared the breathtaking view from its elevation of 600 feet to that from the masthead of a ship. The Hopis themselves he found friendly and attractive; as at San Ildefonso he felt as if he were stepping back in time.[35]

After another week among the Navajos, the IRA's representatives moved on to Prescott, Arizona Territory, and to Whipple Barracks, on its outskirts. They were drawn there by correspondence Welsh had had with General and Mrs. George Crook. The general at that time commanded the Department of Arizona, and the Crooks had concerned themselves with the Hualapais, a small tribe against which he had once campaigned. The previous spring Crook had contacted the IRA about dangerous food shortages among the Hualapais, and the association had donated $150 for emergency relief.[36]

In 1884 the Hualapais made their home in a short stretch of the Grand Canyon and drew rations at nearby Hackberry. After a futile effort at Prescott to organize an IRA branch, Welsh and Gardiner traveled more than a hundred miles to the ration issue point for a brief visit with "this unfortunate and degraded tribe."[37] This episode concluded the southwestern trip, and Welsh was back in Philadelphia by the middle of June.

Although the Pueblos, Navajos, and Hualapais whom he had encountered were far different in personality and circumstances than the Sioux, Welsh saw no reason to alter his views on Indian policy. Even the persistence of Pueblo culture at San Ildefonso and among the Hopis, despite the presence of whites in the area for nearly three centuries, did not seem to faze him. What Welsh saw in the Southwest simply reinforced his belief in the assimilation doctrine and, to achieve it, the necessity for schools and the introduction of private property. The latter he believed would be a deterrent to the Navajo war-making propensity, for "a man will not enter lightly into a quarrel who jeopards his property thereby."[38]

In the Southwest, as in Sioux country, Welsh was impressed by the role of the Indian police and by the overriding importance of the agent. Only fifteen Navajo policemen patrolled an area of 10,000 square miles occupied by a population of 17,000. He concluded that not only were the police efficient but the people were comparatively well ordered.[39]

Agents Riordan of the Navajos and Pedro Sanchez of the Pueblos made highly favorable impressions on Welsh. Unfortunately, Riordan was quitting the Indian Service, in part because of the poor pay and unsatisfactory housing conditions. In his report written for public consumption Welsh denounced quarters for employees at the Navajo Agency as "scarcely fit for cattle" and urged better salaries for Indian Service personnel.[40] He thought it absurd to expect honesty and competent administration from a man inadequately paid. "The Indian Agent is the pivot of the Indian problem," Welsh insisted on his return from the Southwest, and this view was fundamental to his analysis of the Indian problem.[41]

He was not the only one to trvael in the Southwest for the IRA during its first two years of operation. General S. C. Armstrong spent seven weeks in the area in the fall of 1883, visiting the tribes of Indian Territory as well as many in New Mexico and Arizona. The association published Armstrong's account of his tour, which foreshadowed some of Welsh's judgments on the Native Americans of the region. The general was most impressed by the Navajos, whom he described as "the richest of all our Indians. . . . the Jews of their race."[42] Like Welsh, he favored better salaries for agents and greater expenditures on education. For the Five Civilized Tribes, whom Welsh did not visit, the general advocated allotment in severalty, predicting that perpetuation of their holding of land in common would be a "disastrous failure."[43]

Similar sentiments were expressed about the Apaches of the White Mountain reservation after they were visited in the fall of 1884 by Robert Frazer, an IRA representative. Frazer was a mining engineer, a member of the executive committee, and Fanny Welsh's brother. His visit to Arizona was at the invitation of General Crook, and he traveled over the reservation with the general's annual inspection party. Once again the report was that the Apache was "prepared by intelligence and inclination to become in time and with the acquirement of the English language, a law-abiding and useful citizen." The mining engineer even managed to detect that "to own their land individually is their heart's desire." Frazer concluded that the process would be complete when the Apache acquired the ballot. The Philadelphian's experience with machine politics had taught him that "he will then always have a protector in one political party or the other who may desire his vote."[44]

Painter's only investigative trip in this period paid for by the Philadelphia office was to the Northwest. He was sent there in response to reports of starvation among the Blackfeet. Painter confirmed the tragedy and provided additional lurid details of desperate fathers prostituting their daughters to the soldiers at Fort Assiniboine to get money to buy food. Witnesses swore that they, in Painters' words, "could hear their screams from the teepees and bushes under the brutal usage they were receiving."[45] The IRA blamed the starving conditions on the inadequate congressional appropriations, and Painter on his return to Washington lobbied for increased support.

The IRA did not wage this battle, or any other, alone. During these first two years the association developed staunch allies in the Women's National Indian Association, the Board of Indian Commissioners, and the Conference at Lake Mohonk. The WNIA, through Mrs. Quinton, had welcomed the IRA's entrance into the field, and the two organizations cooperated closely. The WNIA distributed to its members IRA publications, and Welsh and other IRA members spoke at meetings of the women's association and aided them in furthering their projects.

Even closer ties between the IRA and the WNIA were considered late in 1883, when Mrs. Quinton formally submitted a proposal for a union of the two organizations which yet would leave each to its own work under its own officers.[46] The first annual meeting of the IRA saw the acceptance of such a proposal, but it was so hedged in by qualifications as to be meaningless. A joint board was appointed, although there is no evidence of its functioning. The WNIA did change direction somewhat, leaving more of the political agitation to the IRA, while the women's group branched out into the subsidizing of missionary work and the building and repairing of Indian homes. Welsh referred to the division of duties as appropriate: "There are some things which, in the present age, can be pushed better by men, but the two societies stand side by side, the slight divergence being that men have more to do with political matters."[47]

Mrs. Quinton was more concerned about the impact of the IRA on WNIA membership. At her request the IRA decided not to accept female members, although it would accept donations from them.[48] This restriction seems to have been in force only briefly, and Mrs. Quinton implied on more than one occasion that the WNIA was getting the short end of the stick in its association with the IRA.

Welsh's view of politics as a male preserve had been expressed at the fourteenth annual meeting of the Board of Indian Commissioners with representatives of missionary societies and Indian rights organizations. Usually taking place at Washington hotels—the Riggs House and later at the Ebbitt House—the one-day January meetings had since the founding of the board provided an opportunity for friends of the Indian to harmonize their views and activities. It is significant that only a month after its birth the IRA thought it necessary to send a representative to the January 1883 meeting. J. Topliff Johnson, a member of the executive committee, described the new organization's general objectives for the benefit of the commissioners and their guests. Johnson enlivened his account with a description of a young Navajo's first encounter with oysters on a trip to Philadelphia, a bit of ethnic humor typical of episodes recounted by whites, who found a constant source of amusement in the reactions of Native Americans to a strange culture.[49] Johnson, like most of those indulging in such humor, did not deliberately intend to degrade another people. He had taken more than a passing interest in Indian causes and had been somewhat upset not to have been invited to the organizational meeting of the IRA.[50]

The response of the head of the Board of Indian Commissioners, General Clinton B. Fisk, to Johnson's statement of IRA objectives was interesting: "Your association is endeavoring to do what this Board has been trying to do for the last ten years."[51] And, indeed, the endorsement of severalty, education, and the improvement of Indian educational opportunities had been heard at Riggs House routinely every year the meeting had been held. Beginning in October of 1883 many of the people gathering at Riggs House every January would have an opportunity to meet again at Lake Mohonk in the fall to discuss their mutual interests amid the glorious fall colors of upstate New York.

The famed Lake Mohonk conferences grew out of the meeting at Santee participated in by Welsh and several others in early June of 1883. As Welsh remembered it several months later, their principal discussions took place in an all-day session in the parlor of Congregational missionary Reverend Alfred Riggs.[52] Among those present were General Eliphalet Whittlesey and Albert K. Smiley of the Board of Indian Commissioners, Bishop Hare, Charles Painter, Dr. M. E. Strieby of the American Missionary Association, and Dr. William Hayes Ward, editor of the religious weekly *The Independent*. Two local missionaries rounded out the group, whose principal topic was the Sioux Agreement pending in Congress.

Welsh found reason for hope in a meeting that could attract so many people to a site as isolated as the Santee Reservation. Albert K. Smiley likewise found the discussions rewarding and decided to try to resume them in the fall by hosting a conference. Held at the rambling lodge Smiley had constructed on beautiful Lake Mohonk in the Shawangunk Mountains, just west of New Paltz, New York, it lasted for three days. So successful was the conference, and the Smiley generosity so boundless, that it was repeated every fall until brought to an end in 1917 by the disruptions of World War I. As the conferees were the guests of Albert Smiley and the setting was one of the most scenic in the country, invitations were prized and most spouses (not including Fanny Welsh, however) were happy to attend.

The first two conferences set the tone for those that followed. Vigorous discussion sessions continued throughout the three days, punctuated with opportunities to socialize at meals and during walks or carriage rides over the beautiful estate. Twelve men signed the report of the 1883 conference, and the one for 1884 lists thirty-one in attendance.[53] At both conferences Welsh served as secretary, and IRA members were prominent on the program committee. In 1883 Welsh, Rhoads, and Painter served on the five-man committee, and the next year Welsh, Rhoads, Painter, and Henry Pancoast served on a sevenman body. Welsh was secretary for both conferences, and he and the association were responsible for the preparation and dissemination of their reports.

There were no surprises in the conclusions reached by the conferences. Nor should there have been, as the participants were the same people, or those of similar views, who had been active in the group meeting at Riggs House every January since 1870 under the sponsorship of the Board of Indian Commissioners. For example, nearly half of those at Lake Mohonk in October 1884 were reunited at the Riggs House in Washington the following January, among them Welsh, Painter, Rhoads, and General Armstrong. At Lake Mohonk the main thrust was the Indian need for land in severalty, education, and the full privileges of citizenship, including the ballot. The importance of getting good agents also was emphasized. Not unexpectedly, given the overlapping attendance, the general tenor of the resolutions at the Riggs House was the same.

Although the first two years saw the IRA's establishment of close relations with the Lake Mohonk Conference, the WNIA, the Board of Indian Commissioners, and reformers in general, its relations with Captain R. H. Pratt and with Dr. T. A. Bland began to deteriorate. In Captain Pratt's case the IRA was not sufficiently enthusiastic about off-reservation boarding schools like Carlisle to suit its sensitive founder. Herbert Welsh admired Pratt and defended him on many occasions; however, Welsh did feel that there also was a role for reservation schools. The two men likewise disagreed over careers for graduates of schools like Carlisle and Hampton. Welsh, like General Armstrong, believed that educated Indians could make a contribution by returning to their reservations. Pratt vehemently opposed this view. "The way to do it is to get out of the woods and stay out," Pratt insisted because he feared the degrading influences to which young Indians would be subjected if they returned to their tribes. The captain accused the IRA of vacillating on the issue and said:

> If the Indians are never to have the liberty of the land, and to be allowed the props and stays which surround you and me, nor to enjoy the inestimable privilege of sweating for daily bread as we do, and that too in competition with the rest of us, they will always be a care upon us, and paupers and vagabonds.[54]

When Welsh was quoted in a newspaper article as criticizing the off-reservation school concept, Captain Pratt reacted strongly. In a letter to Welsh in the summer of 1884 Pratt implied that Welsh had more public standing as an authority on Indians than he had knowledge of the Native Americans. He concluded his short, sharp note, "I wish you would give yourself a year's experience as an Indian teacher or Agent at an agency (ten years would be better), and feel on your own person some responsibility for the progress of your charge."[55]

Welsh's more lengthy response was typical of the man—cool, well-reasoned, courteous, but firm. He mentioned the fact that he had spoken in favor of the eastern boarding schools and of Pratt personally many times. Indeed, at Welsh's suggestion an IRA committee had included Carlisle's appropriation as one of its concerns when it appeared before the Indian committee of the United States Senate. As for Pratt's challenge to him to take employment as a teacher or agent, Welsh turned the other cheek: "I have no doubt that for such work I am unsuited and that I should make a miserable failure of it." "In this Indian Question," he observed, "I regard myself simply as an advertising medium, but even for such I trust that there may be a work to do."[56]

Captain Pratt backed down. "I thank you with all my heart for your 'soft answer' letter," he responded, "and beg you will pardon me for the slightest doubting of your interest, upon such baseless evidence." And he added a revealing comment: "I am greatly taxed and get a little morbid at times."[57] For the moment peace was restored, but Pratt demanded complete loyalty to him and Carlisle, which Welsh could not give. This dispute was only the first of a long series of clashes that would become more bitter with the passage of time.

Welsh's relations with Dr. Bland were going downhill even more rapidly. *The Council Fire* had cordially welcomed the IRA to the work, and there had followed the aborted negotiations for the purchase of the journal by the association.[58] However, even before the birth of the IRA, Dr. Bland had sided with Chief Red Cloud of the Oglalas against Agent McGillycuddy, a man whom Welsh judged to be one of the most effective members of the Indian Service. The Oglala chief's accusations, that McGillycuddy had appropriated government supplies for his own use and had favored certain Indians in the distribution of annuities, were investigated by the Indian Bureau, which found insufficient evidence for action against the agent.[59] As the Bland-Red Cloud campaign against McGillycuddy accelerated, the agent's admirers, Welsh and Senator H. L. Dawes among them, rallied to his support. The Massachusetts senator published a letter in the *Springfield Republican* in which he described Bland as "a very strange man." The senator believed Bland "as wild in his attempts to state facts as he is in his ideas of what is the proper policy toward the race he thinks he serves."[60] Moreover, Dawes cited reports by Welsh and Painter to buttress his defense of McGillycuddy. Welsh further alienated Bland by distributing nearly 3,000 copies of Dawes's letter. Bland's response was an editorial in *The Council Fire* entitled, "The Indian Rights Association—Is The Name A Misnomer?" He appealed to the rank-and-file IRA members, whom he described as good and honest people who had not known that their support of the association "would be used to defend a thieving Indian agent" against charges brought by Red Cloud. Bland suggested that the "Indian Rights (?) Association" might better "have given the Indian's side of this story instead of the agent's."[61]

Welsh and Henry Pancoast replied to Bland in interviews granted the local press.[62] Another member of the executive committee, Philip Garrett, brought the matter to the attention of the secretary of the interior. Garrett assured the secretary that he believed Bland honest, but "of very weak judgment, carried away by prejudices and impulses, so as to be of no practical value."[63] Garrett defended Welsh and Rhoads (now president of the IRA, having succeeded Wayne MacVeagh) as informed and true friends of the Indian. The harsh exchanges between Bland and IRA leaders further divided the eastern friends of the Indian and led the editor of *The Council Fire* to launch his own organization in 1885, the National Indian Defence Association. In the several years of its existence it never seriously rivaled the IRA, but any division weakened the cause in which they all had enlisted.

CHAPTER FOUR

First Battles
Over the Sioux Agreement

In the first two years of its existence the IRA involved itself in a variety of issues of varying significance. They usually were brought to its attention by people in the Indian country, although fact-finding trips by IRA personnel uncovered others. As mentioned earlier, it was at the initiative of General and Mrs. Crook that the organization interested itself in the plight of the Hualapais of Arizona. Not only did the association make the donation the Crooks requested for emergency relief, but Painter tried to get a congressional appropriation for the tribe, and Welsh circulated a flyer on the Hualapais to women who might be able to collect clothing for them. This kind of an appeal for donations of money, clothing, Christmas boxes, or school materials became a routine chore for the IRA. Welsh tried to respond to each request from a reservation, usually contacting the WNIA, or what he referred to in the appeal for aid for the Hualapais as "the Christian women of the country."[1] They seldom failed him.

The starvation among the Blackfeet that took Painter to Montana in 1884 was on a scale beyond the competence of private charity. The Interior Department did not deny that the Indians were starving, but seemed most interested in laying the responsibility at the door of Congress for failing to provide sufficient appropriations. The IRA must be credited with a vigorous publicity campaign that focused the public's attention on the disaster and helped pressure Congress into action. After Painter's report on his Montana trip confirmed the famine conditions, Welsh moved quickly. He and other IRA officers made two trips to Washington to impress on officials the gravity of the situation.

Late in November 1884, Welsh and Robert Frazer were able to see Secretary of the Interior Teller and President Arthur regarding the needs of the Blackfeet as well as those of the Chiricahua Apaches reported by General Crook. In the middle of December they were back again accompanied by Painter, General Armstrong, and Clement M. Biddle, the last a Quaker merchant long active in Indian affairs and now a member of the association's executive committee. This time they presented the Blackfeet predicament to influential members of the House of Representatives, including E. John Ellis of Louisiana, who chaired the subcommittee on Indian appropriations. When Ellis failed to move promptly, Painter wrote him an open letter charging the chairman with prolonging distress among the Blackfeet.[2] Welsh circulated the letter to editors, and Ellis saw a copy of it in the New York *Tribune.* He retaliated on the floor of the House with a sneering reference to Painter as an IRA member and "one of those self-constituted friends of the Indian." The congressman accused Painter with loosing on his head "the anathemas of the press East and North" with a letter containing "the grossest misrepresentations and statements . . . utterly and infamously false."[3] That in turn brought down upon the congressman a *Harper's Weekly* editorial defending the IRA.[4] It was typical of the support Welsh would be able to mobilize among editors of influential eastern publications, and he promptly circulated hundreds of copies. Such pressure must be given some responsibility for Ellis's change of tactics from delaying to expediting a $50,000 appropriation to aid Montana Indians.

Meanwhile the IRA was making its weight felt on another important issue, the Sioux Agreement of 1882. Negotiated by a three-man commission in the fall of 1882, it provided for the sale to the United States of 11,000,000 acres of land. This strategically located purchase would open for settlement and railroad construction a belt of land connecting Missouri River communities like Pierre and Chamberlain with the Black Hills, acquired in 1876. It had the fervent support of local settlers and the two railroads serving the area, the Chicago and Northwestern, and the Chicago, Milwaukee and St. Paul, both of which hoped to extend their lines to Deadwood. But first the agreement would have to be accepted by both houses of Congress.

The commission, headed by former governor of Dakota Territory Newton Edmunds, had no sooner begun its work among the Sioux than Welsh was warned against it by Reverend H. Burt, the missionary Welsh had met on his first visit to Dakota.[5] Moreover, Bishop Hare had informed him that the commission's interpreter was one Reverend Samuel D. Hinman, who had sued the bishop for libel and caused him great anguish.[6] Hinman's affiliation with the commission could only prejudice Hare and Welsh against it. However, there were serious objections to both the terms of the agreement and to the way it had been negotiated. By the time it had been presented to Congress, the eastern friends of the Indian were closing ranks against the agreement.

Less than two months after the IRA's organizational meeting, Welsh had begun to inspire opposition to the Sioux Agreement. A Boston woman wrote Senator Dawes at Welsh's suggestion, informing the senator that Reverend Hinman was not to be trusted.[7] Welsh himself visited Washington late in February 1883 to lobby against the bill, but it slipped through the House as an amendment to an unrelated measure. When Charles Painter learned of the bill's passage, he hastily rallied General Whittlesey of the Board of Indian Commissioners, Bishop Hare (who happened to be in town), and Alice C. Fletcher, an ethnologist and active reformer who was lobbying for her own bill to allot land in severalty to the Omahas. Together they helped convince key senators to take no action for the moment on the Sioux Agreement.[8]

This move was only the first stage of a fight that would ebb and flow for the next six years and see two other groups dispatched to treat with the Sioux. The IRA's position was typical of that taken by the reformers. It did not oppose the government's contention that the Sioux held more land than they needed, and that they themselves would profit by selling some of it and investing the proceeds in livestock, farm implements, and educational facilities. Nor were the interests of the settlers ignored. When in Dakota Territory on his second visit, Welsh, along with Bishop Hare, had conferred with a small group of Pierre residents.[9] Welsh and Hare had assured the anxious settlers that the need to open the area to further development was understood, but they had also insisted that the terms proposed by the Edmunds Commission were unfair. The response of one of the citizens was that they wanted only a Sioux cession and were not concerned about the terms. Such expediency was repugnant to Welsh and Hare, although they labored to be "practical." Welsh quoted approvingly to those assembled with the Board of Indian Commissioners at Riggs House in January 1885 the bishop's view that the Sioux reservations must be diminished in size; they could not remain "like blocks of granite in the way of civilization."[10]

Like others who gathered at Riggs House and Lake Mohonk, Welsh believed that one salutary result of the reduction in Indian land holdings would be their closer contact with the white population. However, the cessions must ensure a fair return to the Indians, and the feeling among their friends was that the Sioux Agreement of 1882 failed to do so. Captain Pratt, with his usual bluntness, referred to it as a "scheme to rob the Sioux."[11]

Another undesirable feature of the agreement related to the Lower Brulé Agency. It would be part of the cession, and Indians living there would have to seek residence at other agencies with no guarantee of fair compensation for improvements on the land from which they would be forced. As a result no Lower Brulé had consented to sign the agreement.

Welsh was particularly distressed at the commission's failure to honor the provision in the 1868 Sioux treaty requiring consent of three-fourths of the adult males to any land cessions. On his travels among the Sioux he had heard from a number of people, including missionaries, Indians like George Sword and American Horse, and the mixed-blood interpreter Billy Garnett, that the commission had included the signatures of a number of boys.[12] Garnett also confirmed Captain Sword's statement that Newton Edmunds and his colleagues did not make it clear to all the Indians that what was being negotiated was a cession of lands, as well as a provision permitting individual Indians to take allotments. Bull Eagle, a warrior of imposing physique, pantomimed the pressure he had been under to sign by seizing the surprised Welsh by the wrist and jerking him to his feet.[13]

Bishop Hare raised still another objection to the agreement, one which the IRA and those who gathered annually at the Riggs House and Lake Mohonk accepted as valid. He pointed out that the document made no provision for compensating the churches operating among the Sioux for their improvements in the form of cleared fields, fences, and buildings.

Recognizing that the real issue was the terms for the reduction of the Sioux holdings, and that the railroads and settlers could not be completely denied, Welsh and the IRA sought a fresh approach. With the help of Charles Painter, Senator Dawes drafted a new bill incorporating the improvements sought by the association and the Mohonk Conference.[14]

The Dawes Sioux Bill was ready for submission by March 1884. Welsh prepared a supporting pamphlet, 3,000 copies of which were printed, and which was included in the 1884 report of the Mohonk Conference. Welsh opened the pamphlet with an obvious bid for western support, a sensible recognition that any Sioux agreement would have to be approved by a Congress more responsive to the needs of settlers than those of Native Americans. He waxed eloquent, referring to the proposed cession as a "magnificent highway . . . between the civilization of Eastern and Western Dakota."[15] Settlers were further

Senator Henry L. Dawes
Courtesy National Archives

soothed by compliments on their "splendid pluck in their battle with the wilderness."[16]

Welsh also claimed that the Dawes proposal would provide "ample justice" for the Sioux, who would be asked to give up about half of their holdings.[17] The bill provided that each of the various Sioux tribes would receive a patent to its remaining land, the patent to be held in trust by the government for twenty-five years. Meanwhile, Indians wanting to hold land individually might get it from the tribal holdings.

The compensation proposed for the land to be surrendered was increased and this time included a million-dollar permanent fund to be placed in the United States Treasury to draw five percent interest, the $50,000 to be paid annually to the Sioux. Nevertheless, this amount still was substantially less than Welsh had calculated the land to be worth.

The Dawes Bill had other new features. Not only were the Indians to be compensated for improvements in any land ceded, but if individual Sioux wished to remain in the areas to be sold they could choose allotments and receive title to them. This clause was not likely to be welcomed by the settlers, although few Indians could be expected to take advantage of it. On the other hand the churches would certainly capitalize on the provision in the bill which guaranteed that those which had maintained schools or missions could secure up to 160 acres.

The Senate passed the Dawes Sioux Bill in April 1884. A House committee proposed changes and returned it to the Senate without taking further action. Meanwhile Senator Dawes was becoming more involved in the drafting of a general allotment in severalty act which might render bills for particular reservations unnecessary.

General allotment bills had been before Congress since 1879. Senator Richard Coke of Texas had introduced a bill in 1880 which was still pending when the IRA came into being. Like all other reformers, including Dr. Bland, Welsh and his colleagues supported allotment because, as the IRA's first annual report declared:

> This measure . . . would act as a powerful stimulus to individual industry, secure the Indian in his possession of land, strengthen his individuality, weaken the tribal bonds, and have a general tendency to place him more upon a footing with the rest of the community.[18]

The IRA published and distributed a pamphlet advocating the Coke Bill in 1884[19] The Lake Mohonk Conference included the pamphlet, as it had the IRA statement on the Dawes Sioux Bill, in its own 1884 report, thus assuring it an even wider circulation.

It was assumed by friends of the Indian that allotment in severalty would have to be accompanied by introduction of the American legal system to safeguard the Indian's newfound property rights. Formalizing marriage relationships and coping with crime on reservations were other objectives of reformers. Henry Pancoast, the young attorney who had accompanied Welsh on the trip to the Sioux agencies in 1882, headed the association's law committee, which reviewed this problem area.

Welsh and Pancoast were disturbed about another facet of the problem, the role of the Indian agent, whom Welsh had referred to as the "pivot of the Indian problem." The agent had tremendous potential for good—or evil. "The Indian is at present almost completely at the mercy of his caprice or tyranny should he be an unjust or hot-tempered man," observed Welsh.[20] The Indian police, whom Welsh endorsed, were totally under the agent's control, as were the Courts of Indian Offenses introduced by Secretary Teller in 1883. Clearly a new legal system was an imperative. Pancoast quoted approvingly Bishop Hare's dictum: "The efforts of civil agents, teachers and missionaries are, like the struggles of drowning men, weighed down with lead so long as by the absence of law Indian society is left without a base."[21]

After months of conferring, the IRA's law committee finally drafted a bill to meet the need. It provided judges, not necessarily Indian, appointed by the president and administering the criminal codes of the territory or state in which the reservation was located. There was some flexibility on treatment of minor offenses, but capital offenses of Indian against Indian were to be subject to federal jurisdiction. This last feature reflected the shock at the recent dismissal of charges against Crow Dog, who had murdered Chief Spotted Tail on the Rosebud Reservation. In December 1883 the United State Supreme Court had ruled that the United States had no jurisdiction over crimes committed on reservations by Indians against Indians.

Pancoast and his committee circulated their draft and discovered that, while the need for law was generally recognized, there was little agreement on the form it should take. Only on two points did there seem to be consensus, and one of these was the provision for federal law to cover capital offenses. Under the circumstances the executive committee decided not to push the bill for the time being. Senator Dawes was willing to try to have the two points on which there was consensus added to other legislation as amendments.[22] The IRA then sent copies of the proposals with an accompanying letter to members of the House and to leading newspapers. The House responded by tacking the Major Crimes Act onto the appropriation bill, and in that form it became law. The IRA congratulated itself on achieving at least this much.[23]

Getting the proper personnel in the Indian Service to execute laws and policies was becoming one of the overriding concerns of the association. From his travels and correspondence Welsh inevitably formed opinions as to the worth of particular Indian Service employees. And very soon individuals began to approach the IRA to support their professional ambitions or protect them from inequitable treatment. Just how far to go in the effort to improve the quality of Indian Service personnel was the question. Painter believed that the association should attempt to get the incompetents out, but he opposed backing specific candidates for positions on the grounds that the government and not the IRA must be held responsible for the quality of personnel.[24] This was a difficult line to draw, however, and Welsh found himself increasingly drawn into campaigns in behalf of or against particular individuals. Inevitably he was at odds with those controlling those appointments—commissioners of Indian affairs, secretaries of the interior, Indian agents, or members of Congress, depending upon the position involved and who controlled the patronage at the time.

Although Welsh discovered that Secretary Teller did not welcome suggestions from the IRA on appointments, the secretary recognized the growing power of the association. The association had been hardly a year old when Teller invited Welsh to confer with him in Washington and used the occasion to seek the assistance of the infant group. The secretary was meeting resistance in Congress to his proposal to provide Native Americans the educational benefits guaranteed them by treaty. Teller suggested that the IRA circulate a petition to try to create some pressure. The executive committee concurred, and signatures were collected in Philadelphia and in other communities by the association's branches, particularly the signatures of leading citizens whose names had recognition value.[25] In addition Welsh distributed 2,000 copies of his and Teller's correspondence on the subject, which inspired favorable stories in newspapers. The IRA asked for an additional $500,000 for Indian education, and Congress did appropriate $400,000 more, a significant improvement for which the association took credit.[26]

By the spring of 1885, the IRA had emerged as a force to be reckoned with. Its membership numbered two hundred and fifty and was still growing. This number did not count those signed up by the twenty-three branches, which provided at least some support. Charles Painter was impressing officials in the national government with association concerns, and the Philadelphia office was rounding into shape as the youthful Matthew Sniffen began to provide continuity and efficient administration. However, Welsh's contribution had been the critical element. His willingness to devote his full time and energies to the IRA had made it go. His religiosity and his social standing in Philadelphia gave him entree to the church members and patricians who were the mainstay of reform movements in the late nineteenth century.

Recognition of the IRA's growing importance was apparent in the willingness of editors of newspapers and magazines like *Harper's Weekly,* the *New York Times,* and the *Springfield Republican* to print association contributions and to editorialize along lines suggested by Herbert Welsh. The IRA's influence at Lake Mohonk and with the Board of Indian Commissioners was manifest. Its own meetings were attracting people concerned with Indian affairs. Commissioner of Indian Affairs Hiram Price graced the first annual meeting in Philadelphia, and Bishop Hare and an occasional missionary or Indian agent put in an appearance at executive committee meetings. Among those calling upon the association for help had been H. B. Whipple, the renowned Episcopal Bishop of Minnesota, whose work for Indians had begun twenty years earlier in the Lincoln administration.[27]

IRA representatives also had found doors open to them in Washington. President Arthur, Secretary Teller, Commissioner Price, and a number of representatives and senators had received them. Under the circumstances it is not strange that early in 1885 President-elect Grover Cleveland should be willing to grant an interview to the corresponding secretary of the association. The Democrats were returning to power after a quarter-century in the wilderness, and good Republicans like Herbert Welsh, who made up the bulk of the patrician reformers, were more than mildly apprehensive.

CHAPTER FIVE

Resolution of the
Sioux Land Problem

The period 1885–1889 was one in which the IRA underwent its most dramatic growth in membership and influence. It also was a period of great frustrations for Herbert Welsh and his co-workers, who were learning that, despite their best efforts, success frequently eluded them. As wards of the United States, the Indians could be dealt with only through the government, and Welsh could not even visit a reservation without authorization from Washington and the cooperation of the local agent. The size and complexity of the Indian Service, and opposition from other groups—whites seeking land or reservation timber, for example—often meant that the association's most impressively mounted campaigns achieved little.

The complex relationship of the executive and legislative branches posed a whole congeries of problems for those interested in the welfare of the Native American. The executive branch had responsibility for the day-by-day administration of Indian affairs. However, Congress, by its control of the purse strings and by enacting legislation, determined the broad outlines of policies to be pursued. In this period Congress was split, with the Democrats holding a majority in the House and the Republicans controlling the Senate. On several occasions bills supported by the IRA managed to get through one chamber only to die in the other.

What impact the IRA had was due to the respect it commanded from people in government who were impressed with its ability to mobilize public opinion. The association more than quadrupled its membership by 1889 (reaching nearly 1,200, if membership in the branches is included). Most of the increase came from people contacted by Welsh and other association officials at speaking engagements. An attempt was made to solicit membership among particular groups, army officers and Jews among them. Welsh obtained a list of officers from his friend Captain John G. Bourke, and his approach to them produced a few recruits. Anna L. Dawes, the senator's daughter, suggested soliciting New York Jews, as she was acquainted with Cyrus and Agnes Sulzberger.[1] The Sulzbergers did join, and Cyrus had an appeal for aid for the IRA published in *The American Hebrew*. Agnes Sulzberger, however, vetoed Miss Dawes's hopes for a Jewish branch on the grounds that it would not be proper "to organize sectarian societies for non-sectarian purposes."[2]

The income of the IRA did not keep pace with its membership, although it more than doubled to about $11,000 a year. Contributors of $50 or more still were essential and were approached annually by Welsh, in some cases semiannually. Among the larger donors were R. Fulton Cutting, a New York financier who gave $300 a year, and his fellow townsman William E. Dodge, Jr., heir to a copper and iron fortune, who was usually good for $250. The John Jacob Astors contributed $450 during this period, and one year J. Pierpont Morgan donated $250. The most generous contributors were two sisters, the Misses E. F. and Ida M. Mason of Boston, who together gave a total of $4,000 during the four years under discussion.[3]

A few of the branches—Cambridge, Boston, and Providence, particularly—made significant contributions to the Philadelphia office. But of the twenty-eight listed in the 1888 annual report, well over half were moribund. Some chose to cease operations, the one in Los Angeles after being able to recruit only seven members, the Newark branch because, in part, of the presence of an active WNIA group. Even the Boston branch, headed by the historian Francis Parkman, had its problems. Welsh usually could count on good news from the Providence group, led by John Nicholas Brown with Thomas J. Morgan as corresponding secretary. But that sort of participation was rapidly becoming the exception, and by 1889 Welsh no longer sought to establish new branches or fought to resuscitate the older ones. His strategy now was to recruit individuals into the national association's membership, regardless of their residence.[4]

Herbert Welsh continued to play the principal role in IRA activities. He recruited members and raised money, determined the causes to be supported, and mobilized the IRA's forces behind them. He also found time in 1885, 1887, and 1888 to visit Sioux agencies, one of the visits an extended trip during which he covered more than 600 miles in the saddle. Welsh also returned to the Southwest in 1888 to observe conditions among Apaches, Hopis, and Navajos, and the year before had visited Florida for the first time to check upon Chiricahua Apaches held there in the custody of the army.

Throughout the period Welsh drove himself to the physical limits. On occasion he went beyond them. Once his writing hand became disabled from overuse.[5] A year later his physician prescribed a two-week vacation as a remedy for exhaustion.[6] Although in the hot summer months the Welshes always retreated from Philadelphia to a pleasanter climate in Maine, New Hampshire, or western Massachusetts, even then Herbert kept up his IRA correspondence and made occasional forays into neighboring areas to recruit members and funds.

His family continued to be a cause for concern. The Welshes had a daughter, "my poor, afflicted little Bessie," whose condition required her to be placed in another household for continuous care.[7] Fanny's health remained poor, and for several months in the fall of 1887 her husband had to assume responsibility for running the household. Their relationship was not a subject Herbert discussed freely, although it clearly was not a source of satisfaction to either spouse. At one point in her illness he was barred from even entering her bedroom. A friend in whom he confided his family problems once tried to reassure him: "try and appreciate any change for the better, though not manifested towards you."[8]

Fanny could have found no consolation in Herbert's deepening commitment to public affairs. She apparently preferred that he spend the time freed by his inheritance at painting or other home-related activities. However, despite those periods when his own or Fanny's health forced him to curtail his work, Herbert was drawn more and more into public affairs. He helped found a Pennsylvania forestry association and was made a vice president of the national organization. The Law and Order Society of Philadelphia commanded some of his fund-raising talents, and he served on the Board of Managers of the City Parks Association. Clearly Welsh was one of those to whom sponsors of good causes inevitably turned for help.

One reason Welsh was able to indulge his sense of civic responsibility was that the IRA's Philadelphia office ran smoothly. Matthew Sniffen, under Welsh's supervision, assumed most of the burden of the correspondence and of the printing and distribution of the association's publications. He was assisted by a stenographer and by part-time help when a heavy mailing required it. For nearly three years the association also employed J. B. Harrison, who was able to do some of the things that only Charles Painter and Welsh had done before.

Harrison was a Unitarian clergyman whose career resembled that of Painter, both having moved from the ministry to involvement in social causes. An accomplished writer and public speaker, Harrison was available to cover the Philadelphia office when Welsh was absent. Sniffen, despite his efficiency, did not have the maturity or stature to speak for the IRA at this time. The differential in their wages reflects the relative worth Welsh placed upon them. Late in 1888 the clerk's salary was only $780 a year, while Harrison commanded $2,000. To Welsh, Harrison was worth every penny of it, "an indefatigable worker, and a most intelligent, broad-minded, and wise man."[9] One of Harrison's inspection tours for the association, of six months duration and covering fourteen reservations from Nebraska to the Pacific Northwest, resulted in *The Latest Studies on Indian Reservations.* Although Welsh had had to invest more time and energy in fund-raising in order to employ Harrison, he deeply regretted learning in the fall of 1888 that Harrison's wife's illness would force him to give up his position with the IRA.[10]

Charles Painter was, of course, another IRA employee well worth his salary. It was Welsh's opinion that "half, or more than half, the value of our organization would be gone if Professor Painter left it."[11] Certainly his contribution was great. His investigations of reservations were carried out while Congress was not in session, and he traveled widely in the four years under consideration, visiting the Southwest and California twice, as well as the Cherokees in North Carolina and tribes of the Great Lakes area. It took a wily Indian Service employee to fool a close observer like Painter. His reports featured colorful and sometimes caustic descriptions of government personnel which made his pamphlets widely read on the reservations. One teacher was limned as "a little mite of a man—sallow, spiritless," who "looked as if he had gotten out of his grave to find 'a chaw of terbacker,' and had lost his way. . . ."[12] A school superintendent was characterized as "a Christian—a tobacco-chewing, nicotine-spitting one indeed—who throws his feet over the desk in front of him and squirts away with the grace and precision which long practice can give alone to a true son of the South. . . ."[13]

Painter's greatest service to the IRA and the Indians it represented was as its Washington agent. Already familiar with the Capitol scene and the legislative process when first employed by Welsh, by 1889 he was truly an expert in extracting information from Indian Office personnel and from the clerks who made up the Indian division of the office of the secretary of the interior. He was equally adept at tracking a bill through Congress and determining when and where to apply pressure to facilitate its passage or kill it, as the case might be. As few bills emerged from committee, it was here that much of the work had to be done, by testifying or by educating individual members on the merits of the proposed legislation. If a bill made it to the floor of the House and Senate, Painter might request Welsh to inspire a wave of editorials and letters in the hope of influencing the outcome.

Painter was a lobbyist and a highly successful one whose access to men of power would be the envy of his modern-day counterparts. He had audiences with President Cleveland several times and routinely conferred with the commissioner of Indian affairs and the secretary of the interior. Before one of his trips to the Southwest he was briefed by both the president and the secretary as to information they would like him to bring back.[14] Congressmen and senators came to Painter for guidance on Indian legislation, and he was known to help those arranging the calendar for pending bills. He also knew how to "browse around" the Indian Bureau, extracting tidbits of information from clerks when their superiors were occupied elsewhere.[15]

When Congress was in session, the IRA's Washington representative was a very busy man. Painter's report for a typical month listed thirty-five projects which had required his attention.[16] Some were major bills involving land cessions. Others were less vital, except to the Indians involved—for example, those few Indians on the small California reservation Painter was trying to get fenced to keep out intruders. He also found time for the handful of Sioux seeking compensation for military service they had performed for the United States twenty years earlier. Nor was he too busy to try to get improvements in laundry and kitchen facilities at one Indian school, and a new matron at another. In literally hundreds of ways the association worked to improve the efficiency of the Indian Service, to redress old grievances, and to prevent new injustices from being perpetrated.

In no area was the IRA's work more important than Indian land. By the time the association came into being, the Native Americans had been stripped of most of their holdings on the continent, but the pressure mounted in the late nineteenth century for further reduction. In large part the pressure was a corollary of the nation's increase in population. In twenty years, from 1880–1900, the country's population increased fifty percent, from 50,000,000 to more than 75,000,000. Six new states were created, and the western half of what would become Oklahoma was opened to settlement. The Sioux in Dakota Territory were under particular pressure as the population of the territory rose from 135,000 to 500,000 in the 1880s.[17]

The IRA's position, simply put, was that it was impossible to stay the flood; the only thing to do was to get the best possible terms for the tribes and protect their claims to at least some of the property by allotment in severalty. The association also took a firm stand against the removal of Indians to new sites, arguing that such moves were serious disruptions in what were at best rather ineffective civilization programs. At Crow Creek, Dakota Territory, it blocked one such move early in President Cleveland's first administration.

During the last week of the Chester A. Arthur administration Herbert Welsh received a telegram from Charles Painter. The Washington agent was alerting him to a disturbing development. Without consultation with appropriate congressional committees or even the commissioner of Indian affairs, Secretary Teller had prevailed on President Arthur to hastily issue a proclamation, dated February 27, opening 500,000 of the 635,000 acres of the Crow Creek Reservation to settlement. Fortuitously, an IRA executive committee meeting was scheduled to take place within hours of Welsh's receiving the telegram, and that body directed the law committee to prepare a formal protest and submit it to the secretary of the interior.[18] Meanwhile, Painter already had called on Secretary Teller to express the association's disapproval of the unexpected action. Something had to be done quickly, as word of the proclamation had leaked out before it was officially promulgated. On February 28 several hundred whites rushed onto the reservation and began staking out claims and throwing up any kind of shanty to establish their homestead rights. By the time Welsh had learned what was happening, there were 2,000 squatters on the reservation and more coming.

The approximately 1,000 Yanktonai Sioux who inhabited Crow Creek were not the Indians for whom the reservation originally had been set aside. Nevertheless, they had been living on it for twenty years, and the 1868 Sioux Treaty could be interpreted as recognizing their title to Crow Creek. Because of the pressure in the early 1880s to reduce Sioux holdings, the Yanktonais had begun to worry about the validity of their claim. The Edmunds Commission visited them early in 1883 and proceeded to capitalize on this fear by getting some of the chiefs and headmen to agree to a cession of part of their land in return for a clear title to the rest. It was the commission's claim that the Yanktonais did not have a clear title, and knew it, that was used by Secretary Teller to justify his precipitate action just before leaving office. It also was reported that his brother James, secretary of Dakota Territory and involved with another Dakota politician in a land-development scheme, actually had drafted the February 27 proclamation and persuaded Henry Teller to take it to President Arthur.[19] Operating on information from James Teller, boomers had stormed onto the reservation forty-eight hours before Arthur's proclamation had been officially promulgated.

Energized by the news, the IRA moved promptly to try to right the wrong it believed to be taking place. The law committee, headed by Henry S. Pancoast, hastily drafted a legal brief opposing the action and dispatched it to newly inaugurated President Grover Cleveland and his secretary of the interior, L. Q. C. Lamar, asking them to stay the opening until its legality could be determined. Pancoast also sent a copy to Senator Dawes and requested his help.[20] Copies likewise were mailed to all association members and a number of newspaper editors. Pancoast then made a hurried trip to Washington to check on details and do some personal lobbying.

The IRA's activities were having an impact. Secretary Lamar issued an order suspending implementation of the Arthur proclamation until it could be examined. The action was none too soon, as the squatters were reported by Agent John G. Gasmann to be locating even on allotments that had been made to individual Indian families. Gasmann thanked Welsh for the association's support, which he valued particularly because his own efforts to protect his Indian charges were bringing down upon his head considerable abuse from the newspaper editor of nearby Chamberlain.[21]

After Secretary Lamar's suspension of the proclamation, the matter was submitted to the Justice Department for study. During this period an IRA delegation consisting of Welsh, Pancoast, and Dr. Rhoads went to Washington to confer with Cleveland and Lamar. The secretary also arranged for them to talk to the assistant attorney general in charge of the study.[22]

Early in May, Welsh was back in Washington at the invitation of Secretary Lamar, who wanted his judgment on the draft of a proclamation to be issued by President Cleveland revoking the opening of Crow Creek.[23] On April 18 the president issued it, and Welsh, Pancoast, Painter and the other IRA people who had been involved in the fight had reason to rejoice.

The association's role in reversing the opening did not go unnoticed among whites in Dakota Territory. The same Chamberlain editor, John H. King, who had harassed Agent Gasmann, now vented his spleen on Welsh and his colleagues. In an editorial King damned "these Eastern saints that know so much and tell the truth so easy," "these Christians so-called." "Why bless your dear souls in the far East!" said editor King patronizingly, you simply do not have the facts straight. King applauded Secretary Teller as the first man prepared to take on an "Indian ring" (the phrase of the day for corrupt groups operating at Indian expense) consisting of Senator Dawes, Bishop Hare, Henry Pancoast, and Herbert Welsh. Editor King disposed of Welsh as a man who "parts his hair in the middle and carries a silk umbrella."[24] On another occasion the hard-hitting editor obviously had Welsh in mind when he referred to "the philanthropist that lives off his dead father's hard earnings and Sunday-school collections."[25]

Although President Cleveland signed a proclamation revoking the one of February 27, that did not in itself remove the estimated 3,000 squatters who had rushed to the area in response to the news of the original proclamation. Many of them would undergo real suffering if driven from their claims, on which they were now living and had planted crops. The same situation had developed hundreds of times since the inauguration of the federal land system. In virtually every instance the government had shown more concern for the squatters who inadvertently or otherwise had illegally taken up land than for the Indians whose land rights had thus been violated. These squatters were pioneers in the American tradition and glorified as such. A Chicago newspaper printed a poem about the plight of a family which sold its house in the East and made its way to Crow Creek and a new life, only to have its dreams shattered by Cleveland's proclamation.[26] The secretary for the Crow Creek Settlers' Union appealed to Welsh to act for "the cause of humanity" and do something in behalf of the squatters, "many of whom stood nobly by the flag when their country was in peril."[27] A reference to the Civil War was obligatory in the 1880s, regardless of the issue.

A citizen of Pierre, two years removed from Connecticut, wrote the Hartford *Courant* to protest its editorial on Crow Creek. The writer portrayed Dakota Territory as the "victim of Eastern prejudice and narrow-mindedness coupled with Southern jealousy." He admitted to having come to Pierre with the eastern idealized view of Indians inspired by James Fenimore Cooper's novels. However, after two years in Pierre he recognized the Indians for what they were: "a lazier, dirtier, and more scoundrelly set of human beings do not exist than the Sioux Indian and his half brothers." He made clear that his sympathies lay with the settler, whose taxes enabled the government to provide the "Indian more value in the shape of rations, clothes, blankets, agricultural implements, stock and seed every year, than the white man can possibly make by the hardest kind of labor, in the same time."[28]

Congregational ministers in Dakota Territory, including the long-time missionary Alfred L. Riggs, also pled the cause of the "innocent white settlers."[29] Meeting in Sioux Falls, they called upon Cleveland to suspend his own order and asked people in the East to be more careful of their facts in attacking the actions of Secretary Teller and President Arthur.

Welsh responded by defending the IRA's position while at the same time expressing sympathy for the plight of the settlers who had gone onto the reservation expecting it to be opened officially. He reminded Reverend Riggs that the association had backed government efforts to negotiate a reduction of Sioux holdings: "We sought to secure in an open and honorable manner far greater advantages to the whites than the outgoing administration would have secured for them by rash, secret, and unlawful means."[30] Welsh pledged to support any move in Congress to compensate those squatters who had been misled by the government's own actions. Specifically, the IRA's executive committee agreed to back a solution proposed by Senator Dawes as an amendment to his bill to reduce the Sioux holdings, then pending in the Senate.[31] The amendment would give the squatter preemption rights to his land claim if it was included in any tract ceded to the United States. Such support only encouraged the squatters to hang on, and three years later 400 remained on Crow Creek, unintimidated by the less-than-strenuous efforts to remove them. In 1888 Welsh's mild criticism of the then Crow Creek agent for this state of affairs led that official to include in his annual report so harsh a blast at the Philadelphian that the commissioner of Indian affairs forced the agent to rewrite it.[32]

One reason for the unseemly haste Secretary Teller had exhibited in pushing the Crow Creek opening had been the fear of its supporters that Congress was going to adjourn without acting on the Dawes Sioux bill. A year had elapsed since Senator Dawes, with the support of the IRA, had introduced his bill to achieve what the Edmunds Commission had failed to do, reduce Sioux landholdings roughly by half. No single issue except the constant fight to improve the quality of personnel in the Indian Service commanded more of the time and energies of Welsh and his colleagues nor proved more complicated and unsatisfying.

The views of Herbert Welsh and the IRA on the subject underwent little change. They still believed that it was impractical to think that the Sioux, numbering fewer than 30,000 people, could hold on to an area four times the size of the state of Massachusetts in the face of the demands of settlers whose interests were represented by the government. "The waves of an importunate civilization, that cannot long be either staid or stopped . . . are beating incessantly upon the border. . . ." declared Welsh, and "sound policy now demands the opening of a lawful channel for the advance of this mighty tide."[33] Get as good a financial deal for the Sioux as possible, but do not waste energy opposing the inevitable, was the IRA's position. And from the association's viewpoint there were positive elements about a Sioux land cession. It would provide them funds for civilization programs and lead to an intermingling of industrious settlers and Indians which would provide the latter the role models they badly needed if they were to become self-supporting farmers and stockraisers.

That the Great Sioux Reservation would be substantially reduced in size was a foregone conclusion, the only question being the terms on which it would be accomplished. The Forty-ninth Congress wrestled unsuccessfully with the problem, and not until late in the Fiftieth was it resolved. Henry L. Dawes did not require much assistance from the IRA in getting his bill through the Senate; it was the House that required the work. The major hurdle was getting a favorable report from the House committee for the right draft of a bill. The next task was to secure for it a place on the legislative calendar to give it some chance of coming up for a vote. Then, and only then, would Welsh worry about getting the votes to pass it while Painter worked to stave off any undesirable amendments.

Senator Dawes reintroduced his Sioux bill in the early days of the Forty-ninth Congress, and in February 1886 it received Senate approval. The IRA had circulated a pamphlet supporting it and came up with another when the fight shifted to the House. Both publications were aimed principally at the settlers and their supporters in Congress. When in Dakota Territory in September 1883, Welsh had conferred again with Pierre citizens and reassured them of the association's desire to see more land opened to settlement.[34] Welsh visited Washington three times in the spring of 1886 to appear before House committees attempting to frame a Sioux bill and to confer with Senator Dawes and other congressional allies. Charles Painter was doing the same thing on a daily basis, interspersing these meetings with his work on dozens of other projects relating to Indians all over the country.

The IRA had the support of the Board of Indian Commissioners and the WNIA in pushing the Sioux bill. At one point in the long struggle Mrs. Quinton estimated that her organization had been responsible for thirty to forty petitions addressed to the House.[35] A month later she reported sending IRA circulars on the Sioux bill to people on her mailing list.[36] One of the most important WNIA state organizations, that in Connecticut, required some persuasion from Welsh. Its head was Sara T. Kinney, an able advocate of Indian causes and wife of the editor of the Hartford *Courant.* Unfortunately for Welsh, in the spring of 1886 she had some misgivings about the Sioux bill. When he learned of them, Welsh immediately wrote Mrs. Kinney explaining the association's position and begging her to bring to bear on Olin Wellborn, the chairman of the House Indian committee, "those powerful influences" that she commanded.[37] His plea was successful, and it was the beginning of a relationship as warm and productive as the one Welsh enjoyed with Mrs. Quinton.

Welsh's relations with Dr. Bland and his National Indian Defense Association were neither warm nor productive. When Welsh testified before the House committees early in 1886, NIDA witnesses also appeared. Testifying the first time, Welsh found himself opposed by Dr. Bland. The second time Welsh appeared, Reverend Bryan Sunderland, NIDA's vice president, testified against the bill, calling for "a wall of adamant, high as the stars and permanent as heaven" to surround and protect the Great Sioux Reservation.[38] Bland also opposed the Sioux bill in the columns of his monthly, *The Council Fire,* and singled out Welsh for uncomplimentary remarks. Bishop Hare believed that much of the Indian resistance to a land cession was due to *The Council Fire,* copies of which were circulating on the Sioux reservation.[39]

Welsh felt himself under attack from both sides. He was abused by Bland and the NIDA because the IRA, from its own viewpoint at least, worked "to save the Indian . . . from that isolation which is the best guardian of barbarism."[40] He was likewise assailed by the Dakota Territory settlers who wanted land regardless of Indian rights. Welsh perhaps had reason for believing that the IRA was following

> the *via media* between a lawless and unjust Indian policy—that which would deny to the Indian all rights and responsibilities . . . on the one hand, and on the other, a sentimental and fantastic policy, which, under a show of kindness, would flatter the pride of chiefs and tribes, seeking vainly to retain the Indian in a condition intolerable to civilization.[41]

As the fight to reduce the Sioux landholdings progressed, Welsh found himself in an uneasy alliance with the representatives of the settlers. The Dakotans dispatched a delegation to Washington headed by Mayor P. F. McClure. The mayor and Welsh corresponded frequently in the next two years in an effort to coordinate their lobbying efforts. Both wanted a Sioux cession to take place, with Welsh insisting the Indians get the best terms possible, and McClure wanting the land obtained at the cheapest possible rate for the settlers. In March 1886 Welsh informed the mayor that he was willing to go to the Sioux agencies, if the bill cleared Congress, to try to persuade the Indians to sell.[42] McClure was pleased with that news but wanted even more—Welsh to serve on the commission that would actually negotiate with the Sioux. Secretary Lamar invited Welsh to lunch and asked him if he was willing to serve in that capacity.[43] Welsh eventually declined, in part because Bishop Hare thought that it would be unwise.[44]

By early May of 1886, Welsh had written so many letters in behalf of the bill that he temporarily lost the use of his right hand. Nevertheless, some of Welsh's enthusiasm was beginning to ebb. In committee the bill was amended to reduce from five percent to three percent the interest rate on the permanent fund to be set up for the Indians from the proceeds of the sale of their land. Welsh's proposal to compensate the Indians by raising the price of the land to the settlers from fifty cents an acre to seventy-five cents was then opposed by Mayor McClure. The Dakotans did not object to the government's paying five percent interest on Indian funds, but they were not happy with the prospect of paying twenty-five cents more an acre themselves.[45]

Meanwhile, Dr. Bland was still sniping away at Welsh and the IRA, charging them with selling out the Indian. Furthermore, all the reports from the Sioux agencies indicated that there would be considerable Indian opposition to a cession on the expected terms. Reverend Cleveland, the Episcopal missionary at Rosebud, further dampened Welsh's enthusiasm. Cleveland warned him he would get a "cool reception" if he tried to persuade the Indians to sell. Moreover, Cleveland was concerned about the impact of the issue on Episcopal misison activity. "What I regret," he said, "is that the church should be mixed up in the minds of these people with a transaction" they regard as unfair.[46]

The first session of the Forty-ninth Congress closed in August 1886 with the bill still bottled up in committee and Welsh discouraged. He still felt deeply the need to bring the Indians out of their isolation, as was evidenced in his revelation to Mayor McClure in an unguarded moment that, if the Indians flatly refused to negotiate, he would be willing to let Congress impose equitable terms on the Sioux.[47]

When the second session of the Forty-ninth Congress opened in December, Welsh did not respond enthusiastically to McClure's call to arms. Charles Painter was of the opinion that if no Sioux bill was passed that session perhaps the desired reduction could be accomplished under the general severalty bill, which seemed to have a better chance of passage and indeed did become law in February 1887. Nevertheless, with the IRA's help in the form of pressure on key congressmen, the Dakotans did get the Sioux bill before the House, only to have it defeated.[48]

The Fiftieth Congress opened in December 1887 and closed in March 1889 and saw two laws enacted authorizing negotiations with the Sioux. The role of Welsh and the association in the passage of the first act was relatively low-key but significant. It was only one among 130 Indian bills introduced early in the session. A further complication was that the House Indian committee had undergone considerable change. The job of educating members would have to be repeated, and new allies in the House would have to be sought. A Massachusetts representative who had been helpful had left the committee, but the IRA was fortunate to find a replacement for him in a freshman from Pennsylvania.[49]

As usual Dawes was able to get his latest version of a Sioux bill through the Senate. In the House a new bill drafted by John H. King was introduced. This was the same King who as editor of the Chamberlain paper had so belabored Welsh over Crow Creek. His bill had one serious defect in the eyes of Welsh and Senator Dawes. Although providing the Indians a better return on the land, it ignored the 1868 treaty requirement for consent of three-fourths of adult males for any land cession. Despite his concern over Sioux intransigence, Welsh still believed the principle of Sioux consent more important than the additional income. "The moral effects of such a violation of faith would be lamentable," he observed.[50] Welsh at once wrote several House members that the King bill would "meet with the determined opposition of our association and of the friends of the Indian generally over the country.[51]

The alternative Painter had suggested of using the Dawes Severalty Act to reduce the Sioux holdings was objected to by Senator Dawes himself. Dawes argued that this approach would be too time-consuming and that the settlers of Dakota Territory were not prepared to "brook any further delay."[52] It also was true that the Indians could get better terms under special legislation than they would under the general act. The senator's logic apparently convinced Welsh, and the IRA shifted position and threw its weight behind efforts to amend the King bill so as to require Sioux assent.

In contrast to his frenetic activity during the previous Congress, Welsh stayed out of Washington this time. He did try through correspondence to mobilize forces at critical points but generally left the personal lobbying to Charles Painter. Painter did well. Confronted with his threat to beat the unamended King bill if it came to a vote, its supporters withdrew it from the floor and redrafted it to require approval of any deal by three-fourths of the adult Sioux males.[53]

Welsh rejected a last-minute bid by Bland's NIDA to cooperate in trying to stop the King bill. He responded to the invitation of the president of the NIDA, Alexander Kent, by saying that Dr. Bland's record, particularly his attacks on Welsh, made cooperation impossible.[54]

The Sioux bill became law on April 30, 1888, not before, however, it had required Painter's vigilance to prevent undesirable changes in conference committee. Welsh was reasonably satisfied with the result. Whether or not the Indians would accept it remained to be seen.

For the previous two years Welsh had been telling any Sioux who asked his advice of the advantages of a cession. For example, early in 1886 he assured a native Episcopal deacon at Pine Ridge that the Dawes Sioux bill would be "one of the grandest things for the Dakota people possible."[55] Another Sioux with whom Welsh corresponded was Reverend Philip Deloria, who had had charge of an Episcopal mission at Standing Rock and more recently had been stationed at the Yankton

Sioux Commission of 1888. *From left to right:* Reverend William J.
Cleveland, Judge John V. Wright, Captain Richard H. Pratt.
Courtesy Smithsonian Institution

agency. Deloria suggested that an Indian delegation be invited to Washington if a Sioux bill became law, and Welsh passed the idea on to the secretary of the interior and the commissioner of Indian affairs.[56]

Joseph Fast Horse and Asa Kills-A-Hundred, both of Pine Ridge, also sought counsel from Welsh, as did High Eagle of Standing Rock.[57] A mixed-blood who contacted Welsh was told that the present offer was probably the best the Indians would receive and that they should accept it.[58] To facilitate negotiations, the IRA employed Reverend William Cleveland to translate a summary of the Sioux Act into Lakota and distributed copies on the reservation. Welsh again volunteered to visit all of the agencies and speak in behalf of the cession. A new secretary of the interior, William F. Vilas, while appreciating his "patriotic and generous offer" decided not to accept it as he did not wish to alert opponents of the agreement before the commission could reach the agencies.[59]

It was generally recognized that the Sioux would need a lot of persuasion. Secretary Vilas had asked Welsh's opinion on the makeup of the commission which would have the chore of negotiating.[60] Vilas had not named any of Welsh's nominees, but Reverend Cleveland, Welsh's fellow Episcopalian, was selected. Why Cleveland consented to serve, given his earlier concern about the adverse impact of such activity on his church, is difficult to understand. The secretary chose Carlisle's founder Richard Pratt to head the three-man body.

Some of the advice the IRA received from the reservation area as to how the commission should proceed was revealing. As it came from people who regarded themselves as friends of the Indian, it was suggestive of the rule of expediency over principle that characterized government negotiations with the Native Americans. Former Agent McGillycuddy, of whom Welsh thought highly, advised the distribution in the right quarters of a few spring wagons to guarantee a favorable bargaining climate.[61] Cheyenne River Agent McChesney, another IRA favorite, thought that extra rations for the Indians while the commission was negotiating with them would be appropriate.[62] Reverend John Robinson, Episcopal missionary at Pine Ridge, proposed buggies and teams for a dozen of the Indian leaders at his agency. For Lieutenant Fast Horse of the Indian police, who was using his influence in behalf of the move to settle families on their own allotments, Robinson suggested carpeting and papering the lieutenant's house.[63] As the weeks passed and Sioux opposition to any cession became more apparent, Reverend Robinson decided it would take not a dozen but about 250 buggies to do the trick: "there can be no bargain made with these folks without some such 'skull duggery.' "[64] As he confided to IRA employee J. B. Harrison, the missionary would rather see them bribed to sell their land than have it "taken from them either by force or legislation."[65] This was not the seminary solution to such a problem, but the Pine Ridge Agency in 1888 did not replicate seminary conditions. Clearly there was the feeling that Indian leaders could be bought and that the circumstances justified it.

The Pratt Commission was no more successful than the Edmunds Commission had been six years earlier. Secretary Vilas, who wanted the IRA's goodwill for the commission, provided Welsh an advance copy of its instructions.[66] Reverend Cleveland kept Welsh informed of the commission's progress, or lack of it, and others from Dakota helped round out the picture of the commission's operations. From the standpoint of those desiring a cession, the reports were discouraging. James McLaughlin, agent at Standing Rock, the first stop for Pratt's party, predicted that the Indians would unite against the agreement.[67] When united opposition occurred, Reverend Cleveland blamed it in part on McLaughlin's failure to throw all the power of his position behind the commission and on Indian threats directed against their fellow Sioux who otherwise would have been willing to sign.[68]

Reverend Charles S. Cook, a Sioux Indian and Episcopal missionary at Pine Ridge, confided to Welsh his unhappiness with Reverend Cleveland's presence on the commission. Reverend Cook reported that the Catholics and the Presbyterians were using it to undermine the Episcopalians, telling the tribesmen that the "White Robed Church" was behind the effort to buy their land. The IRA was tarred with the same brush, opponents of a cession arguing that it was an Episcopalian-dominated organization and largely responsible for the commission's enabling legislation. Cook himself had mixed feelings about the proposed terms, and he predicted accurately that "the Indians will overwhelmingly decide *not to sign*."[69] Welsh forwarded a copy of Cook's letter to Secretary Vilas, who in turn extracted portions of it for the benefit of Captain Pratt. A month after the Pratt Commission's arrival in Dakota Territory, Vilas wrote Pratt that, if the Sioux really opposed accepting the government's proposition, he did not want them "misled or forced into signing."[70] Another effort to reduce the Sioux reservations was about to collapse.

The IRA role in the aborted negotiations drew the fire of Dr. Bland. Welsh's first defense was to impugn Bland's abilities and integrity: "I think I am doing Dr. Bland no injustice when I say that he is not a man of balance or judgment and that his statements frequently are inaccurate." Having disposed of Bland, Welsh argued as usual that the Indians would profit by disposing of land no longer needed for hunting. He blamed intermarried whites and "heathen Indians" for most of the opposition to the commission.[71]

In December 1888 Welsh sought the views of Bishop Hare on still another bill before Congress. This one would reduce Sioux holdings without their consent. "I am much perplexed," responded the bishop, as indeed were many friends of the Sioux who sincerely believed that a reduction of the reservation and allotment in severalty were in the best interests of the Indians. "I cannot oppose the opening," concluded Hare and indicated that he would assume a passive stance "and leave events to take such shape as others may give them."[72] While visiting in the East a few weeks later, he discussed the matter further with Welsh. Hare believed the white settlers dangerously close to invading the reservation. To avoid what he feared might be a bloody confrontation, the bishop had decided not to oppose any Sioux bill enacted, whether or not it required Indian consent.[73]

Once again Welsh followed the lead of Bishop Hare. Despite the very considerable effort the IRA had put into obtaining a satisfactory Sioux bill in earlier sessions of Congress, it now stood quietly on the sidelines and permitted Dr. Bland and his people to shape new legislation. As with preceding bills, this one was a little more liberal in its provisions for the Indians than was its predecessor. However, Welsh did not embark on any campaign to sell it to the Sioux. To Asa Kills-A-Hundred, who again had written seeking his advice, he did describe the bill as "very favorable to your people" and endorsed the new commission headed by General George Crook as "men of reputation and character."[74] Nevertheless, this time there was no volunteering to stump the reservation in behalf of the commission, no printing of circulars at IRA expense. Even when an Indian delegation was brought to Washington and he was asked by General Crook to come down and help close the deal, Welsh declined.[75] He did not want the association identified in the minds of the Indians with the Sioux Agreement of 1889.

When Bishop Hare reported that the Crook Commission had made unauthorized promises to the Sioux, Welsh had the matter investigated by Charles Painter.[76] Before Painter could respond, Senator Richard Pettigrew of the new state of South Dakota inquired about the IRA's stance on the agreement. When Pettigrew was territorial delegate, Welsh had regarded him as the embodiment of the grasping frontier population threatening Indian land. But now Welsh assured the senator that the agreement was "directly in the line of those things which this Association has always tried to secure for the Indians."[77] Like other friends of the Indian, Welsh could take refuge in the pious hope that the president and congress would treat the Native Americans fairly. In February 1890 President Harrison proclaimed the acceptance of the Sioux Agreement, by which the tribesmen sold about half of their reservation. The IRA's long involvement in Sioux negotiations ended not with a bang, but with a whimper. It is significant that the 1888, 1889, and 1890 association annual reports, while endorsing reduction of the Sioux reservation, contained no discussion of the association's expenditure of time and energy on the protracted negotiations. When correspondents attacked the IRA's role in the matter, Welsh's response was to argue that "it is practically out of the question in many cases to gain for the Indian ideal justice in this process, but nothing could be worse for him than that he should be permitted to seclude himself on immense tracts of land from the influence of civilization."[78]

Throughout the eight-year period the IRA's position had been consistent. Welsh and his colleagues believed that it was inevitable—and it was—that the Sioux would have to surrender another large block of land. Welsh made no apologies for his dealings with the likes of Pierre's Mayor McClure. Welsh prided himself on his freedom from sentimentality and his businesslike approach to Indian questions. Nevertheless, it was his Christian conscience that had gotten him involved in Indian work to begin with, and clearly his connection with the Episcopal Church had affected his stand on the Sioux negotiation. However, it is almost certain that, but for the IRA, the Sioux would have had an even more undesirable deal forced upon them. Such damning with faint praise says something about the hopelessness of the Indian position in the 1880s.

CHAPTER SIX

Defending Indian Land
and Natural Resources

The Sioux reservation opening was just one of many cases involving Indian land in which the IRA became involved between 1885 and 1889. If the association soft-pedaled its role in the Sioux agreement, it proudly claimed a share of the credit for the passage of the Dawes Severalty Act of 1887. This act was designed to apply generally and thus did not inspire the conflict that inevitably resulted when a specific reservation was targeted for allotment and sale of its surplus land. Dr. Bland and the NIDA did oppose the general bill unless it included a provision for Indian consent, but they were the exceptions among the eastern friends of the Indians. Those who met in Washington every January under the sponsorship of the Board of Indian Commissioners and those who gathered at Lake Mohonk every autumn were virtually unanimous in their endorsement of the principle of allotment in severalty, imposed by fiat if necessary.

The IRA had endorsed the early versions of the bill and, indeed, had secured alterations in the Senate version to meet criticism of its law committee. At least four of the association's 1885–1886 publications were designed to help severalty legislation through Congress. As with the Dawes Sioux bill, hopes rose and fell in the sessions of the Forty-ninth Congress. Again the House was the problem, and much depended on the willingness of the congressional leadership to push the bill. As Congress approached recess in June 1886, Painter reported ruefully that no House severalty bill would be voted on that session. Olin Wellborn of Texas, the committee chairman involved, had exhausted all the zeal he could muster getting through two bills opening Indian Territory to railroads serving his home state.[1]

It was only a matter of time until some sort of severalty bill would be enacted into law. Not only were the friends of the Indian overwhelmingly in favor of it, but so were the secretary of the interior and the commissioner of Indian affairs. Secretary Lamar wanted as much done as was possible on those reservations that already had provisions for allotment in the treaties creating them. In pressuring the commissioner of Indian affairs to push allotment "with utmost vigor," Lamar argued that "the encroachments of the whites upon Indian reservations in almost every instance are in cases where the lands are held in common and not in severalty."[2]

When Congress reconvened in December 1886, the stage was finally set. Painter again testified before the House committee and stressed the need for a general severalty bill. He left the committee room fairly confident that success was in sight.[3] And indeed it was, although by a very narrow margin. Two days later the bill was finally brought up for a vote in the House; it passed with only one minute remaining on the legislative clock. If it had not made it then, a friendly congressman believed, the severalty bill would not have been brought up again that session.[4]

The House and Senate versions still had to be reconciled in conference committe and then receive President Cleveland's approval. Dr. Bland still fought to stop the legislation, and Welsh felt impelled to respond to him in a letter to a Boston newspaper. In this communication Welsh asked if it was best that Dr. Bland should have his way and

> leave this defenseless race helpless amid the crush of an irresistible civilization, with no individual right to the ground on which they stand, virtually unaccountable before the law and unprotected by it, and disinherited of the common privileges of freedmen and citizens?[5]

When on February 8, 1887, President Cleveland did sign the severalty act into law, the IRA's pleasure was manifest. Painter engaged in a little hyperbole by ranking the severalty bill with Magna Charta, the Declaration of Independence, and the Emancipation Proclamation.[6] The association's annual report hailed it as "the beginning of a new order of things" and proudly claimed "a large measure of the responsibility of its enactment."[7] When a *Catholic Columbian* editorial termed the the Dawes Severalty Act "a monstrous measure," Welsh informed the editor that

> This bill is the bridge over which the Indian may be led from barbarism to civilization. . . . The Indian must become in all respects like ourselves, or else become extinct under the action of those unrestrainable forces of civilization which will not tolerate savage and tribal life.[8]

The IRA warned that the passage of the act did not "change the condition of a single Indian" and that implementation would have to be monitored carefully.[9] Senator Dawes himself was worried about the impact of the legislation that carried his name. As he phrased it, with considerable prescience, for those who gathered at the Riggs House in Washington in January 1887, if the severalty act

> is administered in bad faith, and by bad men, it first wipes out all of the heritage of the Indian, and then it scatters him among our people without preparation for citizenship, and without the capability of maintaining himself, really in a worse condition than he can be in now.[10]

To try to ensure that good men administered the act, Herbert Welsh recommended several people to Secretary Lamar for the position of allotting agent. None of them was employed, but the IRA kept an eye on the allotment process and managed to prevent at least some of the abuses of the act.

There were many other instances during the years of the first Cleveland administration of the association's intervening to try to protect Indian land. Among them were cases involving Menominees, Chippewas, Puyallups, Hopis, Mission Indians of California, tribes in Indian Territory, and Southern Utes.

The Southern Utes were the last of the Utes to remain in Colorado. Nearly 1,000 of them occupied a 1,100,000-acre reservation adjoining the New Mexico boundary. Perhaps a third of the land was arable if irrigated with the available water. The Utes, however, had shown little interest in farming, and this fact provided the citizens of Colorado with a rationale for opening the reservation to settlement by whites. The plan was to remove the Indians to a larger but admittedly poorer reservation in Utah. Still in the territorial stage, Utah was unable to defend itself from states like Colorado, which wanted to use it as a dumping ground for unwanted Indian populations.

A Ute delegation had visited Washington in 1886 seeking removal to Utah, but it was rebuffed, in part because of IRA opposition.[11] Probably most Utes wanted to move to Utah because the game population of their Colorado reservation had been sharply reduced and they envisioned the Utah site as one enabling them to resume their old ways. This plan, of course, the IRA opposed, confident that it knew better than the Utes themselves what was good for them. In 1887 the association blocked in committee a Ute removal bill. A Colorado senator was successful the next year, however, in getting a bill through Congress. Painter blamed Senator Dawes for failing to stop the legislation and tried unsuccessfully to convince President Cleveland that the law did not mandate him to appoint a Ute Commission.[12] Nevertheless, Cleveland did so, and the commission spent five months in late 1888 on the reservation negotiating an agreement with the three Ute bands. The IRA attacked the resulting Ute agreement as moving the Indians to poorer land and as having been carried out solely to satisfy the land hunger of Colorado whites. Welsh's stand on this issue was particularly awkward as one of the Ute Commission members was Reverend T. S. Childs, a friend in whose Washington home he had been a guest. At the January 1889 meeting at the Riggs House hosted by the Board of Indian Commissioners, Welsh and Painter disputed openly with Reverend Childs over the agreement. Welsh regretted finding himself at odds with an old friend, but, as he wrote Childs, "a question of such moment must over-ride considerations of personal friendship and regard." Welsh held as a cardinal principle that Indians should not be removed just to suit the conveniences and needs of whites, "if the ground on which they are living is capable of furnishing them homes and self-support."[13] The association circulated a pamphlet written by Painter, who employed all of his wiles to block the bill in the House committee after it passed the Senate. The *Durango Herald,* which was one of the Colorado newspapers behind the Ute removal effort, paid tribute to Painter's "cunning art of the lobbyist" and credited him with preventing the bill's reaching the House floor in time to have a chance of passage.[14] Temporarily, at least, the IRA had blocked this attempt to move Southern Utes to Utah. Others would take place.

Welsh's trips to the Southwest led him to champion another Indian group, the Hopis. Their land was threatened not by whites but by other Indians, the Navajos, whose reservation totally encompassed a Hopi enclave. When he visited the Hopis in 1888, he heard complaints that Navajo livestock ate Hopi grass and that the Navajos themselves robbed Hopi melon patches, cornfields, and peach orchards. When a party of Navajos stole fifteen horses, Welsh reported the theft to the agent, who was able to recover the Hopi property.[15] At Welsh's request, Secretary Vilas interceded with the secretary of war to send troops to oust Navajo livestock.[16] Welsh also prevailed upon General Nelson A. Miles, now Department of Arizona commander, to support the Hopi position. Welsh had met General Miles while touring the Southwest in 1888 and was very impressed by the officer, whom he described as a "wise and earnest friend of the Indians."[17]

General Miles had been of assistance to the IRA in 1885, when it undertook to do something for the Mission Indians. That was only the beginning of an involvement with those distressed groups. Charles Painter had included California in his tour that year and called on Helen Hunt Jackson in San Francisco a few weeks before she died. Mrs. Jackson had been delighted to hear of the IRA's interest in the Mission

Indians, whom she had brought to the country's attention in her novel *Ramona*. Painter found the real-life Ramona to be less beautiful and less intelligent than the woman portrayed in the novel.[18]

The Mission Indians desperately needed help. The titles to their twenty-odd reservations were being challenged. Their agent was stationed as much as a hundred miles from some of them and was either ignorant of their problems or unwilling to oppose the whites overrunning the reservations. Mrs. Jackson had been able to get the Justice Department to take some interest in the plight of the Indians; nevertheless, when Painter visited California in 1885, little was being done by the government to protect them. One case required immediate action. The Soboba band of about 160 people lived on 200 acres, part of a larger tract purchased by a Californian, M. R. Byrnes, when a Mexican land grant was subdivided. Despite the fact that the Indians had occupied the site for at least a century, Byrnes brought suit to eject them. The Soboba dispute was regarded as somewhat of a test case for several bands whose reservations were caught up in the legal tangle of Mexican land grants.[19]

That the Soboba case was pursued successfully in the courts was due principally to the persistence of the IRA. When Painter visited California, he found that the Indians had lost the case by default, and it was only through the association's pressure that it was reopened. When Painter returned east, the legal problems of the Mission Indians were brought to the attention of the association's law committee, which studied the brief prepared by Shirley C. Ward, the attorney then representing the Soboba band.[20] The firm which had originally handled the case had lost interest when the government could not promise it that it would ever be compensated. Ward had agreed to take the case on anyway. Dr. Rhoads and Welsh went to Washington in January 1886 where Painter joined them in calls on Commissioner of Indian Affairs J. D. C. Atkins and President Cleveland to impress upon them the gravity of the problems of the southern California Indians. Both officials appeared receptive, and President Cleveland suggested that Attorney General Garland be contacted.[21] Despite the interest manifested by the president and the Indian commissioner, the attorney general was unable to find any money in his budget to retain Shirley Ward. The IRA finally was reduced to guaranteeing Ward that it would pay him $500 and that it would try to persuade Congress to appropriate more substantial compensation.[22] Painter provided help by doing research in Washington on the case and sending his findings on to Ward.

In addition to working to provide legal counsel for the beleaguered Soboba band, the association sought to mobilize eastern public opinion behind the Mission Indians. Painter reported on the situation to those gathered at Lake Mohonk in 1885, and Welsh did so the following year. The conference responded by creating a legal fund to be administered by a committee which included Philip Garrett.[23] The following January, Painter brought the subject to the attention of the Board of Indian Commissioners' meeting at the Riggs House. The IRA also issued two pamphlets, *The Case of the Mission Indians in Southern California* and *A Visit to the Mission Indians of Southern California and Other Western Tribes*, both distributed widely.

Painter bore the brunt of the IRA battle for the Mission Indians, although it was Welsh who took a significant financial risk for them. In August 1886 Shirley Ward notified Welsh, who was vacationing at New Hampshire, that the court had ruled against the Soboba band and that, unless a bond of $3,300 could be raised immediately for an appeal, the Indians would be ejected from their homes. Unable to get executive committee action on such short notice, Welsh took the responsibility upon himself and wired Ward $3,300 of his own funds. When he was able to convene the excecutive committee, it authorized the collection of a special fund to compensate Welsh, but until it was raised the risk was all his.[24]

The court's decision could only have encouraged those whites seeking squatter's rights on other Mission Indian reservations. Painter pressed the issue with the president and the secretary of the interior and managed to get an order to the military authorities in California to clear the intruders from the reservations. He also came to the rescue of some of the natives of the Coahuilla Reservation who found that their traditional homesteads had been included in one of the alternate sections assigned to the Southern Pacific Railroad. Working as an intermediary between the railroad and the Indians, Painter managed to get the Southern Pacific to accept another section and restore the one in question to the reservation.[25]

In June 1887 Painter returned to southern California, this time with some financial support from the Boston Indian Citizenship Committee, which, because of Helen Hunt Jackson, had a longstanding interest in the Mission Indians. At the Santa Isabel Reservation he found that the Indians had been cut off from their fields by a wire fence constructed by claimants to the grant. On the Capitan Grande Reservation, white men's stock was grazing, squatters were selling liquor to the Indians, and a flume to carry water for white settlers was being built across Indian land. Painter despaired of getting remedial action from the agent for the Mission Indians and, working with a representative from the Department of Justice, took the case personally to General Miles, who evicted the intruders.[26] Painter was willing to credit the president and the secretary of the interior with good intentions, "but between the issuance of the order and its execution, at such great distances there are a great many unreliable people. . . ."[27]

Early in 1888 Shirley Ward reported that he had been successful; the California Supreme Court had overruled the lower court, and the Soboba band was safe. It also meant that the $3,300 bond would be returned to Welsh. There still remained the matter of compensating the attorney for his work beyond the $500 given him by the IRA. With the help of Senator Dawes, Painter was able to get an appropriation for $2,500 for Ward tacked on to another Senate bill. However, even so simple a project required two days and an evening of lobbying by Painter. It had finally ended up in the hands of a conference committee, and he had had to contact each of the six members. Painter's task was eased by the fact that one of the senators involved was a friend of Shirley Ward's father, while a congressman on the committee was an admirer of Painter's father.[28] Such serendipity is the stuff of lobbyists' dreams.

While the Soboba case was being settled in the courts, the IRA was throwing its weight behind a Dawes bill, first introduced with the prompting of Helen Hunt Jackson in the Forty-eighth Congress, that got to the root of the problem. The bill would provide each Mission Indian band with an unclouded title to its reservation and find additional reservations for those many Indians left in limbo by the upheaval that had followed American occupation of California. In the next two congresses the association lumped the Mission Indian bill with the general severalty and Sioux bills as ones to get priority. Nevertheless, not until 1891 would Congress come to the relief of the Mission Indians. In the interim Painter spent countless hours appearing before committees and approaching members of Congress in behalf of the bill.

In contrast with the Mission Indian case, the IRA's intervention in behalf of the Puyallup Indians was one of its minor operations, although typical of the forces with which it contended. In 1885 there were fewer than 600 Puyallups on their reservation adjoining Tacoma on Puget Sound. The reservation already had been divided into allotments encompassing all of the tribal holdings, leaving nothing for land-hungry whites.[29] However, the Puyallups as yet had not received their final titles despite their lacking only the signature of Secretary Lamar. His excuse for not having completed the patenting process was that he was under considerable pressure not to do so from Senator J. H. Mitchell of Oregon. The senator, in turn, was responding to pressure from the Northern Pacific Railroad, which was interested in the excellent land.[30] Charles Painter took up the Puyallup case and was able to help convince Secretary Lamar that he should issue the Indians their patents, ensuring them their land at least for the present.[31]

The IRA again confronted whites with designs on Indian resources in the case involving Wisconsin lumbermen and the Menominees. This tribe's reservation contained some of the finest pine timber in the nation and was the target of numerous schemes for exploitation. A leader in the effort was Philetus Sawyer, a wealthy lumberman from Oshkosh who had served five terms in the House before being sent to the Senate in 1881. As a representative he had sponsored legislation giving whites access to Menominee pine, and he did not let the obvious conflict of interest dissuade him from doing the same in the Senate.

In 1887 Senator Sawyer introduced a new bill to permit lumbermen to buy Menominee timber at ridiculously low rates and then arranged to have the congressman from his home district introduce it in the House. The Indians opposed this move, preferring to do the logging themselves if it was to be done, and their agent supported them. Nevertheless, the bill probably would have become law had it not been for the IRA. Painter testified against the bill before the Senate and House committees. To his shock he found that it had the support of Senator Dawes, whom he accused of viewing Sawyer as an "Angel engaged in lumber business."[32] Although Painter took a representative of the tribe by to see Dawes and make clear the Menominee opposition to the measure, Dawes not only got Sawyer's bill through the Senate, he amended it so as not to require Indian consent. Painter described himself as in a "state of rage" as a result of Dawes's action.[33] Fortunately for the Menominees, the association found an ally in Robert M. LaFollette, the young Wisconsin representative, who had a seat on the House Indian committee and who arranged for the bill to die there. Painter was able to report to Welsh, "I think I have effectually headed off the Menominee timber steal. Had most grateful expressions from their Representatives the other day."[34]

The IRA moved rapidly to help the Menominees, and incidentally other tribes, on another issue involving timber. In 1873 a federal court decision had barred Indians from selling a reservation's grass, minerals, or timber, limiting the Indians by what came to be called the "life tenancy doctrine."[35] This ruling, however, had been so interpreted as to exempt "down and dead" timber. The Menominees had capitalized on this interpretation every winter, and the proceeds from the sale of down-and-dead timber was a significant part of their annual income. To their dismay they learned that in November 1888 the Justice Department had issued an opinion removing the exemption and limiting their use of such timber to the satisfaction of their own personal needs for fuel and building material. Secretary of the Interior Vilas noted this opinion in his 1888 annual report and, in an offhanded way, suggested that Congress might consider corrective legislation.[36] Shortly afterwards, Welsh wrote Secretary Vilas that, judging from what Painter had seen in a recent visit to the Menominees, "there is likely to be serious suffering" if the Indians could not market the down-and-dead timber.[37] Vilas responded that there indeed was a problem and that legislation was needed, but apparently he left it to the IRA to take the initiative.[38] Welsh did not dally. He sought the help of Senator Dawes and then wrote Senator Jonathan Chace of Rhode Island requesting that he prod Senator Dawes on the issue.[39] Painter had convinced Welsh that Dawes would bear watching on timber legislation, and Welsh intended to take no chances.

Within less than two months of Welsh's inquiry to Secretary Vilas, there was a law permitting Indians to sell down-and-dead timber, and a record had been set for expeditious action. Apparently Senator Sawyer saw no need to oppose the bill because it would mean more business for those like himself who operated sawmills. Early in January 1889 Painter had gone to the Indian Office and, with the help of personnel there, actually had drafted a bill for which he obtained the endorsements of the Indian commissioner and Secretary Vilas. Painter then had the bill introduced into both houses, and by mid-February it had become law. Painter's last chore on this project was to see President Cleveland to make certain that he signed it.[40] In his annual report the Indian commissioner diplomatically gave his superior, the secretary of the interior, credit for the legislation, although it was clearly Welsh and Painter who were responsible.[41] Indians on scores of reservations would benefit.

Despite its good intentions, the IRA was limited by its small staff and budget in what it was able to do for the more than a quarter of a million Indians on over 160 reservations. It simply was unable to properly investigate all of those cases brought to its attention. Its experience with the Chippewas of Wisconsin and Minnesota in this period is illustrative. Lumbering interests also were involved in the confused affairs of these Indians, who were living on a dozen widely scattered reservations administered by two agencies, one in Minnesota and the other in Wisconsin. The physical distances involved in a largely undeveloped area made adequate supervision impossible even by conscientous agency officials. Most of the Chippewa reservations had large stands of valuable timber, and this fact guaranteed that there would be constant finagling on the part of lumbermen to get access to these tracts. Where they did so legally, they were supposed to employ native labor exclusively. Nevertheless, the unwillingness of the Chippewas to submit to regular employment and their demands for higher-than-customary wages made them undesirable employees for the lumbermen,[42] who sought every opportunity to evade or twist the regulations set up to protect the Indians.

At least some of the Chippewas did well during this four-year period, those at four Wisconsin reservations receiving $1,000,000 in cash and goods for logs cut on their land, plus a large share of the $3,000,000 spent by the lumbermen in cutting and removing the logs. Unfortunately, few of the Chippewas had any long-term benefit from the large income they briefly enjoyed, almost all of it going for consumer goods, including liquor.[43] It also is true that the Indians were not receiving full value for the timber cut. Many of the contracts were tainted with fraud, and in some remote areas illegal logging operations were common.

Welsh had not visited any of the Chippewa reservations, and, although J. B. Harrison and Charles Painter had, together they had not seen them all. What Painter had observed convinced him of the wisdom of trying to concentrate the Chippewas of Minnesota on the two reservations of that state with the most arable land. Therefore he was happy to assist in the passage of a law in 1886 leading to the establishment of a commission to negotiate with the Chippewas and other tribes of the Northwest.[44] He and Welsh were reassured on learning that a member of the commission would be Episcopal Bishop Henry B. Whipple, who had been a staunch friend of these Indians for a quarter of a century.

The Chippewa reaction to the commission was mixed. C. H. Beaulieu, of White Earth Reservation, spoke for the progressive element, assuring Welsh that consolidation followed by allotment was what was needed, although he expected trouble from the "Blanket Indians" until "we can bring them gradually into the traces to make good citizens."[45]

Beaulieu did not speak for the majority of the Chippewas on the reservations the commissioners visited. However, they did return to Washington with two agreements which Congress then declined to ratify. The IRA, despite its general approval of the government's plan for the Chippewas, did not push for ratification of the agreements. Instead, Painter backed a substitute bill designed to achieve the same objectives, a bill which also failed.[46] The only recourse left was for Congress to authorize another commission, which it did in January 1889. This group would go to work that summer.

In February 1888, while the first Chippewa agreements were awaiting congressional action, members of the tribe from the La Pointe, Wisconsin, agency came to Washington to protest Agent T. J. Gregory's collusion with lumbermen. Painter accompanied them when they appeared before congressional committees, and Welsh directed him to persevere in his efforts to stop "the robbery of these people of their lumber."[47] Painter did bring the agency's problems to the attention of a Senate investigating committee and arranged for Chippewas to testify.[48]

The demands for access to Chippewa timber generated pressures on members of Congress, but they were slight compared with what the members of that body were subjected to in connection with the opening of the land that eventually would become Oklahoma. When the IRA came into being in 1882, the area was known as Indian Territory, and a movement to open it to settlement by whites was well underway. The principal argument was the familiar one that large areas in Indian Territory lay idle and that the tribes would profit by disposing of their surplus acreage. Every session of Congress saw several bills introduced to get whites access to some of the land.

The Indian Office's response was to propose its own plan to open up the western half by removing the Indians from it into the eastern half. The IRA opposed this idea, adhering to the principle that had governed it in the dispute over the future of the Southern Utes: Indians should not be moved around the country simply to suit the convenience of settlers. The association's position was presented to the public in 1888 in a pamphlet by Charles Painter.[49]

Painter's publication inspired an editorial in *Harper's Weekly*. The editorial's opening sentences affirmed the propriety of reducing Indian landholdings there: "The vast domain of Oklahoma will be and should be made accessible to settlers. Upon this point there is no serious difference of opinion." However, it continued, "in making the great change we must have the courage and honor to defend the Indians against ourselves." The editorial closed with a plea that Congress take into account "the views of those who, like Professor Painter and the Indian Rights Association, have made a complete and disinterested study of the subject."[50]

Although the IRA made its views known, it did not play the role in the fight over opening Indian Territory that might have been expected. It expressed its opposition to moving Indians from the western to the eastern part of the territory, but the scheme actually was stopped by Kansas and Arkansas, which did not care to see warriors of the calibre of the Comanche and Cheyennes located near their state lines. Nevertheless, the influence of the association was recognized by a convention held in Kansas City in February 1888. It was claimed to represent people from the region who wanted Indian Territory, or at least a part of it, opened to white settlement. When J. B. Harrison prepared an IRA handout responding to a convention position paper, a spokesman for the Kansas City group invited the association to send a committee to Washington to confer with their lobbyists. Welsh declined, nor did he accept an invitation to send Harrison to the annual meeting of the Commercial Club in Kansas City, a group also interested in opening Indian Terrtory.[51]

Meanwhile Painter had been conferring with William M. Springer of Illinois, chairman of the House Committee on Territories, who was preparing his own bill. They met with another congressman in the committee room, and Painter was able to get the bill changed to meet some of his objections.[52] One of the arguments subsequently used by its supporters was that the bill had the approval of the IRA. At least one of the association's members protested its support of the bill, but Welsh assured her that Painter's amendments made it acceptable.[53] When a Pennsylvania congressman queried Welsh about it, he responded with a statement of the association's general policy: "Where Indians possess more land than is necessary for their maintenance when living in a condition of civilization, it is desirable that the surplus lands be opened to white settlers under terms which are equitable."[54]

Welsh was disturbed by the activities of the "boomers," those whites who several times organized illegal expeditions into Indian Territory in an effort to pressure the government and to stake out claims. He suggested to Painter the advisability of seeking a law to punish the intruders, only to learn from the Washington representative that a law already existed.[55] Unfortunately, it provided for fines only and thus did not deter the boomers, who had no property to be assessed anyway.

In March 1889 the Springer bill became law, opening for settlement the Oklahoma district of Indian Territory. It was only a small portion of the total territory, but a beginning. Over the next twenty years the pressure would be maintained to complete the process, and the issue would prove to be a divisive one for the IRA.

Issues in Personnel
and Education

Of all the issues taken up by the IRA, those associated with land and
resources were unquestionably the most important to the tribes. However, there were others with which the association itself was equally
concerned. The quality of its relations with the administration in power
and with members of Congress was always vital if the IRA hoped to do
more than expose inequities and lament them. Efforts to improve the
personnel in the Indian Service, from the commissioner of Indian
affairs down to agency blacksmiths, consumed much IRA time and
energy. It regarded education as the most important single tool for
advancing the civilization of the Indians, and everything about it—
appropriations, choice of personnel, and basic policies—were concerns of the association. The IRA also sought the development for the
reservations of a framework of laws compatible with those of the states
and nation. Special issues such as the future of the Chiricahua Apaches
held in Florida likewise demanded attention. Considering how thin the
resources of the association were spread, its impact was remarkable.

President Cleveland certainly accorded the IRA respect. Even
before his inauguration he had granted an audience to Herbert Welsh,
who took the opportunity to stress the importance to the Indians of
land tenure, a system of laws, and good agents. After returning to
Philadelphia, Welsh sent Cleveland some reading material, including a
list of five agents whom the association particularly would like to see
retained in office.[1]

The president needed guidance in this area as he was entering
office relatively uninformed, not being acquainted, for example, with

the functions of the Board of Indian Commissioners.[2] Nevertheless, initially Welsh was quite pleased with Cleveland. The president had responded quickly to the IRA's request that he block the Crow Creek opening, and Welsh thought he had acted "nobly" in trying to clear the herds of Texas cattlemen from the reservations in Indian Territory.[3] Other friends of the Indian had comparable impressions. A committee appointed at the Lake Mohonk Conference of October 1885 met with the president the following month. The committee members were pleased to have Cleveland invite them to submit their proposals to him, and they were touched when tears appeared in the president's eyes as he discussed the role of Christianity in civilizing the Indians.[4]

By mid-term the IRA was less happy with the Cleveland administration. The president still made the right statements and was willing to make room in his appointment schedule for association representatives. Charles Painter spoke with the president at least half a dozen times in the second half of his term, usually about appointments to the Indian Service. Welsh and Dr. Rhoads also had discussed this subject with the president early in 1886, but were unable to see that they had made much impression on Cleveland.[5]

There was general disappointment with the quality of presidential appointments, not only among the friends of the Indian but also among the Mugwumps, the liberal Republicans who had deserted their party in 1884 to support Grover Cleveland. The IRA submitted to the president at his request a list of what it regarded as unfortunate Indian Service appointments or discharges.[6] After the passage of nearly a year with no significant improvement in the quality of appointments, the Philadelphia reformers obtained permission for a committee to call on the president and present him with another list of deplorable personnel decisions. This time, if the president failed to give the committee satisfaction, Welsh was prepared "to make our appeal to the public."[7] The committee's report of its visit and the president's failure to even mention the subject in his annual message to Congress did not suggest that Cleveland intended to reform his appointment policies. Welsh therefore decided to go public and began providing editors, among them Dr. William Hayes Ward of the influential religious journal *The Independent* and George William Curtis of *Harper's Weekly,* with lists of abuses and urging them to speak out.[8]

Despite candidate Cleveland's implications that he supported the civil-service concept, his administration had been only a few months old when it became apparent that, as far as the Indian Service was concerned, it was going to be partisanship as usual. The Democrats were in power for the first time in a quarter-century, and there were mouths to be fed. A record of service to the Democratic Party seemed to be the principal qualification for appointment to the Indian Service, which was reputed to have more patronage than any other agency in the government. Among the incompetents who surfaced was a Mississippian assigned as a farmer to a Mission Indian reservation. Painter described him as a farmer "who neither knows Spanish, Indian, nor farming east or west."[9] Welsh, who believed that "the solution of the whole Indian problem lies quite as much in the wise, unpartisan administration as in wise legislation," was increasingly unhappy as the Democratic policy became apparent.[10]

The terms of Republican agents usually were not renewed regardless of the agents' competence. Some agents were asked to resign before completing their four-year terms. One of the first to fall by the wayside was R. H. Milroy, an able official by IRA standards, who complained to Welsh that his troubles stemmed "from having fought on the wrong side in our last war" as far as the Democrats were concerned.[11] Among the other casualties highly regarded by Welsh were James G. Wright and V. T. McGillycuddy, who had headed the Rosebud and Pine Ridge agencies, respectively. McGillycuddy was one of the five agents whom Welsh had singled out for recommendation to president-elect Cleveland as unusually able. With that kind of support McGillycuddy might have survived the Democratic sweep had he not refused on principle to accept a chief clerk appointed from Washington.

One of the most controversial Democratic innovations was the transfer of the power of appointment of agency chief clerks, physicians, and additional farmers from the agent to the commissioner of Indian affairs.[12] The justification offered was that it would improve quality and, in the case of the chief clerks, help prevent collusion and fraud. The agents, however, resented the loss of patronage and were particularly disturbed at having a stranger, perhaps incompetent, appointed chief clerk, who was in effect deputy agent in charge of administration. The agents had to make heavy bonds, up to $100,000 for the large agencies, and now they felt that both their bonds and their reputations were placed in jeopardy.

Agent McLaughlin of Standing Rock had two chief clerks in succession supplied him from Washington, neither of whom was competent to do the job. The first, a young Tennessean, the agent described to Welsh as "inexperienced in all kinds of business, except politics. . . . writes a more wretched hand than I do and his orthography is that of a school-boy; while in computing figures he is equally poor."[13] The young man explained his appointment to McLaughlin as due to

Commissioner J. D. C. Atkins's desire to woo support from his fellow Tennesseans for a bid for the United States Senate. This clerk in time was replaced by another Tennessean dispatched from Washington. McLaughlin and other agents made their unhappiness with this policy known in Washington, and Agent McGillycuddy flatly refused to accept a chief clerk selected for Pine Ridge. Faced with this challenge to his authority, Secretary L. Q. C. Lamar fired McGillycuddy despite the IRA's protests.

Welsh's view of Secretary Lamar was that, at best, he was "an amicable, well-disposed gentleman" without real control of his department.[14] At worst, he was a "chronic blunderer."[15] For his part, the secretary, an ex-Confederate from Mississippi, made an effort to be on good terms with the IRA. Painter believed him sincere and sought to reconcile Lamar and Welsh after the two had exchanged strong letters concerning an article Welsh had written for the *Civil Service Record*. Welsh did assure the secretary that he was not acting as a partisan Republican in criticizing the Cleveland administration and pledged his willingness "to do any thing in my power to serve you, so as to bring about the advancement of this cause to which I am giving all my strength."[16] Richard Henry Dana, editor of the *Civil Service Record*, had wanted to publish the letters exchanged by Lamar and Welsh, but the latter had declined to release them because "I am willing and anxious for peace with him."[17] Lamar reciprocated and invited Welsh to lunch when he was in Washington and on one occasion gave Painter a lift in his carriage. Lamar needed the IRA's support for projects like the opening of the Sioux reservations, and the administration could not have enjoyed the hostile press comments inspired by the association. Nevertheless, Lamar could not satisfy both the IRA and the Democrats clamoring for office. He kept Morris A. Thomas, accused of stuffing ballot boxes, in one of the most sensitive positions at his disposal, inspector, and he did not restore McGillycuddy or Wright to their agencies. One of the association's few triumphs was the secretary's grudging removal of an agency physician who earlier had been conicted of corruption while holding public office in Connecticut.

Welsh could not forgive Lamar for what he termed the secretary's "dreamy acquiescence" in the patronage policies of the Indian Office, which inflicted on the agencies "large numbers of Tennesseans and a liberal sprinkling of Mississippians."[18] Those the IRA held responsible for this practice were Indian Commissioner Atkins, with his senatorial ambitions, and his assistant, Alexander B. Upshaw. Both were Tennesseans who, according to the IRA, "regarded the Indian reservations as a green pasture where their political herds might comfortably browse and fatten."[19] Welsh considered Atkins, like Lamar, well-meaning but ineffective. The real villain he believed to be Upshaw, "insolent and arbitrary" and a "thorough spoilsman" who controlled Atkins.[20]

Given the patronage policies of the Cleveland administration, Welsh became an enthusiastic supporter of the movement for civil-service reform and the extension of the Pendleton Act to cover the Indian Service. Charles J. Bonaparte, who was influential in the Baltimore reform group, had brought Welsh's attention to the case of Inspector Morris A. Thomas, charged with election fraud while active in Maryland politics. The appointment required Senate confirmation, and the IRA unsuccessfully lobbied against Thomas.

Welsh also established relationships with three important figures in the civil-service movement, Dorman B. Eaton, Richard H.Dana, and George William Curtis. Eaton had drafted the Pendleton Act and in 1886 was the head of the Civil Service Commission. After reading his study of the reform in Great Britain, Welsh approached him in June 1886 for suggestions on how to proceed to obtain the extension of civil service to the Indian Service.[21] From Curtis, Welsh solicited advice on further reading, stating that he was "anxious to make a careful study of the whole subject of reform in the civil service."[22]

Editor of *Harper's Weekly,* Curtis would be a valuable ally in several fights taken on by Welsh. As president of the National Civil Service Reform League also, Curtis appointed a committee of himself, Carl Schurz, and Theodore Roosevelt to discuss issues with the IRA. When the meeting took place in New York, Roosevelt was unable to be present. Welsh came away from the meeting reassured that the IRA should fight Inspector Thomas's confirmation.[23] Dana, who edited the *Civil Service Record,* also opposed Thomas. Dana had published the previously mentioned article by Welsh which had aroused the ire of Secretary Lamar.

Civil-service reform for the Indian Service became almost an obsession with Welsh. Probably due to his efforts, the National Civil Service Reform League passed a resolution at its 1886 annual meeting proposing the extension of civil-service rules to include Indian agency clerks.[24] Welsh also brought the subject before the Mohonk Conference the same year and secured a resolution from that organization. Not content with that, he had his remarks at Mohonk published in a separate flyer and circulated.[25]

Not everyone had Welsh's faith in the merit system. Painter still believed that the IRA should concern itself with the individual's performance after he was in office rather than with the process of his appointment. As he pointed out, Secretary Lamar's defense of Morris Thomas was that he was his most effective inspector, whatever may have been Thomas's failings before assuming that position. When Welsh sought Sara Kinney's view on Painter's stand, she tended to side with the Washington representative. That must have disturbed Welsh, and he was "staggered" to read J. B. Harrison's evaluation of Welsh's panacea for the problems of the Indian Service.[26] It was J. B. Harrison's judgment that "if there is anything in the world that . . . would be any more useless, ineffective and impracticable than competitive examinations for determining the fitness of people for work on an Indian Reservation, I do not know what it is."[27] Nevertheless, Welsh was committed to the idea. He was convinced that entrance into public service though competitive examinations would greatly reduce the chances of incompetent personnel.

As the election of 1888 approached, the IRA was providing ammunition to the opponents of Cleveland's attempt to remain in the White House. The New York *Daily Tribune* carried an editorial quoting Welsh's charge that "the service has been confided to narrow and greedy partisans whose selfish policy has brought it to a condition of deplorable degradation."[28] Nevertheless, on election day Welsh cast his vote for Grover Cleveland, although he knew of only one other member of the executive committee who did so.[29] Probably Welsh was won over by Cleveland's choices late in his term of both a new commissioner of Indian affairs and a new secretary of the interior.

Welsh recognized that the real power lay with the secretary, but only if he chose to exercise it. General Armstrong once had described the commissioner of Indian affairs as a mere clerk to the secretary, and Welsh agreed.[30] Indeed, Welsh would go further and argue that in most instances it was the clerks in the office of the Indian commissioner and in the Indian division of the secretary's office who really ran the show.[31]

The changes in the top positions that occurred in 1888 were salutary in Welsh's judgment. Lamar had been moved from the Interior Department to the Supreme Court, where he exhibited the same bland mediocrity. As predicted, J. D. C. Atkins resigned the Indian commissionership to seek election to the Senate. Welsh must have been pleased that, despite Atkins's lavish use of Indian Service patronage to build support among fellow Tennesseans, his campaign failed.

Cleveland's new team in the Interior Department was headed by William F. Vilas, who had been serving, with full consideration for the position's patronage potential, as postmaster general. Unlike his diffident predecessor, Secretary Vilas intended, in Painter's phrase, "For weal or woe . . . to run the business."[32] But Vilas also thought it wise not to alienate the IRA. Within a few months Welsh had received several friendly letters from the secretary, and they had a pleasant conference in Atlantic City.[33]

Welsh believed Vilas to be a distinct improvement over Lamar; however, he was very concerned that Upshaw might succeed in moving up to occupy the position Atkins was vacating. John H. Oberly, a member of the Civil Service Commission and formerly superintendent of Indian schools, was favored to replace Atkins. Welsh would take no chances, however, and launched a campaign to ensure that Upshaw did not become Indian commissioner. A letter to the president was drafted to protest that Upshaw's "complete subservience to the spoils system" placed him at odds with Cleveland's own declaration on civil service.[34] Editorials in *Harper's Weekly* and the New York *Daily Tribune,* critical of Upshaw, demonstrated that Welsh's campaign was having some effect.[35] Perhaps because of the opposition of the IRA, Cleveland decided that Upshaw should not get the job. Painter saw the president in late June, and Cleveland assured him that Upshaw would not become Indian commissioner and that he had told the Tennessee senators to quit prodding him on the subject.[36] In September the president nominated John Oberly to be commissioner, and he took office in early October.

Welsh was delighted with the new commissioner. Within a week of assuming his new duties Oberly had responded to an overture from Welsh by inviting the IRA to send a representative to a meeting he was calling with the Board of Indian Commissioners. Welsh was soon writing Dana of the *Civil Service Record* that the association had "a high opinion of Mr. Oberly's ability and character" and was confident that a new day had dawned with regard to appointments in the Indian Service.[37]

It was Oberly's career as superintendent of Indian schools which first had attracted the attention of Welsh. Only the second occupant of that position, Oberly endeavored to exercise some real control over the government schools and make it a system in more than name. This effort inevitably put him at odds with the agents who had had a relatively free hand with reservation schools and also produced confrontations with boarding-school heads like Captain Pratt.

Captain Pratt's resentment of any effort of the Washington bureaucracy to influence the operation of Carlisle and his caustic attacks on anyone who disagreed with him inevitably created an anti-Pratt lobby in the Indian Office. In 1886 his opponents retaliated by attempting to have the captain's name struck from the appropriation bill. Pratt had been able to secure supplementary pay as head of Carlisle and its elimination might well have been the first step in his recall to regular duty. The army was never happy with special duty assignments which took officers away from their regiments for extended periods.[38]

Welsh, on learning of the threat to Pratt, promptly went to his defense. He contacted Senator Dawes and Byron M. Cutcheon, a member of the House from Michigan, and both promised help.[39] The IRA also rushed into print a laudatory pamphlet entitled *Captain Pratt and His Work for Indian Education.* [40] Pratt's name, which had been dropped from the House version of the appropriation bill, was restored by the Senate. Meanwhile, Welsh was mobilizing some of the same people to oppose an attack on the eastern boarding schools.

In 1886 there were three eastern boarding schools with contracts to educate Indian youths. In addition to the well-known Hampton and Carlisle, there also was Lincoln Institution in Philadelphia. Headed by the strong-willed and energetic Mary McHenry Cox, the school had a boys' department which in 1886 enrolled fifty whites and almost twice that number of Indians. The IRA was not happy with the Philadelphia school's operation but rallied to its support when appropriations for all three boarding schools were threatened.

The attack on the eastern boarding schools was led in the House by William S. Holman of Indiana and Joseph G. Cannon of Illinois. Their favorite tactic was to disparage the performance of the "returned student," the young Indian restored to his reservation after schooling in the East. Holman and Cannon maintained that, unless employed by the government, the returned students quickly lapsed into barbarism. In holding this view, Cannon and Holman saw eye-to-eye with Senator Preston B. Plumb of Kansas, who could not be counted upon to support any Indian schools, but particularly those in the East. The IRA already had distributed Hampton teacher Elaine Goodale's rebuttal of Senator Plumb, which had appeared first in *The Independent.* [41] Now the association mobilized its forces against Holman and Cannon.

To counter the congressmen, Welsh fed information to their colleague Byron M. Cutcheon. He also commissioned Helen Ludlow, another Hampton teacher, to write a pamphlet, sent to each member of the House, on the virtues of the returned students.[42] The House passed the appropriation for the schools by a very wide margin, and Welsh later insisted he had not really been worried. Nevertheless, the IRA circulated a letter claiming credit for a victory over Cannon and Holman.[43]

Despite the IRA's support of Captain Pratt and Carlisle, its relations with the prickly captain worsened. One problem continued to be the association's support of reservation schools as well as off-reservation schools like Carlisle. Pratt could see no good in the reservation experience in any form. Welsh, on the other hand, believed that reservation schools could play a valuable role and that the day schools were "like so many candles glimmering in the darkness of the Reservation night."[44]

Pratt also resented the competition from Welsh and the IRA for support from eastern philanthropists. The captain was very upset late

in 1887 when he learned that Welsh was approaching for funds some of
the same people Carlisle looked to for support. Pratt was outraged by
the $12,000 fund-raising goal Welsh had set for the association for
1888. The captain scorned those who, like Welsh, chose to try to shape
public opinion on the Indian issue rather than work with the Indians
themselves. "I'd give a damned sight more to see Welsh and Company
cleaning the Indians than cleaning White folks, eating good dinners,
spreading their quack remedies, and heading off those who are heart
and soul in the nasty part of the work up to their eyes," Pratt fumed.[45]

Welsh again chose to turn the other cheek. To General Armstrong
he observed that Captain Pratt seemed incapable of refraining "from
saying unkind and harmful things of those who have never done
anything but wish him well and work in his behalf." Welsh concluded,
"I wonder that a man of such noble qualities does not feel the in-
gratitude and the unwisdom of such utterances; however, I suppose he
is made that way and cannot help it."[46]

When the revered General Armstrong and his Indian work at
Hampton became the target of Captain Pratt's spleen, Welsh was less
forgiving. He called upon Senator Dawes to defend Armstrong from
the "cantankerous" Pratt and solicited letters supporting Hampton
from Mrs. Mary McHenry Cox.[47] Both Dawes and Cox responded
affirmatively, and Armstrong and Hampton appeared to be none of
the worse for Pratt's attack.

Sometimes it was the IRA that appeared to be in the role of
character assassin. At least this was the way Elizabeth P. Peabody viewed
the association's stand on Sarah Winnemucca, a Paiute Indian. In 1885
Miss Peabody, active in behalf of many good causes in Boston, raised
$1,200 for a school Sarah was to operate. Working with Senator Dawes,
Miss Peabody also was able to get government support for the school.
But then she made the mistake of asking Charles Painter to inspect the
facility on one of his trips to California. Painter's visit convinced him
that Sarah was guilty of a variety of "immoralities and vices," had no
claim to leadership among the Paiutes, and was "an unmitigated
fraud."[48] What made it particularly awkward was that Miss Peabody
had used her Boston contacts to help Painter secure railroad passes for
this western trip. Nevertheless, he did not feel that he could fail to
report what he had found. In the IRA publication embodying his
findings on this trip, Painter said that he and Mr. and Mrs. Joshua Davis
of Boston, who had accompanied him to Sarah's school, had concluded
"that the confidence placed in her has been misplaced." Painter added,
unfortunately, with the touch of acid of which he was capable, that he
had reported the facts to "these good, but strangely-infatuated ladies,"
that is, Miss Peabody and her followers, but that they had refused to
accept them.[49] Miss Peabody was even more disturbed when J. F. B.

Marshall, who headed the American Unitarian Association's Bureau of Southern and Indian Education, cited Painter's report as evidence that contributions to Sarah Winnemucca's project would be charity wasted. Painter reported to Welsh that this development had led Miss Peabody to open fire upon him with her "patented self-cocking, manifold repeating gatling gun."[50] The eighty-four-year-old Miss Peabody doggedly defended Sarah while denouncing Painter's "utter incompetence" and "utter carelessness."[51]

The Sarah Winnemucca affair was a minor matter as compared to the issue of the use of native languages in mission schools, a controversy that surfaced in 1887. In July of that year an Indian Office circular reminded agents and school personnel of the ban on instruction in any language except English. As Commissioner Atkins later would explain it:

> The intention is to prevent the waste of valuable time by Indian children in schools, in learning a barbarous tongue which is not comprehensive enough to embrace civilization or to comprehend it, and to utilize that time in school in learning the language of the country of which they are about to become citizens—a language in which not only the scriptures can be read, but all the extensive literature of the civilized world.[52]

The order was not a new one, having first been issued in 1880 and reiterated on several occasions. However, it had not been enforced, and many mission schools, particularly Protestant ones among the Sioux, employed the vernacular. The July 1887 directive seemed to ban all use of the native languages even in those institutions supported by private funds. Zealous reservation officials appeared ready to include in the ban even preaching in the vernacular.

The reformers faced a dilemma, as was apparent at the Mohonk conference in the fall of 1887. The final report of the business committee of the conference emphasized the importance of instruction in English in the Indian schools. However, it warned:

> No policy can be endured which forbids Christian men and women to teach Christian truth, or to prepare instruction in it in any way they deem right, in any part of this Commonwealth that is consistent with that civil and religious liberty which is unhampered in every other part of our land, and must hereafter be unhampered within all Indian reservations.[53]

The conference also agreed to appoint a committee to seek an interview with President Cleveland regarding the work of religious and philanthropic groups among the Indians.

Charles Painter had attended the conference, but Fanny Welsh's illness had kept Herbert in Philadelphia. Welsh was anxious to learn of any action taken at Mohonk against what he regarded as "an arbitrary and unwise" order as applied to mission schools. Indeed, he viewed it as "an astounding example of unwarranted interference upon the part of the civil authorities with personal and religious liberty."[54]

Welsh's orchestration of opposition to the vernacular order was typical of his approach. He exchanged information on the subject with the American Missionary Association, the Board of Foreign Missions of the Presbyterian Church, the American Bible Society, various missionaries and editors, and Bishop Hare and General Armstrong. Reverend William Hayes Ward, editor of *The Independent*, editorialized on "this atrocious order" and published a letter to Welsh from a missionary at Pine Ridge.[55] The *Springfield Republican* also addressed the issue and printed a letter written by President Cleveland, together with comments on the letter by Welsh.[56] As always, Welsh's position was that of the true reformer: "I believe that in all these troubles our stronghold is public sentiment," he wrote, "and that with a fearless and impartial spirit the facts should be continually brought home to the minds and hearts of our people."[57]

On this issue, also, Welsh and Captain Pratt found themselves on opposite sides. Reverend Cook, in seeking help from the IRA mentioned that Carlisle would not deliver to its students letters written in the native languages. Through William Hayes Ward, Welsh learned that Pratt was completely in sympathy with the vernacular order, although he claimed to be censoring only those letters in the Lakota language thought to contain undesirable material.[58]

As usual the pressure generated by Welsh and his allies achieved some results. Bishop Hare and a committee representing the Mohonk Conference discussed the issue with President Cleveland, and another committee, representing the Board of Indian Commissioners and missionary organizations, met with Commissioner Atkins. Some concessions were made to the missionaries, although Welsh still found intolerable the president's insistence that he had, in Welsh's words, "the legal and moral right to regulate even the petty details of missionary work."[59] In the columns of the *Springfield Republican* Welsh expressed his pleasure with the modification of the vernacular order, regretting only "that the principle which has been contended for by those who opposed the original order is [not] recognized in the president's modification of it. . . ."[60]

Congress had the final word on the controversy. The appropriation bill for the Indian Service enacted in June 1888 contained a section authorizing the use of the Bible in the vernacular by church schools.

The controversy also had the effect of bringing to the surface Herbert Welsh's latent fears of the Roman Catholic Church. Ever concerned about the Episcopal missions among the Sioux, Welsh wrote

Reverend Ward of *The Independent* that the "secret motive" behind the vernacular directive was "the desire to hamper missionary work of Protestant bodies, and so indirectly to favor that of the Romanists."[61]

In Cleveland's first term a number of Protestants involved in Indian work had convinced themselves that the administration was favoring the Catholic Church. Reverend F. F. Ellinwood, corresponding secretary of the Presbyterians' Board of Foreign Missions, expressed concern in 1886 about Roman Catholic competition with his church's missionaries among the Umatillas. Reverend Ellinwood even went so far as to suspect that Catholics had been indirectly responsible for the death years earlier of the famed Dr. Marcus Whitman. Ellinwood indicated that he had recently seen a letter by Welsh on the subject of Catholic activity on reservations.[62] Another Presbyterian, Dr. T. S. Childs, the man with whom Welsh differed on the Southern Utes, raised the issue at the 1887 Mohonk Conference. Dr. Childs expressed alarm that Catholics, although less than one-tenth of the population, controlled two-thirds of the contract schools.[63]

In the summer of 1886 Herbert Welsh had begun to fret as a result of communications from Bishop Hare about Catholics obtaining additional positions on Sioux reservation staffs. Welsh responded by calling upon Charles Painter and J. B. Harrison, the former in Washington and the latter about to make a trip to the Northwest, to be on the alert for evidence of undue Catholic activity.[64] After the issuance of the vernacular order and the appointment of more Catholics to reservation posts, the Protestant unease intensified. Painter, writing Welsh on the topic, declared: "It comes from all points of the compass that this process is going on, a decanting of Protestant influence from the control and education of the Indian and an injection of Catholic. It is not accident but evident design."[65]

Welsh responded with one of his flurries of letters. He contacted Reverend Ward of *The Independent,* General Armstrong, and Anna Dawes, among others. When General Armstrong responded with the observation that "the under current of the Indian Office seems wrong and almost suggests insincerity in their relations to Protestants," Welsh promptly sent that also on to Reverend Ward.[66] To Miss Dawes, Welsh made a plea for financial help for Reverend Philip Deloria, who hoped to erect an Episcopal school at Standing Rock, a reservation where Welsh claimed the Catholics were opposing Episcopal missionary work.[67]

At least in part as a result of Welsh's prodding, *The Independent* ran two articles on the subject. In the first, Reverend Ward cited statistics obtained from General Whittlesey to demonstrate the disproportionate influence the Catholics were exerting in Indian education. He believed the source of the influence to be both the efficiency of the Bureau of Catholic Indian Missions located in Washington and the Indian Office's partiality to Catholics designed to woo political support for the administration.[68] In the second *Independent* article Welsh was quoted as agreeing that politics was a probable explanation for the increase of Catholic appointments to the Indian Service. His advice was for the Protestants to establish in Washington an office to counterbalance the Bureau of Catholic Indian Missions.[69]

Welsh's anti-Catholicism was not the blind hostility of the real bigot. He spoke highly of the work of Catholic sisters with Apaches being held at Fort Marion, Florida.[70] At one point he was prepared to back James McLaughlin, the veteran agent at Standing Rock and a Roman Catholic, for the post of commissioner of Indian affairs. Indeed, Welsh approached McLaughlin's bishop to see if his church would have any opposition to the IRA's support of the agent's candidacy.[71] And when Welsh was in Pueblo country in September 1888, he was reminded that the Church was not a monolith. He and a Catholic appointee to a government school in Albuquerque found themselves in agreement. Both were disturbed by the zeal with which local priests were persuading Indian children to attend parochial schools rather than the government school. Welsh was upset that some of the Mexicans teaching at the parochial schools could not speak English and even concluded, "Now is the time for an enforcement of the language order!"[72] Apparently even that detested mandate had its uses.

Captain Pratt was also unhappy with the role of the Catholic Church in Indian education. He estimated that three-fourths of the employees in the church's school system were foreign-born and that many of them had difficulty using English. "The outlook for Americanizing the Indian under such conditions is not promising," was the captain's opinion.[73]

Neither Welsh nor Pratt was among the reformers who gathered at the Lake Mohonk lodge in late September 1888. However, Welsh's idea of having an agent in Washington to represent the Protestants did surface. A resolution was introduced calling simply for a secretary for the Mohonk Conference to be stationed permanently in Washington. Nevertheless, the discussion accompanying the motion made it fairly clear that everyone realized that the position called for lobbying to assure Protestant groups their share of the government funds going to contract schools. Senator Dawes's wife, Electa, who was present, assured her husband that this was the intent, and she endorsed it.[74]

It also was clear that Electa Dawes and the senator did not like the prospect of Charles Painter in that role. The conference executive committee, to which the resolution had been referred, did approach

Painter about taking the job. Painter described the duties as being "to watch Roman Aggression, and all matter relating to Indian interests."[75] He was prepared to assume the position as an additional duty to his IRA job, with supplementary pay and secretarial help. The project never got off the ground, possibly because there were others who agreed with General Whittlesey that it would be undesirable if it put the Mohonk group "in a position of antagonism to one of the great denominations of the country."[76]

During Cleveland's first term it was patently clear that the Catholic Church's share of the funds going to contract schools had increased and the number of Catholics in the Indian Service had grown. But Welsh and his allies did not come up with the evidence to back their charge that it was all a play for the Catholic vote. When Dr. Childs wrote the president after raising the issue at Mohonk in 1887, he received a reply from Secretary Lamar. The secretary denied any favoritism to the Roman Catholic Church, maintaining that, if the Catholic role in Indian education was growing while that of the Protestants was declining, it was due to Catholic zeal and efficiency.[77] Welsh wrote Secretary Vilas the following year to complain that Protestant missions among the Indians were "being put in jeopardy, or actually robbed of fruition" by appointment of Catholics to the Indian Service.[78] Vilas responded in less detail than Lamar, but the message was the same. No favoritism was intended, Lamar maintained, and "the relative share which any sect may secure in this work must, therefore, depend upon the zeal and labor they bring to it."[79] Bishop Hare, for one, was not convinced. While awaiting the returns of the presidential election in November 1888, he expressed to Welsh the hope that the Republicans had won, "in view of the increasing power of Rome with the Democratic Administration."[80]

The IRA's concern for education for the Indian was almost matched by its concern for law for the Indian. As discussed earlier, the association had framed a bill to provide for a system of reservation courts, but had ceased to push it when it became apparent that the proposal lacked a consensus among the reformers. In February 1887 Welsh learned of a new plan drafted under the aegis of the Boston Indian Citizenship Committee and generally associated with the name of one of its members, James Bradley Thayer, a distinguished Harvard Law School professor.

The Thayer plan called for the abolition of the Bureau of Indian Affairs, the administration of reservations to be transferred to two individuals for each reservation, a trustee and a commissioner appointed by the local United States circuit court judge. Welsh's immediate reaction was that such a sweeping change would have "all the well known disadvantages of a revolution without compensating advantages."[81] In typical fashion he communicated his doubts to several people and sought their opinions. Among those whom he contacted were Dr. James E. Rhoads and Henry Pancoast of the IRA, President Merrill E. Gates of Rutgers College, Carl Schurz, Senator Dawes, and General Armstrong. All agreed that the Thayer proposal had major flaws. Schurz thought that it had no chance of serious consideration by Congress, a view confirmed by Senator Dawes's hostility to the proposal.[82] The senator indicated to Welsh that he would not like to oppose Thayer publicly but did hope that his ideas might be "disposed of." Welsh was ready to try, and, with the senator's permission, incorporated part of one of Dawes's letters in an attack on the Thayer plan published by the *Springfield Republican*.

Welsh's criticism brought a rebuke from the Boston committee's Frank Wood, who also wrote Senator Dawes. Wood charged Welsh with launching his campaign against Thayer without really knowing what the professor had proposed. And, Wood said, "We intended to consider the bill in all its details in conference with you [Dawes], Herbert Welsh and other friends of the Indian before making the bill public."[83]

By this time Welsh and Thayer had exchanged letters on the subject, and Thayer also had published a letter in a newspaper. Welsh had concluded that perhaps he had been too hasty in going public with the dispute. He went to Boston to confer with Thayer and other members of the Boston committee, and the professor visited Philadelphia to discuss his bill with IRA leaders. The result was that Thayer consented to significant modifications, dropping the proposal to abolish the Indian Office and limiting the bill to the creation of reservation courts.[84] However, it was February 1888, a year after the debate got underway, before the compromise was agreed upon and both the Boston committee and the IRA were prepared to try to get it through Congress.

Despite the best efforts of the association and the Boston committee the bill got nowhere. Welsh sent copies of it to various senators and representatives, and called upon John Nicholas Brown of the Providence branch, Mrs. Quinton, Mrs. Sara Kinney, and others for help. Mrs. Kinney had been approached by Frank Wood also, but refrained from doing anything until she learned from Welsh "if this Bill is in accordance with the views of the IRA Assn. and Senator Dawes and others who should approve it before we try to push it."[85]

Senator Dawes had agreed to introduce the bill and did so. Nevertheless, it quickly became apparent to Painter, who was pushing the bill in Congress, that Dawes had serious objections to the proposal. Painter, Thayer, and others appeared before the Senate Indian committee in defense of the bill, but Senator Dawes virtually ended its chances of passage by opposing it before the committee.[86] To his wife,

Dawes confided his distaste of the reformers' "impracticable schemes" and of "Prof. Thayer's aerial project" in particular.[87] Once again the IRA had invested considerable time and energy in a plan to provide reservation courts and had little to show for its efforts. The Thayer plan did not quietly die; for several years it would be on the agenda of the reformers.

One reason that Welsh had been willing to compromise his differences with Professor Thayer was that he had been seeking the support of the Boston group on a project in which he and the IRA had invested considerable time and energy—the plight of the Chiricahua Apaches held prisoner at military installations in Florida and later at Mount Vernon Barracks in Alabama.[88]

The association's involvement in the Apache affair had grown out of Herbert Welsh's trip to the Southwest in 1884, when he met Captain John G. Bourke, then of General George Crook's staff. Captain Bourke was one of those army officers who became interested in the Native Americans he had been assigned to subjugate. General Crook encouraged Bourke's study of the southwestern tribes, and in the spring of 1886 the captain was assigned to Washington to write up his ethnological findings. Several valuable papers on aspects of Apache culture resulted.

Captain Bourke's arrival in Washington coincided with the movement of the first detachment of Apache prisoners to Florida. Ultimately nearly 500 Apaches—men, women, and children—were located at two military installations. Most of them were at Fort Marion at St. Augustine, where they attracted the attention of crowds of tourists. A small group of adult males, including Geronimo, was held under tighter security at Fort Pickens on Santa Rosa Island in Pensacola Bay.

In April 1886 Welsh went to Washington in connection with the IRA's interest in promoting congressional action on negotiations for reduction of the Sioux reservations. However, he also had been in touch with Captain Bourke, who had persuaded him to visit Secretary of War William C. Endicott to discuss the Apache situation. Welsh obtained the appointment, but the interview was unsatisfactory. Captain Bourke had hoped that the government would not just incarcerate the Apaches, but would inaugurate an educational program similar to Captain Pratt's for southern Plains Indians held at Fort Marion in the late 1870s. Secretary Endicott was not very receptive to Welsh's concern for the Apaches. Indeed, it was his opinion that hanging would be best for the men, although he thought something might be done for the children.[89]

Welsh had found another cause for the IRA, one which intermittently over the next eight years would take time, effort, and money.

And if he had been inclined to let the matter slide while absorbed in affairs of the Southern Utes, the Menominees, the Sioux, and a dozen other tribes, Captain Bourke was always there to remind him of the plight of the Chiricahuas.

Under Bourke's tutelage Welsh began to see other facets of the problem. It was not just a question of rehabilitation of prisoners; there were serious questions about the guilt of many of the prisoners and about the morality of the government's imprisoning them in Florida. Most of the Apaches had agreed to the transfer after having been promised a 600-square-mile reservation, only to end up in a fortress prison less than 100 yards square. Included among the prisoners were many who had served as enlisted army scouts, some of them actually on the government's payroll when seized and transported to Florida. Incredibly, two of the scouts who had been instrumental in running down the last group of hostiles had themselves been disarmed and thrown onto the train headed for Florida.[90] Finally, there was the case of Chato, which Bourke brought to Welsh's attention. Chato, an Apache chief, had come to terms with the government in 1883 and subsequently had faithfully adhered to its policies, even serving as a scout in one campaign against Geronimo. Persuaded to head a small delegation to Washington in the summer of 1886, Chato refused to agree to the removal of his people from Arizona. As a result, his trip home was interrupted at Fort Leavenworth and, after some bureaucratic shillyshallying, he and the other members of the delegation also were seized and shipped to Fort Marion. Bourke denounced it as "a most contemptible outrage."[91]

During the last two and a half years of the first Cleveland administration, Welsh worked to improve the lot of the Florida prisoners. He hoped to ameliorate their situation in Florida while working to get them established at another location where they could become self-supporting. Although he regarded the Geronimo party at Fort Pickens as deserving of punishment, Welsh wanted the government to live up to its promises and at least unite Geronimo and his fellow prisoners with their families, who were with the main body at Fort Marion.

To achieve some relief for the Apaches, Welsh resorted to his already familiar tactics. As it was primarily an army problem, he hoped to win over Secretary Endicott. To this end he exploited his contacts in Boston, the secretary's home town. The need for support from Bostonians was one reason Welsh was anxious to preserve good relations with the Boston Indian Citizenship Committee despite differences over the Thayer plan. Among those from whom he solicited letters to Endicott were Leverett Saltonstall, Collector of the Port of Boston, and Professor Francis Parkman of Harvard College. Parkman, the western historian and a member of the association's Cambridge branch, was a colleague of Endicott's on the Harvard Corporation. J. Randolph Coolidge, Jr., secretary of the Boston branch of the IRA and a member of a prominent Boston family, also was asked for a letter of introduction to the secretary of war.[92]

Welsh himself, accompanied by Captain Bourke, made a visit early in 1887 to Fort Marion, where he interviewed Chato and the two shanghaied government scouts. Welsh described himself as "much struck" by Chato's appearance and spoke of his having a "well-shaped head and a manly, open expression."[93] As usual Welsh took advantage of the visit to establish relations with local officials, including an army officer and an interpreter who would later provide him a flow of information about the situation at Fort Marion. When the *Army and Navy Register* published a letter from Welsh on the Apaches, he also began to hear from Lieutenant Colonel Loomis L. Langdon, commander at Fort Pickens. Colonel Langdon asked IRA assistance in getting the wives and children of the prisoners under his charge brought over from Fort Marion. "You and your friends are welcome to all the credit if you will only get me those poor devils' wives and children," he pled.[94]

As he became more involved in the Apache prisoner affair, Welsh had difficulty avoiding being drawn into the internecine warfare of the officer corps. He was acquainted with generals George Crook and Nelson Miles, admired both, and considered them enlightened on Indian issues. However, they were rivals in the army and had differed openly on how to handle the Apache hostiles, particularly on the wisdom of employing Indian scouts. As a former aide to General Crook, Captain Bourke was very partisan, but Welsh managed to remain friendly with both generals and the captain who provided him with background material.

Following his trip to Florida in March 1887, Welsh wrote a sixty-two page pamphlet summarizing the situation and printing extracts from many of the key orders and reports.[95] In addition to circulating the publication, Welsh was able to get selections from it reprinted in the New York *Daily Tribune* and other newspapers. Painter spoke to President Cleveland about the Chiricahuas but got no satisfaction from the chief executive. Painter also talked to Secretary Lamar about the problem, and Lamar at least agreed to bring it before the cabinet.[96]

It was Painter's opinion that more pressure was needed, and Welsh was prepared to inspire it. On a swing through New England he discussed the topic with Senator Dawes and interested parties in Cambridge, Worcester, and New Haven. He also stirred up Providence's John Nicholas Brown, who could always be counted upon to contact his congressional delegation in a good cause. The Boston reformers sent to

Washington their own delegation, including Mayor Prince, for an interview with Secretary Endicott.[97]

The public discussion forced the administration to address itself to the issue. Captain Bourke specifically credited Welsh's pamphlet with bringing the subject before the cabinet. President Cleveland's decision was to reunite the Fort Pickens prisoners with their families, and to move the rest of the Fort Marion prisoners to a better location. But, before the move would be made, Captain Bourke was ordered to inspect the recommended site, Mount Vernon Barracks, about twenty-five miles north of Mobile Bay. The captain made a hasty trip south and approved the new location, although he did conclude that the soil was too sandy for most agriculture. It was pine land, however, and Bourke was confident that the Indians could find employment in lumbering.[98]

The transfer of the Fort Marion prisoners to Mount Vernon Barracks was speedily accomplished, and after a year it was felt safe to send those at Fort Pickens to the same post. The first transfer was no sooner underway than Captain Bourke asked Welsh to try to persuade some prominent Boston ladies to form a committee to help the Apaches. The captain was still insisting that a program of education be developed. About sixty of the young Chiricahuas had been sent to Carlisle, but Bourke wanted something for those children and adults remaining at Mount Vernon Barracks. Both he and the interpreter who accompanied them to Alabama pictured the prisoners as idle and stagnating.[99]

Together, Bourke and Welsh were able to interest Mrs. Augustus Hemenway of Boston in the Apaches. A wealthy philanthropist, Mrs. Hemenway contracted with a young Hampton teacher to go to Mount Vernon Barracks to work with the women and children.[100]

Welsh endorsed all of this activity and particularly the enrollment of the children at Carlisle. Despite his differences with Captain Pratt, he had gone out of his way in his report on the Apaches to commend Pratt's transformation of the young Chiricahuas from "wild, untrained, filthy savages" to "clean, neat and decently dressed" children.[101]

Nevertheless, there remained the problem of the ultimate location of the Apaches. The demands of white Arizonans that former hostiles be tried for murder and assorted crimes made their immediate return to the territory impossible. Welsh suggested that a likely interim location might be in "the dry elevated plains region of the West," possibly an abandoned military post in Nebraska.[102] However, that was too near Arizona to be acceptable to settlers of that territory. A better location might be an 800-acre farm adjoining Hampton Institute, where they could be supervised by General Armstrong. The general was willing, and Welsh endorsed the idea after an inspection of the proposed settlement, only to have the plan blocked by Captain Pratt's criticism that the area would be unhealthy. Most of 1888 was consumed in debating the merits of the location near Hampton versus sites farther west. Pratt seems to have been the first to suggest Fort Sill as a possibility because of the location there of the Kiowa Apaches, a culturally related group.[103]

As the controversy dragged on, Welsh even sought help from President Cleveland's sister, whom he got to intercede with Secretary Endicott.[104] Endicott's response was to accuse the IRA of misrepresenting the facts on the Apache issue.[105] Although Cleveland was defeated at the polls in November, Welsh continued to try to get action from his administration. He promoted the cause of the Apaches before the Riggs House conference in January 1889 and wrote letters to newspapers and magazines calling their attention to the issue. he also kept up his drumfire on secretaries Vilas of the Interior Department and Endicott of the War Department and sent one last appeal to President Cleveland. Although he doubted that Cleveland would respond, Welsh felt he must play this "last card" with the departing administration.[106] It was typical of him that, once convinced of the righteousness of a cause, he would persevere despite disappointments that would have discouraged a lesser man.

CHAPTER EIGHT

Adjusting to the
Harrison Administration

During the Benjamin Harrison administration, 1889–1893, congressmen and commissioners of Indian affairs not only would pay heed to the causes the IRA championed, but would seek association help on matters before Congress such as appropriation bills for the Indian Service. The membership of the Philadelphia association grew to over 900, and, when those in the branches were included, the figure approached 1,500. Income of the IRA did not rise proportionately, averaging about $6,500. The association still depended heavily on large donors. While the dues-paying members became more numerous, those willing to give significantly more did not.[1]

At least some of the increase in membership came from the ranks of the Indian Service. Employees in the field were beginning to request membership in significant numbers. One can only speculate as to their motivation, but, as more and more of them were turning to the IRA for redress of grievances or help in retaining their positions, it is reasonable to assume that these reservation employees were inspired by more than interest in Indian welfare.

Although nominally only the corresponding secretary, Herbert Welsh continued to be to a large degree the heart and the brain of the organization. It was he who had the major voice in determining what causes the IRA assumed and how its resources would be allotted. The other officers appeared prepared to permit him to run the show, probably because they all had demanding professions while he was able to devote his full time and energies to his avocations. Welsh went so far as to ask President James Rhoads to step down because he was unable to attend many executive committee meetings, and arranged his replacement by Philip C. Garrett. Rhoads was not unhappy to step aside, as his duties as president of Bryn Mawr College left him little time for the IRA.[2] But Welsh did not find the relief he had sought. Executive committee meetings continued to attract perhaps a half dozen of the twenty members, sometimes only two or three. Despite his being a member of the Board of Indian Commissioners and having strong views on Indian policy, the new president did not have the time or inclination to take over from the corresponding secretary the real direction of the association. As Garrett assured Welsh on one occasion when a difference of views developed, he was not only willing but anxious to change his own to make them "harmonious" with those of Welsh: "yours should govern, so far as the utterances of the Indian Rights Association are concerned."[3]

As that rarity, an able man with excellent connections who was prepared to devote his full energies to good causes, Welsh found himself recruited for other work at the expense of the IRA. During the years 1889 to 1893 he was superintendent of his church's Sunday school in Germantown, continued as a vice-president of the Forestry Congress and as a member of the board of managers of the City Parks Association, and worked with the local Board of Education. He also joined the Universal Peace Union after his support for arbitration had been confirmed; however, he resisted invitations to lend a hand to the movements for postal saving banks and the relief of Russians exiled to Siberia.

Somehow Welsh found time to become involved in local politics. One fight he enlisted in was against the introduction of a trolley system powered by overhead lines. He helped raise money to oppose the plan and in the spring of 1892 was so busy with the campaign that he was unable to accept all of his invitations to speak on Indian affairs.[4]

State politics also engaged Welsh's attention. In 1890 he helped organize the Lincoln Independent Republican Committee, which had as a nucleus old friends and IRA associates such as Dr. Rhoads, Henry S. Pancoast, and N. DuBois Miller.[5] Their objective was no less than the defeat of Matthew "Boss" Quay's handpicked Republican gubernatorial candidate. With their help the Democratic candidate won. Emboldened by its success, the group set its sights on Quay himself, one of the shrewdest politicians Pennsylvania ever produced. The plan was to try to elect to the Pennsylvania legislature anti-Quay people whose votes would then retire Boss Quay from the U.S. Senate. In the fall of 1891 Welsh was heading this campaign to oust, as he told Theodore Roosevelt, "the fount and the stronghold of corrupt politics" in Pennsylvania.[6]

The following year Welsh permitted himself to be offered as a candidate for the legislature on an independent ticket. Although he had neglected his Indian work to organize the opposition to Quay and had diverted some of the energies of the IRA office personnel into it as well, Welsh waged a very diffident campaign for himself. He depended on his friends to solicit votes while he remained above the battle. In September 1892, as the campaign was developing in intensity, Welsh went off to South Dakota and Denver on Indian work. Not that the election results suggested that more active campaigning might have won him the seat. The Republican machine candidate drew more votes than Welsh and the Democratic nominee combined. Even Welsh was surprised at how few votes he had drawn. He attributed his failure to the "most barefaced falsehoods" circulated by his opponents, and his overestimation of the anti-Quay sentiment and of his own "hold upon the confidence of my fellow-townsmen."[7] In the aftermath of his political drubbing Welsh concluded that he had made a mistake in running for public office and that he was temperamentally unsuited for it.[8]

The corresponding secretary's preoccupation with politics for extended periods threw more responsibility upon Charles Painter and Matthew Sniffen. Painter still received a steady stream of subjects for investigation which originally had been referred to the Philadelphia office. Now Welsh's growing involvement in other causes left Painter more often on his own. This change did not pose any problem, as the basic philosophy of the IRA was well established. Many of its causes, like the opposition to the removal of the Southern Utes or the effort to do something for the Apaches held in Florida and Alabama, were around for several years. Welsh's preoccupation, and then Painter's absence in California on Mission Indian business for nearly a year, also meant a growing role for Sniffen. Welsh delegated more of the detail work to the young clerk and by 1892 was authorizing him to send out letters over his own signature as "Clerk" of the association.

Welsh still retained the power to direct the strength of the IRA into any channel he chose, even though it might be one viewed with misgivings by others. This control was made abundantly clear in the vigorous fight the association waged in early 1889 to persuade newly elected President Harrison to retain John Oberly, a Democratic appointee, as commissioner of Indian affairs. It was quite unlikely that Harrison would do so, and there were some of Welsh's normal allies who did not share his view of Oberly's superior qualities. Nevertheless, Welsh decided to wage the fight as a matter of commitment to the principle of civil service.

Commissioner Oberly had made a real effort to earn Welsh's support. He had made himself available for conferences with Welsh and Painter and had responded promptly to Welsh's suggestions regarding the Indian Service. For example, a Welsh nominee became Navajo agent, and the White Mountain Apaches gained an industrial school and those at San Carlos a sawmill that their agents had asked the IRA to help them to secure.[9] When the commissioner committed himself to work for the extension of civil service to the Indian Service, any reluctance Welsh might have had to back a potential loser vanished.[10]

By January 1889 Welsh had thrown himself into the campaign to secure Oberly's retention and was "writing in every direction."[11] It was really a remarkable effort, particularly considering the odds against its success, which Welsh himself set at about nine to one. An eight-page pamphlet was printed and circulated, and literally hundreds of letters were dispatched to friends of the Indian urging them to write their congressmen and to circulate IRA petitions.[12] If an individual was known to have any special relationship with the president-elect or any member of his cabinet, he was asked to exploit it. For example, someone in Philadelphia who knew the pastor of the church in Indianapolis attended by Harrison was approached to solicit a letter from the pastor.[13] Editors were supplied with lengthy defenses of Oberly's records as well as copies of pertinent correspondence.

As always, Welsh tried to make the campaign an appeal to reason. He was a man with a strict code of ethics, one who even in the heat of battle would try to deal with the issue objectively and with complete devotion to the truth. Nor was he for sale in an era when American public life was replete with those who were. He was approached once by a Pine Ridge agency employee with a proposal to enter the cattle business. The man would supply the management know-how, and Welsh would supply the capital and the contacts that would enable them to secure the beef contracts for several Indian agencies. Welsh was promised handsome profits in a range-cattle industry which had attracted hundreds of wealthy easterners like Theodore Roosevelt, but he dismissed the idea offhand. "I could not with propriety," he wrote the man at Pine Ridge, "invest in any enterprise in which I sought to use whatever influence I may have acquired in my efforts for the civilization of the Indians, to promote my private financial interest."[14]

Welsh did have one definite weakness. Many people were surprised to find portions of their letters to him appearing in his correspondence with other people, or even in newspapers. Those who knew him well frequently headed their letters with some injunction like "Strictly Private" or "Not For Publication." Even these designations did not always stop Welsh. One of Commissioner Morgan's letters, which carried the warning *"strictly confidential . . . destroy as soon as read,"* Welsh promptly shared with editor William Hayes Ward and later filed with other IRA correspondence.[15] Apparently such injunctions had little or no significance for him. One of his own letters to Commissioner Morgan, marked "Personal," he promptly had copied and sent to Theodore Roosevelt.[16]

The IRA's Oberly campaign did generate considerable public support for the commissioner. Pro-Oberly letters or editorials appeared in at least twenty newspapers and journals, including the *Springfield Republican, Harper's Weekly*, the Boston *Post*, and the Indianapolis *News*. As usual, Welsh made use of the network of religious journals such as the *Baltimore Methodist* and the *National Baptist*. In Philadelphia a committee of "very influential ladies" was recruited to circulate petitions, and it secured the signatures of 262 of the leading local Republicans.[17] The WNIA distributed to its members copies of the Oberly petitions, and Mrs. Quinton assured Welsh that the Pennsylvania congressional delegation had been contacted.[18]

The efforts to mobilize support for Oberly among senators were generally unsuccessful. The usual response was one still heard today, that the president should make his own choice and thus be held completely responsible for administration policy. Among those who responded, senators H. M. Teller of Colorado and Preston B. Plumb of Kansas wrote at length to explain their opposition to Oberly.[19] Senator J. J. Ingalls of Kansas was more succinct: "I am in favor of the prompt removal of Mr. Oberly, and hope soon to have the opportunity of voting for a Republican successor in that office."[20]

Not all of the eastern friends of the Indian united behind Oberly. General Armstrong, whose opinion Welsh always valued, was most unenthusiastic about making a fight in Oberly's behalf.[21] Dr. Rhoads, at the time still serving as president of the IRA, was advising retreat a month after the battle got underway.[22] The Boston Indian Citizenship Committee had asked only for the appointment of a good man and refused to alter its stand by specifying Oberly.[23]

Two public officials from whom Welsh solicited help also disappointed him. Newly appointed Civil Service Commissioner Theodore Roosevelt, with whom Welsh at that time had only a slight acquaintance, declined to support Oberly because of some adverse comments about him made by George Bird Grinnell, the author, publisher, and expert on plains tribes. Roosevelt proved immune even to a personal visit from Charles Painter, earning that Washington veteran's observation that he "was not favorably impressed either with the good sense or fairness of the Hon. Theo," whom Painter termed "immensely green."[24] After an exchange of letters with Roosevelt, Welsh confided to George William Curtis, with whom he shared Painter's account of his talk with Roosevelt, that the New Yorker lacked a "judicial faculty."[25] Like most people, Welsh found it difficult to respect the judgment of individuals who disagreed with him on significant issues. However, in time he would become a great admirer of the irresistible TR.

Senator Dawes was another who responded negatively to the Oberly campaign. He maintained that the president should be able to select his own subordinates. While suggesting that Oberly had flaws, Dawes tried to soften his response to Welsh: "I know your entire honesty in this matter and I have no reason to doubt that you believe I am equally sincere." The senator added, "There I beg you to let it rest as between us."[26]

Dawes must have known that this was not Welsh's style. Welsh insisted that the senator spell out his reservations about Oberly, while circulating far and wide copies of their correspondence. Editors Samuel Bowles and George William Curtis were invited to read it, as well as various other individuals, among them Dr. Henry I. Bowditch, a Boston physician who had had his own exchange with Dawes on the issue. Welsh confided to Dr. Bowditch that in his judgment Dawes's conduct for the past year "in reference to various Indian bills, has . . . been . . . such as to seriously threaten the welfare of the Indians, and to embarrass our efforts in their behalf."[27]

Senator Dawes tried twice to terminate the acrimonious discussion with Welsh. The second time he protested that it was "fast approaching an angry discussion" and that, while he believed Welsh mistaken in the matter, he knew Welsh had "the best interests of the Indian at heart." Dawes did chide Welsh about getting people to write him about Oberly and then circulating and even publishing the responses: "They all seem to be treated as public property. . . ."[28] Welsh promptly sent out copies of *that* letter, and the controversy boiled on. It came to a head when the *Springfield Republican* published a Dawes letter in which he vented his anger at Welsh's tactics:

> Herbert Welsh has failed by persistent letter-writing and importunate personal pressure to draw me into public arraignment of the official conduct of Mr. Oberly. . . . I do not intend that he shall be any more successful by circulating as public property letters he has drawn out of me, or by twisting extracts from them out of their context for the material for editorials in the columns of newspapers whose good opinion I esteem, and whose influence among my constituents helps to form their opinion of me.[29]

Welsh did not respond to the *Springfield Republican* letter, as he believed that Samuel Bowles's accompanying editorial comment had made a reply unnecessary. He did, however, send to the Boston *Post* a defense of his actions.[30]

While supporting Oberly, Welsh had maintained all along that the real issue at stake was not Oberly's record but the iniquitous spoils system that made it impossible to consider keeping a Democrat in a Republican administration. At the least he hoped to force the new administration to pick an able replacement. In this effort he was successful.

One of the IRA members from whom Welsh received support in the Oberly campaign was Thomas Jefferson Morgan, the corresponding secretary of the Providence branch. A Civil War veteran who was addressed by his army rank, as was the custom in this period, General Morgan was the head of the teacher-training school at Providence. Back in November, Welsh had mentioned him as a possible superintendent of the Indian school system.[31] Two weeks later Welsh informed the president-elect that Morgan, who had served under Harrison during the war, would be acceptable to the IRA as commissioner of Indian affairs, although he preferred Oberly.[32] Welsh battled to the end for the incumbent, but by June 1889 it was all over. Oberly resigned after being told he would not be kept by the new administration. Welsh was "most cast down by this, as it seems to me a great calamity."[33] However, a day later he was taking comfort, even pride, in the belief "that our fight . . . has done much good, and it has forced the President to appoint the Republican whom we thought best suited, if Mr. Oberly was to be removed."[34] Welsh promptly telegraphed Morgan congratulations on the appointment and followed with letters in which he promised the cooperation of the IRA and was careful to point out that as early as December 4 he had recommended Morgan to the president-elect should Oberly not be reappointed.[35]

When Morgan's confirmation by the Senate faced opposition, with no embarrassment at all Welsh launched a campaign in his behalf comparable to the one he earlier had waged to keep Oberly in the position. He had ample reason to do so because Commissioner Morgan equaled or exceeded Oberly in his efforts to be responsive to IRA queries and suggestions and had asked Welsh's assistance in securing qualified personnel for particular positions. Morgan explained he had been appointed by Harrison "from his conviction that I would administer the office in such a way as to satisfy the philanthropic and Christian sentiment of the country."[36] General Morgan certainly tried, at least so far as the IRA was concerned.

Although appointed in June 1889, Morgan was not confirmed by the Senate until the following February, after an unexpectedly hard fight. The same was true of Daniel Dorchester, whom President Harrison had nominated as superintendent of Indian schools and whose confirmation was sometimes linked with that of Morgan. The opposition came principally from the ranks of the Roman Catholics.[37] They

were understandably alarmed at the prospect of two Protestant clergymen, Dorchester a Methodist and Morgan a Baptist, being appointed to positions so crucial to the Catholic interest in the education
of Indians. Moreover, Dorchester was notorious among the Catholic
hierarchy as the author of an anti-Catholic diatribe. Morgan's known
bias in favor of public schools also was disturbing to the Catholics, who
soon were accusing him of unjustified removals of Catholics from the
Indian Service schools. Morgan's proposal to reduce the scope of the
contract school system further alarmed them. The Catholic Church
had the country's most extensive contract school system, in 1889 receiving $347,672 of the total of $476,765 available for all such Indian
schools. In contrast, the Presbyterians, although they ranked second,
received only $41,825.[38] The elimination of such support obviously
would have had a catastrophic effect on the Catholic schools, and thus
the Catholics opposed Morgan strenuously.

   Like Welsh and the IRA, the Catholics strove to bring pressure on
Congress and the administration to achieve their ends. The leadership
in the fight against confirmation of Morgan and Dorchester was provided by Reverend Joseph A. Stephan, the German-born head of the
Bureau of Catholic Indian Missions, headquartered in Washington.
He galvanized the Catholic press into an all-out attack on Morgan. The
commissioner was accused of bias in his discharge of Catholic teachers
and, to discredit him, the press regaled the public with details of a Civil
War court-martial Morgan had undergone. Even after Morgan was
confirmed, he continued to be a target of Catholic criticism, which did
not abate when the acerbic Father Stephan took leave from his post at
the Catholic Bureau. Despite the opposition, and perhaps because of it,
Commissioner Morgan persevered in his efforts to expand the government school system at the expense of the contract schools. In the
1892 presidential campaign the Catholic Church urged the defeat of
Harrison, in this fashion striking at Morgan, and Catholic spokesmen
denounced both as anti-Catholic bigots.[39]

   Throughout his difficulties with the Catholics, Morgan looked to
the IRA for help and received it. The commissioner preferred not to
respond directly to attacks but was happy to provide Welsh with ammunition. For his part Welsh never showed any hesitation to engage in
protracted debate through the mails or in the public press with anyone
or any subject.

   In supporting Morgan's confirmation, Welsh employed his usual
tactics. He ordered mailings to all the members of the Philadelphia
organization and to the IRA branches as well. He exploited his newspaper contacts, and the New York *Tribune* and the *New York Times,* as
well as the *Springfield Republican* and other papers, carried Welsh-

inspired editorials or letters over his name. Welsh also turned to his friends among Protestant journal editors and circularized a number of Baptist and other Protestant ministers as well as all of the Episcopal and Methodist bishops.[40]

Welsh's campaign did generate a lot of mail to members of Congress. It also generated a great many expressions of bigotry. Episcopal Bishop William C. Doane of Albany responded to Welsh's appeal with an expression of his deep concern and the observation that

> Rome is pursuing in this country exactly the same course that had destroyed her influence in all other countries. Namely, meddling in political affairs. I am abundantly satisfied that nine out of every ten of the martyrs of Rome have not died for the faith but have been duly punished for political meddling.[41]

Methodist Bishop Willard F. Mallalieu of New Orleans was another who spoke with some heat. He described Archbishop John Ireland, who was taking a leading role in the fight against Morgan, as "a consistent Jesuit i.e. without honor or conscience."[42]

Although their reactions were less quotable, most of the others to whom Welsh turned for help for Morgan responded affirmatively. Amelia Quinton and Sara Kinney both indicated that they had been working for Morgan even before Welsh contacted them.[43] Anna Dawes, who had been acting as a mediator between her father and Herbert Welsh, assured the latter that the senator was solidly behind the commissioner.[44]

Morgan attributed much of his difficulty to John A. Gorman, a Catholic who had been discharged from the Indian Bureau on Morgan's recommendation. The commissioner supplied Welsh with information which led him to refer to Gorman, in a letter published in a Philadelphia paper, as having been discharged for "inefficiency, gross insubordination and intoxication."[45] Gorman challenged Welsh, who cited Morgan as the source of his information. Welsh thought that Gorman was trying to establish a basis for a libel suit, but nothing came of it.[46]

Captain Pratt came to Commissioner Morgan's aid with a telegram to a senator stating that he had seen Gorman drunk in the bureau.[47] Pratt did not care for Morgan, but he cared less for the Catholic Church and Father Stephan, whom he regarded as working for the overthrow of the public school system.[48]

Both Dorchester and Morgan were confirmed by the Senate. Morgan, even before victory had been achieved, had expressed his gratitude to Welsh: "You have fulfilled your task admirably."[49] For his part Welsh advised Morgan to be generous to the Catholics in victory,

although in his correspondence he did not attempt to conceal his own
anti-Catholic sentiments. During the confirmation fight he had denounced Bishop Ireland as having difficulty telling the truth.[50] After
the Senate had confirmed Morgan, Welsh confided to Episcopal
Bishop Doane, "The whole struggle . . . impressed me deeply with a
sense of the unscrupulous audacity of the Roman Church in pulling
political wires."[51]

Despite these views Welsh demonstrated his willingness to work
with Catholics for the common good. Early in Commissioner Morgan's
tenure Welsh had sought and obtained Cardinal Gibbons's support for
an employee faction at Rosebud Agency, one of whose prominent
members was a Catholic teacher.[52] On the basis of his own familiarity
with Rosebud, Welsh had championed two employees there who were
threatened by dismissal, the superintendent of the local school and a
farmer. The commissioner found himself caught between Welsh and his
allies on the one hand, and, on the other, the Rosebud agent, who was
insisting that the employees be discharged. Morgan during this period
was receiving from the IRA advice on personnel matters on almost a
daily basis. The commissioner finally told Welsh that he had other
sources of information and that on occasion these might lead him to act
contrary to IRA recommendations.[53]

Ultimately the Rosebud agent won, and the farmer, whom the
agent described as not knowing the difference between a breaking and
a stubble plow, or how many potatoes to plant to an acre, was fired. So
was the school superintendent, who was depicted as having "lost the
respect of every person on the agency, the Indians included," to the
point that even those with whom he boarded would not converse with
him.[54] But Welsh was not easily discouraged, and he continued to carry
on a voluminous correspondence with Commissioner Morgan on personnel matters, invoking the aid even of Catholics on occasion.

Welsh had sought out Cardinal Gibbons when he first heard
rumors of Catholic unhappiness with Commissioner Morgan. As the
controversy became more heated, Welsh, through the good offices of
his friend and prominent Catholic layman Charles J. Bonaparte, arranged to visit Baltimore and confer with Bishop Ireland and Bishop
Patrick W. Riordan of San Francisco. That meeting did not allay the
fears of the prelates, who had an appointment to see President Harrison about the administration of the Indian Bureau.[55]

During the confirmation fight Welsh had tried to influence the
Catholic hierarchy through another layman, Peter L. Foy of St. Louis.
When Welsh learned from Foy that Archbishop Patrick J. Ryan would
be staying with him when the bishop visited St. Louis in January 1889,
Welsh tried to make the case for Morgan to Foy. Declaring that "your

Church is doing an extended and excellent work in the direction of Indian civilization," the IRA spokesman attempted to establish his credibility with Foy. "I am personally acquainted with several Roman Catholics who are laboring in the Indian field, with whom I have had delightful and cordial relations," Welsh enthused.[56] All of that introduction, of course, was preliminary to a ringing endorsement of Morgan and a denial that the commissioner was discriminating against Catholics. Whether the letter convinced Foy, or whether Foy discussed it with Bishop Ryan, is not known. It does demonstrate that Welsh was ready to try to reason with his opponents as well as to attempt to overwhelm them in the press.

Morgan's confirmation by the Senate in February 1890 did not end the struggle. In September, Senator Dawes reported to his wife that "the quarrel between General Morgan and the Catholics has broken out anew, and I am to give Father Stephan an audience today."[57] For the remainder of his tenure Commissioner Morgan had to deal with Catholic efforts to remove him from office. Welsh stood by him loyally, praising the commissioner's record and responding to specific Catholic attacks. When Morgan reacted to a strongly worded communication from Father Stephan by refusing to deal with the Catholic institutions through the bureau Stephan directed, Welsh lauded the commissioner's decision. "I cannot see how any other course is open to you," he wrote Morgan. "The insolence of the director's letter to you is unparalleled," Welsh concluded.[58]

Father Francis M. Craft, who took up the cudgels against Commissioner Morgan early in 1891, had been working for many years on the Sioux reservations where Welsh had come to know him as "a very unreliable and mischevious [*sic*] person."[59] To support this evaluation of the priest, Welsh depended on James McLaughlin, the long-time agent at Standing Rock and a Catholic himself. Agent McLaughlin dismissed Craft's "wild ravings," which he attributed to the priest's "very poor judgement."[60] Nevertheless, Father Craft played a role in inspiring a move in the House of Representatives to have Morgan's conduct of the Bureau of Indian Affairs investigated.

Curiously, Morgan also was being criticized for being too easy on the Catholic Church. Morgan admitted that he had failed to fire some inefficient employees *because* they were Catholic.[61] Captain Pratt, an extremist in this issue as in everything else, denounced Morgan for claiming to oppose the Catholics while actually increasing the dollar amount of their contracts to educate Indian students. Pratt's description of priests engaged in Indian education work as an "unmitigated unscrupulous body of liars and tricksters" brought Catholic wrath down upon his head.[62] In 1892 Painter reported a move inspired by the

Church to persuade House members to omit from the appropriation bill a salary for Pratt as Carlisle's superintendent.[63]

Despite his own extreme annoyance with the anti-Morgan campaign, Herbert Welsh continued to turn to Catholic prelates for help on other issues. Early in 1892, while preparing literature to oppose a congressional reduction in the Indian school appropriation, Welsh obtained Cardinal Gibbons's permission to quote him.[64] The IRA executive, despite his differences with the Catholic Bureau, even appealed for help to Bishop Martin Marty, president of the bureau, citing promises of aid from Bishop Fitzgerald of Little Rock and from Archbishop Patrick J. Ryan. Bishop Marty assured Welsh of his sympathy but declined to write any letters because, "as the Catholic Hierarchy is a unit, the Cardinal's letter sufficiently expresses our sentiments."[65] That statement simply bore out Welsh's prediction that Gibbons's permission to quote him "will, of course, be equal to a command to the Roman Catholics and the Roman Catholic press of the country to oppose the threatened reduction."[66]

Even as Welsh continued to support Morgan publicly, privately he was manifesting a growing disenchantment, despite their having visited in each other's homes and despite Morgan's efforts to respond to Welsh's every suggestion regarding reservation matters. Indeed, Captain Pratt regarded the commissioner as the "creature of the Indian Rights Association."[67] Nevertheless, in some respects it was inevitable that a rift should develop between Morgan and the IRA's corresponding secretary. Welsh was free to make judgments purely on an evaluation of what was in the best interest of the Indians or the Indian Service personnel involved. In contrast, Morgan, as a political appointee, had to answer to the secretary of the interior and to the president. And, as he had informed Welsh early in his tenure, on occasion Morgan got reports from others that conflicted with those coming from Welsh.

Welsh's principal criticism of Morgan was that he confined himself too much to school matters, where Welsh acknowledged he had done an excellent job. It was difficult to please a true reformer of the Welsh variety. He could say of Morgan that, "take him all in all, he has done better work than any of his predecessors," but Welsh always wanted more.[68]

Evidence that the Morgan-Welsh relationship was cooling was to be found in Welsh's travel plans for the fall of 1892. He and Civil Service Commissioner Theodore Roosevelt had been corresponding for months about a trip, several times postponed, that would include the Sioux reservations in South Dakota. Morgan suggested that he accompany them. Although three years earlier it had been Welsh who was pushing Morgan to join him on a trip to reservations in Arizona, Welsh now told the commissioner that he did not think it would be wise for them to visit the Sioux together.[69] As he explained it to Roosevelt, his traveling with the commissioner would "compromise me as the representative of an organization which is supposed to make independent investigations, and to be impartial in its judgement."[70] Morgan took the rejection in good grace, although it must have irked him. He recognized the advantages accruing from a good relationship with the head of the most active Indian reform organization in the country and was willing to tolerate a great deal from Welsh. Nor was Morgan above flattery, arranging to have a boarding school at Fort Mojave, Arizona, named the Herbert Welsh Institute.[71]

If the two had visited Pine Ridge together, they might have been able to reach an understanding about the commissioner's difficulty with the agent there, Captain George Leroy Brown. An army officer assigned temporary duty as agent, Captain Brown was well known in eastern reform circles, having served on the staff of Hampton Institute for three years. The captain and Welsh were personally acquainted, and the two had communicated often since Brown's assignment to Pine Ridge. Captain Brown was one of a number of agents who felt free to call upon Welsh for a little help outside official channels when he had a problem at his agency.

Like other army officers assigned such duty, the captain found it difficult to accept orders from civilians in the Interior Department. He and Commissioner Morgan were soon at odds, with the commissioner accusing him of insubordination. Welsh, at least initially, could see both sides of the issue. Morgan tended to be "domineering and hasty"; however, Brown "no doubt is in error in the stand he has taken."[72] Nevertheless, the captain was an efficient agent, and, since it was not Welsh's authority that was being challenged, he opposed Brown's removal as a loss to the Indian Service. The ousting of competent agents to make room for local political favorites was something that could always be calculated to stir Welsh to action.

The dispute dragged on for months and further damaged the Morgan-Welsh relationship. The difference had originated in a report from Bishop Hare to Welsh that Brown would be replaced by a local cattleman. Welsh, assuming that the commissioner would have no more to do with this change of agents than he normally had—that is, nothing—hastily dashed off a letter which was published in an eastern newspaper. Morgan rebuked Welsh mildly for taking a stand on Captain Brown before hearing Morgan's side of the dispute. The commissioner admitted that he usually learned of the appointments of agents from reading them in the newspaper, but he claimed to be consulted occasionally about removals.[73]

Captain George LeRoy Brown
Courtesy National Archives

When Welsh, in company with Roosevelt, visited Pine Ridge in the fall of 1892, he had an opportunity to make a personal judgment about one of the principal issues dividing Commissioner Morgan and Captain Brown. In question was the quality of 70,000 pounds of bacon purchased by the government for issue to the Pine Ridge Indians. Brown had refused to issue it, claiming the bacon was unfit for human consumption. Welsh examined some of it while at Pine Ridge and declared it "very revolting in appearance" and "wholly unfit for human food."[74]

Welsh had an ally in Theodore Roosevelt in his fight to keep Brown at Pine Ridge. TR and Welsh had traveled together for ten days over the Sioux reservations, and Welsh found him "a remarkable man, and one of the most delightful companions."[75] Roosevelt later promised to do all he could to prevent Brown's removal and suggested that he and Welsh get together soon for a "war talk."[76]

The Brown case was complicated by a controversy within a controversy. Just as Commissioner Morgan was accusing Captain Brown of insubordination, the agent was leveling the same charge at his agency physician. The doctor was not the usual political appointee, but Charles A. Eastman, a Santee Sioux closely associated with Frank Wood of the Boston Indian Citizenship Committee. Also, Dr. Eastman was now the husband of Elaine Goodale, superintendent of Sioux day schools since leaving Hampton Institute and an active member of the IRA. When they became engaged, Miss Goodale had written Welsh, "I am sure that you are one of the real friends who will rejoice in my happiness, and so I will tell you of it myself."[77]

While at Pine Ridge, Welsh had agreed to hear out the Eastmans' complaints of harrassment at the hands of Captain Brown. The conference resulted only in their concluding that Welsh was predisposed to favor Brown. The IRA executive now found himself involved in another quarrel that would be fought out in the newspapers. Once again Welsh would expend an inordinate amount of time in a public dispute, this time with people whom in the past he had befriended and indeed had fought alongside in other battles. He seemed to lack the capacity to choose which fights were worthwhile and, as a result, was almost constantly embroiled in a running battle with someone. For a man with pacifist tendencies, he had a remarkable propensity for at least verbal combat.

As the quarrel between the Eastmans and Captain Brown waxed, Welsh became more and more deeply involved. Captain Brown inundated him with copies of his correspondence with his agency physician. Mrs. Eastman published a letter in the New York *Evening Post* detailing their side of the controversy. Welsh first declined an invitation by the editor to respond, saying he wished to avoid "public exhibition of disagreement between the friends of the Indian."[78] However, he reconsidered, and early in December the *Evening Post* published his rebuttal to Mrs. Eastman. Bishop Hare praised Welsh's letter, but it infuriated Frank Wood and Mrs. Eastman.[79] The latter wrote a twenty-page response, which the paper declined to print so Mrs. Eastman sent it directly to Welsh.[80] Wood defended Dr. Eastman before a meeting of the Boston committee, as if his own son had been attacked, according to a witness. When Eastman chose to resign from the Indian Service rather than be transferred from Pine Ridge, Wood asked bitterly if Welsh were "proud of having secured the removal from the Indian service of the best educated Indian this country has yet produced . . . whose highest purpose in life was to Christianize, civilize and help his people."[81] Mrs. Eastman contented herself with the public announcement that she was resigning from the IRA.

The Brown-Eastman dispute had gradually overshadowed the original Brown-Morgan difficulty. This controversy had not been resolved, and Captain Brown was still in office when Commissioner Morgan resigned his post in December 1892.

Throughout the Brown troubles Welsh had turned to Theodore Roosevelt for advice and help. Roosevelt had assured Welsh time and time again of his support for the agent. However, unlike Welsh, TR had limits as to how far he would go in badgering officials in behalf of Brown. Nevertheless, Welsh was grateful for his help and sent TR a Navajo blanket "as an evidence of my very warm and deep feelings for you."[82] A few days later Welsh described Roosevelt to a correspondent as "a very unusual man, with great power of observation, good sense and force of character; one of the very best young men that we have in political life to-day."[83] Roosevelt obviously had come a long way in the three years since Painter and Welsh had first met him and concluded that he was a greenhorn lacking political judgment.

Not even Roosevelt was any help to Welsh in his dealings with Harrison's secretary of the interior, John W. Noble. Another Civil War general, and an attorney from St. Louis, Noble was not disposed to try to humor eastern do-gooders. Welsh attempted in vain to establish a relationship with the secretary comparable to the one he had enjoyed with Noble's predecessor, William F. Vilas. In Noble's first months in office in 1889 he had received from Welsh a number of recommendations for discharging or retaining Indian Service personnel. Welsh also was a member of a delegation which called upon the secretary to share with him their views of how the Native Americans should be handled.[84]

One former agent for whose reappointment Welsh mounted a substantial campaign was James G. Wright, who had served at Rosebud. Unfortunately, Wright's residence was Chicago, and Secretary Noble informed Welsh that this fact made him unacceptable to the citizens of South Dakota.[85] This case was the IRA leader's introduction to the principle of "home rule," which was a reaction against giving federal jobs in the West to non-westerners. In the Harrison administration it became the practice to appoint only local residents to such positions as Indian agent.

Welsh responded in typical fashion to Secretary Noble's announcement of the home-rule policy. He first sought an evaluation of the new practice from a number of people, including editor Samuel Bowles, law professor James B. Thayer, and John Davis, one of the mainstays of the Boston Indian Citizenship Committee. Welsh then prepared a critique of home rule for Secretary Noble. He pointed out that the policy would endanger Indian interests by placing over them men likely to be responsive to their fellow westerners who, for example, might be cattlemen anxious to get access to reservation grass, or land speculators interested in getting a good deal on Indian land. In addition, Welsh questioned a policy which would severely handicap the chance of getting able personnel by restricting the choices to the limited population of a single territory or state.[86]

Secretary Noble did not respond directly to Welsh's argument. A few days later, however, he did inform Welsh that J. George Wright, a seven-year resident of Dakota Territory and the son of James G. Wright, whom Welsh was pushing for the Rosebud agency, had been named Rosebud agent on the recommendation of the Sioux Commission headed by General George Crook. The secretary observed tartly, "I suppose that he will be acceptable to his father, and I hope that he will be to the Indian Rights Association."[87] Welsh promptly wrote Commissioner Morgan for confirmation: "I can hardly persuade myself that there is not some mistake about the matter."[88] But true it was, and home rule would be the Harrison administration's policy.

The IRA did not have a friend in Secretary Noble. Indeed, nearly two years after taking office he had not made the acquaintance of its indefatigable lobbyist, Professor Painter. When Welsh favored Noble with letters about the Sioux and the causes of the Ghost Dance uprising, the secretary dismissed them as of "no importance" and "mere surmises and based upon rumors."[89] With no influence with the secretary, Welsh was forced to depend more heavily on the commissioner. And this circumstance led to tension between Welsh and Morgan because the commissioner simply did not have the power to do many of the things Welsh desired. As Welsh himself later was forced to admit, Morgan "is little more, under present conditions, than a chief clerk in his own office."[90]

Welsh, however, was not a man easily discouraged. The home-rule policy only inspired him to greater efforts to bring about the extension of civil service to all employees of the Indian Bureau. Even before the announcement of home rule, Welsh had been working on a quixotic scheme to mobilize public opinion behind civil-service reform. It was an idea that came to Welsh one Sunday in April 1889. His plan was to get ministers all across the country to preach a sermon during the Thanksgiving season on the need of civil service. He raised a separate fund of more than $1,000 to finance the mailing to ministers of all faiths, an added chore for Matthew Sniffen and his helpers in the Philadelphia office, who sent out 23,000 letters. Welsh's appeals to the Catholics through Cardinal Gibbons and Archbishop Ryan were in vain, but twenty-eight Episcopal bishops and leaders of other denominations did consent to lend their names to the enterprise. Only 250 ministers directly responded to the mailing, and not all favorably. Nevertheless, Welsh estimated that thousands of sermons were delivered on the civil-service theme.[91] The whole affair was just another example of Welsh's expenditure of a great deal of energy on relatively unprofitable projects in behalf of noble ideas.

Welsh did feel very deeply that recruiting able personnel for the Indian Service was essential. From the beginning he had made this a main thrust of the IRA, as evidenced by the thousands of letters in its files relating to personnel matters. That Welsh himself sometimes backed losers was demonstrated by the case of the Navajo agent who owed his appointment to Welsh's sponsorship, but who later became addicted to morphine and had to be discharged. Welsh also was somewhat embarrassed when Dorchester and Morgan, whom the IRA leader was investing much time and energy in backing, proceeded to employ their wives as special agent and clerk, respectively.

Through it all Welsh remained committed to the civil-service principle. To the editor of a Hartford paper he urged a change in the system which saw "thieves, adulterers, fornicators, and drunkards and, in large numbers, wholly inefficient persons appointed to . . . the Indian service . . . [with] the power to curse and blight those whose morals and lives were committed to their keeping."[92] Complaining once to Theodore Roosevelt, Welsh cited some examples: farmers who did not know how to plant potatoes or who passed their time spinning war stories, and physicians who treated throat problems by having their patients drink tincture of iodine or carbolic acid.[93] Roosevelt agreed that "the patronage system is degrading at the best; but when applied to the poor Indians it is simply infamous."[94] Welsh, with some help from Roosevelt, doggedly persevered in his campaign to extend civil service over more Indian Bureau personnel. The troubles on the Sioux reservations in the winter of 1890–1891 provided an unexpected boost to his campaign.

CHAPTER NINE

The Association Responds
to the Ghost Dance Crisis

In the summer of 1890 the reservations of the Plains Indians were alive
with excited reports of a new messiah, a Paiute Indian named Wovoka.
His testimony was that he had died the previous year, had gone to
heaven, and then had been restored to earth with a message for his
fellow Native Americans. If they obeyed a few simple rules of conduct
and engaged in a ceremony, which came to be known as the Ghost
Dance, the plains would again teem with buffalo and other game, and
generations of dead Indians would be resurrected. There were varia-
tions in Wovoka's message as it was disseminated on the many reservations. However, only among the Sioux did it take on a belligerent note
and feature the use of bulletproof Ghost Dance shirts.[1]

The unrest among the Sioux which culminated in the tragic
Wounded Knee Massacre did not engage the IRA's attention until
November of 1890. Within the next few weeks, as events moved toward
their climax at Wounded Knee Creek on December 29, Herbert Welsh
received a steady flow of information about conditions on the reservations in the Dakotas. The association began to send out reports informing the public of the crisis and considered dispatching its own
investigator to the scene. Eventually it was decided to employ a local
missionary. His reports were used in a public relations campaign Welsh
directed to try to capitalize on the momentary public interest in Sioux
affairs to secure a further extension of civil service over reservation
employees. The IRA also would become involved in defending an
Indian accused of murdering an army officer and in trying to ensure

prosecution of white men who had attacked a small party of peaceful Indians.

The build-up of tension among the Sioux had gone virtually unnoticed by the IRA until it reached critical proportions. In the spring of 1890 Herbert Welsh had spent a month on the Navajo reservation, and Charles Painter had spent several weeks in the Oklahoma area. After his summer vacation Welsh threw himself into the anti-Quay campaign in Pennsylvania, which absorbed his energies during September and October. He dispatched Painter on another trip to Kansas and Oklahoma; clearly the possibility of an outbreak of violence on the Sioux reservations was not one of Welsh's concerns in the summer and early fall of 1890.

Since assuming a low profile relative to the final negotiations for the reduction of the Sioux reservations, the IRA was principally interested in ensuring that the new administration retained those agents the organization had rated as competent. In June 1890 Charles E. McChesney, of whom Welsh approved, was removed from the Cheyenne River Agency. When the IRA sought an explanation for the dismissal, Secretary Noble firmly refused to provide any.[2] The administration also removed the Pine Ridge agent, H. D. Gallagher. Welsh was not happy about this action either, although he did not have much respect for Gallagher. Of all the Sioux agents, however, only Gallagher had the prescience to refer in his annual report, prepared in August, to possible trouble with the Ghost Dancers.

Gallagher's successor at Pine Ridge, Dr. Daniel F. Royer, had hardly taken office before he was considering the necessity of calling for troops to support him against the increasingly bold Ghost Dancers. Reports of their going armed and making threats against whites quickly circulated among the towns near the reservations and led to requests for troops by governors and congressional delegations. At Standing Rock, veteran agent James McLaughlin was having trouble with the celebrated Sitting Bull, who was a participant in the new movement. McLaughlin hoped to avoid calling for troops, something he prided himself on never having done.

Agent Royer had no such scruples; indeed, he was pleading for troops. On November 17, after Dr. Royer had telegraphed one more time asking for at least a thousand troops, the army did begin to move units to Pine Ridge and to Rosebud, which adjoined it.[3]

Meanwhile Welsh had received his first communication from the Dakotas indicating that a crisis was brewing. It was a letter from IRA member Thomas Stewart, the harness maker at Standing Rock. One of those Indian Service personnel who wrote freely to Welsh relative to matters at his agency, Stewart warned that trouble could be expected in the spring "if something in the mean time is not done to divert there [*sic*] minds from this religious Excitement."[4] The harness maker was particularly disturbed by McLaughlin's problems with Sitting Bull, whom Stewart tended to champion against the agent.

With this report in hand plus newspaper stories about Indian troubles and possible troop movements, Welsh sought further information. He turned to Reverend Cook, the Sioux at Pine Ridge who was a member of the Episcopal clergy, as well as to Agent McLaughlin, Bishop Hare, and General Nelson A. Miles, commander of the Department of the Missouri, which would provide any troops needed. Welsh also asked them if he could be of any help by visiting the reservations.[5]

Agent McLaughlin did not request a visit from Welsh, although he described the situation as serious and an effort by those who had opposed the Sioux Agreement of 1889 to take advantage of the "Messiah Craze" to reopen the issue. However, McLaughlin did not want to move against the faction at Standing Rock led by Sitting Bull until cold weather had sapped the enthusiasm of the Dancers. In a telegram General Miles also described conditions as "serious" but did not see any role for Welsh. Reverend Cook's reply was a lengthy description of a potentially explosive situation and an invitation to Welsh to come out to Pine Ridge. Bishop Hare did not think Welsh was needed, being at this point inclined to play down the seriousness of the Sioux threat and attributing the army's reaction possibly to presidential ambitions on the part of General Miles.[6]

The IRA's president, James Rhoads, suggested that Charles Painter be sent out to the Dakotas, but Painter was not feeling well, having just returned from a difficult two months inspecting schools and agencies in the Southwest. Welsh did not push him nor did Welsh decide to go himself since he had received no encouragement from anyone except Reverend Cook.

Welsh already had concluded that much of the problem among the Sioux could be attributed to the administration's spoils system, which had placed inexperienced agents at the Pine Ridge and Cheyenne River agencies just in time to confront the crisis. Welsh's panacea was to extend civil service to include all positions on Indian reservations. This was the line he took in letters to IRA members and newspaper editors in November and December, having decided the time had come "to press forward our demands for an Indian Service founded upon right principles."[7] The IRA also printed and circulated items from a Sioux Falls, South Dakota, newspaper quoting Bishop Hare and another clergyman to the effect that the threat of an Indian uprising had been exaggerated. Another mailing consisted of an editorial from a St. Paul newspaper blasting the spoils system.

The reports from Pine Ridge all questioned the actions of Agent Royer in the crisis, and Welsh seized the opportunity to seek the reinstatement there of Dr. Valentine T. McGillycuddy, who had preceded Gallagher and had been a casualty of the Cleveland administration.[8] He sought the aid of several editors in this campaign, but these efforts were in vain. Dr. McGillycuddy did go to Pine Ridge to represent the governor of South Dakota, and Welsh received from McGillycuddy frequent letters about what was transpiring among the Sioux.

Meanwhile Welsh reacted to two proposals that had arisen, one of them directly related to the troubles in the Dakotas. It stemmed from General Miles's insistence that the Sioux agencies be turned over at least temporarily to the army for administration, reviving the old debate between the War and Interior departments as to which could better administer Indian affairs. When the issue first surfaced, Welsh assured a Philadelphia editor that, while he favored the use as agents of judiciously selected officers, he could see no long-term benefit from giving the army full responsibility for administering Indian affairs.[9] Commissioner Morgan protested to Secretary Noble about such a transfer, and Welsh informed Morgan that he was in agreement. Welsh added that he thought that what was needed was an end to the spoils system, more money for education, and "undivided responsibility in the management of the Indians."[10]

This reference to "undivided responsibility" clearly related to a proposal Commissioner Morgan's wife, Caroline, had made to Welsh. She, in turn, claimed that she had been inspired by an earlier use by Welsh of the expression. What she proposed was that the commissioner's responsibilities be greatly expanded, giving him control over inspectors and the other Indian Service functions that fell directly within the jurisdiction of the secretary of the interior. Moreover the commissioner would head an independent agency with direct access to the president, a realignment that would have its advocates in the 1960s and 1970s.[11] Welsh could recognize the merit in an idea he had inspired and was soon propagating it himself. Such a sweeping reform had little chance of accomplishment, particularly when the government's attention was centered on the dangerous situation developing on the plains.

Despite the flow of letters from McGillycuddy and others, Welsh still was attracted to the idea of the IRA's having its own investigator on the scene. The man he finally turned to late in December was Reverend William J. Cleveland, Episcopal missionary at Rosebud who had spent seventeen years among the Sioux, was fluent in Lakota, and had served on the Sioux Commission of 1888. After securing permission from his superiors, Bishop Hare, who specified the financial terms on which Cleveland could serve, he was ready to go to work.[12]

The course of events in December gave Reverend Cleveland ample subjects for investigation. Midway in the month an attempt by Indian police, backed at a discreet distance by troops, to take Sitting Bull into custody had produced a brief although intense firefight. Sitting Bull and five policemen were among the fourteen Sioux killed, and a debate promptly got underway as to the wisdom of the tactics Agent McLaughlin and the army had employed. Thomas Stewart, no friend of the agent, wrote Welsh that the authorities need not have acted, as Sitting Bull had had but few followers and the chief himself had been losing enthusiasm for the movement. "I strongly believe in god's justice and he will not let this crime go unpunished. . . ." was the harness maker's judgment.[13] However, Stewart was regarded by his fellow employees as somewhat eccentric, as Welsh was aware. A female counterpart to Stewart in eccentricity, Emma C. Sickels, reported on conditions at Pine Ridge, the site December 29 of the infamous Wounded Knee Massacre which occurred when troops attempted to disarm a band of Ghost Dancers.

Welsh described the bloodshed there to Theodore Roosevelt as "a horrible sequel of the whole wretched affair."[14] His shock and dismay at the death of twenty-five soldiers and nearly two hundred Indians, many of them women and children, only intensified his campaign to secure reforms in the system. In the next three months he would hammer on this theme in mailings to IRA members, editors, ministers, and prominent citizens who might have influence with the administration and members of Congress.

A day after he had learned of the bloodshed on Wounded Knee Creek, Welsh composed a long letter to the editor of *The Civil Service Record* which embodied many of the views he would hold on the tragic events. He described the Sioux as divided into two principal factions, "a Christian and progressive party" and a "pagan and non-progressive" group. The former had been growing rapidly in numbers and influence, but this growth had only "tended strongly to tighten the bands of conservatism and opposition among the pagan Indians." At Pine Ridge the unrest had been complicated by turnovers in agency personnel, particularly the replacement of Agent McGillycuddy by H. D. Gallagher, who had permitted the agency police force to deteriorate. Then the Harrison administration had replaced Gallagher with Daniel Royer, whose skill at controlling a county convention greatly exceeded his abilities as an Indian agent. Royer took office just as Pine Ridge was brought to the verge of violence by a combination of circumstances. They included, according to Welsh, resentment against the 1889 agreement providing for the diminution of Indian landholdings and the introduction of severalty, a cut in government rations that reduced some Sioux to real hunger, and the agitation of leaders of the pagan and non-progressive faction.[15]

Welsh's letter to the editor went on to detail his own futile efforts to secure the appointment of Dr. McGillycuddy as a special agent in charge of Pine Ridge until the excitement could subside. Meanwhile the situation had continued to deteriorate. The "hostile and frightened Indians" fled the troops, looting the homes of the progressive Sioux on their way to rough terrain in the western part of the reservation, where they prepared to resist the soldiers. "I ask no pity for those ignorant and frantic creatures whose fierce act of resistance to disarmament [on Wounded Knee Creek] was the last link in a series of causes which produced this horror," declared Welsh. However, he asked, was not the real villain "the spoils system in the management of Indian affairs, with its foolishness, its selfishness, its ignorance, and its last frightful outcome?"[16]

Civil-service reform was a long-range goal; the IRA would be called upon to do something immediately about the Indian casualties at Wounded Knee. Within days of the fighting Welsh had reports on it from Bishop Hare and Elaine Goodale. The bishop had been shocked out of his optimism by the scene that met his eyes in the Episcopal church at Pine Ridge which was being used as a hospital—"a chamber of horrors" was how he described it.[17] Miss Goodale, whose break with the IRA had not yet occurred, had turned to the association for financial help in caring for the wounded. Welsh promptly wrote Commissioner Morgan asking that the Indian Bureau do something and placed notices in eastern newspapers asking for donations to help the Wounded Knee victims. About $1,200 was raised, and part of it was used to support a trained nurse brought in to help the wounded.[18]

In assigning blame for Wounded Knee, Welsh strove to be fair to all parties. the IRA reproduced and circulated Dr. Eastman's letter to Frank Wood, in which the Indian physician stationed at Pine Ridge described going to the battlefield three days later and finding the bodies of women and children, and also eleven wounded Indians, including two infants, who somehow had survived.[19] In his correspondence Welsh referred to the "horrible butchery of women and children" and asked Captain Bourke to use his sources in Washington to try to determine what really had happened at Wounded Knee.[20] Nevertheless, while admitting that women and children had been killed far from the original scene of action, Welsh supposed that "in a fierce sanguinary hand-to-hand fight common soldiers would become unrestrainable."[21] In a letter to the editor of *The Washington Post* Welsh spelled it out in more detail:

I, personally, should be very slow to criticize those who are risking life and limb in suppressing an Indian outbreak which was not of their making, and should be altogether unwilling to make any reflections upon the Army as a whole, knowing well as I do that many of the officers are not only honorable and brave men, but are serious, steadfast and judicious friends of the Indian; men who are advocates of humane treatment for the Indian race, and of all wise efforts for its education and development.[22]

In the aftermath of Wounded Knee, Welsh also urged discrimination in dealing with the Sioux. Those progressives who had suffered at the hands of the hostiles should be compensated, and the leaders of the Ghost Dancers should be punished. The IRA spokesman was particularly upset that some of the leading Ghost Dancers, who had been held in custody at Fort Sheridan in Illinois, had been released to travel in Europe with Buffalo Bill's wild-west show. Meanwhile the "loyal Indians" would "pass a dull and penurious summer on the prairie."[23]

Welsh's sense of justice also was outraged that Plenty Horses, a young Brulé Sioux who had killed Lieutenant Edward C. Casey, would be dealt with severely while white cowboys who had killed the Indian Few Tails would go unpunished. At the time of his death early in January 1891, Lieutenant Casey had commanded a detachment of Cheyenne scouts that had been keeping the ghost dancers' camp under surveillance. There had been no fighting for several days, and the authorities were hoping to persuade the Sioux to abandon their stronghold in the Badlands and return to the agency. It was to further this objective that Lieutenant Casey had tried to make contact with some of the hostile chiefs, only to meet Plenty Horses, who, after some conversation and without warning, killed the young officer. Plenty Horses, who had attended Carlisle Institute only to discover that like other returned students he met rejection from his people, had chosen this way to reestablish himself with his fellow Sioux.[24]

Four days later, in an unrelated affair, two Sioux families returning from an authorized hunting trip off the reservation were attacked by cowboys. In the shooting that followed, Few Tails was killed and his wife and another woman were wounded. Few Tails's wife was left for dead by the attackers but managed to make her way a grueling seventy miles in midwinter to safety. The men primarily responsible for this unprovoked assault were three brothers, the Culbertsons. They claimed to have been tracking Indian horse thieves but apparently were prepared to kill any tribesmen so unfortunate as to cross their path.[25]

Welsh and the IRA became involved after General Miles took steps to see that both Plenty Horses and the Culbertsons were punished for their crimes. As the shooting of Lieutenant Casey had been committed on a reservation, Plenty Horses would be tried in a federal court. The attack on the Few Tails's party, however, had taken place off the reservation in an area under the jurisdiction of South Dakota state courts. Initially Welsh's principal concern had been to see that the Culbertsons did not escape justice, frontier juries being notorious for overlooking crimes by whites against Indians. Welsh wrote Secretary Noble insisting that the "white desperados" who had murdered peaceable Indians be sought out and punished.[26] In April 1891 the IRA distributed a four-page circular on the Few Tails incident contrasting the treatment of the Culbertsons, who still were free, with Plenty Horses, who was being held in the Fort Meade guardhouse. "Evidently," the circular commented, "there is one law for the white man and another for the Indian. . . ." The IRA stated that there was ample evidence that the case had attracted public attention. Thirty papers from all parts of the country had demanded that Few Tails's killers be punished.[27] Not everyone, however, reacted with such heat as Theodore Roosevelt, who advocated martial law if it was otherwise impossible to get action against whites in local courts. He also favored permitting the Indians to retain their weapons until they could be guaranteed protection. "The hanging of a few white scoundrels implicated in such deeds as that of the murder of Few Tails's party would do incredible good," stormed TR. He was careful, however, to make it clear to Welsh that he did not want his views publicized.[28]

In addition to seeking prosecution of the Culbertsons, the IRA was drawn into the defense of Plenty Horses. Within two days of the young Sioux's indictment for murder, both an attorney at Deadwood, South Dakota, and the officer commanding the installation where the prisoner was being held had written Welsh seeking help for Plenty Horses. Attorney John H. Burns indicated that he had been approached by the accused and his father to serve as defense attorney. Burns already had decided that Plenty Horses's best defense would be that the killing had occurred in time of war. He was willing to take on the case but wanted at least $500 compensation and for this reason was turning to the IRA. Lieutenant Colonel E. V. Sumner, in charge of the prisoner, reminded Welsh that he had met him several years earlier when Sumner had commanded Fort Robinson in Dakota Territory. The officer remembered Welsh for his "kindly feelings for the helpless" and thus felt he could ask the Philadelphian for aid for Plenty Horses.[29]

Welsh first approached the Indian Bureau on the grounds that, as an Indian, Plenty Horses was a ward of the government and should be provided counsel. The association also dispatched executive committee member Edward M. Wistar to Washington to plead the young Brulé's case with the Interior and Justice departments. The response to Wistar and to Welsh's letters was that it was not clear that the government legally could provide counsel to Indians accused of crimes, and even if it could be done it would require a special congressional appropriation.[30]

The IRA also was having trouble determining whether it could or should spend its funds to defend Plenty Horses. It first offered Burns $200 to serve as defense attorney, but he held out for $500. Meanwhile the association's law committee had studied the situation and concluded that defending individuals accused of crimes was not a proper function for the IRA and would set an expensive precedent.[31]

A court-appointed attorney defended Plenty Horses in his first trial, which ended in a hung jury. The IRA wrestled with its conscience and concluded that while it still could not pay attorney's fees it could send $325 to the law firm defending the Brulé to be used for expenses incidental to the second trial. When it ended with Plenty Horses's acquittal on the grounds that Lieutenant Casey had died in the course of military operations, the IRA allowed the Sioux's attorneys to retain as a fee any of the $325 which had not been used for expenses.[32]

Welsh was not happy with the trial's outcome. From the beginning what he had sought for Plenty Horses was a fair trial. He did not believe that the Brulé, who had shot Lieutenant Casey in the back of the head as the young officer rode away, should go free, but neither did Welsh think that a death sentence was warranted. Justice, not charity, was what the IRA sought. As Welsh assured one of his South Dakota correspondents who had been a juror in the first trial, "We are not sentimentalists."[33] Welsh particularly regretted the impact the acquittal would have, as did Reverend Cleveland and Dr. McGillycuddy, on the effort to convict the Culbertsons.

Using the same wardship argument that he had used to try to get government counsel for Plenty Horses, Welsh tried to persuade Attorney General W. H. H. Miller to provide assistance in the prosecution of the slayers of Few Tails. The attorney general responded that as a result of a request from the Interior Department he already had taken the action Welsh desired.[34]

A particular reason for Welsh's interest in the Few Tails case was that it would "test the possibility of securing justice in crimes committed against Indians."[35] And Welsh maintained that there was a world of difference between the actions of Plenty Horses and the Culbertsons:

> The former case was the killing of an armed military officer who most imprudently rode within the lines of hostile Indians in time of war. The latter was the deliberate ambushed slaughter of an old Indian known to be friendly travelling under a safe conduct from Gen. Miles after hostilities had ceased.

Welsh had inquired of the Indian Bureau if it had any record of a white man's being hanged for murdering an Indian. Its response was in the negative. "What a confession for a civilized nation to face the civilized world with," declaimed Welsh to a Philadelphia editor, "that the Indian may look in vain for redress in an American court of justice!"[36]

The Culbertson brothers and two accomplices. were indicted. Nevertheless, acquittal of Plenty Horses made it extremely unlikely that a South Dakota jury would convict the white men. A concerned Welsh wrote Attorney General Miller to ask what steps the Justice Department was taking to aid the prosecution. Miller did not provide any details. He did give Welsh a lecture on justice in the United States, pointing out that in several states it would be difficult to find an instance of a white man's being hanged for killing a Negro. Welsh's indignant reaction was that the attorney general could do better than extenuate the plight of the Indian by allusions to the plight of the black.[37]

Despairing of much help from the Justice Department, Welsh did what he could to stir up public sentiment. The IRA purchased 500 copies of a letter he had published in a Philadelphia paper describing the "cold blooded murder" and sent them to newspapers whose readers included Dakotans, as well as to clergymen of all the denominations represented in the two states.[38] Welsh's efforts were in vain. A jury promptly acquitted the Culbertsons and their accomplices. Welsh made one last futile attempt to extract some reform from the miserable affair. He approached Winifred Jennings, a young writer, with the suggestion that she use the Few Tails tragedy as the subject of a novel which might "prevent in the future such a tragic miscarriage of justice."[39]

The IRA could feel some satisfaction in at least having helped bring the Culbertsons to trial and in securing a degree of justice for Plenty Horses. The association also claimed some credit for the extension of civil service over additional positions in the Indian Service, an extension undoubtedly expedited by the public outcry over violence on the Sioux reservations in the winter of 1890–1891. Welsh had stepped up his efforts in behalf of civil service in January 1891. He already was claiming credit for the removal of Dr. Royer, whose "inefficiency and cowardice" as Pine Ridge agent were blamed by the IRA for precipitating the violence.[40] With the encouragement of Commissioner Morgan, who thought the time "fully ripe" for an all-out drive to bring the Indian Bureau under civil-service rules, Welsh put his machine into motion.[41] Letters went out from Philadelphia plugging civil service and requesting recipients to write President Harrison. Welsh also had petition forms developed and sent to people who might circulate them. He sought to ensure Senator Dawes's support by bringing pressure to bear on him from his Massachusetts constituents. It was Welsh's judgment that Dawes would do little without prodding; indeed, Welsh believed the senator would attempt to defeat the reform "by affected superior wisdom, good humored sneers, and the attempts to place us in the position of well-meaning but indiscreet enthusiasts."[42] Prompted by Welsh, the Boston Indian Citizenship Committee did prevail upon Dawes to deliver an appeal for the reform directly to President Harrison. Harrison's response was that he did intend to do something about the matter, and in April he issued an executive order.[43]

The presidential order did not achieve all that the reformers had sought, although it did extend civil service over 600 additional Indian Service personnel, mostly school employees and physicians. Still uncovered, however, were nearly 2,000 other posts at Indian agencies, among them the position of agent. Bringing Indian agents under civil-service rules would necessitate special legislation, as such appointments required Senate confirmation. Nevertheless, Welsh was pleased. The IRA annual report for 1891 referred to the president's action as the "silver lining to the otherwise dark cloud of the Dakota outbreak."[44]

The annual report carried a summary report by Reverend Cleveland, whose letters from the Dakotas had been so influential in shaping the IRA's view of the whole affair. Cleveland had been given some general guidelines for his investigation as well as specific questions for which Welsh wanted answers. For example, had Sitting Bull been scalped by the Indian police? How important a factor was hunger in driving the Indians to resist? Had black cavalrymen sexually assaulted Indian women?[45]

Reverend Cleveland's investigations began at Standing Rock, which he reached on January 13 after a cold trip of sixty-six miles, facing the wind in an open wagon the whole way. From Standing Rock he went south to Cheyenne River, then to Crow Creek and Lower Brulé, and ended up at Pine Ridge and Rosebud in March. As Cleveland's letters arrived in Philadelphia, Welsh compared them with reports he was receiving from Bishop Hare, Agent McLaughlin, Dr. McGillycuddy, and others, and he liked what he saw. Excerpts from Cleveland's letters began to show up in the material Welsh was sending out in his media blitz, and he congratulated the missionary on the quality of his reporting—"in the highest degree thorough and intelligent."[46] Cleveland had been an excellent choice for the mission. In his residence on the Sioux reservations he had developed the essential contacts among both Indians and agency employees. For example, when he reached Pine Ridge he found in charge Captain F. E. Pierce, "my old friend," who "has put everything in his power at my service and gives me free access to all papers, letters, people, etc."[47]

Welsh was so pleased with Cleveland's performance that he arranged to bring the missionary east on a speaking tour which included Baltimore, New York, and Boston, as well as the Princeton campus.

The tour was still another expense for the association and it had to make a special appeal for funds.

Some idea of what Reverend Cleveland's eastern audience heard can be deduced from his rather disjointed statement in the association's 1891 annual report. His conclusion was that, rather than an Indian outbreak, the Ghost Dance episode was a case of the Indians' "having been broken in upon." He believed it was true that a faction led by chiefs like Sitting Bull, Big Foot, Crow Dog, and Red Cloud was planning some action for the spring of 1891 and was using the Ghost Dance movement to advance its own aims. However, he blamed government mismanagement for swelling the ranks of the discontented, detailing sixteen instances of everything from the spoils system to the supply of poor-quality tools and clothing. A great man for lists, Cleveland also provided one of general conditions that had set the stage for the trouble, including failure of crops two years in succession and epidemics which had produced unusually high death rates. The major contributor to Indian discontent had been the 1889 agreement by which the Sioux sold about half of their land. Moreover, the government had been slow to comply with its side of the bargain. Cleveland quoted one Sioux who had expressed his bitter disillusionment: "They made us many promises, more than I can remember, but they never kept but one; they promised to take our land, and they took it."[48]

The whole sordid affair had demonstrated the range and nature of IRA concerns and how it could react to a crisis. Welsh had been caught by surprise but had acted quickly to apprise the association of the nature of the emergency. The sympathies of the IRA, as could have been predicted, were with the Sioux who were not Ghost Dancers, many of whom were members of Welsh's own Episcopal Church. Nevertheless, the association had raised more than a thousand dollars to help provide medical care for the victims of the Wounded Knee Massacre. To enlighten the public about what was happening among the Sioux and the causes of the unrest, the IRA had published 18,000 copies of seven circulars that related to the Sioux troubles. Its intervention in the cases involving the deaths of Lieutenant Casey and Few Tails had publicized the failure of Indians to be assured justice in American courts. Most important from Welsh's perspective, the IRA had taken the lead in molding public opinion which helped convince President Harrison that the time was ripe for an extension of civil-service rules over more positions in the Indian Service.

CHAPTER TEN

Ute Removal and
Other Land Issues

The issues discussed in the previous two chapters were just some of those which commanded the attention of the IRA during the presidency of Benjamin Harrison. Another was trying to ensure that Indians retained at least a part of their land and natural resources. During the tenure of an administration which boasted of reducing reservations by 23,000,000 acres in its first three years, this was a task of no mean proportions[1] The association also did what it could to back the tribes being threatened by large lawsuits for depredations alleged to have been committed by their members in the era of frontier warfare. In turn this situation led to a need to protect the tribes from the swarms of lawyers attracted by the fees the depredations claims and other tribal troubles could generate. The Apache prisoners in Florida and Alabama also continued to absorb association time and effort.

The IRA continued to try to help Indian Service personnel, such as the man who was fighting to remain in charge of a Cherokee school in North Carolina, or the woman discharged from her position at another school after what would be referred to in a more enlightened period as a case of sexual harassment.[2] These cases, particularly that of the Cherokee school superintendent, consumed the energies of Welsh and Painter and distracted them from more worthy causes. Almost daily the mail brought the Philadelphia office similar pleas for assistance in getting or retaining jobs, or soliciting other forms of aid. The approach of the Christmas season always was heralded by requests from school superintendents in remote areas of the West for presents for their pupils. A remarkable number of these requests did not go unheeded.

No single issue between the years 1889 and 1893 consumed more time and energy of the association than did the continued efforts of the people of Colorado to rid themselves of the Southern Utes. During Cleveland's first administration a commission had negotiated an agreement with the Utes to effect their removal to a new reservation in Utah Territory. The IRA fought to block ratification of this agreement in the Fiftieth Congress, as discussed in Chapter 6. The struggle would be renewed in the Fifty-first and Fifty-second congresses, and the issue would not be resolved until the closing days of the Fifty-third Congress in early 1895.

The fight ebbed and flowed with the tempo of the congresses. There would be months during which nothing would be done, and then there would be a frantic burst of activity with hearings before the House and Senate Indian committees. Sometimes an intense lobbying effort would have to be mounted on short notice to try to influence the scheduling of the Ute bill on the legislative calendar. The make-up of both committees was crucial in the legislative process, and Welsh and Painter were particularly concerned about the House committee in these congresses. Senator Dawes headed the Senate committee and usually could be counted upon to support the IRA viewpoint, although rarely with the enthusiasm the reformers demanded.

Throughout the campaign the IRA's position remained unchanged. To move the Utes would violate the government's commitment to civilizing the Indians and would be solely to satisfy "the greed of white men for Indian land."[3] The new reservation, three times the size of the one in Colorado, would not provide as much arable land, and removal to it could only further delay the Utes' conversion to farming. Above all, there was the "fatal precedent" the removal would establish for future government action. "If it yields now," Welsh wrote, "it will be but a few years before the Indian's neighbors in Utah will demand his removal from the proposed reservation, to some more inaccessible and worthless spot."[4]

That the Utes themselves, practically all of whom were hunters and gatherers, favored removal by a large majority made more difficult the IRA's effort to defeat the agreement. But, as from the beginning, Welsh argued that Ute compliance was based on ignorance and susceptibility to bribes. The agreement they had accepted included a provision for a $50,000 payment to the members of the tribe, plus $2,000 specifically earmarked for the chiefs. Such payments were routinely employed by government agents to weaken tribal opposition to land cessions. When it was proposed that the bill be amended to permit the Utes who wished to remain to be allotted on the Colorado reservation, Welsh refused the compromise, arguing that the Indians did not know what was best for them and wanted to move in order to continue their life as nomadic hunters. As he wrote Cardinal Gibbons when soliciting support from the Catholics, for the government to act only as the Utes desired "would be precisely the same as though a father were to ask of his boy eight or ten years of age whether he preferred to be instructed in religion and sent to school, or whether to remain in ignorance and idleness."[5]

The IRA was not trying to save all or even most of the 1,000,000-acre Colorado reservation for the Utes. In line with its consistent policy it was prepared to advocate the sale by the tribe to the government of whatever land remained after the Indians had received their allotments. The proceeds from the sale of the land would then be used to outfit the farms of the Utes, to educate their children, and for other worthwhile purposes. Eighty-acre allotments were deemed sufficiently large in this case as it was assumed that these tracts would be irrigated.[6] Presumably the Ute allotments would be made from the best land available; nevertheless, the arrangement still would leave more than 90 percent of the reservation open to white settlement. In retrospect it is revealing that this amount was not sufficient to satisfy the Coloradans.

As always, the IRA first mobilized the facts in the case and then tried to convince the public of the rectitude of its position. In October 1889 Charles Painter spent a week on the proposed reservation in Utah Territory and found the experience "very hard *sledding*."[7] He covered 300 difficult miles in a wagon, crossing high divides in snowstorms. On three of the nights Painter camped out with cowboys. Another night he spent on the floor of a Mormon's cabin before the fire, and twenty long hours were passed in the company of railroad section hands at a remote location. The personal knowledge of the area thus gained gave credibility to his charge that, excluding the San Juan Valley, no more than 500 acres of the 3,000,000-acre Utah reservation could be irrigated and thus were adaptable to agriculture.[8]

Two years after Painter visited the proposed Ute reservation, the IRA sponsored another inspection of the area by Francis Fisher Kane and Frank M. Riter. Kane served on the association's executive committee, and Riter was a member of the Pennsylvania legislature. Both active young men, they rode horseback for two weeks over the rough country and evaluated it in much the same terms as Painter. Like him, their firsthand acquaintance with that part of Utah Territory gave weight to their testimony against the proposed reservation.[9]

To get the IRA's view of the issue before the public and members of Congress, Welsh resorted to a number of mailings. These ranged from one or two pages to more than thirty and were usually printed in lots of

1,500, although there were 7,000 copies of one and 3,000 of another.[10] Most of the literature went to the members and friends of the association. Sometimes particular audiences were targeted. All members of Congress received a few of the mailings, and those belonging to the Indian committees got additional handouts. All bishops of the Episcopal and Methodist churches were recipients of one pamphlet, and about fifty residents of Colorado and Utah got another.

The bulk of the more than 20,000 pieces of mail sent out in this period to protest removal of the Utes consisted of reports by Welsh and Painter or others representing the association. The IRA also circulated articles from friendly newspapers, and Welsh wrote literally hundreds of letters relating to the Ute issue.

Needless to say, the association's activity did not endear itself to those seeking Ute removal. Newspapers in Durango, on the edge of the Colorado reservation, were most virulent, but editors elsewhere in the state also got in their licks. The Denver *Times* was sweeping in its denunciation:

> The Indian Rights Association people are so bound up in their pre-conceived ideas and prejudices that they are absolutely incapable of telling the truth as to any matter pertaining to the Indians. They have never done anything in the Indian business, but misrepresent, slander, villify, meddle and make mischief.[11]

The association itself reprinted and circulated, with their rebuttal, an item from another Denver paper, *The Colorado Sun*. The *Sun's* editor maintained that the IRA had never done anything constructive for the Indians, such as sending missionaries or building schools or churches. It had only interfered, charged the editor, "in an officious, meddlesome, hurtful and seemingly malicious way." He even claimed that by contributing to tribal unrest, the association was responsible "for outbreaks and murders.."[12]

The Durango newspapers made much of an obviously questionable IRA ally. Both the Painter and the Kane-Riter tours of the proposed reservation in Utah were greatly facilitated by the Pittsburgh Cattle Company, which provided transportation, housing, and guides. The company was one of several which grazed large herds of cattle there and had an obvious interest in keeping it free of the Utes. Painter recognized the danger in the relationship but was unwilling to forgo it: "The charge of working in their interest we can not avoid . . . we can accept all helps and facilities for learning the truth, and then stick to the truth no matter who is hit by it."[13] This was the course the IRA pursued, and throughout the battle Welsh and Painter were in correspondence with officers of the Pittsburgh Cattle Company on tactics to be employed. The association also was happy to receive support from settlers in Montrose, Colorado, near the Utah line, whose prosperity depended upon the cattle companies.

One critic of the IRA's position was not a westerner. J. P. Dunn, Jr., was the secretary of the Indiana Historical Society, state librarian, and the author of a history of Indian wars in the West. He raised an issue that did not often occur to the white friends of the Indian. "I did not imagine," he wrote Welsh, "that your society assumed to decide what was best for Indians and urged that course without respect to the wishes of the Indians."[14] Dunn believed more harm than good might come in forcing tribes into agriculture before they were ready for it, and he cited the origins of Nez Percé and Ute wars to sustain his contention. This approach did not dissuade Welsh. The association's position was that hunters did not necessarily have to pass through the pastoral stage before becoming farmers. As one of its pamphlets on the Ute issue pointed out: "The Navajos . . . are rich in herds, but in nothing else pertaining to civilized life, and it is almost impossible to reach them with schools or missionaries, because of their nomadic habits."[15] No, regardless of their personal desires, these wards must accept the dictates of a wise guardian and trade the bow for the hoe and the plow.

Such criticism of the IRA as Dunn's was rare outside of Colorado. The association compiled a list of a hundred newspapers and magazines which had published material friendly to its position on Ute removal.[16] They were generally eastern publications like Samuel Bowles's *Springfield Republican* and George William Curtis's *Nation.* However, the Augusta (Ga.) *Chronicle,* the Burlington (Iowa) *Hawk-Eye,* and the San Francisco *Call* appeared on the list. As usual there was a good representation of religious publications.

The IRA was not alone in this fight. Welsh had turned to his customary allies for support. Amelia Quinton rallied the WNIA to oppose something so "manifestly wicked and foolish" as this attempt "to imprison in perpetual barbarism a thousand souls!"[17] Like Welsh, she regarded it as a repudiation of the severalty program embodied in the Dawes Act of 1887. General Whittlesey of the Board of Indian Commissioners brought the issue before the conference at Lake Mohonk in 1889, and in 1891 opposition to Ute removal was made one of the planks in the platform of the conference.[18]

While not taking a leading role, Indian Commissioner Morgan made a significant contribution by opposing Ute removal in a thirty-four page letter to Secretary Noble.[19] He shared a copy with Welsh, who reproduced its conclusions in the association's "Protest," which it mailed in March 1890. Morgan repeated his stand in his annual report for 1890.[20]

Senator Dawes was of help, although not to the extent Welsh and Painter had hoped. They particularly blamed him for having introduced in the Senate in 1889 a bill to ratify the agreement. Dawes's defense was that he had done so to accommodate a colleague and that he had reserved the right to oppose the bill when it reached the floor. The senator confessed to being in a quandary. He believed the Utes were making no progress where they were located, in part because of their demoralizing contact with the white population of Durango. Nevertheless, he considered the proposed site in Utah Territory to be even less desirable in terms of potential for self-support. Unlike Welsh, Dawes thought that severalty should be applied only after some evidence of progress in civilization. In his judgment the Utes, whom he described as "shiftless, lazy, roving, hunting, thieving," were clearly unready.[21] Above all, Dawes believed that the votes were there in both chambers to pass the bills if they could get out of committee. The senator compared his attempting to stay ratification to the task confronting the legendary Mrs. Partington and her broom.[22]

Welsh was not impressed. To Amelia Quinton, Welsh depicted the senator's posture as "weak and vacillating" and said that "while he nominally holds the position of the friend of the Indian . . . he has betrayed Indian interests and dealt them a more serious blow than they could have received from an open enemy."[23] Welsh accused Dawes, in a statement published in the *Springfield Republican,* of being partially responsible for the lack of progress of the Utes because of his ambivalence on the issue. The senator protested to Samuel Bowles about this item, but the editor defended the IRA leader as "one of our most careful and conscientious contributors."[24] In a letter to Welsh, Anna Dawes vigorously defended her father from what she called "the most peculiar apprehension of Father's position."[25] The exchange did seem to stiffen the senator's backbone. In 1892, when Wolcott of Colorado attacked on the Senate floor the IRA and its agents, Dawes rose to their defense. He even described Charles Painter, someone whom he disliked, as a man of intelligence and "honesty of purpose."[26] Welsh dropped the senator a note thanking him for his "generous and courageous defense" of the IRA's Washington agent.[27]

That the Ute agreement of 1888 was not ratified in either the Fifty-first or Fifty-second Congress was due more to the IRA than to Senator Dawes. In the Fifty-first, bills to ratify were introduced in both houses, and Painter appeared before the committees to testify against them. Neither visit was a pleasant experience. At the Senate hearing he was the only one to appear in opposition and for several hours stood his ground alone, "abused and vilified by Honorable Senators and Drs. of Divinity and other Colorado magnates."[28] Although the House committee favorably reported the bill, it did not reach the floor for a vote that session.

Fearing that the bill would pass if it ever got out of committee, Welsh proposed to Commissioner Morgan that he approach Secretary Noble about the possibility of allotting the Utes where they were, thus forestalling any threat of removal.[29] Morgan's initial response to this suggestion was negative, but several months later he did propose allotment to the secretary. Morgan's argument was that "uncertainty as to their future can but be extremely damaging to the Indians."[30] The Utes had no inducement to go to work on their Colorado reservation to try to make homes and open farms, nor was the government inclined to assist them in the absence of any certainty of their tenure in Colorado.

When Morgan wrote that letter, the Fifty-second Congress was underway and bills to ratify the agreement already had been introduced. Early in 1892 Francis Fisher Kane went to Washington to testify before the House committee. Painter, who also was busy trying to present sharp reductions in funds for Indian education, was feeding information to the few opponents of removal on the committee. One statement was the joint product of Painter, General Whittlesey, Delegate Caine from Utah Territory, and the ex-governor of that territory. During the same period Welsh had several mailings prepared in the Philadelphia office and was trying to inspire southern clergymen to circulate petitions against Ute removal. Welsh also was "working like a beaver" to get people from Boston, Baltimore, and Philadelphia to travel to Washington to testify.[31] Theodore Roosevelt, at Welsh's request, spoke to a South Carolina representative on the issue.[32]

Despite the campaign, the House committee favorably reported the bill. But Painter did not give up easily and persuaded members of the committee who had voted against the bill to present a minority report—one which Painter himself had drafted.[33]

Then the embattled agent for the IRA received an unexpected assist. The chairman of the House Indian committee went back home to Arkansas to mend his political fences. He was gone for several weeks, and during his absence no action was taken on the Ute bill. It was just as well because some of Painter's allies were losing enthusiasm for the fight. The Utah delegate and the ex-governor were soft-pedaling their opposition because of a new Utah statehood bill introduced in the Senate by Henry M. Teller—who also had introduced the Ute bill in the Senate. The Utah people were not prepared to risk their long-delayed statehood by alienating Teller over the Ute bill. And, as that old

Washington hand Painter pointed out, probably others would be un-willing to oppose Teller on the Ute issue because he had been "right" on the tariff, on silver, and on the Lodge federal elections force bill.[34] The legislative process was never simple.

Despite the complications, the IRA forces again were able to pre-vent ratification of the Ute agreement. Senator Dawes's committee declined to take action until the House passed the bill. Painter was able to get it placed at the bottom of the list to be brought to the House floor for action. He then helped ensure that the bills coming up earlier were *thoroughly* discussed, which meant that the House never did get to the Utes.[35] In January 1893 Painter could report that gold had been discovered on the proposed Utah reservation and that citizens of Durango were pouring into the area.[36] At least temporarily they were unlikely to be urging the removal of Utes to the region. Two more congresses had passed into history, and the Ute agreement still was not law. The same congresses failed to take action on another scheme to move Indians, this time the Lower Brulés.

In the summer of 1891 Reverend Luke Charley Walker, a full-blood Sioux in charge of an Episcopal mission on the Lower Brulé reservation in South Dakota, alerted Herbert Welsh to an attempt to move "my people."[37] Welsh promptly sent a copy of Walker's letter on to Lyman Abbott and asked him if he would print something in *The Christian Union* which might help stay this action. In Welsh's opinion, it was the Southern Ute story all over again: "The whites know these lands are good and so wish to get them for themselves and to have these Indians removed to another place."[38] It was the beginning of the IRA's involvement in another issue which would drag on for years.

Nor was it as simple as Welsh first presented it to Abbott. By the Sioux Agreement of 1889 what had been a solid mass of Sioux land-holdings had been divided into five blocks comprising about half of the original acreage. The Lower Brulés, about 1,000 people, had possibly received the least consideration of any of the several tribes on the original reservation. Most of the Lower Brulés had lived along both sides of White River within a dozen or so miles of their agency. But the 1889 agreement provided them a new reservation about thirty miles north of White River. The south bank of that stream now lay in Rosebud Reservation, and the north bank was in the area purchased by the United States. When the Crook Commission had come to the Lower Brulés in 1889, the Indians had asked if they could join their close relatives the Upper Brulés on their Rosebud Reservation. General Crook seems to have held out to them some hope that this move might be accomplished later. But meanwhile they would have to go to their new location, which was across the Missouri River from the Crow Creek

Sioux Delegation of 1891. Included are Indian Commissioner T. J. Morgan (4), American Horse (5), Reuben Quick Bear (13), David Zephyr (19), One-to-Play-With (28), George Sword (35), Reverend Luke Walker (38), Alexander Rencountre (40).

Courtesy Smithsonian Institution

Reservation of the Yanktonai Sioux, with whom the Lower Brulés had relatively little in common.

Welsh, as usual, had little difficulty in seeing the issue as crystal clear. When he and Theodore Roosevelt visited the Sioux in September 1892, Welsh spent four days riding around the new Lower Brulé Reservation. He reported that the Indians already there, acknowledged to be a minority of the tribe, were making good progress. These progressives should be supported in their willingness to remain at the new location, and the non-progressive element should be required to leave the ceded area and the Rosebud Reservation and go to the new reservation. Reuben Quick Bear, a young Upper Brulé who had been educated in the East, strengthened Welsh's resolve by insisting that the Rosebud Indians did not want to share their reservation with the Lower Brulés.[39] Indeed, a Rosebud council had rejected a Lower Brulé overture in June 1892.

Welsh's cast of villains for his latest morality play was headed by Senator Pettigrew of South Dakota, an old adversary who seemed to Welsh to spend most of his waking hours figuring out how to defraud the Sioux of their land. As his cat's-paws in his latest maneuver the senator was employing a Lower Brulé named One-to-Play-With and also David Zephyr, a mixed-blood. Zephyr, in moments of indiscretion, was heard to say that he would get $2,000 if all of the Lower Brulés moved to Rosebud, thus opening the Lower Brulé Reservation to settlement by Senator Pettigrew's constituents.[40] Reverend John Eastman, brother of Dr. Charles Eastman and himself a Presbyterian missionary, was recruited by Senator Pettigrew to come to Washington and lend some respectability to the removal effort.[41]

That Eastman was a Presbyterian was significant. John P. Williamson, a long-time missionary of that church among the Sioux, had a different perspective than Welsh's on what was good for the Lower Brulés. He pointed out that the Episcopalians, Welsh's church, had three facilities on the new reservation and understandably wanted the Lower Brulés concentrated there. In contrast the Presbyterians had been operating in the White River Valley and favored permitting the Lower Brulés to remain in that vicinity by moving over to the Rosebud Reservation on the south bank. Moreover, it was Williamson's judgment that the land along White River was superior for agricultural purposes to that of the new reservation.[42]

Rather early in the contest Charles Painter was persuaded that a compromise was in order: if the Rosebud Indians were willing, permit those Lower Brulés who so desired to move south of White River while allowing the others to remain on the new reservation.[43] Welsh was not prepared to consider any such plan. As had been the case with the Utes, he regarded the pleas of the faction of the Lower Brulés who wanted to remove to Rosebud as just another ploy on their part to delay their opening farms and shedding their old ways. As he explained it to Theodore Roosevelt. "The Indians who are anxious to go to Rosebud are poor, ignorant people whose real welfare depends upon their being told firmly and positively . . . that they must settle down on their own lands."[44]

Welsh's hopes rose and fell. When the Rosebud Indians indicated that they were unwilling to receive the Lower Brulés, and the latter failed to obtain the consent of three-fourths of the adult males to such a move as was required by the Sioux Treaty of 1889, it appeared that the matter was settled. But the project refused to die, and a typical IRA operation was mounted to oppose it. Welsh called on Mrs. Quinton's WNIA, the Boston Indian Citizenship Committee, and various editors for help. Twenty-five hundred copies of a pamphlet opposing Lower Brulé removal were printed and circulated.[45] Meanwhile Painter was trying to offset the parliamentary maneuvering of Senator Pettigrew. With the help of Senator James K. Jones of Arkansas, Painter was able to block passage of a Lower Brulé removal bill in the closing days of the Fifty-second Congress. Once again Senator Dawes had been of no help, and even Commissioner Morgan had been on the wrong side of the issue, which helped explain his decline in Welsh's favor late in his tenure as Indian commissioner.[46]

Unlike the Utes and the Lower Brulés, the Stockbridge Indians who sought assistance from the IRA wanted to be readmitted to their old reservation. Numbering only about 200 people, they were members of a group which had been persuaded by a government commission in 1874 to give up its claims to its tribe's 11,520-acre Wisconsin reservation in return for per capita payments of $672.71 and full citizenship rights.[47] The trade had taken place under questionable circumstances, and those Stockbridges who had participated almost immediately regretted it and sought re-admission to the reservation and the tribal rolls. There was a loophole which encouraged them to work for re-enrollment, and to accomplish it they agitated for twenty years. However, it required an act of Congress and was opposed by lumbering interests in Wisconsin. Presumably the reservation would ultimately be allotted, and the surplus land would then be available for purchase by the lumbermen. The fewer Stockbridges on the tribal rolls, the fewer allotments to be made, and the more pine land to which the lumbermen would finally have access. The IRA normally was happy to expedite the transformation of reservation Indians into allotted citizens; nevertheless, it would not do so simply to satisfy the greed of white men.

In 1886 the association had used its influence to thwart one effort by the lumbermen to remove Indians from the reservation.[48] In the Fifty-first and Fifty-second congresses Painter worked to secure legislation to enable the "terminated" Stockbridges—to use a term that would gain grim significance in the 1950s—to get back on the tribal rolls. It was a long-drawn-out and frustrating business, as were most issues requiring legislation. Painter spent hours before unfriendly committees and, as had been the case with the Utes and the Lower Brulés, he did not feel he had all the support from Dawes which the senator could have provided him. In the Fiftieth Congress Dawes seemed to Painter to be unnecessarily sensitive to the wishes of a Michigan senator who represented lumbering interests and whose name by strange coincidence was Francis Brown Stockbridge. By March 1889 Painter was denouncing Dawes's conduct as "dishonest and disreputable," although he lacked proof.[49]

Legislation designed to remedy the wrong done to the Stockbridges was introduced into four congresses before finally being enacted. This issue was not considered sufficiently important to merit the type of effort generated for the Ute cause, or even that of the Lower Brulés. However, in behalf of the proposed legislation Painter did what he could, testifying before committees, shepherding Stockbridge delegations through the bureaucratic maze, and drafting bills. When Congress finally acted, Painter took no chance on a presidential veto. Learning that President Harrison had sent the bill to the Interior Department for an opinion, Painter and General Whittlesey rushed there in time to counteract Wisconsin Senator Philetus Sawyer's effort to influence the secretary against the bill. They then followed the bill over to the White House, where they consulted with the president about it and agreed to prepare a brief justifying his approval of the law.[50] Painter still feared Harrison might veto it; however, the president affixed his signature to the bill the Stockbridges had long sought.

Painter had one last chore to perform to help restore the terminated Stockbridges. The law made no provision for the salary of someone to conduct the re-enrollment of Indians scattered as far east as reservations in western New York. Painter and Whittlesey had been concerned that the addition of an appropriation to the bill for this purpose might tip the balance against it.[51] With no pay associated with the job of revising the Stockbridge membership rolls, the position did not attract the usual crowd of job-seekers. Painter himself, in his capacity as a member of the Board of Indian Commissioners, was delegated by the government to perform the task.[52] It was appropriate that someone associated with the IRA, which had fought so long and hard for the legislation, should help implement it.

Charles Painter also played a major role in bringing some relief to the Mission Indians in California. As detailed in Chapter 6, the IRA had become interested in the plight of these Indians as a result of

Painter's visit among them in 1885. In an effort to salvage something for the more than 3,000 of them still lacking legal title to their village sites, Helen Hunt Jackson had drafted a bill to require the government to establish a commission to work on the problem. She gave it to Senator Dawes, who had maneuvered it through the Senate three times before the House finally passed it in January 1891. Through three congresses it had been one of the Indian bills on which Painter had expended some effort.

On the recommendation of Commissioner Morgan, Secretary Noble appointed Painter to a Mission Indian commission. The two other members were A. K. Smiley, the genial host of Mohonk Mountain House who was developing property at Redlands, California, and Judge Joseph B. Moore of Michigan, a political appointee, although one who did an excellent job, in Painter's judgment.

Painter was to spend nearly a year on the assignment. During this period he drew the government pay that went with the duties of a member of the commission, supplemented by half of his salary as an agent of the IRA. He had asked for his full salary, but the executive committee of the association was not willing to be that generous.[53] Painter earned his joint income. Smiley and Judge Moore were on the job less than half of the time, and Painter was left to carry on alone during the hot summer. Much travel was involved as the Indians were scattered throughout southern California from the coast east to the desert areas. Painter did have the help of Frank D. Lewis, an attorney originally employed by a Mohonk Mission Indian committee and now on the government payroll.

The commissioners had hoped to consolidate all of the Mission Indians on a few reservations. However, as Painter reported, "No matter how poor their lands, or how small they want to stay where they are."[54] One group steadfastly refused to leave its ancestors' graves in a desolate desert area where the temperature could exceed 120 degrees in the summer.[55] For these and more than thirty other bands, reservations were assigned. Many individual families were allotted grants from the public domain. At the conclusion of his work Painter declared that "The promise made to Mrs. Jackson I feel I have fully redeemed, and . . . the trouble of the Mission Indians will be greatly reduced."[56]

There still remained serious problems, such as those facing the occupants of several villages on Warner Ranch faced with eviction by a former governor of California who had title to the land. Nor were the Indians happy that the commissioners recommended reducing the size of some of the reservations previously established. Morongo was slashed from 88,475 acres to only 14,560, and Agua Caliente from 60,870 to 4,480. From these two reservations alone the Indians would lose more than 130,000 acres, which would be placed in the public domain where it would become available to white settlers. "For the comfort of those friends of the Indian," observed Painter sarcastically, "who believe that the way to civilize him is to give him a vast territory over which to roam," the Indians would still be free to settle on the tracts which would become a part of the public domain.[57] Once Congress had given legal sanction to the work of the commission, allotting agents began to assign individual tracts to those Indians on the reservations held in common. That and the effort to provide legal protection for the Mission Indians against continued encroachment by whites would occupy the attention of the reformers for years to come.

Charles Painter also was in the forefront of the fight to provide justice for the Sisseton and Wahpeton scouts. The Sisseton and Wahpeton tribes, together with the Mdewakatons and Wahpekutes, made up the eastern, or Santee, Sioux. It was Indians principally from the two last-mentioned tribes who were responsible for the bloody outbreak in Minnesota in 1862. With a few exceptions the Sissetons and Wahpetons had refrained from joining in the attacks on the white settlers; indeed, hundreds of warriors from these two tribes had served in the army which put down the uprising. Nevertheless, they had been lumped with the hostiles in being denied the payment of annuities due them for a sale of land to the United States in 1851.[58]

Early in 1888 Gabriel Renville, the chief of the Sissetons and Wahpetons, called on Painter in Washington to solicit the IRA's help in securing the restoration of the annuities to the former scouts. Painter drafted a bill for this purpose and later accompanied Renville to the Bureau of Indian Affairs, where he learned to his surprise and disgust that the bureau was about to recommend against the bill. Painter's protests were so vigorous and well-reasoned that Commissioner Atkins asked him to prepare his own analysis of the issue, which he did. Painter's report persuaded Atkins to revise his own response to the committee's request for information and incorporate in it Painter's brief. It was a good demonstration of Painter's versatility as a lobbyist. He had drafted the original bill and then helped write Commissioner Atkin's reaction to it! Leaving nothing to chance, the association then published a seven-page pamphlet, *How We Punish Our Allies*, urging Congress to enact the bill into law.[59]

Then the move to provide simple justice to the Sisseton and Wahpeton scouts became hopelessly entangled in negotiations for the purchase of the surplus of their reservation after allotment. For this "very perplexing and complicated mess" Painter blamed his friend General Whittlesey, who was a member of the commission which completed the negotiations in November 1889.[60]

A year and a half elapsed before the agreement was ratified by Congress. At one point it was being held up by the opposition of Representative Joseph G. Cannon, who was chairman of the appropriations committee. Cannon did not think the annuities should be restored. When reminded that the Sissetons and Wahpetons were impoverished and suffering from hunger, his response was "Damn them! Let them starve!"[61] The Senate already had passed the bill, and the IRA issued another flyer on the subject in which it called on "every citizen who feels a sense of shame . . . and who has a touch humanity . . . to join in an earnest petition to the House of Representatives that it perform this act of justice.[62] Within a month Congress had ratified the agreement, and the association could claim credit for another successful lobbying effort.

Before the scouts could be compensated, however, a final issue had to be resolved. Attorney John B. Sanborn was asking a share of the sum Congress had awarded the Sisseton and Wahpeton scouts. Sanborn originally had individual contracts with 206 of the Indians to represent them in return for one-third of any judgment the scouts received from the government, the contracts to run for twelve years. The secretary of the interior reduced Sanborn's fee to ten percent and then approved the contracts. When Congress appropriated the money in 1891 the Indians believed the contracts to have lapsed, even though provision was made in the law to satisfy Sanborn's claim. The IRA championed the Indian version, and Secretary Noble, who had been ready to go along with Sanborn, was forced to submit the case to the Court of Claims.[63]

Both Painter and General Whittlesey testified in the case. Sanborn admitted that the IRA had played a major role in securing satisfaction for the Indians, but he claimed credit for having sent Chief Renville to Painter originally. The court finally ruled against Sanborn, and Painter congratulated himself and the IRA on having saved the Sissetons and Wahpetons nearly $50,000[64] His work still was not done, however.

Reverend John Robinson, an Episcopal missionary at the Sisseton and Wahpeton reservation, had alerted the IRA to an effort by the individual sent to make the payment to the Indians to collect the ten percent Sanborn was claiming. "It is sufficient to make a much more saintly man than myself cuss," was Painter's exasperated reaction to the news.[65] More than six months after the Court of Claims had invalidated Sanborn's bid for ten percent of the $700,000, Painter was still investigating complaints of Indians who had given checks to the disbursing agent. As the IRA agent had remarked at the time of his triumph in the Court of Claims, "I am sure I have worked harder, in this case, first to secure this money, and secondly to prevent its being stolen, than the lawyers did who secured a fee of $76,500 from the Cheyennes and Arapahoes."[66]

The fee to which Painter referred was a sore point with him. He had learned of it several months earlier while nosing around the Interior Department and immediately concluded that it was something that needed to be "thoroughly investigated, and as thoroughly ventilated."[67] It was part of an emerging pattern of contracts between hustling attorneys and apprehensive tribes. In some instances the Indians had sought legal counsel in their dealings with the government. In others they were seeking protection from the depredations claims for white losses in the Indian wars. These claims were being filed in alarming numbers—more than $20 million worth—since Congress's transfer in 1891 of jurisdiction over such suits to the Court of Claims. Painter viewed the developing situation as "an unbounded vista of assault . . . upon the funds of various bands of Indians."[68]

The attorneys for the Cheyenne and Arapahoe tribes included two former agents and an ex-governor of Kansas. They submitted a bill for their services which Painter regarded as completely unjustified. In his judgment they had done little more than use their influence to help persuade Indians who did not wish to do so to sell most of their reservation to the United States. But Painter, who could not possibly investigate all such cases, might not have further pursued this one had he not been requested to do so by John H. Seger and Captain J. M. Lee. Captain Lee was assigned to the headquarters of General Nelson A. Miles in Chicago; however, he had served as acting agent of the Cheyennes and Arapahoes for a year. During his tenure as agent he worked closely with Seger to encourage the Indians to take up farming and stock-raising. John Seger was that rare agency employee who managed to establish some rapport with his Indian charges. Both he and Captain Lee were genuinely interested in Cheyenne and Arapahoe welfare and disturbed at what they regarded as efforts of the attorneys to fleece the Indians.[69]

However, this would be a battle that Painter would not win, despite some real effort. He went to Chicago to interview Captain Lee and General Miles and returned with a number of pertinent documents. The general believed that the best approach would be to seek resolutions from Congress blocking the payment to the attorneys.[70] To prepare the public to bring pressure on the members of Congress required further work. Painter made a trip to the Cheyenne and Arapahoe reservation in Indian Territory, obtaining information that, with the testimony of Lee and Miles, would be the basis for his report to the Mohonk Conference in October 1892 and for a sixty-two page pamphlet the association distributed the following March.[71] With Painter's coaching, the 1892 Mohonk Conference platform contained the statement that the government had a duty to protect the Indian "from robbery, through deceit or extortion, by scheming lawyers or greedy land claimants."[72] Despite the pressure the IRA helped generate, it had no success in getting congressional action rescinding the fees of the Cheyennes' and Arapahoes' attorneys. As Painter had predicted, "The enterprising but no-longer-to-be impecunious shyster" would have a field-day bringing suits against the tribes or defending them against raids on their property by the government or private citizens.[73]

Although at the height of its power and influence, the IRA had little success with two other issues with which it was concerned for years, the Apache prisoners and the recruitment of Indians for wild west shows. After the shift of the Apaches to Alabama following the vocal protests of the association over the conditions under which they were held in Florida, Welsh concluded belatedly that the Alabama site might be a distinct improvement in terms of health but provided too few employment opportunities. Prodded by Captain John Bourke, Welsh pressured the War Department to move the Indians to still another location east of the Mississippi. Unlike his predecessor in the Cleveland administration, Secretary of War Redfield Proctor indicated his willingness to relocate the Apaches if the IRA would come up with a practical proposition.[74] In June 1889 the Boston Indian Citizenship Committee, after a visit from Charles Painter, tentatively agreed to purchase as a home for the Apaches either a property near Hampton Institute or another not far from Wilmington, North Carolina. Painter and Captain Bourke were to decide between the two sites after an inspection trip. When they recommended instead a tract owned by the North Carolina Cherokees, months were lost before the Boston people, who had scattered for their summer vacations, could reconvene and consider the proposition.[75]

Meanwhile the North Carolina press began to object, and the governor of the state suggested slyly that perhaps Vermont, the home of Secretary Proctor, would be a better location.[76] Just as this opposition was beginning to subside, army politics completely stymied the association's efforts. General O. O. Howard, commanding the Eastern Department, took a hand and appointed his son, Lieutenant Guy Howard, to represent him. Although Lieutenant Howard sought out Painter and promised to cooperate with the IRA, the chance of a move to North Carolina was fading fast.[77] It was abruptly ended when General Crook persuaded the War Department to propose a move to Fort Sill. In turn this plan was opposed strenuously by General Miles, who had originally suggested North Carolina to Welsh. Welsh himself was not happy with Fort Sill because he predicted that Arizonans would oppose that location, which they did when a bill favoring the Fort Sill site was introduced into Congress.[78] Welsh's optimism that the new Harrison administration would provide an opportunity for the IRA to find a satisfactory, permanent home for the Apaches east of the Mississippi had completely dissipated within a year. President Cleveland's abrupt decision in 1894 to shift the Apaches to Fort Sill came as a surprise to Herbert Welsh, and he did not attempt to have the decision reversed. The whole affair had been a drain on the association's resources for several years, and the IRA had very little to show for it. The same might be said of its opposition to the recruitment of Indians by promoters of wild-west shows.

Even as the difficulties the Ghost Dancers on the Sioux reservations were having with the government had been building to a climax in late 1890, Welsh had found himself placed in a humiliating situation. At the request of the Indian Bureau he had met a steamer bearing Buffalo Bill Cody's troupe back from a European tour. Welsh's assignment was to check on the condition of the Indian members of the cast, but he was refused cooperation by the show's manager and indeed was treated with "great insolence."[79]

Commissioner Morgan had attempted to introduce several minor reforms in the administration of the reservations. One was to discourage the recruitment of Indians for exhibitions and shows similar to "Buffalo Bill's Wild West." Secretary Noble had approved Morgan's proposed ban on further recruitment, only to have the Sioux crisis come along and upset the new policy.[80]

In the aftermath of the fighting in South Dakota a number of the Ghost Dancers had been shipped to Fort Sheridan, near Chicago. When Cody proposed to hire nearly thirty of them for his show, Commissioner Morgan was opposed. Nevertheless, Buffalo Bill got them since they were prisoners in the custody of the War Department, and Morgan's stand was not supported by Secretary Noble.

On learning of the action, Welsh wrote several people soliciting their opinion of Buffalo Bill's taking the Indians to Europe. Welsh's own views were clear. he thought it would be viewed by other Sioux as "rewarding those who have been fomenting revolt and depredation."[81] Welsh also was not convinced that Cody's morals were sufficiently high to be entrusted with responsibility for Indians. Bishop Hare had informed Welsh that back in December, when Cody had been dispatched there by General Miles to assist in the arrest of Sitting Bull, Buffalo Bill had arrived at Fort Yates drunk. According to the bishop, Cody had been kept intoxicated while at the fort in order to prevent his playing a role in the dealings with Sitting Bull. But Welsh's most serious objections were that such employment "widely advertises the wild and bad side of Indian lives . . . keeps up shiftlessness and a love of excitement . . . promotes dissipated and evil habits. . . ."[82]

Armed with further information from Mary C. Collins, a missionary at Pine Ridge, on the impact of such show experience on Indians, Welsh began doing what he could to arouse public opinion. He sent out a circular calling for petitions to President Harrison, got a letter published in the New York *Evening Post,* and printed editorial references by the *Springfield Republican,* the Boston *Post,* and *Harper's Weekly.*

One man who saw the letter in the *Evening Post*—and did not like it—was Nate Salsbury, Cody's associate in show business. He caught Mary Collins in an error and made the most of it. In a letter to Welsh, Salsbury accused him of hiding behind a woman's skirts by citing Miss Collins as his authority. The showman maintained that, when Cody's troupe had visited Philadelphia, Salsbury had been called upon by "a party of bald and benevolent gentlemen who desired to investigate our method of treating the Indians" and that he had cooperated with "these worthy cranks." Salsbury concluded by warning Welsh to stay away from Pine Ridge or risk attack from relatives of Buffalo Bill's employees who had been receiving money from them.[83] Salsbury estimated that since 1885 Sioux had earned $74,300 performing for Cody.[84]

Welsh was not intimidated by Salsbury's blast, although an episode Matthew Sniffen had to handle during the corresponding secretary's 1891 summer vacation might have made him more cautious. Three Winnebagos appeared in Philadelphia police headquarters to complain of being stranded in the city by G. W. "Pawnee Bill" Lillie's wild west show. City authorities had turned to the IRA for help, and Sniffen wrote the Indian Bureau only to have it deny any responsibility.[85] Just when Welsh was preparing to direct Sniffen to circularize association members about this latest outrage, further information brought into question the validity of the Winnebagos' account. An Indian interpreter for Lillie's shows, and Pawnee Bill himself, testified that the Indians were drunken troublemakers who previously had been employed at a Wisconsin sawmill and were recognized as full citizens with no special claims on the government.[86] The IRA declined to further concern itself with these questionable characters.

In April 1892 Painter called Welsh's attention to Secretary Noble's approval of a new batch of circus contracts and advised reopening the issue. Welsh's response was to circulate to members and interested parties a protest addressed to President Harrison and signed by officers and executive committee members of the association.[87] Secretary Noble fought back with his own handout which contained endorsements of wild-west shows by General Miles, the agent at Pine

Ridge, and Secretary of State James G. Blaine. Secretary Blaine had visited with Cody's Indians in London and had reported in glowing terms on the condition of their quarters.[88] Welsh solicited the aid of Commissioner Morgan in refuting Secretary Noble on the issue but to no avail. Morgan, because of what his wife described as the "exceeding delicacy of his position," chose not to publicly oppose his superior.[89]

Nevertheless, Welsh decided to seek the views of a wide range of people qualified to comment on the issue—agents, traders, missionaries, and others. The responses did not provide the consensus for which Welsh had hoped. Roman Catholic Bishop Martin Marty, the trader Thomas V. Keam, and missionary John Robinson were some of those who defended the practice of permitting Indians to join show troupes. Among the reasons advanced was that it did provide employment opportunities for people who, if they remained on the reservation, would lead lives of idleness. Certainly agents were happy to see some of their more boisterous charges profitably employed at a distance from the reservation.

Other Welsh correspondents, such as Amelia Quinton, Alice Fletcher, and missionary Alfred Riggs, believed the practice should be forbidden. In the shows, the Indians reenacted attacks on stagecoaches and performed scalp dances. In Riggs's opinion such activities led the Indian to conclude "that the old wild ways are equally good with the sobriety, industry and economy that civilization requires, and a good deal more profitable."[90] Even though Welsh claimed that the "general tenor" of the responses was critical of the wild-west shows, he clearly was discouraged by the fact that people whom he respected, including former agent Valentine T. McGillycuddy and Captain George LeRoy Brown, failed to line up with him on the issue.[91] The project to prepare another IRA publication on the subject was quietly shelved.

As President Harrison's term drew to a close, Herbert Welsh and the association could look back on the four years with mixed feelings. Thomas J. Morgan, despite weaknesses in areas other than Indian school administration, had proved to be "the best Indian Commissioner that we ever had."[92] Against this positive aspect had to be weighed President Harrison's and Secretary Noble's decision to turn over reservation patronage to local politicians—the notorious home-rule policy, which the IRA had unsuccessfully opposed. Welsh blamed that spoils system for the maladministration which could result in a Wounded Knee Massacre and only grudgingly credited Harrison with subsequently extending civil-service regulations over additional positions in the Indian Service.

Charles Painter indicated his preference for Cleveland in the 1892 presidential campaign, and it is reasonable to assume that Welsh agreed with him.[93] After four years of Harrison, Herbert Welsh remembered Cleveland as a president genuinely interested in the welfare of the Indians and in implementing this concern by "courageous acts in defense of their rights."[94] True, Cleveland had appointed spoilsmen Commissioner Atkins and Assistant Commissioner Upshaw; however, when convinced of the damage they were doing by Welsh and other reformers, Cleveland had taken reservation patronage out of their hands. Welsh looked forward to having Grover Cleveland back in the White House.

CHAPTER ELEVEN

Association Leadership
Begins to Falter

At the height of its power at the beginning of Cleveland's second administration, the IRA would begin to lose influence during the next four years. Its able Washington agent Charles Painter died in 1895, and Herbert Welsh was led by a restless conscience into other avenues of reform. The association's membership remained fairly constant, although the activity of the branches continued to decline. The IRA remained dependent upon the largesse of a very few contributors. For the four years between 1893 and 1897, the total of dues and contributions was almost $25,000. However, three donors were responsible for $13,000 of this amount. The Misses Ida and E. F. Mason each gave $1,000 a year, and Mary D. Fox willed the association $5,000.[1] Without the generosity of these philanthropists the IRA clearly would have had to severely restrict its activities.

The focus of the IRA's operations continued to be in Washington. As Welsh phrased it, "the Government is the great machine of power through which we ought to work."[2] This emphasis placed much of the burden on the Washington agent, as Welsh freely acknowledged: "Perhaps the most vital part of our work is that represented by our Washington agent, Mr. Painter, a man of experience, discretion, high character and courage."[3] Painter had been exemplary in the role, and Welsh was generous in his praise, describing the agent a year before his death as having "as much practical knowledge of Indians and the ins and outs of Government management of Indian affairs, both executive and legislative, as any man in the country."[4]

As more of his time and energy went into other projects, Welsh inevitably had to leave the bulk of IRA business to the discretion of

[148]

Painter. Less and less was he inclined to try to direct the agent's activities, Painter being given great latitude even in determining his summer itineraries. More and more frequently letters sent to Welsh were simply forwarded to Washington for the agent to respond to as he judged best.

The interest Welsh previously had exhibited in local politics, civil-service reform, and other good causes continued to grow. If Indian affairs were not beginning to bore him after a decade's immersion in them, at least he now found them less exciting and challenging than other reforms. The range of those new interests was impressive. On the local level Welsh was dismayed by the "dreadful evils" in Philadelphia but determined to do something about them.[5] In the spring of 1893 he was engaged in local campaigns to clean up the city and improve its water supply to try to head off a possible cholera epidemic that summer. Later that year he was busy planning a national conference of municipal reformers to be held in January 1894. He emerged from that meeting as chairman of a committee to lay the groundwork for a National Municipal League, which appeared in May with Welsh as a member of its executive committee. The winter of 1894–1895 saw him secretary of a committee attempting to elect a reform candidate as mayor of Philadelphia.[6] Although the candidate was "overwhelmingly defeated," Welsh found it possible to feel that the campaign had had some educational value.[7] A few weeks later he initiated a lawsuit charging corruption in the construction of a municipal reservoir. Meanwhile he was seeking funds for a variety of organizations besides the IRA—the Culture Extension League (to improve recreational facilities for the poor), the National Civil Service Reform League (of which he was the finance chairman), the Civil Service Reform Association of Pennsylvania, the Pennsylvania Forestry Association, and the National Municipal League. It is not strange that Welsh should remark ruefully: "My days seem to be past in continuous beggary."[8]

Two additional causes that engaged Welsh's interest were international arbitration and Armenian relief. He served as the secretary of a committee organized in Philadelphia early in 1896 to raise funds for the Armenian victims of Turkish atrocities. Welsh's arbitration work grew out of American intervention in the boundary dispute between Venezuela and British Guiana, an intervention which raised the possibility of war between the United States and Great Britain. When this concern led to the creation of an International Arbitration Commission, Welsh was turned to for "initiative and to supply earnestness and work."[9] Not surprisingly he ended up helping plan a conference held in Philadelphia in February 1896 and traveling to New York and Washington for other meetings of the commission.

All of these activities combined did not distract him from Indian affairs as much as what he first referred to as "a little newspaper project."[10] This journalistic enterprise was a weekly paper which Welsh launched in the spring of 1895 and for which he served as publisher and managing editor until he closed it down in 1904. *City and State*, the first issue of which appeared May 9, 1895, grew out of Welsh's unremitting effort to arouse reform sentiments in Philadelphia. It was a constant source of frustration to him that Philadelphians simply did not seem to care—unlike Bostonians, as he once noted.[11] Perhaps a weekly—he first intended to call it *Public Spirit*—could rouse them from their sloth. He envisioned its providing "continuous education for the people," being "the means of uniting and stimulating our various reform elements" and in this fashion helping "purify politics in Philadelphia and Pennsylvania."[12] While striving to be independent politically, *City and State* would "seek to apply fundamental Christian principles to public affairs."[13] Welsh early decided "to give the greater part of my working time to its service."[14] As usual he drew on his friends and acquaintances, soliciting items from Bishop Hare, Charles Bonaparte, and others. Francis Fisher Kane, N. Dubois Miller, and F. Hazen Cope, all IRA stalwarts, took over the financing problems, and Matthew Sniffen was drafted to serve as business manager.

Within a month of its appearance *City and State* had a subscription list of about 700 and another 600 copies were distributed to newsstands.[15] Much of Sniffen's time went into soliciting advertisements and trying to increase circulation by such devices as having copies of *City and State* sent to Philadelphia's principal barbershops.

Although he had an associate editor, Welsh set the paper's tone. Thus it was he who decided, in a most atypical mood, to duck the tariff issue, which he thought could be "fatal" for his enterprise in protectionist Philadelphia.[16] However, such timidity was rare, and Welsh lived up to his pronouncement that for reformers, as for the French revolutionary Danton, the watchword should be "audacity, audacity, and still audacity."[17] Before *City and State* would cease publication, Welsh would have managed to alienate some of his oldest supporters by the paper's stand on such emotional issues as American atrocities against Filipinos.

The IRA's Indian work could only suffer from Herbert Welsh's preoccupation with other projects. Despite the importance he had attached to travel in the West to gain firsthand acquaintance with problems of Native Americans, he visited no reservations in these four years. He did, however, make two trips to Europe and take his annual eight- or ten-week summer vacation at Sunapee.

Welsh also was speaking much less frequently on Indian subjects, something which he had done regularly in the early years of the association. He had regarded speaking engagements as a high priority, as they not only helped shape the public opinion he valued so highly but also helped recruit members and raise funds for the IRA. Welsh continued to travel to speaking engagements in New York, Boston, Detroit, and even as far west as St. Louis, but more often now he spoke on topics other than Indians. When invited now to address a group about Native Americans, Welsh usually declined, pleading other commitments. On a few occasions he accepted the invitation but asked if he could speak on another subject. To a Yale audience he chose rather to talk about municipal reform, and Moravian seminarians heard him discourse on the role of women in reform movements, a topic in which he was much interested.[18]

There was no question but that Welsh had overcommitted himself. In the spring of 1894 he again was under doctor's orders to reduce his workload. More and more frequently what suffered was his Indian work, and his correspondence contained many references to being overwhelmed with other assignments and having temporarily to abandon the association's business.

Something more difficult to evaluate, but important, was the effect on the IRA of Welsh's use of his association contacts to solicit support for his other projects. Few letters left the Philadelphia office in the spring of 1895 which did not contain a plug for *City and State*. Indeed, frequently the association's business would be dismissed in a sentence or two and the balance of the letter would be related to Welsh's latest enthusiasm. After J. P. Morgan contributed to a fund which Welsh was collecting for the Navajos, he sought to approach the financier for a donation for the National Civil Service Reform League.[19] Reuben Quick Bear, the Rosebud progressive, was solicited by Welsh to join the IRA—and also to subscribe to *City and State*.[20] Quick Bear, who sought the association's aid in keeping his reservation free of Lower Brulés, both joined the IRA and subscribed to the paper. This constant equation of Indian problems with those of municipal reform or the plight of Armenians could only detract from the cause for which the IRA had been established.

Welsh's use of association facilities and staff for other than IRA business raised a more immediate problem. However, President Philip Garrett and members of the executive committee were not prepared to protest volubly because Welsh received no compensation for the time he himself devoted to the association. But Matthew Sniffen was on the payroll, as was Emma Register, a clerk. A committee appointed by Garrett to study the problem concluded that about half of Sniffen's time and one-third of Miss Register's was going into *City and State*. The demands of the civil-service associations and the other Welsh projects that occasionally absorbed staff time were not considered sufficiently burdensome to be computed. The committee concluded apologetically that *City and State* must pay twenty percent of the Sniffen and Register salaries and the same proportion of the rent for the IRA offices.[21]

The IRA did derive some direct benefit from *City and State*. Virtually every issue carried items relating to the association's Indian work, and the Washington agent frequently summarized his activities for *City and State* readers. However, Welsh had enjoyed considerable success in getting access to the columns of journals and newspapers with greater circulations than *City and State*. What the Indian reform movement needed, particularly at a time when it was losing by death such leaders as Hampton's General Armstrong, was the full commitment of Herbert Welsh, and that it would no longer receive.

The unexpected death of Painter in January 1895 posed real problems not only for the IRA but for Welsh, who needed the association's Washington office in the hands of someone who did not require constant supervision.[22] Deeply involved in the Philadelphia mayoral campaign, he did not have the time to devote to the selection of Painter's successor that the importance of the position merited. As he phrased it in a letter to General Whittlesey, "Local duties here of a very critical and pressing nature . . . absolutely tie my hands."[23] Less than a week after Painter's death, Welsh, with the approval of the executive committee, approached Charles F. Meserve about the opening.

Merserve had had a background in business and education in Massachusetts before his selection in 1889 by Commissioner Thomas J. Morgan to head the Haskell Indian training school at Lawrence, Kansas. He served in that capacity until 1894, when he left the Indian Service to become president of Shaw University, a Baptist-supported school for blacks in Raleigh, North Carolina. In the spring of 1894 Welsh had considered employing him to make a summer tour of reservations that Welsh was too busy to visit. To executive committee members whom he was trying to sell on this proposition Welsh had described Meserve as having the ability, experience, and appearance required to do the job, as well as having been a member of the association for several years.[24] Although this employment did not materialize, it was no surprise that Meserve should be considered as a replacement for Painter less than a year later. At that time Welsh made clear to Meserve that he had other interests which "largely occupied" his time although he still hoped to "guide all essential operations."[25] To Welsh's obvious relief Meserve accepted the appointment, only to back out a few days later when the trustees of Shaw University protested strongly his leaving.

Welsh immediately turned to Francis E. Leupp, the Washington correspondent of *Nation,* head of the Washington bureau of the New

York *Evening Post,* and also editor of *Good Government,* the voice of the National Civil Service Reform League. It was in the last capacity that Leupp had made Welsh's acquaintance, Welsh being on the journal's publication committee. For more than a year before Painter's death, Welsh and Leupp had corresponded occasionally, and *Good Government* carried an essay Welsh had read at the 1893 Mohonk Conference. When the IRA's Washington position became vacant, Welsh had asked Leupp to suggest a replacement. Leupp decided that he himself might be interested and discussed it with his friend Theodore Roosevelt, who then proposed Leupp to Welsh as "the very man for it."[26] By that time, however, the offer had been made to Meserve. When that arrangement fell through, Welsh quickly turned to Leupp, there apparently being no one else being considered and Welsh anxious to get someone as soon as possible to head the Washington office.

The problem with Leupp's appointment was that he was no more prepared than Welsh to give the association his full energies. He took on the position in addition to his responsibilities to the *Evening Post* and *Nation.* (Apparently he gave up his editorship of *Good Government* at about the time he entered the employment of the IRA.) Although he received from the IRA a $2,000 annual salary, almost as much as Painter's $2,500, it was clear that his loyalties were first to the *Evening Post.* Leupp could talk of putting in fifteen-hour days, and indeed he was capable of an inordinate amount of work, but nevertheless the IRA was getting in place of Painter a part-time employee and one who still had a lot to learn about Indian affairs. He also had his own office arrangements, which meant that the association's agent no longer shared rooms with General Whittlesey, the secretary of the Board of Indian Commissioners. That daily contact with Whittlesey had helped keep Painter abreast of what was going on in Indian affairs and had given him another avenue for influencing the course of events.

During the last year of his life Painter was a member of the Board of Indian Commissioners. Welsh had suggested the appointment to Secretary Hoke Smith as a means of giving the association's agent "a certain official authority in making investigations."[27] There was no salary attached to membership on the board, although Painter was reimbursed for travel on board business, which sometimes coincided with IRA business.

For a time in early 1895 it had appeared that Painter might become commissioner of Indian affairs. As usual Welsh had been interested in seeing the new administration appoint good people as secretary of the interior and commissioner of Indian affairs. Using Carl Schurz as an intermediary, he contacted President-elect Cleveland. According to Schurz, Cleveland remembered Welsh "as a man with whom he might not always have been in perfect agreement, but who could always be counted upon to be animated with perfectly honest and proper motives."[28] Within a few weeks Welsh received through a mutual friend, Reverend Charles Wood, a message from Cleveland that he would be happy to consider anyone the IRA would care to suggest as commissioner.[29] At this point Welsh could come up with only two possibilities: James McLaughlin, agent at Standing Rock, and the former agent at Crow Creek, W. W. Anderson. As he confided to Painter, McLaughlin, although a Catholic, could be expected not to favor his church. Painter had another name to propose: his own. He quoted someone who had questioned the association's support of a Catholic, whom most of its members would oppose because of his church affiliation, and had then suggested Painter as a candidate.[30] When Professor James Thayer contacted Welsh on behalf of the Boston Indian Citizenship Committee about arriving at a candidate they jointly could support, Welsh proposed Painter. The Boston committee agreed, and, in addition, General Armstrong communicated from Hampton his support of Painter. Bishop Hare also endorsed Painter and helped lower McLaughlin's stock by suggesting that the agent lacked the "education and refinement" needed by a commissioner.[31]

Early in January, Welsh had an hour-long interview with Cleveland in New York. The president-elect already had been primed by Reverend Wood with the possibility of Painter as commissioner. In the conversation with Welsh, Cleveland referred to advice and counsel on Indian affairs that he had received from Painter in his first administration. Welsh was reluctant to push Painter, given his connection with the IRA, but did speak warmly of his qualifications. He came away from the meeting believing that Painter had a chance for the appointment.[32]

Charles Painter also received support from a group speaking for the Ebbitt House conferees. Then Welsh, to his great surprise, learned from Reverend Wood that Cleveland had about decided to offer the commissionership to Welsh himself. The president-elect had concluded that Painter's many years in Washington as a critic and investigator of the Indian Service might handicap him in an administrator's role. After recovering from his surprise, Welsh told the association's executive committee that he would not accept the appointment if it were offered him, believing himself unfit for such responsibilities.[33]

After his inauguration President Cleveland again contacted Welsh, this time to get his reaction to returning John H. Oberly to the commissionership. Despite the strenuous campaign he had waged in 1889 to persuade President Harrison to retain Oberly, an appointee of Cleveland's first term, Welsh now turned thumbs down on him, citing statements from Theodore Roosevelt and another member of the Civil

Service Commission.[34] Unknown to Welsh, Captain Pratt would also oppose Oberly, arguing that he had favored Catholics when he was superintendent of the Indian school system. In his usual caustic fashion Pratt told the president that he should appoint a commissioner who would not be beholden to either the Catholic Church or the IRA.[35]

Not willing to appoint Painter and presumably not impressed by the credentials of Francis Fisher Kane and Charles Meserve, both men with IRA connections who had been suggested by another group, President Cleveland bypassed the reformers completely. He appointed Daniel M. Browning, an Illinois politician who had sought the position of land commissioner. Browning knew nothing of Indian affairs. Welsh regarded this outcome to his four-month-long effort to get a qualified person into the job as quite disappointing: "I think he [Cleveland] has treated us with rather scant courtesy."[36] Nevertheless, Welsh wrote the new commissioner to offer him the association's cooperation, and Browning responded promptly and appropriately.

Daniel Browning had even less influence than most commissioners of Indian Affairs, a weak office at best. He had the fortune—or misfortune—to have in General Frank C. Armstrong an assistant commissioner who had been born on a reservation, had been in the Indian Service several years, and was convinced he knew all that there was to know about Native Americans. The Washington insiders were soon circulating the report that Armstrong really ran the Indain Bureau. After his first meeting with Armstrong, Welsh described him as "wholly satisfied with the absolute correctness of his own opinions on every point, and quite intolerant of any difference of view that might be entertained by others perhaps as well qualified to judge as he."[37] Since Welsh and Painter were confident of their own grasp of Indian affairs, it was inevitable that they would be unhappy with the new leadership in the bureau.

As usual, however, the really important decisions, and many that were not, had to be passed up the line for the judgment of the secretary of the interior. The new secretary was Hoke Smith, a Georgian who also knew nothing of Indians. Smith was young, vigorous, and determined to run his department. The IRA leaders would cultivate Secretary Smith, and their relationship with him was much pleasanter than it had been with Secretary Noble. As was his custom when administrations were changing, Welsh had written Secretary Smith as soon as he took office, urging him to retain certain agents of whom the association thought highly. In June the secretary telegraphed Welsh an invitation to come to Washington to confer with him on possible personnel changes at the agencies. This flattering invitation could only have predisposed Welsh to see the better side of Hoke Smith. Predictably he found the secretary "frank, straight forward," although the IRA's spokesman was clearly shocked at Smith's ignorance of "names of Indians and places that are very familiar to persons of ordinary culture."[38]

During a lengthy discussion Welsh took the opportunity to strike a blow for an agent whom the new administration was considering demoting from that rank to chief clerk. Secretary Smith, who had been referring to a list of changes proposed by Assistant Commissioner Frank Armstrong, called General Armstrong in to attempt to rebut Welsh's defense of the agent. The result was a heated exchange between Armstrong and Welsh. The latter concluded that, with Commissioner Browning and Secretary Smith both uninformed on Indian matters, Armstrong would have unusual influence for an assistant commissioner. "Given Armstrong's evidently violent and crude way of handling things," the situation caused Welsh to "rather tremble for the future."[39]

Secretary Smith, however, was a quick learner, and he received a steady flow of advice and counsel from the IRA. Six months after his first invitation to confer with the secretary, Welsh was again asked to Washington by Hoke Smith, this time to discuss at length the government's Indian school system.[40] Twice in 1894 Welsh was able to get an appointment with the secretary. Smith also solicited his help in lobbying Congress for funds and personnel for his department.[41] The relationship showed some strain when the secretary took exception to IRA attacks on inspectors operating out of his office and warned Welsh about "excessive zeal."[42] Such admonitions were wasted on someone like Welsh, and he and Hoke Smith would again be at odds a few months later over criticism of the government's handling of the Navajos. Like most people, the secretary appreciated compliments but was restive under criticism. Welsh assured him that he could expect from the IRA whatever his conduct merited.[43] Despite these disagreements the association's relationship with Hoke Smith was as good or better than it had been with any other secretary of the interior, which was fortunate given Commissioner Browning's ineffectuality.

Overall the IRA was pleased with Cleveland's appointments in his second term, particularly that of William N. Hailmann to be superintendent of Indian schools. Daniel Dorchester had held this position under President Harrison, and the association had played an active role in countering Catholic opposition to his confirmation by the Senate. Three months after Cleveland's accession, Dorchester was still in office, although his wife had lost her government job, and he was beginning to hope that he might survive. Possibly to improve his odds Dorchester wrote Welsh a warm note of congratulations on his report of a visit to the Sioux reservations and took the opportunity to expand on his own accomplishments. Welsh replied on cue and promised to help him retain his office. General Whittlesey also interceded with Welsh in behalf of the superintendent, and a few days later the IRA sent out a circular to nearly 200 people asking letters and petitions in support of Dorchester.[44]

Six months later Welsh reversed himself. Secretary Smith had written him a personal letter asking him for the names of people he might recommend for the post of superintendent of Indian schools.[45] Hoke Smith indicated that he would prefer a layman and one with no discernible sectarian bias. As Dorchester was both a Methodist clergyman and the author of an anti-Catholic tract, this statement did not bode well for him, but Welsh was clearly pleased to have been consulted. For the record he prepared a statement to the secretary opposing Dorchester's removal, yet in the same letter he suggested two men as possible replacements. Theodore Roosevelt helped rescue him from his dilemma by passing on a secondhand report of lack of perceptiveness on Dorchester's part.[46] It was of no great consequence, but it offered Welsh the excuse he needed to abandon the superintendent. A few days later Welsh spent five and a half hours in Hoke Smith's office, during which time the secretary introduced him to William N. Hailmann, whom Smith had chosen to succeed Dorchester. The secretary also had asked Dr. W. T. Harris, the head of the Bureau of Education and the man who had proposed Hailmann's name to Smith, to join them for a time. Welsh was impressed that the Democratic secretary was willing to continue Harris, a Republican, in office and even to accept recommendations on personnel from him. Before Welsh left, Secretary Smith had prevailed on him to prepare a letter to President Cleveland endorsing Hailmann.[47] Welsh followed it up within a month with a four-page circular lauding Hoke Smith and rationalizing the shift in IRA support from Dorchester to Hailmann.[48] The wily Georgian had demonstrated how to handle Yankee reformers.

One Cleveland policy, the frequent use of army officers as agents, Welsh claimed some credit for shaping. During his meeting with the president-elect in January 1893 Welsh had informed him of a recent law (enacted in July 1892) which authorized the president to fill these positions with officers unless he preferred to use civilians, and urged Cleveland to use it.[49] Like Hampton's founder, General S. C. Armstrong, Welsh believed that this policy was a means of undercutting the iniquitous spoils system, as the officers had no political ties. Moreover, they frequently were familiar with the tribes to which they were assigned, a very rare thing for civilian agents. Within six months of his inaugural, President Cleveland had appointed army officers to twenty-seven of the fifty-seven agencies.[50] Unfortunately, many of the officers quickly became unhappy in their new positions and sought reassignment, resulting in an even higher rate of turnover of agents than was normal with civilians, which was bad enough.

The IRA waged its usual fight to keep in office those agents of demonstrated competence. J. George Wright at Rosebud, whose father had been another association favorite, and George Steell, who administered the Blackfeet reservation, received particular support. Welsh wrote several prominent Democrats soliciting letters in behalf of Wright, whose initial appointment had so shocked him. When he had his interview with Hoke Smith in June 1893, Welsh presented the secretary with several endorsements of Wright by army officers and challenged Assistant Commissioner Frank Armstrong's criticism of the agent. The following March the IRA put out another circular praising Wright and asking that letters in his behalf be written to Cleveland and Hoke Smith. Welsh was careful to include in his mailings a number of Episcopal bishops in southern states who might be persuasive with the secretary from Georgia.[51] J. George Wright's job was saved, but Welsh was not able to do the same for George Steell.

Agent Steell had an active defender in George Bird Grinnell, the journalist and student of Indian cultures. Since 1889 he had contacted Herbert Welsh on occasion about Plains tribes, and Welsh recently had written a favorable review of a book by Grinnell. At that time Welsh had solicited information about the author from Theodore Roosevelt, a mutual friend. Under the circumstances Grinnell had no difficulty rallying Welsh's support for Steell. The IRA executive wrote both Secretary Smith and Commissioner Browning in Steell's behalf, although this time in vain. The army officer sent to relieve Steell was reluctant to do so because of the agent's patent ability, but even this support could not move the administration. Nevertheless, Welsh continued to press the issue, referring to it at the 1893 Mohonk Conference and trying to involve Amelia Quinton and the WNIA in the campaign. This pursuit of what was obviously a lost cause was vintage Welsh. As he explained it to President Daniel C. Gilman of Johns Hopkins University, Cleveland was not likely to admit his error, "but I do believe that by following out this course pertinaciously we shall at least cause the reform slowly to advance."[52]

The IRA had ample opportunity to take on similar causes, as many Indian Service employees turned to the association when they had been fired or felt their jobs were endangered. One ex-agent asked to be enrolled as a member of the association and in the same letter sought help in being reinstated.[53] Others were less blatant, but either way they contributed to a surge in membership applications when administrations changed.

George Bird Grinnell
Courtesy Library of Congress

Between the letters from people trying to hold on to their jobs, and others from people seeking the help of the IRA in getting into the Indian Service, it frequently appeared that the association was an employment agency. In this capacity it had a mixed record with the Cleveland administration, as reference to just a few of its clients indicates. Welsh was able to secure the appointment of his nominee to head the Santee agency. He interceded in behalf of a discharged school superintendent, but then backed off this cause when he was convinced that the firing had resulted from the superintendent's inability to get along with the agent. The office seeker who had been turned down for an agency and then left it to Welsh "to get me what you can" was ignored.[54] Welsh did take up the case of a Miss Caryl and that again put him at odds with the redoubtable Captain Pratt.

Miss Caryl had been discharged from her teaching position at Carlisle and had appealed for help to the IRA. Welsh turned to Theodore Roosevelt in his role as a civil-service commissioner. Roosevelt attributed the dismissal to Pratt's "ferocious effort" to have Carlisle exempted from civil-service regulations.[55] Roosevelt believed Pratt had become too much of a burden to the reformers and should be "turned away."[56] Miss Caryl, meanwhile, was saved by being transferred to another government school.

Captain Pratt's vituperations continued to plague the reformers. Hostile to anyone willing to assign any role in the civilization process to reservations, he classified the IRA and the WNIA both as "harmful influences in Indian management."[57] Nevertheless, he invited Welsh to a celebration of Carlisle's fifteenth anniversary in 1894. Welsh declined, pleading other commitments, but he spoke in glowing terms of the school's "marvelous work."[58] More importantly, Welsh asked Painter to extend Pratt what help he could, "although he has so frequently sought to injure and disparage us."[59]

Toward the end of Cleveland's second term, Captain Pratt's attacks reached a crescendo. Outraged at efforts to impose employees upon him through the operation of the civil-service system, Pratt at one point refused a direct order of the assistant commissioner of Indian affairs. The IRA's advice to Secretary David R. Francis, who had succeeded Hoke Smith in August 1896, was to reprimand Pratt rather than send him back to the army.[60] Secretary Francis did so, and apparently the tempestuous capatin had escaped again. Then an issue of *Red Man*, a Carlisle organ, carried blistering attacks on the Civil Service Commission, Superintendent Hailmann, and the IRA. Hailmann was accused of mailing copies of *City and State* to Pratt and Indian Service personnel under government frank. This issue of the *Red Man* Pratt sent to members of the association and many employees in the Indian Service.

Pratt made a particular point of calling the franking issue to the attention of Senator Matthew S. Quay, whose Pennsylvania political allies were constantly criticized in *City and State*.[61]

The association's Washington agent, Francis Leupp, was furious at the attack on Hailmann. Leupp wanted Pratt not only removed from Carlisle but discharged from the army "if necessary to stop the spread of his pernicious vagaries."[62] When Welsh counseled a more moderate reaction, Leupp declared that he would work to get rid of Pratt even if he had to do it as an individual. He did press the secretary of war as well as Secretary Francis to take action and managed to have the issue brought up at a cabinet meeting.[63] However, the administration had only a few weeks remaining to it, and there was no eagerness to alienate Pratt's supporters by discharging him at this late date. He was left to the incoming McKinley administration to discipline or discharge.

Pratt was unrepentant. In a letter to someone who had protested his attacks, the captain denounced the failings of the civil-service system and identified particular villains. "There is no more conspicious and inveterate office seeker in the country than 'Teddy Roosevelt,' and Mr. Herbert Welsh follows close after," he declared.[64] At least in Welsh's case this charge was clearly unfair. An IRA committee drafted a response for public circulation, but by now Welsh was privately expressing the opinion that Pratt's "mind is becoming more or less unbalanced."[65] He counseled Leupp to moderate his assault on the captain, although the association did circulate an article by Leupp reprinted from the New York *Evening Post* and the IRA's own committee report. When the February 1897 *Red Man* charged Welsh and Leupp with running the IRA without regard to the wishes or interests of the membership, Welsh answered through the columns of *City and State*. He argued unconvincingly that the association actually was "managed" by a twenty-member executive committee.[66]

Despite Pratt's opposition the IRA would see its long battle to extend civil-service regulations over the Indian Service finally won during the second Cleveland administration, but not without one final skirmish. At the 1893 Mohonk Conference both Welsh and Philip Garrett delivered papers calling for the further extension of civil service. After returning from Mohonk, Welsh learned from Theodore Roosevelt that Secretary Hoke Smith had proposed to him that school superintendents be removed from the classified list and that a few Smith nominees for positions be exempted from examinations. Welsh was properly alarmed at what he referred to as the administration's attempt to "use the service as a partisan purse from which to pay their political friends."[67] When Commissioner Browning included the proposal relating to school superintendents in his annual report,

Roosevelt urged Welsh to attack it since he could do so now without citing Roosevelt as his source. [68] Welsh responded with 3,000 copies of a seven-page pamphlet, entitled *A Dangerous Assault Upon the Integrity of the Civil Service Law in the Indian Service,* and a petition to the president signed by members of the IRA's executive committee.[69] At his December interview with Hoke Smith, Welsh took the opportunity to personally press the secretary on the issue. And in the association's own annual report for 1893 it was pointed out that Commissioner Browning had dropped two teaching positions at Chilocco from the classified service, replaced them with two assistant positions not so covered, and then filled them with his niece and the son of a friend.[70]

The association's pressure must have contributed to President Cleveland's action in June 1894 placing all assistant teacher positions under civil service. Even though Secretary Smith had let his school superintendent proposal quietly die and Welsh was pleased at the order relating to assistant teachers, early in 1895 the association issued two more circulars on civil service.[71] But the end was in sight. In March and May 1896 President Cleveland issued executive orders extending the classified system over virtually all remaining positions, exempting only agents and inspectors. Indians applying for positions in the Indian Service would be exempted from the examinations which were the heart of the classified system. Although Leupp was unhappy with the Indian preference policy, Welsh was exultant over extension of the system. The association's annual report that year bragged, "We do not think it is transgressing the law of modesty to regard this as a decided victory for the Indian Rights Association."[72] Many other organizations and individuals had contributed to the fight, but certainly none had done more than the IRA and Herbert Welsh.

In this administration Welsh and the IRA faced one other issue relating to operation of the Indian Service: the Teller Bill, a proposal to replace the Indian commissionership with a three-man team, one member of which should be an army officer, one a Democrat, and one a Republican. Apparently the idea was originally conceived by a former army officer, Major Meredith Helm Kidd, and then taken over by Secretary Hoke Smith, who presented it in his annual report for 1895. It was introduced into the Senate by Henry M. Teller of Colorado, himself a former secretary of the interior.

The IRA's handling of the issue reflected some of the problems resulting from Welsh's concentration on other than Indian issues. The Teller Bill was first discussed in detail at the Ebbitt House conference in January 1896. Welsh did not make this meeting, and Leupp, without guidance from Philadelphia, threw the weight of the association behind the bill. He then prepared a circular discussing "Secretary Smith's excellent plan" which the IRA distributed widely.[73] Ten months later Welsh informed Leupp that N. Dubois Miller, the attorney and his longtime friend, had convinced him that the bill might be a mistake.[74] Welsh arranged to have a committee of five, including himself and Miller, help the association formulate a position. Thus composed, the committee recommended opposing the measure. Leupp fell in line and arranged for a parliamentary maneuver in the House by which the bill was killed.[75] The episode revealed an indecisiveness in IRA leadership which had been unknown when Herbert Welsh was devoting his full energies to the association. The same quality would be manifested in the IRA's handling of issues that touched the Indians more directly.

CHAPTER TWELVE

Successes and Failures During Cleveland's Second Term

Some of the IRA's causes in Grover Cleveland's second term were carryovers from earlier administrations—for example, those relating to the Lower Brulés and the Southern Utes. There were fewer issues involving reduction of reservations because much tribal land already had been surveyed and allotted and the surplus sold to government.

Colorado's pressure on the Southern Utes was renewed early in 1894. The scheme to move them to Utah had been abandoned, but the Coloradans had gotten a bill introduced into Congress to concentrate the Utes on the less desirable western part of their reservation. Those prepared to farm would be permitted to take allotments in the eastern section. However, the settlers were confident that only a few Indians would elect to do so, which would mean that nearly all of the good land ultimately would be opened for white occupation.

Charles Painter was able to get amendments attached to the bill which made it only somewhat less unsatisfactory in his judgment. The IRA's position had been that all of the Utes should receive allotments on the best land on the reservation. The bill that became law in February 1895, however, left it to each Indian to decide if he wished to take an allotment in the eastern part of the reservation or join other Utes in holding land in common in the western area.[1]

When the time came for the Utes to make their decisions, Painter had been replaced by Francis Leupp, who went to the reservation to observe the process. He took the opportunity to speak to the Indians before the polling began and tried to make clear the gravity of the choice they had to make, and the responsibilities as well as privileges which would go with allotment and citizenship.[2] Nearly half of the thousand Utes decided to take their allotments, ten times as many has had been expected to by the Coloradans who had backed the enabling legislation. It was a victory of a sort for the IRA. Now the association would have to be alert to ensure that the Utes who chose to remain got access to irrigation water, without which their allotments would be unproductive.

The course of events with the Lower Brulés was also disappointing to the IRA. Welsh's old nemesis Senator Pettigrew was at it again. Now chairman of the Senate's Indian committee in the Fifty-fourth Congress, the South Dakotan was using his new position to re-open the issue of permitting no Lower Brulés to move back to Rosebud Reservation. Such an action would accommodate those Indians who wished to go to Rosebud and open more Lower Brulé reservation land to white settlers.

In July 1896 Reverend Luke Charley Walker, the Episcopal missionary at Lower Brulé, warned the association of Senator Pettigrew's latest moves. Herbert Welsh was aboard a steamer in mid-Atlantic, and Matthew Sniffen forwarded the letter to Francis Leupp, together with some literature on the issue.[3] Unfortunately, Leupp was en route to St. Louis to cover the Republican national convention and could do nothing to hinder Pettigrew's adding an amendment to the appropriation bill. The addition not only authorized Lower Brulés who wished to do so to take allotments on Rosebud, it provided that the Upper Brulés of that reservation would be compensated at the rate of one dollar an acre, the money to come from Lower Brulé tribal funds. More than 500 Lower Brulés immediately rushed to take advantage of the law and moved south to Rosebud. Welsh later lamented that Pettigrew "has stolen a march upon us, and accomplished what I hoped had been permanently prevented."[4] Certainly the senator deserved congratulations on his persistence and parliamentary skills, but the IRA clearly was not as effective in Washington as it had been when its Washington agent devoted his full energies to association business.

Lower Brulés of the progressive persuasion, such as Benjamin Brave and an old friend of Welsh's, Alexander Rencountre, would continue to press the association to try to reverse what had happened. In early 1897 there was a flurry to letters among Lower Brulé Reservation, Philadelphia, and Washington, although Leupp was not optimistic that anything could be done either in Congress or the courts.[5] Pettigrew and the forces of greed had triumphed over Welsh, whom the senator had once referred to as "the spasmodic self-constituted philanthropist who has a fit of virtue about the Indians once a year."[6]

Leupp was prepared to accept what had happened as reflecting the desires of the majority of the Lower Brulés. For his part Welsh continued to believe that the Indians should not be permitted the luxury of doing what they chose. The government should not take a neutral stance and watch a non-progressive tribal majority impose its will on those Indians who were willing to follow the civilizing policies fostered by the government.[7]

The same logic lay behind the IRA's interest in the Senecas of western New York. These Indians had managed to escape allotment in severalty because of a preemption claim on their land held by the Ogden Land Company. Early in the nineteenth century this company, in a confusing series of deals among land speculators and the states of New York and Massachusetts, had acquired the right to purchase land still held by the Senecas. In 1893 these Indians held land in common on three reservations in western New York. Two of these reservations, Cattaraugus and Allegany, constituted the Seneca Nation of Indians as recognized by the United States in 1849. In discharging his assignment to enroll the Stockbridges, Charles Painter had visited the reservations in western New York for the first time. In his portion of the 1893 IRA annual report Painter had noted that a political faction he referred to as the Christian Party sought allotment and citizenship. It, however, was in the minority. The majority party, the Pagans, favored continuation of tribal relations and communal ownership of land. According to Painter, whites had leased much land from the Senecas, although there were complaints that most of the proceeds disappeared into the pockets of leaders of the majority political faction. He believed there existed a general pattern of political preferment at the expense of the Christian Party. Painter suggested that the IRA use its influence to persuade the government to extinguish the Ogden Company claim. This action would open the way to the allotment of the reservations with the individual Indians receiving clear titles to their farms—whether the majority of the Senecas wanted them or not.[8]

In March 1894 Herbert Welsh's attention was again called to the Senecas by a newspaper story. It apparently reminded him of Painter's reference to those Indians in the annual report, and he directed Painter to give thought to the issue and prepare some literature which could be circulated. On his own initiative the Washington agent already had had discussions relative to the Ogden Land Company claim with the congressmen from western New York. They had agreed that as soon as they could get some sense of what the company would demand they could then go to Congress for an appropriation and "provision for a speedy allotment of land."[9]

It proved more complicated than Charles Painter had expected. The Pagan Party sent a delegation to Washington to counter the petitions sent in by the Christian Party, and some New York congressmen sided with the supporters of the status quo. The most Congress would do in 1894 was to attach an amendment to the appropriation bill calling for the secretary of the interior to make an investigation of the Ogden Land Company claim.[10] Then in January 1895 Painter, the member of the IRA leadership who had brought the question to the fore, died. By that time, however, others, including the Board of Indian Commissioners, had become interested in the issue. The appropriation bill for 1895 carried a provision authorizing the secretary of the interior to negotiate with both the land company and the Senecas for purchase of the company's interest. Philip Garrett, the association's president and a member of the Board of Indian Commissioners, was appointed by Secretary Hoke Smith to conduct the negotiations. The heirs of the owners of the original company demanded five dollars an acre to surrender the preemption claim and this amount Congress was unwilling to pay.[11] Thus the drive by the reformers to impose severalty on the Seneca Nation was effectively squelched for the time being. Ironically, the dubious preemption claim of a defunct land company had enabled the Senecas to stave off an attack on the communal ownership of land which was the foundation of their nation and their culture.[12]

That the IRA was not in favor of severalty at any price was demonstrated in its opposition to the agreement with Kiowas, Comanches, and Kiowa-Apaches negotiated by the Cherokee Commission in the fall of 1892. One of several agreements arranged by the commission, headed by David H. Jerome, to extend the blessings of severalty to southwestern tribes and open additional land to white settlement, it was called to the association's attention a year later by James Mooney. A member of the staff of the Smithsonian's Bureau of Ethnology, Mooney had done considerable fieldwork among the Kiowas. While the agreement was awaiting action by Congress, Mooney asked the IRA to try to block it, maintaining that the majority of the Indians had opposed it and that the commission had employed "threats, bribery and deception" in obtaining it. Moreover he believed it would lead to the "speedy destruction" of those tribes if implemented. Mooney suggested that Welsh contact Captain J. M. Lee of General Nelson A. Miles's staff or Lieutenant H. L. Scott of Fort Sill for additional information.[13]

Welsh contacted Captain Lee, who, while not claiming personal knowledge of the negotiations, expressed the opinion that the agreement had been obtained by "threats, cajolery, misrepresentation and possibly bribery."[14] Welsh also wrote Commissioner Browning and launched Painter into action. The Washington agent visited Browning twice and asked to appear before the House's Indian Committee, which was considering a bill to ratify the agreement. Painter also had several interviews with Mooney, who filled him in on some of the shabby techniques the Cherokee Commission had employed. In the spring of 1894 Painter secured permission for Lieutenant Scott, who commanded an Indian scout company at Fort Sill, to escort a delegation of Kiowas and Comanches to Washington to protest the agreement. Once they had arrived, Painter arranged for them to appear before the House committee and to see Secretary Hoke Smith. The association's Washington agent personally accompanied them to the capitol and to the secretary's office.[15] The agreement was blocked at least temporarily, and the IRA could take some credit, although there were other factors which gave Congress pause, including Choctaw and Chickasaw claims to the area and active lobbying by Texas cattlemen who leased about half of the reservation for pasture and thus opposed allotment.[16]

The IRA also was taking an interest in the future of the Five Civilized Tribes, which occupied Indian Territory recently diminished in 1890 by the creation of Oklahoma Territory. These tribes had been specifically exempted from the operation of the Dawes Severalty Act, although few people believed that the Cherokees, Choctaws, Chickasaws, Creeks, and Seminoles could escape allotment and continue indefinitely under their tribal governments. As the House Committee on Indian affairs phrased it in 1892, "The obvious policy of the United States is to bring all of the territory within its limits, with the exception of the District of Columbia, to statehood."[17] The following year Congress created a commission to negotiate with the Five Civilized Tribes, a commission which came to be known by the name of its chairman, former Senator H. L. Dawes.

The Dawes Commission began its work in Indian Territory early in 1894. Its first report, which appeared in November, called for a change in status of the Five Civilized Tribes while recognizing that the Indians would not willingly cooperate in such a plan. Charles Painter's reaction to the issue was sought by Herbert Welsh; Painter's initial response was that he had not been in the Indian Territory for several years and was reluctant to take a stand on the report of the Dawes Commission. Welsh had never been among these tribes; however, he had "long held the view that the government of the so-called civilized tribes . . . would sooner or later have to give way, and conditions there become the same as those which governed the rest of our people." Welsh cited General S. C. Armstrong as his authority for maintaining that there was "very little pure Indian blood . . . left in the so-called civilized nations."[18]

The opposition of the Five Civilized Tribes to the Dawes Commission quickly became apparent. They closed ranks and refused to negotiate, leaving the commissioners to conduct hearings and gather information as the basis for another report. In this one the commission called on Congress to create a regular territorial government to supplant the tribal governments and to give federal courts civil jurisdiction to match the criminal jurisdiction they already had in Indian Territory. Implementation of these recommendations would mean the end of tribal self-government.

The fact that such a plan would be carried out unilaterally by the United States, despite the existence of treaties seeming to grant autonomy to the Cherokees and other tribes, caused some distress among the white friends of the Indians. It was an article of faith among them that the Native Americans ultimately would have to merge with the majority population and lose their identity. However, the reformers also had striven to protect Indians' treaty rights, and the Dawes Commission was recommending that in the case of the Five Civilized Tribes these should be ignored.

It was a dilemma that most friends of the Indian solved by somewhat reluctantly deciding that the end justified the means. Others tried to dodge the issue. The report of the Board of Indian Commissioners for 1895 accepted the judgment of the Dawes Commission that the tribal governments in Indian Territory were pawns in the hands of a selfish minority who employed them to monopolize tribal natural resources. Nevertheless, the board called for an investigation of "the legal rights of both parties under the treaties" on the assumption that "the American people wish to do nothing prejudicial to the rights of the Indians."[19]

Two members of the ten-man board that prepared this statement were Philip Garrett, the IRA's president, and Francis Leupp, its Washington agent. Garrett had joined the board in 1890, and Leupp had just been appointed. Garrett had real misgivings about any government action which might infringe on clearly defined treaty rights, whereas Leupp accepted the Dawes Commission conclusion that conditions in Indian Territory merited drastic action.[20]

The need to formulate an IRA position on the future of the Five Civilized Tribes became obvious early in 1896. Given the gravity of the issue, the association probably would have formulated a policy on it promptly, had Welsh not been preoccupied with other matters. Both Welsh and Leupp were willing to go along with the government's unilaterally substituting a territorial government for the tribal governments as a preliminary to allotment in severalty and statehood. Welsh argued that it was impractical for the Five Civilized Tribes to maintain governments within a government.[21] Both he and Leupp stressed the corruption of the tribal governments and the need to protect the minority of full-bloods from the exploitation of the mixed-bloods, intermarried whites, and adopted whites. Indians of whatever blood quantum had become a small minority in Indian Territory by 1896, perhaps only 65,000 of a total population of 365,000.[22]

A different view within the association's executive committee was represented by Mrs. Brinton Coxe and Mrs. John Markoe, who were influenced by critical reports on the Dawes Commission by a reporter for the Philadelphia *Press.* Maria Coxe and Matilda Markoe were two of the first three women to be appointed to the executive committee and owed their positions to Herbert Welsh. Over the years he had become increasingly impressed with the need for reform movements to draw upon the resources of the female segment of the population. In an article on the municipal reform movement that he wrote in early 1894, Welsh spoke of the contribution being made by "intelligent, experienced, and enthusiastic women." As he phrased it, "Women are needed,—and if their efforts are guided wisely they may become invaluable allies in this work." They would need to learn "the self-restraint necessary to those who work effectively in organized bodies," but he had no doubt of their ability to do so.[23] Welsh matched his words with action and arranged the appointment of Miss Susan P. Wharton to the executive committee of the IRA and promised that the next vacancy also would be filled with a woman.[24] He more than fulfilled his pledge, and by 1896 Mrs. Coxe and Mrs. Markoe had joined Miss Wharton on the committee. After what followed, Welsh must have been reminded of his observation on their need to be "guided wisely."

In the spring of 1896 Mrs. Coxe and Mrs. Markoe began to press the association to take a stand against the recommendations of the Dawes Commission. At a meeting of the executive committee June 2— a meeting missed by Welsh, who was in Europe—Mrs. Markoe was able to get a resolution adopted instructing Leupp to do what he could to prevent anything adverse to the Five Civilized Tribes being added to the appropriation bill being drafted in Congress.[25]

Leupp took no action, and the appropriation bill did emerge with a rider ordering the Dawes Commission to prepare new membership rolls for the five tribes, rolls which would be necessary if the Indians were to be allotted land. Congress also took the opportunity to enunciate policy: "It is hereby declared to be the duty of the United States to establish a government in the Indian Territory which will rectify the many inequalities and discriminations now existing in said Territory. . . ."[26]

The ladies had an ally in Professor Thayer of the Harvard Law School. He advised Mrs. Markoe that "those Indians have the strongest moral right to be allowed to work out their own salvation under the old treaties." Moreover, he said, "how they shall hold their land, and whether they shall keep it or sell it, are their questions and not ours."

Thayer had nothing but scorn for H. L. Dawes, whom he dismissed as "too petty a person, too much concerned for his own personal name and fame to be trustworthy."[27] When Mrs. Coxe also cited the Harvard law professor's criticism of Senator Dawes, Welsh countered by disparaging Thayer's lack of any personal experience with reservation life and "opportunity to study the question from its more practical side."[28]

Coxe and Markoe wanted a public meeting on the issue, but Welsh insisted that it should be preceded by a fact-finding mission to Indian Territory. He tried to involve Leupp in this assignment despite the agent's earlier declaration that he was "utterly out of sympathy with the single-sided sentimental view" represented by the critics of the Dawes Commission.[29] It was not Leupp's lack of objectivity but his inability to visit Indian Territory before the end of the presidential nominating conventions which led Welsh to look elsewhere for an investigator. He even was willing to send the Philadelphia reporter who had originally stirred up Mrs. Coxe and Mrs. Markoe, but the newspaperman was unable to go. Welsh also approached unsuccessfully Francis Fisher Kane, a member of the executive committee and Mrs. Coxe's nephew, who believed that his aunt and Mrs. Markoe had "worked themselves up into a most unnecessary excitement."[30] The man Welsh finally turned to was Charles Meserve, who hoped to find time in the summer to leave his responsibilities as president of Shaw University.

Meserve agreed to undertake the mission for the association, although he admitted to being predisposed to accept the findings of the Dawes Commission.[31] Welsh already had concluded that sending anyone to Indian Territory was "simply superfluous and a waste of money."[32] However, the ladies now insisted upon an investigation, and an investigation they would get. So, Charles Meserve headed for Indian Territory, and Hebert Welsh left for Sunapee, New Hampshire, for his extended summer vacation.

Predictably, Meserve returned from Indian Territory endorsing the work of the Dawes Commission in a report the association published in a pamphlet which also included a speech on the subject by H. L. Dawes.[33] Mrs. Coxe and Mrs. Markoe were distinctly unhappy. Mrs. Markoe earlier had offered her resignation from the executive committee because she had moved to New York City, and residence in Philadelphia or its vicinity had previously been a criterion for service on the committee. Mrs. Coxe was now in what she dubbed "rather a hopeless minority" and considered resigning herself. In a letter expressing her disappointment with Meserve's report, she asked Welsh to waive the residency requirement in the case of Mrs. Markoe.[34] Welsh defended Meserve as having been "quite unprejudiced in this matter," which was not entirely true. Welsh did voice deep regret at the prospect of the executive committee's losing the services of either of the women and assured Mrs. Coxe that Mrs. Markoe's moving to New York need not disqualify her from membership.[35]

Both women remained on the committee, although they were still displeased with the association's policy on Indian Territory. Mrs. Coxe referred to the IRA's position on the Curtis bill, which Congress was considering in 1896 to implement portions of the Dawes Commission's recommendations, as "perfectly incomprehensible to me," and charged Francis Leupp with withholding information on related bills.[36] But she and Mrs. Markoe had few allies in the association. Philip Garrett had abandoned his opposition after hearing the issue thrashed out at the Mohonk Conference in 1896. As Welsh had predicted, Garrett could be "convinced by evidence," whereas Mrs. Coxe "takes a purely sentimental view of this whole question," and sentimentality was the worst failing which Welsh could ascribe to a friend of the Indians.[37]

The IRA's position on the future of the Five Civilized Tribes was not at odds with that of other reform groups. The platform of the 1896 Mohonk Conference called for the abolition of the tribal system "everywhere as soon as possible, and the Indian incorporated into the citizenship of the States and Territories." The conference specifically endorsed the Curtis bill and stated that the "utter failure of these tribes to protect the rights of citizen Indians in the tribal property" imposed an obligation on the United States to intervene.[38] The Board of Indian Commissioners, meeting with secretaries of missionary societies and other friends of the Indian in January 1897 at the Ebbitt House in Washington, heard Dawes on the work of his commission and urged Congress to enact legislation "to bring order out of chaos in the Indian Territory, in accordance with the recommendation of the Dawes Commission."[39] However, the Curtis bill would not make it through Congress until 1898, and the implementation of the Dawes Commission recommendations would be a concern of the IRA for several years to come.

Herbert Welsh had had no firsthand knowledge of the Five Civilized Tribes, which perhaps helps explain his initial procrastination on their relations with the Dawes Commission. He did know the Navajos from travels on their huge reservation in 1884, 1888, and 1890, and he lavished more attention on them than on any other single tribe during Cleveland's second term.

Welsh had returned from his 1890 visit to the Navajos impressed with the failure of any of the Christian missionary organizations to have representatives among those Indians. During the next two years he worked with the Episcopal women's auxiliary of Westchester County,

New York, to raise funds to support a missionary to the Navajos. Earlier Welsh had been able to secure the position of agent for the Navajos for a man who would grievously disappoint him by being discharged for drug addiction. Two agents later the incumbent was Lieutenant E. H. Plummer, an army officer assigned to that duty. Welsh's Episcopal connections provided him a means of approaching Lieutenant Plummer, as the officer had been confirmed in that church by Bishop J. M. Kendrick, an acquaintance of Welsh's whose diocese included the Navajo Reservation. Welsh had been in contact with Bishop Kendrick often in relation to their church's struggling missionary project for the Navajos.

In April 1893 Welsh wrote Lieutenant Plummer, who had just taken office. Welsh mentioned the names of Bishop Kendrick and his "warm friends" among the officer corps, generals George Crook and Nelson A. Miles, as well as captains John G. Bourke, J. M. Lee, and others. "If at any time our Association can co-operate with you in the work of improving these people," volunteered Welsh, "we shall be very glad to do so."[40] It was the beginning of an active relationship.

Until Lieutenant Plummer asked to be relieved of the responsibility for the agency late in 1894, he called upon Welsh and the association for assistance on a number of occasions. The first was a plan to bring a small party of Navajos east to help convince them of the need to accept the white man's civilization and to recognize the futility of opposing it. Welsh approached the Interior Department about the government's funding this travel only to be told that there was no money available.[41] With government approval Welsh then committed the association to raising a fund to subsidize a delegation's visit to the Chicago World's Fair. His target was to raise $700, and at his suggestion the executive committee contributed $100 of IRA funds. A letter to prospective contributors was prepared and sent out emphasizing that such a project also would help reduce the chances of bloodshed in view of recent troubles on the Navajo Reservation. While Welsh was at Sunapee in the summer of 1893, Matthew Sniffen presided over the drive, which finally raised about $750.[42] In October, courtesy of the IRA, Lieutenant Plummer led a delegation of fourteen Navajos to Chicago, where they were permitted to camp on the grounds of the exposition. Welsh had conceived the unlikely scheme of persuading Congress to send a delegation to Chicago to meet with the Navajos. To head this group he hoped to secure Henry Cabot Lodge, who had succeeded to H. L. Dawes's seat in the Senate. Welsh tried to enlist Theodore Roosevelt to pressure his friend Lodge, but to no avail. Roosevelt declined to do so, and Lodge pled the necessity of remaining in Washington to cope with the silver issue then before the Senate.[43] Meanwhile the delegation of

Navajos had visited Chicago, and their agent reported the eleven men and three children of school age much impressed. Lieutenant Plummer attributed a big increase in enrollment in the Navajo boarding school to the "wonderful effect" of the Chicago experience.[44]

That trip, however, was just one of the projects in which Plummer enlisted the association. Others ranged from obtaining a primer in braille to enable a blind Navajo youth to learn to read, to trying to obtain major increases in agency funding to expand farming operations among the Navajos. Welsh was able to secure the primer; indeed, one of the people he approached proposed to bring the boy east for schooling. Welsh, however, declined this offer because of the tragic mortality rate among Navajos enrolled in eastern schools.[45]

The proposals to increase agency funding were much more difficult to implement. Lieutenant Plummer drafted an ambitious plan to increase the level of farm instruction for the Navajos. He asked for a supplementary appropriation of $5,000 to pay the salaries of four additional farm instructors and to buy seeds, fencing, and farm implements. At Plummer's request Welsh wrote Hoke Smith endorsing the agent's plan, and he circularized editors asking them for publicity which might generate some pressure on the secretary. Before that request had been satisfied, Welsh again petitioned Secretary Smith in behalf of the Navajo agent, this time to provide an additional clerk, an interpreter, and a laborer.[46]

Even before the Chicago trip Lieutenant Plummer, in a fit of frustration, had requested to be relieved of the Navajo duty. A major was sent to Fort Defiance, site of the agency, to replace him; however, the transfer of responsibility never took place. The major's wife was shocked at the appearance of her new home, and, meanwhile, Plummer had received some indication that the Indian Bureau would at least improve the salary of his clerk, which had been another issue the agent had raised. The major, with Plummer's blessing, telegraphed his superiors that the lieutenant was highly competent and should not be replaced. At the same time the major asked for and was granted other duty.[47] Plummer remained with the Navajos—for another year. In May 1894 the lieutenant again threatened to resign, and in October he did so. This time his replacement actually assumed the duties, and Lieutenant Plummer joined the ranks of army officers who had become Indian agents expecting to make great changes, only to become disillusioned and ask for reassignment.

Welsh might have heaved a sigh of relief, as Plummer was becoming something of a problem. Rumors were circulating that the officer, whose family had not accompanied him to Fort Defiance, was having an affair with an attractive young teacher. Moreover, he had a rival for her affections in an engineer assigned to Fort Defiance to supervise an irrigation project. Some of the bad blood between Plummer and the engineer—the officer had sought Welsh's help in getting rid of the engineer—might have related more to the man's interest in the teacher than in his incompetence as an engineer.[48] Welsh had strict Victorian views on sexual morality and would have had difficulty long supporting an agent thus accused, regardless of his other virtues.

Plummer's successor was another officer, Captain Constant Williams. In his first month on the job he put in a request for a $25,000 supplementary appropriation for his agency, claiming that many Navajos were threatened by starvation. Like his predecessor, Captain Williams turned to the IRA for help.[49] The association rushed out a circular to its members and friends asking them for letters and petitions to Washington, and Welsh personally called on Commissioner Browning to make an appeal for the Navajos. There was a good response to the IRA's circular, and Hoke Smith was soon feeling the heat and resenting it. He called the attention of the secretary of war to Captain Williams's request for IRA intercession, and that dignitary responded by ordering the officer not to communicate with outsiders about official business. When Welsh protested this effort to muzzle the agent, Secretary Smith chided him for attempting to bring influence to bear upon an official who should be much better informed than the authors of the letters the IRA had inspired. Welsh reminded the secretary that the association on occasion had used similar tactics to defend him from attacks by his critics and asserted the right of the IRA to make known to the public unpleasant facts such as the condition of the Navajos.[50]

A few days later the receipt of another alarming report from Captain Williams stirred Welsh to greater action. He committed the association to underwrite the purchase of 10,000 pounds of flour by Williams if the government refused to reimburse him for his emergency expenditure.[51] Welsh then dashed off letters to Amelia Quinton and Sarah T. Kinney of the WNIA, and President Merrill Gates of the Board of Indian Commissioners, among others, begging their assistance in the crisis. Edward M. Wister, of the executive committee, traveled to Washington to confer with Commissioner Browning about the Navajos. Welsh considered rushing out to Fort Defiance for an on-the-spot investigation but concluded that his other commitments would not permit it. Instead he convinced the executive committee to employ for this purpose one Alfred Hardy of Farmington, Connecticut, a former Navajo agency employee.[52]

Hardy spent five months on the Navajo Reservation providing firsthand reports on the condition of the tribesmen. On the basis of

Hardy's accounts of famine conditions and ill-clad Navajos sleeping on the ground in freezing weather, the association launched a campaign to raise relief funds and collect clothing for shipment to the reservation. About $1,300 was raised, with J. P. Morgan providing $250 of the sum and the Wisconsin branch of the WNIA nearly another $100.[53]

Commissioner Daniel Browning sent to Fort Defiance a special agent who discounted the reports of starving Indians. Nevertheless, Browning did not object to Hardy's use of IRA funds to purchase seeds and tools on an emergency basis or Captain Williams's use of association monies to ease the suffering of the hungry. With 20,000 Indians on the reservation, the association's limited resources could not help a significant number. Captain Williams, however, did credit the IRA's letter campaign with pressuring the government to come to the aid of the Navajos with a special appropriation of $25,000.[54]

The affair had been a real strain on the association's finances. Originally Hardy was to have completed his investigation in two months, but he insisted he needed to remain in Navajo country for an additional three at a total cost to the IRA of more than $2,000. This expense, coupled with a grant to Charles Painter's widow, a commitment of $700 to defend some Indian policemen, and having to go outside the IRA staff to investigate a crisis in Wyoming, meant that 1895 was a rough year financially for the association. At one point its funds were depleted to the point that it was faced with the possibility of having to borrow money to pay its bills. Welsh blamed himself for being so busy with *City and State* and other projects that he had failed to closely monitor Alfred Hardy's activities.[55] It was another illustration of the problems the association faced in the transition from Painter to Leupp, complicated by its leader's many commitments.

There were other Navajo matters that engaged Welsh's attention in these years. They usually were minor problems that individually seemed of little consequence but cumulatively took time. For example, Mrs. Mary L. Eldridge, a field matron among the Navajos, was handicapped in her work by the absence of a ferry across the San Juan River. Alfred Hardy referred the problem to Welsh, who contacted several people for assistance. He was able to raise $150 toward the purchase of a flat-bottom boat and a cable, and Francis Leupp persuaded Commissioner Browning to find another $115 to complete the project.[56] Welsh also had helped raise money for a small hospital at the Navajo agency.[57]

The Bannocks were another tribe whose problems required investigation at some unusual expense to the IRA. In July 1895 Bannocks from the Fort Hall Reservation were hunting elk on public land in Jackson's Hole, the valley between the Teton and Wind River ranges in

northwestern Wyoming. They were hunting as they had for generations, without regard for the game laws of the new state of Wyoming,
much to the distress of local settlers, whose principal source of income
was catering to big-game hunters who came to the area to bag trophies.
With the collusion of local authorities, settlers began rounding up at
gunpoint Indian hunting parties and taking them before a justice of
the peace. One group of Bannocks attempted to escape and was fired
upon; the casualties included an old, nearly blind Indian who was killed
and an infant lost by its mother in the confusion.[58]

    City and State carried an editorial on the tragedy early in August
under the heading "A Mere Matter of Color." The writer, probably
Welsh, pointed out the contrast between Indians, who hunted for
subsistence, and wealthy whites like Boies Penrose of Pennsylvania,
who hunted for pleasure. Claiming that Penrose, one of the favorite
targets of Philadelphia reformers, had killed elk out of season but had
not been prosecuted, the writer concluded bitterly: "Still, ours is the
land of liberty and even-handed justice,—if only your skin doesn't
chance to be black or red!"[59]

    The IRA decided that, despite its straitened financial cir-
cumstances, the affair required investigation. The executive committee delegated to Welsh and N. Dubois Miller the responsibility for
selecting the individual for the mission.[60] Francis Leupp was out of the
question because he was off on a political assignment for the *Evening
Post*. Reverend William J. Cleveland, the association's emissary in the
aftermath of Wounded Knee, agreed to take on the task and spent
about a week in the Jackson's Hole area. His reports appeared in *City
and State* and were reprinted in the association's 1895 annual report.
When Leupp returned to Washington, he interceded with Secretary
Hoke Smith to try to ensure the Bannocks' hunting rights and to bring
the murderers to justice. To avoid such problems in the future, Leupp
proposed to the secretary that the Jackson's Hole area be made into a
national forest by executive proclamation. Reverend Cleveland had
suggested adding it to Yellowstone National Park, but that action would
have required legislation.[61]

    Nothing came of the proposal, nor were legal actions fruitful. A
federal district court upheld the primacy of Bannock hunting rights
over Wyoming game laws only to have the United States Supreme
Court to rule on appeal for the state.[62] The Indians were advised by the
government to give up their traditional elk hunts, and in August 1897
their agent reported their compliance despite the severe loss it meant to
them.[63] The IRA's role in the affair had been primarily to publicize the
injustice, but there was no follow-up. Its resources were stretched thin,

and it simply could not do the job it would have liked with all the issues brought to its attention, particularly with Welsh's relegation of Indian matters to secondary consideration in his own scheme of things.

One case that Welsh did become very concerned about and to which he committed the IRA was that of seven Indian policemen on Cheyenne River Reservation who were accused of murder. In March 1893 William Fielder, an intermarried white man, had been reported to the agent for beating his Indian wife with a club. Seven policemen were dispatched to arrest him, but he resisted with an axe and a pistol and in the struggle was killed. The facts were submitted to a grand jury which found no grounds for indictment. Two years later the policemen again found themselves under arrest, and a new federal attorney was pressing for a conviction. One explanation for the reopening of the case was the anger of Fielder's fellow "squawmen" that intermarried whites would be subject to arrest by Indian policemen.[64]

The case led to a rift between the Interior and Justice departments. The South Dakota federal attorney had sought and received approval of Attorney General Richard S. Olney to prosecute the policemen despite a defense of their actions in a brief prepared by Indian Commissioner Browning and transmitted to the Justice Department by Secretary Hoke Smith. There also seemed to be some questionable practices in the government's handling of the case. Friends of the policemen were convinced that the decision to try the case in Deadwood, at the other end of the state, was designed to handicap the defense. They also were unhappy with the interpreter the government insisted on using. Finally, there was a question of intent in a serious error in the wording of the verdict against the only two policemen, Straight Head and Scares-the-Hawk, who were found guilty.

When Welsh's attention was called to the pending trial, he promptly labeled it a "perfect outrage" and leaped into the fray.[65] A Deadwood editor, Bishop Hare, and Reverend Edward Ashley, the Episcopal missionary at Cheyenne River, were contacted for further information. Through Reverend Ashley the IRA made a commitment to pay up to $700 in attorney fees to defend the policemen if the government refused or was unable to do so.[66] Welsh also stirred up Francis Leupp to bring what pressure he could on Attorney General Olney to get an investigation of the federal attorney's office in South Dakota.[67]

When Straight Head and Scares-the-Hawk were found guilty, Welsh described it as the worst case of injustice he had heard of in thirteen years of involvement in Indian affairs.[68] He already had enthusiastically seconded Leupp's suggestion that an effort be made to have medals awarded the policemen. Three thousand copies of a circular entitled *The Attorney-General and Seven Indian Policemen of Cheyenne River Agency—A Case Where to Serve Faithfully Came Near Meaning the Gallows* were put in the mail and petitions were prepared should the decision be made to seek a presidential pardon.[69] Letters to President Cleveland were sought from Carl Schurz and the Episcopal bishop of New York, and another circular was sent out consisting of a talk made by Leupp on civil-service reform. In it he attributed the decision to prosecute the policemen to the replacement of an able Republican by an incompetent Democrat and was particularly hard on Attorney General Olney.[70]

In this case the IRA worked closely with Commissioner Browning and had the support of other influential people. The commissioner, with the approval of Hoke Smith, asked the IRA to apply for a presidential pardon for the two Indians if they were not freed by a writ of habeas corpus.[71] Through Bishop Hare, Welsh had obtained petitions for a pardon signed by the members of the South Dakota Board of Charities and Corrections, which supervised the state's penal system, the judge who had presided at the trial, and all the members of the jury, save one who could not be reached![72]

The attorneys hired by the association were successful in their efforts to free Straight Head and Scares-the-Hawk from the penitentiary by habeas corpus proceedings. It then remained for the IRA to seek reimbursement from Congress of the $700 it had advanced the attorneys. In devising a strategy, Leupp had the counsel of Commissioner Browning.[73] The decision was made to omit the IRA's name from the bill to be introduced lest the association's enemies in Congress oppose the legislation. As it finally was passed, the act specified Reverend Ashley to receive no more than $700 for money spent hiring attorneys for the policemen. Eighteen months after it advanced the sum, the association was repaid.

The case of the Cheyenne River Seven had demonstrated that the IRA could still move expeditiously if Welsh chose to concentrate his attention on a particular issue. In contrast, the association's role relative to the Florida Seminoles suggested a lack of continuity and perseverance which characterized IRA activities too frequently during Cleveland's second term.

Charles Painter was responsible for the association's passing interest in the Seminoles. He and General Whittlesey had been intrigued by an ambiguous reference to these Indians in the 1892 annual report of the secretary of the interior. According to this source a school among the Seminoles was not being held but at the same time was exerting a beneficial influence on the Indians. As Painter planned to visit the Apaches at Mount Vernon, Alabama, in the spring of 1893, he suggested to Welsh that he travel on to Florida to investigate the Seminoles, about whom the IRA knew nothing. As little additional expense would be entailed, Welsh agreed.[74]

Fewer than a thousand Seminoles remained in south Florida, and they were without any legal status since the government's effort to move all the tribe to Indian Territory in the 1830s and 1840s. The seven-year war which grew out of that removal had embittered the Seminole survivors in Florida, and they regarded the government with fear and mistrust.

In 1891, after a visit to the area by Amelia Quinton, the WNIA undertook an ambitious project to resettle Seminoles on 400 acres purchased about thirty miles southeast of Fort Myers. Eighty of these acres were sold to the government, which agreed to establish an industrial school at the site. The government also agreed to employ to superintend the school one of the missionaries the WNIA had sent to work among the Seminoles. It was this school which actually had not gone into operation but whose beneficial influence the secretary had referred to in his report.

Painter did visit the settlement and concluded that the WNIA's efforts had been wasted. He identified two main problems: the settlement had been established twenty-five or thirty miles from the nearest Seminoles, and, by associating the government with the school, Mrs. Quinton had damned the whole operation in the estimate of the Indians. Painter said that any competent government inspector would dismiss the project as "utter folly, and waste of money."[75] A somewhat milder form of his report to Welsh was published in the association's annual report for 1893. One of its more interesting aspects was its presentation of the life led by the Seminoles in the everglades. Painter depicted them raising hogs and cultivating garden patches and enjoying a better existence than "the great majority of the poor whites and negroes" of Florida.[76] However, they had no title to the land they used, and the growth of the white population posed problems for the future. The state had appropriated $5,000 to buy land for a Seminole settlement, but Painter indicated that this had been done with no consultation with the people whose future was being planned for them. For a man who had served many years as the agent of an assocation which seldom doubted its ability to divine what was good for Indians, Painter raised an interesting question about the Seminole:

> that he will willingly leave the selections he has made when all was open to his choice, and the mode of life he has adopted, the means of support he has found so adequate and congenial, and go out to seek what the Government he so hates, and the Missionary whom he does not want, have to offer, is, to say the least, doubtful.[77]

The report also was significant because of the willingness of the IRA to print it and thereby endanger its relations with Mrs. Quinton and the WNIA. Welsh regularly turned to the group for help when undertaking major projects. And surely Painter and Welsh had learned from their criticism of Elizabeth Peabody's support of Sarah Winnemucca that people did not appreciate having their philanthropic ventures derided in the association's publications. However, apparently Amelia Quinton had a thicker skin. A few weeks after the 1893 annual report was published and she undoubtedly had read it, she and Welsh both spoke to a church group in a Philadelphia suburb. They shared a streetcar ride back to the city and, much to Welsh's relief, at no time did she raise the subject or reveal any annoyance with the IRA.[78]

Despite having made an issue of the Seminoles' future, the association did nothing about it. A year after Painter's death an item in a WNIA publication led Welsh to suggest to Leupp that he investigate what the government might do to protect the Seminoles from white intruders. Leupp responded by checking with the Indian Bureau, which informed him that, while most Seminoles were still squatters on public land and were steadily being elbowed aside by whites, the government was gradually acquiring land for the Indians.[79] Clearly this was a matter that merited investigation, but, despite having raised the issue, Welsh did not pursue it.

The failure to follow through on the Seminole case was symptomatic of the decline in IRA efficiency. The death of Painter and his replacement by a man who had other responsibilities, along with Herbert Welsh's decision to sharply reduce the time he allotted to Indian affairs, were having an impact. The IRA was still performing a very valuable service, as many tribes and individual Indians could testify, but its capacity to help was diminishing at the very time that more and more Indians solicited its assistance.

CHAPTER THIRTEEN

Indian Education
and Other Concerns

Some of the issues that engaged the IRA's interest during Cleveland's second term cut across tribal lines. Among them were the enrollment as tribal members of the children of mixed marriages, the enlistment in the army of Indians, the proposed abolition of selected Indian agencies, fraudulent claims on tribal resources, and efforts to cripple the Board of Indian Commissioners. And, always, Welsh and his colleagues were very interested in the government's policy on Indian education.

President Cleveland had been back in the White House only about six months when Welsh became apprehensive about his administration's handling of the Indian school system. Welsh had left the October 1893 Mohonk Conference in company with the superintendents of the Chilocco and Haskell boarding schools. From them he learned that they were facing staff reductions as an economy measure, as well as new barriers to their recruitment of pupils from the reservations. The superintendents of the several off-reservation boarding schools normally were in competition for the reservation youth. Now the government began to restrict their recruiting to certain regions, and to require that they have the consent of both the agent and the parents before removing a child. In practice the superintendents always had needed the cooperation of the local agent for their recruitment. He had ways of putting pressure on parents reluctant to send their children away for periods up to five years, denial of rations being a favorite tactic. Welsh regarded this new requirement for parental consent as nullifying the compulsory education law.[1]

Convinced that the expansion and improvement of the government school system under Commissioner Thomas J. Morgan in the
previous administration was being undercut, Welsh decided to bring
the situation to the attention of people who might be of some assistance.
One letter went to Reverend Lyman Abbott of the *Christian Union,* with
copies to Reverend William Hayes Ward of *The Independent,* and Merrill
Gates of the Board of Indian Commissioners.[2] To Civil Service Commissioner Roosevelt and to Charles Painter, Welsh expressed not only
his fear of the new administration's education policy but the need to
rally Protestant support for the Morgan reforms to counteract growing
Catholic influence.[3] As a result of the decision by non-Catholic
churches to sever their educational ties with the federal government,
by 1893 only a few of their schools continued to participate in the
contract arrangement. Declining to follow their example, the Catholic
Church had added to its already major proportion of the funding
available for the contract schools. Although the system seemed to be
favoring the Catholics, there was a simple explanation for the attrac-
tiveness of the contract schools for the government. In 1893 it could
educate a child in a church-operated school for $86.66 a year, con-
trasted with an average cost of $116.29 in a government school.[4]

Early in 1893 Charles Painter expressed his unhappiness about
what he perceived to be the failure of the Catholics to spend much on
missionary work; instead, they preferred to proselyte through the
contract school system.[5] In the next several months Welsh would become more alarmed at the Catholic role in the Cleveland administration. Gradually he began to believe there was a Catholic conspiracy in
Washington working to counter the program Thomas J. Morgan had
initiated and which was now being so capably carried out by William N.
Hailmann, the newly appointed superintendent of Indian schools. The
cast of villains in the scenario included Assistant Commissioner Frank
C. Armstrong, former Chief Clerk John A. Gorman of the Indian
division of the secretary's office, and F. T. Palmer, a clerk in the Indian
Bureau—all Catholics. General Armstrong and Palmer were suspected of using their positions to favor their church in a variety of ways,
while Gorman did the same by testifying before congressional committees.

Seeking allies to counter the alleged Catholic menace, Welsh
turned to two of the nativist organizations so active in late nineteenth-
century America. In November 1893 he wrote James M. King, a
Methodist minister and the general secretary of the National League
for the Protection of American Institutions. The league had appeared
in New York in 1889 and was primarily concerned with public education. Unlike other nativist organizations, the National League drew its

membership from upper-class America.[6] Reverend King had been at the Lake Mohonk conferences in 1890 and 1892, and Welsh credited him with being largely responsible for the Protestant withdrawal from the contract system.[7] Reverend King indicated complete sympathy with the IRA's concern and suggested cooperation in dealing with Congress and the Interior Department.[8]

Welsh also shared with Reverend King correspondence he had had with Cardinal Gibbons. The cardinal had been quoted in the *Review of Reviews* for November 1893 to the effect that he wished never "to see the day when the church will invoke or receive Governmental aid." Welsh promptly wrote him that, while the contract system had done some good, it "is not in harmony with the American idea, which seems to me to look with disfavor upon such quasi-alliances between Church and State." Welsh then asked Cardinal Gibbons if, given his statement in *Review of Reviews*, he agreed with Welsh that the contract system should be abandoned.[9] The cardinal's response was that he did not regard the contract system as government aid to a church, a distinction Welsh was unable to detect.[10]

The other nativist group Welsh turned to, the Junior Order of United American Mechanics, was particularly strong in Pennsylvania. In 1894 Welsh actually joined this organization, whose members he described as "full of zeal and the spirit of organization, intensely Protestant and American in feeling." He saw in the group "a most hopeful channel for pressing right measures, if one can wisely suggest and formulate such measures to them."[11] Because of their opposition to sectarian schools, Welsh hoped to use them to build support for the government Indian schools and Superintendent Hailmann.

Despite his association with nativist organizations and his belief in the existence of a "grave crisis . . . in Indian affairs" stemming from "the conflict between the American public school idea . . . and the Roman idea," Welsh believed himself "as free from religious bigotry as any man could well be."[12] Like many Americans concerned with public education, he was genuinely alarmed at the rapid growth in the 1880s and 1890s of both the Catholic parochial school system and its share of government funds used to educate Indian youth. The large number of foreign-born priests and nuns instructing in the Catholic schools also was very disturbing to reformers who stressed assimilating Indians into American society. The question, as Welsh expressed it to Carl Schurz, was how "to help avert the evident design of the Roman Bureau, without bringing the matter to all the unfortunate complications of an open discussion where religious bigotry and bitterness will rage."[13] Specifically, he was worried by the reaction to Catholic expansion "which has taken form among ignorant and unscrupulous people in the dangerous follies of the A.P.A.," a reference to one of the most rabidly anti-Catholic groups, the American Protective Association.[14] Unlike the APA, which singled out Catholic schools as undesirable recipients of federal aid. Welsh maintained that he wanted only to ensure "exact fairness toward all religious bodies."[15]

Despite his protestations about his freedom from "religious bigotry or bias,"[16] Welsh did tend to see Catholic conspiracies where probably none existed, as was evident in the fight over continuing the position of superintendent of Indian schools in 1894. In April 1894 Secretary Hoke Smith requested the IRA's assitance in defeating a move in Congress to eliminate Superintendent Hailmann's position. Welsh responded that he could "act at once with vigor on the lines marked out in your letter."[17] A circular was hurriedly prepared and sent out, and the executive committee drafted a petition and dispatched it to the House Indian Committee. A letter from Welsh to the *New York Times* on the subject was published, as well as an editorial in the same issue. The New York *Evening Post* carried a story by Francis Luepp, and the material from both newspapers was reproduced and also circulated.[18] Finally, Welsh sent letters to a number of people calculated to help inspire a groundswell of public opinion against the move to abolish the superintendent's position.

William S. Holman, chairman of the House Indian Committee, had been prompted by John Gorman to try to eliminate the position. As Hailmann was convinced that Gorman's fellow Catholics Armstrong and Palmer were conspiring against him, Welsh perhaps can be excused for his suspicions of a Catholic plot. Theodore Roosevelt, after a conference with Hailmann, also feared that "the Roman Catholic influence . . . is one of the most potent factors being used against him."[19] Roosevelt was sufficiently alarmed at the situation to wire Welsh, who was attending a National Municipal League meeting in New York, to "come at once." Welsh did hurry to Washington and saw Hailmann and Secretary Smith, as well as Roosevelt. He returned to Philadelphia reassured that Hoke Smith would stand by Hailmann and that the disloyal clerk, Palmer, would be discharged.[20]

The danger to Hailmann faded, although other problems relating to Indian education persisted. Until his defeat at the polls in November 1894, Representative Homan used his position as chairman of the House Indian committee to try to reduce government outlays for Indian education, and the IRA did what it could to oppose him.

A year and a half after Holman's forced retirement, the coalition working to sever the government ties to the church schools began to achieve results. In June 1896 Congress declared it to be government policy not to appropriate for sectarian schools unless non-sectarian schools were unable to do the job, in which case contracts up to only fifty percent of the 1895 level of support could be negotiated.[21] The stage was set for the phasing out of the contract relationship with the churches, and Welsh was pleased. He opposed any abrupt termination, however, as "exceedingly unjust to those who in good faith and at the call of the Government have entered into this work."[22]

In 1894 and again in 1896 economy-minded congressmen also considered withdrawing financial support from the Board of Indian Commissioners. The IRA was opposed not only on the grounds that lack of funds would cripple an agency making a valuable contribution, but also because it had a personal stake in the board.[23] As related in Chapter 11, early in 1894 Welsh had asked Hoke Smith to recommend Charles Painter to President Cleveland for appointment to the board, arguing that it would give Painter "a certain official authority in making investigations."[24] It also would help the IRA financially, as board members received traveling expenses, although no salaries. Probably because of Welsh's request, Painter received the appointment, joining on the board another association officer, President Philip Garrett, who had been a commissioner since 1890. Less than a year after Francis Leupp replaced Painter in the Washington office of the IRA, he also was appointed to the board. As Leupp remarked, the appointment would "give me increased opportunities for usefulness to the Association and save most of the expense of travel when I visit the reservations in the Association's behalf."[25] Given the overlap in membership and the fact that the two organizations actually shared office space in Washington during part of Charles Painter's tenure, it is not surprising that the Board of Indian Commissioners and the IRA frequently cooperated on Indian causes. Indeed, it was difficult at times to determine whether Painter and Leupp were acting as agents of the IRA or as members of the Board of Indian Commissioners. Funding was restored, and the IRA claimed credit.[26]

Two matters that engaged the association's attention in Cleveland's second term both related to broad policy, one being a proposal to permit tribes to enroll the children of Indian mothers and white fathers, and the other being a move to eliminate Indian agencies in Washington State. In the second case the IRA took a stand at odds with its general policy of speeding the end of the Indian's special relationship with the government. After having talked for years of the necessity of Indians' breaking from the tribal and reservation life, in the 1890s the eastern reformers faced the imminent dismantling of agencies and of the scrapping of the inhibiting and protective network of government regulations. The prospect was daunting for both the Indians and the reformers.

A missionary had informed the association of an effort by Representative Holman to save money by eliminating several agencies in

Washington State. Welsh promptly wrote Indian Commissioner Daniel Browning, who responded that he had testified before the House committee against the proposed abolition of the agencies and hoped that the IRA would use its influence to oppose the move.[27] Welsh made copies of the letters from the missionary and Browning and, together with a letter of his own, sent them to sixty people who might communicate with Representative Holman on the subject. Welsh himself wrote Holman stressing the need for a gradual transition in the Indian condition and warning against "any violent, or sweeping action in regard to this change."[28] This economy move, like the efforts to eliminate the office of superintendent of Indian schools and to drop the appropriation for the Board of Indian Commissioners, was successfully blocked.

The IRA enjoyed only a partial success in opposing legislation relating to the children of Indian mothers and white fathers. In January 1897 Francis Leupp warned Welsh that a bill similar to ones he and Painter had stopped in the past had slipped through the House as a rider on the appropriation bill.[29] The new measure would guarantee to the children of such marriages access to tribal property equal to that of other members of the tribe. Leupp suggested that Welsh inspire Indian petitions to the Senate against the legislation, and Welsh got off letters to Philip Deloria, Reuben Quick Bear, and Alexander Rencountre, as well as a number of missionaries and other whites who might be helpful in generating Indian petitions. Among those that came in was one from Pine Ridge signed by Red Cloud, No Water, Short Bull, and five other Oglalla Sioux.[30] Their objection to the proposed law was their belief that the children of squawmen already seemed to get more than their share of any issues to tribal members, as was usually the case on other reservations as well.

The IRA also put out a pamphlet entitled *Let There Be No Backward Step* and sent a letter to members of the Fifty-fourth Congress.[31] The association argued that the rider to the appropriation bill would slow assimilation and vitiate an 1888 law that had specified that Indian women marrying United States citizens would themselves become citizens. Moreover, the proposed legislation would open the door to a rash of claims on tribal property by earlier generations of children of mixed marriages. Despite the opposition, a modified version of the rider became law. The association found consolation in having helped make it less of a threat to "all the Indian tribes in the country that still possess anything worth a white man's stealing."[32]

The IRA's interest in blocking the legislation stemmed in part from its experience with the "Murphy Claims." For ten years the association had opposed efforts of the Murphy family, which had no blood connection with the Sac and Fox, to be admitted to the Sac and Fox reservation in Kansas. Back in 1890 Charles Painter had spent a month on that reservation monitoring a federal investigation of the issue. Both the tribe and the Indian Bureau had fought to keep the Murphys off Sac and Fox tribal rolls, but the claimants had kept their case alive through the cooperation of Kansas politicians. A similar alliance was at the heart of the "Old Settlers" attorneys' claims which engages the IRA's interest in 1896.

Two years earlier a congressional appropriation act had provided $800,000 to satisfy claims of western Cherokees (the Old Settlers) against the federal government. The 1894 law provided that up to thirty-five percent of this amount could be used to pay the fees of those who presumably assisted the Cherokees in prosecuting their case. The Indian Bureau rigorously examined the claims for services and finally allowed $86,000 less than the thirty-five percent the law permitted. The disappointed agents for the Cherokees launched an intensive lobbying campaign to be paid the $86,000 also. It was this "crazy medley of shams" that the IRA opposed.[33] It issued a circular, *On the Verge of a Scandal,* drafted by Francis Leupp, and he lobbied members of both houses.[34] Despite Leupp's activity the Senate passed the appropriation, leaving the House conference committee as the last chance to block the payments. There he was only able to have the final version of the bill written in such fashion so as to delay payment until a thorough examination of the claims could be made. The next Congress, after much discussion, split the disputed $86,000 evenly between the Indians and the attorneys. The IRA reported, "The Indians were robbed, but of only one-half the amount originally demanded."[35] Again, as in the Murphy Claims case, it had been demonstrated that unscrupulous white men could use the political process to pursue ends opposed by the Indian Bureau and friends of the Indian attempting to protect tribal interests.

The IRA's position on the claims cases was no surprise. Its stance on the advisability of the army's recruitment of Indians was somewhat unexpected, given the association's opposition to other forms of off-reservation employment, such as wild-west shows, regardless of how carefully supervised. As was so frequently the case with other issues, the IRA's interest in the army's short-lived experiment with recruiting Indians for regular units (as opposed to the widespread use of Indians as scouts) derived from the initiative of an Episcopal missionary. Reverend George Beecher wrote Welsh in the summer of 1893 to protest the pending disbandment of a company of Indian soldiers at a post in Nebraska.[36] On instructions from Welsh, who was vacationing, Matthew Sniffen sent copies of the letter to various newspapers, Commissioner Daniel Browning, and several army officers. Later, Welsh composed a letter of his own to protest the disbanding of the Indian units, and nearly 200 copies were distributed. He maintained that such service could contribute to their Americanization through "order, discipline, regular habits, cleanliness, proper food." It also, according to Welsh, would bring to bear on them "moral and religious influence," a claim that even a recruiting sergeant would blush to make.[37] To try to save this program, Welsh dispatched Charles Painter to the War Department. The Washington agent did discuss Indian recruitment with the adjutant general; however, that officer offered him no assurances.[38] The army had concluded that the experiment had not demonstrated the value of all-Indian units, and as a result they would be disbanded.

The four years of the second Cleveland term had seen significant changes in the IRA. It no longer ran as smoothly as when Charles Painter had handled the Washington end of its business and Herbert Welsh had given Indian affairs priority in ordering his own schedule. The association still spoke with authority, and secretaries of the interior, commissioners of Indian affairs, and members of congress were reluctant to risk its wrath. However, the machine now seemed to sputter, to run somewhat erratically. By 1896, issues were not being followed through with the old intensity. Leupp had other responsibilities, and he lacked the direction from Philadelphia he would have received a few years earlier. Welsh, though with less frequency, still could be moved to a paroxysm of letter-writing by an issue such as the threat to a valued administrator like William Hailmann. But it seemed that, as his time for Indian affairs diminished, he had difficulty ordering his priorities. Welsh still found himself drawn into projects of little import, such as trying to find a purchaser for an eagle captured by a young Sioux, or peddling a novel of dubious literary merit about the Indian Service.[39]

In terms of the IRA's influence in Washington, Cleveland's second term had provided unusual opportunities. Indian Commissioner Browning had been rather ineffectual, but he had never failed to at least hear the association's views. Secretary Hoke Smith had been the real power, and he had gone out of his way to be cooperative. It remained to be seen whether the association would do as well with the administration of William McKinley, whose election Welsh's *City and State* had supported.

CHAPTER FOURTEEN

Difficulties with the
Mckinley Administration

Even though the IRA suffered a gradual decline in operational efficiency and strength during the second Cleveland administration, it had
not been obvious as long as there was a president, a secretary of the
interior, and an Indian commissioner anxious to please. While William
Mckinley occupied the White House, he exhibited neither an interest
in Indian affairs nor a desire to humor the reformers, and it was
reflected in the attitudes of his two secretaries of the interior, particularly the first. Under these circumstances the decline in the quality of
leadership in the Philadelphia office and the disruption resulting from
another personnel change at the IRA Washington agency assumed
more significance.

Membership in the Philadelphia association dropped slightly to
just over 700. Coupled with the absence of any branch activity, by 1901
it meant the IRA's strength had dropped significantly in the decade of
the Nineties. This drop was reflected also in the receipt of dues and
contributions, which declined about a third between 1897 and 1901
compared to the period of 1893-1897. The original membership and
the ranks of the more liberal benefactors of the association were being
thinned by death.

Another explanation, of course, was Welsh's own unwillingness to
invest as much of his time in the association as he had during its first
decade. Fund-raising had been primarily his responsibility, both for
the IRA's general operations and for the numerous special funds for
association projects. Now he sometimes found himself too busy with
other matters to give fund-raising his personal attention. This was true

even of an appeal from Zuni country which was in the grip of a smallpox epidemic, a call for help Welsh passed on to the Washington agent to do with what he could.[1] He also was too busy to accept membership on a Lake Mohonk committee directed to prepare recommendations for improving the Indian Service. Philip Garrett headed this important group, whose seven members included General Whittlesey, Lyman Abbott, and William Hayes Ward. Despite Garrett's insistence, Welsh refused, pleading "the pressure of other duties" and citing specifically *City and State*.[2]

Welsh did make one trip to the Indian Country in these four years, but it was to the Sioux reservations, with which he already was quite familiar. And this trip appears to have been undertaken principally for the benefit of his daughter Dorothy who, together with one of her friends, accompanied him. Welsh might better have invested the time in acquainting himself with the Five Civilized Tribes or those of the Pacific Northwest, both major Indian groups with which he had had no personal contact.

It was not that Welsh was taking it easier. He was a workaholic and never seemed to completely relax. When at Sunapee in the summer he kept up an active correspondence, and when he went abroad he prepared travel letters for publication in *City and State*. His one diversion was painting, which he usually did only at Sunapee. As he chided an acquaintance who was planning to retire from all public projects, "While we live we ought to work," and he quoted the Prince of Orange's motto, "Rest Elsewhere."[3]

There was no apparent improvement in Welsh's family life. Fanny never accompanied him on his business trips, not even to the Mohonk conferences, which never failed to attract a large quota of wives. She was not in good health, although well enough for European travel. Some idea of their relationship is to be found in a letter he wrote her from the office informing her that he had invited Francis Leupp to their home.[4] It is indicative that he thought it necessary to identify Leupp, who at the time had been the IRA's Washington agent for nearly two years. Such a situation could have been either the cause, or the result, of Welsh's extraordinary commitment.

"My greatest care and concern now is the paper 'City and State', although Indian affairs still occupy me very closely," Welsh wrote in April 1897.[5] Being editor and publisher of a newspaper was ideal for him, as it gave Welsh a platform from which to pronounce on local, national, and even international issues. In the columns of *City and State* he criticized President McKinley for not exhausting all diplomatic openings before going to war with Spain in 1898. Nevertheless, the paper did not actively oppose the prosecution of the war and had its own military hero, Theodore Roosevelt. Even before Roosevelt had seen combat, *City and State* was suggesting that he replace the incompetent secretary of war.[6] After TR's participation in a minor skirmish the paper lauded his "cool bravery and reckless dash" in a story that reviewed Roosevelt's achievements as a public official in Washington and New York.[7]

City and State took a strong stand against United States's annexation of the Philippines and was a harsh critic of the conduct of the campaign against the Filipino guerrillas. As early as July 1898, in a column headed "East American Indians," it predicted a repetition with the Filipinos of our shameful experience with the Indians:

> Such a history runs a well defined course. First comes the intrusion of the individual American, who is usually of the lawless class, and who, under any circumstances, believes that the savage has no rights which he is bound to respect. Then comes resistance and conflict; then the military are called in to suppress the savage for doing what nearly all men do under like circumstances. While this process is going on and while the immoral members of the white race are contaminating the native race with whisky and diseases sprung from vice, the moral members are trying to apply the balm of just treatment and education.[8]

On another occasion Welsh suggested that the United States provide justice for the Chippewas, whose timber resources were being plundered, before taking on responsibility for additional "millions of depressed peoples,"[9] and *City and State* predicted the need soon for a "Philippine Rights Association."[10]

This tack proved to be an expensive one for *City and State*. A number of people cancelled their subscriptions, among them one of Welsh's oldest friends and supporters, Charles Pancoast. But Welsh was armored by a sense of his own rectitude:

> I shall have no regrets for the course pursued. I never was more firmly convinced of anything than that our protest has been justified by the facts, and that the policy pursued by the Administration was essentially in opposition to fundamental American principles, and to the Christian idea.[11]

The IRA clearly suffered by Herbert Welsh's identification with the anti-imperialist movement, which did not enjoy a broad base of popular support. Indeed, he was accused of contributing to the death toll of Americans in the Philippines.[12] Nevertheless, he persisted, serving on the executive committee of a local chapter of the Anti-Imperialist League and authoring a book entitled *The Other Man's Country,* which argued against the annexation of the Philippines.

Despite the agreement in 1895 that *City and State* would assume a portion of the IRA's office costs, questions continued to be raised about the diversion of association resources to *City and State* work, not to mention other Welsh projects. In 1901 a memorandum was prepared, probably by Matthew Sniffen, to answer such critics.[13] It described the financial arrangements between the paper and the association and argued unconvincingly that, principally as a result of the Indian items which appeared in *City and State*, the association actually had the better of the deal.

But *City and State* was just the IRA's principal competitor for Herbert Welsh's attention. He also continued to be active in the National Civil Service Reform League, whose meetings occasionally took him out of Philadelphia. Despite defeats suffered in the political arena, Welsh never gave up hope of converting Pennsylvanians to good government. To this end he devoted much time in 1898 to managing a futile gubernatorial campaign for an independent candidate. Not discouraged, Welsh undertook to assist the Honest Government Committee to save Pennsylvanians from themselves. This organization also would be headquartered in the offices of the association and draw upon its staff's resources. The solution in this case was to hire another clerk, and it became the responsibility of Matthew Sniffen to coordinate the operations of the IRA, *City and State,* the Honest Government Committee, and whatever other good causes in which Welsh became involved.[14]

That his reform efforts were seldom successful did not daunt Herbert Welsh. He explained it as a matter of faith:

> it is the confidence of a certain faith in the Spiritual Power which either guides the world to better things or, in moments of relapse, is a sure witness of its unrighteousness. Of both the nature and the authority of this Divine Law I feel that I have definite knowledge and conviction. We who so feel can afford, while laboring, to wait.[15]

As the United States become more active on the world stage, Welsh was drawn into work in behalf of international arbitration as well as the Anti-Imperialist League. That other friends of the Indian shared in this impulse was manifested by A. K. Smiley's decision to host a conference on international arbitration at Lake Mohonk in June 1900. Welsh attended that gathering, although he was unable to make the Indian conference there in October of the same year.

At the same time that Welsh was being drawn by his restless conscience into international causes, he somehow found time and energy to concern himself with the race issue in the South. As he explained it, "For several years past I have felt a kind of call to take a more practical interest in work for the colored people."[16] What triggered his concern was news of lynchings in the South, a call at his office by the founder of a school for blacks in Alabama, and a chance visit to the campus of Washington and Lee University in Lexington, Virginia. These events led him to embark upon his most ambitious fund-raising drive.

William Benson was a young black who, with the aid of his father, a former slave, had launched a Negro school at Kowaliga, Alabama. More than a year after Benson had seen him in Philadelphia, Welsh decided to visit Kowaliga, and, if possible, Tuskegee Institute. Welsh was personally acquainted with Tuskegee's founder, Booker T. Washington, whom he regarded as the "greatest and safest leader of the negro race" and "the Armstrong idea reincarnated."[17] Such a statement was one of the finest compliments that Welsh, a great admirer of General S. C. Armstrong, could pay a man.

Welsh did visit Kowaliga and lauded the school and its founder in letters to potential supporters and in the columns of *City and State*. However, his original idea of trying to support a struggling Negro school was expanded into a less conventional attack upon what he called "the terrible black problem."[18] This was a bold plan to raise $100,000 for Washington and Lee on the theory that not only did Hampton, Tuskegee, and Kowaliga need help, but so did white colleges like Washington and Lee. As Welsh put it in a letter to Bishop Whipple: "In proportion to the number of educated men in the South, whose minds are not only developed and equipped but whose moral nature is opened to the knowledge of how God can elevate the lowest order of human beings, will be our success in working for the blacks."[19]

That Washington and Lee among all the struggling southern colleges would be the beneficiary of his fund-raising was due to Welsh's having visited friends in Lexington, Virginia, the home of the college. While there in April 1900 he had been invited to address the students on the Philippine issue. The occasion led to a meeting with the chairman of the physical science department who unburdened himself to the northern visitor about the inadequacies of the college's laboratory equipment. It was time well invested. Welsh's active mind linked the "black problem" with the need to educate a new generation of white leaders. Moreover, he was impressed by the reaction of Washington and Lee's faculty to his views of civil-service reform and the need for industrial education on the Hampton-Tuskegee pattern for the South's blacks. A new Welsh project was taking shape.[20]

That Welsh was driving himself too hard became apparent in February 1901. After what was first diagnosed as strain from a fall, and then as appendicitis, he was reported by Sniffen to be "very weak physically and mentally,"[21] and then finally as suffering from "nervous prostration."[22] Although Sniffen kept him abreast of IRA business, it was three months before Welsh again appeared regularly at the office.

In this trying period Matthew Sniffen emerged as more than the chief clerk for the association. He now was responsible for coordinating Welsh's involvement in his various causes. In earlier years Sniffen had simply transmitted Welsh's directives—"Mr. Welsh desires," "Mr. Welsh requests." Now Sniffen was beginning to give the directions himself. A benchmark in his evolution from clerical to managerial status was Welsh's proposal in March 1901 that Sniffen go to Washington to confer with the Indian commissioner on some urgent association business.[23]

Welsh also was more inclined now to delegate tasks to President Garrett. Garrett does not seem to have resented a system in which the corresponding secretary rather than the president was the real head. Even when making committee appointments Garrett deferred to Welsh's judgment. This paradox attracted the attention of others, among them Captain Pratt, who once revealed that an association president had related ruefully that Welsh had scheduled an IRA meeting without even consulting him. But now that Welsh was prepared to relinquish some of his control, there was no rush to take it off his hands. No one had ever been ready to invest as much time in the association as Herbert Welsh.

As the Philadelphia office became less active, and an examination of its letter books reveals a marked decline in correspondence, the Washington office was left to carry a greater burden. Unfortunately Francis Leupp still had other commitments, principally to the New York *Evening Post*. The contacts he had built up in the government during his years as a reporter did make him valuable to the IRA and it was with real regret that Welsh learned in late 1897 that Leupp was being pressured by his paper to give up some of his outside activities.

Leupp was willing to give most of his time to the IRA by severing his relationship with the *Evening Post*—if the association substantially increased his salary.[24] Apparently Welsh was unable to agree to such a plan, and he and Leupp began to discuss possible successors. Leupp suggested a Kansan, S. M. Brosius, an old friend of Charles Painter and someone who had been active in matters relating to Indian reservations in Kansas and Iowa.[25] Welsh allowed Leupp to take the lead in this matter because he was busy trying to organize a fellow reformer's campaign for the governorship of Pennsylvania. Leupp envisioned his being on the IRA payroll until the fall of 1898, while meanwhile grooming Brosius, who would be a part-time employee.[26]

The transition occurred more quickly than Leupp had expected. After being reassured by a letter from Brosius's pastor and a visit to

Samuel M. Brosius
Courtesy Historical Society of Pennsylvania

Philadelphia by the candidate himself, Welsh presented his name to the executive committee, which authorized its corresponding secretary to negotiate the employment of a new agent.[27] The result was that Brosius came on the payroll full-time on May 1, 1898, and Leupp went off in June. Leupp did extend himself to help Brosius learn his new job, but he must have been miffed at what turned out to be a rather abrupt transition. It seems to have occurred in this fashion because Welsh was giving so relatively little attention to association business. Back in January, when Leupp's departure was still in the discussion stage, Welsh had been in Washington on civil-service reform business and had been too busy to see the association's Washington agent. Nevertheless, it was an amicable parting. In the next few years Leupp assisted the IRA on several occasions, and once Welsh stayed with the Leupps when he was in Washington.

Some measure of the relative worth of Leupp and Brosius in Welsh's eyes can be seen in their IRA salaries. Leupp had been paid $2,000 a year for what was really part-time employment. Welsh insisted that Brosius, for $1,800 a year, "give his entire thought and time to the work" and not "have any other business or obligations which would seriously distract his mind . . . or lessen his strength in regard to it."[28]

What the IRA got was a man without the stature of Painter or Leupp and without their contacts and experience in Washington. Leupp had felt a little out of his depth in Welsh's Philadelphia social circles, as evidenced by his not knowing the proper attire for evening wear. The veteran journalist, however, was a sophisticate compared with the man from White Cloud, Kansas. Brosius was aware also of his limitations as a public speaker and writer, but he left nothing to be desired in his energy and dedication to his job. Although he did not have Leupp's personality or his influential contacts such as Theodore Roosevelt, Brosius traveled widely in the West as the IRA's agent and quickly developed a familiarity with conditions on many reservations. He may not have been as effective as Leupp or Painter in the capitol's committee rooms, but he was even more energetic than Painter in uncovering scandal and corruption on the reservations. A Quaker, he had clearly defined moral standards and within two years of assuming the position had filed charges against a number of government employees.

Neither Brosius nor Leupp had much success in working with McKinley's secretaries of the interior, nor did Herbert Welsh. Reading in a newspaper in March 1897 that the appointment was being offered to Cornelius N. Bliss of New York, Welsh immediately dashed off a letter to him expressing the hope that Bliss would accept the position and referring to the "deepest gratification of many friends of the Indian" at the prospect.[29] It did not take Welsh long to regret his enthusiasm for the appointment. Francis Leupp reported Bliss "curt and rather disagreeable," and General Whittlesey, although secretary of the Board of Indian Commissioners, had difficulty getting an audience with Bliss.[30] After being in office less than four months, the secretary asked for Leupp's resignation from the Board of Indian Commissioners. Bliss explained it in terms of the need to make a place for a specialist in agriculture.[31] Leupp and Welsh were convinced that it was because Bliss resented a critical article by Leupp that had appeared in the *Evening Post* and which labeled the new administration very political in its handling of the Indian Service. To Welsh, Leupp described Bliss as a "bitter disappointment."[32]

Welsh responded by taking Secretary Bliss to task in *City and State* for removing Leupp from the board, and in the 1897 annual report of the association the administration was belabored for its political partisanship. In the following year, conditions did not improve as far as the association was concerned. In a most unusual exercise of authority, Secretary Bliss prevented a speech by Leupp from appearing in the Mohonk Conference proceedings, which were published as part of the annual report of the Board of Indian Commissioners.[33] Leupp concluded that the situation had deteriorated to the point that his favoring a course of action was enough to make Bliss oppose it, and vice versa. He hoped that Brosius would do better with the secretary.

Brosius, unfortunately, had no better success with Cornelius Bliss. He found the secretary "most unapproachable" and unwilling to accept any suggestions relative to the conduct of the Indian work.[34] The association's 1898 annual report spoke of its disappointment with President McKinley's and Secretary Bliss's reversion to home rule as a way of selecting Indian agents. The report expressed particular disappointment with the removal of William Hailmann as the head of the Indian school system and reprinted criticism of the administration included in the report of the 1898 Mohonk Conference. Secretary Bliss's response to the tone of the Mohonk Conference proceedings was to refuse to permit them to appear in the report of the Board of Indian Commissioners on the grounds that they were not government business.[35] It was with some relief that Brosius and Welsh heard in December 1898 that Secretary Bliss was leaving the cabinet.

Welsh had hopes for Ethan Allen Hitchcock because the new secretary was the brother of Henry Hitchcock, an enthusiastic civil-service reformer.[36] Armed with a letter of introduction from the brother and accompanied by the secretary of the National Civil Service Reform League, Welsh finally got an interview with Secretary Hitchcock in April. It did not go well, Welsh describing the secretary as being "in a state of bubbling irritation."[37] Hitchcock strongly objected to any suggestion that the Indian division of his office was obstructive and demanded to know the source of Welsh's information on this subject. He also was upset at the prospect of Brosius's visiting the Crow Reservation, where the agent was under investigation. Welsh concluded that despite the secretary's asperity there was hope that he would be an improvement over Bliss. Welsh was therefore somewhat taken aback when Hitchcock refused to provide him a letter of introduction for Welsh's visit to the Sioux agencies in the spring of 1899.[38] Such letters previously had been routinely granted and helped ensure a friendly reception from those reservation officials with whom Welsh was unacquainted.

With the passage of time Secretary Hitchcock did mellow, and meanwhile Welsh took some consolation in William A. Jones's performance as commissioner of Indian affairs. Jones's background in business and Wisconsin politics hardly qualified him to be Indian commissioner. He made no secret on taking office of his relative ignorance of the Native American. Several months later he declined to speak to the annual meeting of the IRA on the grounds that "I do not think there is a member of the Association but that knows a great deal more about Indian affairs than I do. . . ."[39] Nevertheless, Leupp, Brosius, and Welsh all became his supporters. In part it was because his willingness to listen to their advice about the Indian Service was such a welcome change from the chilly receptions they received from Cornelius Bliss and Ethan Allen Hitchcock. There also was an engaging modesty about Jones. Because of a preoccupation with other than Indian causes and the general lack of communication with the McKinley administration, Welsh had had not direct contact with Jones until December 1898. Then the commissioner showed up without warning at the association's annual meeting. Welsh first became aware of his presence when Jones rose and good-naturedly responded to some of the biting comments about the administration which Welsh had just made. In the dialogue that followed, however, Jones admitted to the validity of several of Welsh's points.[40]

It was the beginning of a mutually beneficial relationship. Jones later confessed to having been originally persuaded that IRA people were "well-meaning, but meddlesome people, impracticable in their ideas, and somewhat visionary." He now was willing to recognize that they might be closer to the mark than those "who are disposed to make sport of them, and to discredit their suggestions."[41] Jones claimed to have completely revised his previously held opinion that Welsh was "somewhat of an iconoclast or an Esau."[42] Later that year, when Secretary Hitchcock refused to give Welsh a letter of introduction, Commissioner Jones provided him with one calculated to impress any member of the Indian Service:

I know of no one who has done more toward purifying and elevating the Indian Service than Mr. Welsh, and moreover his labor has been without the hope or expectation of either political or financial recognition, but from a philanthropic and high minded sense of duty.[43]

In taking a stance so different from that of his administrative superior, Jones ran some risks. When Secretary Hitchcock learned of remarks the Indian commissioner had made at the IRA meeting, he called Jones in and persuaded him to write a letter to Welsh in which Jones maintained that he and the secretary did not differ significantly on civil-service reform.[44]

Had Welsh had his choice he would have preferred being on good terms with the secretary of the interior, as that was where the power lay. Welsh had told Jones to his face during their exchange in Philadelphia in December 1898 that as commissioner of Indian affairs he was essentially a clerk, the important decisions being made in the Indian division of the secretary's office. Welsh's position was, as it had been since the days of Commissioner Thomas J. Morgan, that the Indian Bureau should be removed from the Deparment of the Interior and its head report directly to the president.

With neither President McKinley nor his secretary of the interior very receptive to suggestions from friends of the Indian, the IRA won few personnel battles in this administration. Before the appointment of William Jones to be Indian commissioner in 1897, Welsh proposed to the president and the secretary two other names for that position— Theodore Roosevelt and Samuel B. Capen.[45] The latter was a member of the Boston Indian Citizenship Committee and a businessman with reformist impulses. In a letter to Leupp, Welsh, whose own name was being mentioned, had listed Leupp himself as one of four people he was considering backing for the job, the others being Capen, N. Dubois Miller of the IRA, and Roosevelt. Welsh said he would not take the job if it were offered him and spoke of Roosevelt most enthusiastically:

He has every qualification for a first-class Commissioner. His rigid integrity, his fearlessness, his sound judgment in all the details of administration, his hold upon the public, his knowledge of the subject, would make him, perhaps, the most valuable man in the country.[46]

When instead Roosevelt was appointed assistant secretary of the navy, *City and State* spoke warmly of "his manliness, his indefatigable energy, his sweetness of temper, his perfect simplicity of character, and his keen, practical good sense." Its only qualification to the paean of praise was a reference to Roosevelt's being "somewhat of a jingo by disposition and his utterances on foreign policy are not always wise, or at least wholly to our liking."[47]

Theodore Roosevelt was just one of many people to whom Welsh had turned for aid in his fight to save Superintendent of Indian Schools William Hailmann. As usual the IRA was trying to persuade the incoming administration to continue in office competent appointees of the previous president. Described as "unquestionably the ablest educator ever connected with the Indian service," Hailmann was singled out for particular support in a campaign that went on for a year and a half.[48] The IRA began, within a week of McKinley's election, contacting newspaper editors and others who might be helpful. What made this fight particularly awkward was Welsh's conviction that Captain Pratt was making unusual efforts to turn the new administration against Hailmann. Pratt clearly did not like the superintendent and blamed him for trying to implement the civil-service system, which interfered with Pratt's control of Carlisle personnel. Pratt published in the school's paper what *City and State* described as a "virulent and largely unveracious" attack on the IRA, Welsh, and Dr. Hailmann, and mailed copies of this issue of *The Red Man* to members of Congress and others.[49] Welsh responded in kind, and the IRA produced a pamphlet entitled *The Importance of Retaining Dr. Hailmann, Superintendent of Indian Schools, and the Attack Made Upon Him and the Indian Rights Association by Captain Pratt.*[50] Welsh confided to Roosevelt, "I believe myself that Pratt's mind is unbalanced."[51]

In its campaign to save Hailmann's job the IRA was not alone. The WNIA and the Board of Indian Commissioners also petitioned the administration in his behalf. Theodore Roosevelt assured Welsh he was using his influence on Secretary Bliss, but he was no help with McKinley, finding it "almost impossible to see the President."[52] Welsh also used Roosevelt's name in soliciting Senator Henry Cabot Lodge's help for the cause.

After more than a year of this campaign Welsh concluded that he had invested about all the time he could in trying to save Hailmann's job. As he explained it, "The work of the paper is becoming more and more exacting and absorbing."[53] However, Welsh found it difficult to extricate the association from the battle. When he learned that James McLaughlin, the former agent and now inspector operating out of the secretary's office, was going to speak to Archbishop Ireland for Hailmann, Welsh decided to approach Cardinal Gibbons. His letter to the cardinal not only stressed Hailmann's sterling qualities, but also that a possible successor was backed by Captain Pratt. In case it should have escaped the prelate's attention, Welsh reminded him that Pratt had "lost no opportunity to attack in the most virulent and unseemly manner . . . alike the Roman Catholic Church and its members, the Indian Rights Association, the Civil Service Reform . . . and his own superior, Dr. Hailmann."[54] The cardinal responded that he could endorse any letter Archbishop Ireland might write for Hailmann and did so.[55] Welsh published the archbishop's letter in *City and State,* and the paper carried a petition in Hailmann's behalf signed by, among others, Booker T. Washington, J. Pierpont Morgan, and the presidents of Harvard, Johns Hopkins, and the University of Wisconsin.[56]

The administration was not persuaded by the campaign in Hailmann's behalf, although it may have stayed the axe for a few months. In January 1898 Commissioner Jones informed the superintendent that Secretary Bliss wished him to resign. Hailmann, on learning that Jones did not agree with the secretary, decided not to resign but rather wait to be pushed out. By June it was apparent that it would not be long. One candidate to replace him, Estelle Reel, had even approached the IRA for support and had revealed that the job was slated to go to someone from Wyoming or Nebraska.[57] A last-minute appeal was rushed into print, *Answers to Charges Made Against Wm. N. Hailmann,* but within a week Miss Reel's name had been submitted to the Senate for confirmation.[58] Welsh promptly wrote her: "I heard yesterday with the deepest regret of Dr. Hailmann's removal . . . but learned with pleasure that you had been appointed to succeed him"[59] *City and State* accused Secretary Bliss of a "violation of the merit system" while noting that Miss Reel had had a good record as state superintendent of Wyoming schools. Appointing a woman to the federal position, however, "is an experiment, and we trust results will justify its wisdom."[60]

Welsh must have been flattered by Miss Reel's seeking his support and assuring him that "it will be my earnest endeavor to fulfill the duties of the office in a manner acceptable to you and your organization."[61] Nevertheless, before the year was out he was describing her as a politician and a "transparent humbug."[62] Two years later Welsh was warning Brosius to be on his guard against her. Probably recalling her approach to him, Welsh said Reel's tactic was to "come forward boldly, place herself among those whom she has reason to fear may be her opponents and to win them over by her bland ways. . . ."[63] This was one experiment in women's rights which had gone wrong, at least in Welsh's judgment.

The IRA enjoyed only limited success in influencing other McKinley administration personnel decisions. Brosius took more of an interest in personnel than had Leupp and had virtually a free hand from the Philadelphia office as to whom he campaigned for or against.

He filed charges with the department against several Indian Service officials, including an Osage agent and the head of the secretary's own Indian division, making no friends in the bureaucracy in the process. One agent whose conduct was endorsed by Brosius and the association was army officer Captain George W. H. Stouch.

Captain Stouch came to the attention of the association when he was shifted from the Northern Cheyenne Reservation at Tongue River, where he had done excellent work, to the Crow Reservation. Brosius received word from an army chaplain that the move was made to make room at the Northern Cheyenne agency for a political friend of a Montana senator. The new appointee was accused by the chaplain of bringing back unsavory characters whom Captain Stouch had ousted from the reservation and being controlled by a cattle company trespassing on Indian land. Secretary Bliss insisted, however, that the change had come at least partly at Captain Stouch's request and that he was needed to bring some order to a messy situation at the Crow agency.[64] Subsequently the IRA did take credit for getting Stouch assigned to the Cheyenne-Arapahoe agency, which had had a scandal-ridden administration.

A particular Brosius target in the McKinley administration was William J. Pollock, Osage agent, whom Brosius once described as "the most corrupt agent of recent years I truly believe."[65] Pollock's specialty was profitable collusion with cattlemen who leased pasture on the Osage Reservation. The Osages were quoted as being so desperate to rid themselves of the agent that they were willing to pay him $2,000 a year if he would just retire from government service.[66] Pollock had powerful political connections, and, when Inspector McLaughlin brought sufficient evidence against him to lead to a request for his resignation, the agent rallied his congressional supporters and forced the department to reconsider. Brosius then decided to personally investigate complaints and included the Osages in his itinerary for a western trip in the late summer of 1899. He came back to Washington with enough evidence to file charges against Pollock, and the association's executive committee voted $350 to pay expenses of witnesses brought to Washington to testify against the agent.[67] This tactic produced results. Another inspector was sent to the Osage agency, and a senator became interested in the case. Finally, Pollock was prevailed upon to resign. By that time he probably had more than recouped the $85,000 he claimed to have invested in the position. As Pollock had put it so well, "I am not here for my health. . . ."[68]

Another Brosius achievement late in McKinley's first term was helping bring about the resignation of E. E. White, author of *Experiences of a Special Indian Agent,* and head of the Indian division of the secretary's office, a key position in Indian affairs. White, Brosius believed, was shaking down attorneys who were handling Indian claims.[69] He also was suspected of using his access to Secretary Hitchcock to turn the secretary against the IRA. Brosius brought charges against White relating to his dealings with the attorneys, and early in 1900 Secretary Hitchcock forced his resignation. Brosius took credit for his ouster.[70]

Brosius had an opportunity to bring pressure to bear against other undesirable Indian Service personnel through a special committee of the National Civil Service Reform League. Under the leadership of William Dudley Foulke, a friend of Theodore Roosevelt, the committee was looking at all government agencies in the spring of 1901. In the absence of Welsh because of illness, Sniffen could only send Foulke some newspaper clippings relating to two agents who needed to be removed, but he directed Brosius to make contact with the committee. Brosius did so and wrote up three cases in considerable detail for Foulke and his colleagues. One of them was that of the Tulé River agent in California. The man owned a drugstore which sold liquor to Indians, and he maintained the agency office in the same building. Brosius submitted a photograph to document the proximity of the two activities.[71] The IRA would claim that the National Civil Service Reform League's report on the spoils system in the Indian service "was based almost wholly on information furnished by the Association."[72]

The IRA approved one administration solution for troublesome agents—abolish their positions and transfer their responsibilities to the superintendent of the agency's school. The advantage of this move was that school superintendents were covered by civil service. Such a change also contributed to the illusion that the Indian Service was in the process of dissolution. There were still those who thought that the time had arrived for it to wither away, and both the Board of Indian Commissioners and those attending the Lake Mohonk Conference were paying lip service to the idea. By contrast Herbert Welsh continued to argue for the necessity for the time being of an Indian Bureau to protect the Indians: "left without the protection of the Government for a very considerable space of time, their enemies would destroy them in very short order."[73]

Welsh, however, was part of the consensus among reformers in the late 1890s that the time had come to gradually eliminate the issue of rations to reservation populations. The sentiment was expressed freely in discussion and in the form of resolutions and recommendations at the winter conferences sponsored by the Board of Indian Commissioners and the fall get-togethers under the auspices of A. K. Smiley at Lake Mohonk. In January 1899 Herbert Welsh wrote Commissioner Jones about the need to reduce rations and cited Bishop Hare and a missionary on the Cheyenne and Arapahoe Reservation to reinforce his contention.[74] Later that year Reverend Aaron Clark, Episcopal missionary at Rosebud, where Welsh had visited on his spring tour of the Sioux reservations, advised Welsh of the need to abolish the ration system, which Clark said was a "needless crutch" and "favors the ignoble spirit of the professional beggar."[75] Merrill Gates of the Board of Indian Commissioners then asked Welsh for IRA assistance in stopping "needless rations" at agencies which were contributing to the "pauperization of Indians."[76] This sentiment was echoed in the association's 1899 annual report, which also called for the end of the "pauperizing condition of dependence."[77]

Commissioner of Indian Affairs William Jones already had begun in 1898 to reduce the level of ration support. Most reservation occupants never had been issued rations, although those Plains tribes covered by the treaties negotiated by the Peace Commission in 1867 and 1868 had been promised them for varying periods of time. In practice this promise had meant that most Plains Indians received some rations throughout the thirty-year period for which the government had committed itself to compensation for land acquired. With the exception of the Plains Sioux, those commitments were lapsing in 1897 and 1898. The Sioux claim on rations stemmed also from the terms of the coerced purchase of the Black Hills in 1876. The government had promised rations until the Indians involved were capable of self-support.

Despite the popularity of the theory of throwing the Native Americans on their own resources, Commissioner Jones quickly found himself in trouble when he tried to implement it. The war with Spain required the sharp reduction of army strength in the West. As experienced a man as Inspector James McLaughlin thought that perhaps this was not the time to reduce rations for these former warriors.[78] Jones complicated his task by presenting an administrative reform in the procedures for disposing of the hides of cattle killed for the meat portion of the ration. Previously these hides had been issued to the Indians, who used a few to make moccasins and other leather articles and sold the rest to agency traders, earning about $18,000 a year for the Rosebud Sioux alone.[79] Told that the traders frequently did not pay the Indians full value for the hides, Jones ordered that the hides be sold to the highest bidder on a yearly contract, the proceeds utimately to be divided among the tribesmen. This cut off a source of leather to the Indians as well as a steady income. Now they would have to wait up to a year to see any hide money.

Because of Welsh's contacts among the Sioux (and on this topic he heard not only from Episcopal missionaries, but from a Jesuit priest and an agency trader, also), he was most concerned about the impact of ration reduction on those Indians.[80] In the first three years of the new program Welsh was in a dilemma. In theory he subscribed to the idea that rations should be eliminated; however, reports from the Sioux reservations spoke of the suffering that was entailed. There also was a growing recognition of the fact that these reservations could only with difficulty sustain their Indian populations. Brosius, who visited Standing Rock in 1900, informed Welsh of the utter failure of crops that year because of drought. The Washington agent did not expect Indians unskilled in agriculture and stockraising to survive in an area that would not support an experienced white farmer. Brosius finally concluded that a partial answer was to relax the restrictions on their movements and permit them to seek employment off the reservation.[81] Others, however, thought the answer lay in building up Indian herds, which was impossible as long as the Sioux found it necessary to kill breeding stock to avoid starving.

Welsh, who had been urging farming on the Sioux for nearly twenty years, continued to support the idea of ration reduction but warned against implementing it "too suddenly and vigorously."[82] He was reluctant to be critical of Commissioner Jones on the issue because of the commissioner's excellent record in other respects. Jones himself believed that Welsh was receiving exaggerated reports of conditions among the Sioux. He insisted that the truly needy were being cared for and he was stopping rations only for squawmen, mixed-bloods, and others who either were not tribal members or were capable of self-support. The commissioner even offerd to make a special trip to Philadelphia to brief the IRA's corresponding secretary on the subject.[83] That visit never took place, possibly because the offer coincided with the beginning of Welsh's illness in February 1901.

Equally difficult for Welsh, and more embarrassing, was the action which the association found necessary to take against the Educational Home in Philadelphia. Since 1883 this boarding school, the boys' division of Lincoln Institution, had accepted Indians for a training program presumably comparable to that of Carlisle and Hampton. The head of Lincoln Institution was Mary McHenry Cox, who had joined Welsh in the periodic battles with congressmen determined to reduce appropriations for eastern boarding schools. Further complications were that Lincoln Institution had ties with Welsh's own church, and Episcopal Bishop O. W. Whitaker was not only the nominal head of the Educational Home but vice-president of the IRA.

The nasty affair dragged on for three years, beginning early in 1897 when a member of the home's board came to Welsh with stories of cruelty to students. The IRA informed Dr. Hailmann of the charges but did not press the matter at that time.[84] Welsh obviously was reluctant to tangle with Mrs. Cox, who had a fearsome reputation. He once described her as having an "extraordinary combination of undesirable qualities," but also "power of will and such vigor that General [S. C.] Armstrong used to say it was utterly impossible for any man to oppose her successfully."[85] It also would be awkward to press charges against an individual with whom he had been allied so often in the past.

Nearly two years after the abuses had been brought to Welsh's attention, the IRA finally created a committee to investigate the school. Ten weeks later the group was ready to report, and, meanwhile, Matthew Sniffen had visited the home on his own and had seen his young Indian guide physically assaulted by the superintendent, a former Philadelphia police chief. Such direct methods were traditional at the Educational Home, one of whose earlier superintendents had specialized in flogging, explained as a carryover from his days in the British navy, from which he had been dismissed. In its troubled history the school had been investigated by a state board and by the Society for the Prevention of Cruelty to Children.[86]

The committee's report charged not only that students were physically abused but that they were not getting the industrial training promised. Copies of the document were sent in February 1899 to local papers and the congressional Indian committees. Unfortunately its impact was nullified by a telegram from Bishop Whitaker to the conference committee considering the appropriation for the Educational Home. The bishop endorsed Mrs. Cox's operation, and the committee members, claiming to be confused by the contradiction of an IRA report by its own vice-president, voted the appropriation.[87]

Welsh's reaction was to blame Mrs. Cox, whose "powers of persuasion, coercion, and mystification of the truth are such that it is a very difficult thing to contend with her."[88] If he had had any doubt of these powers, she made him a believer by threatening the IRA with legal action. But Welsh was not one to back down, and he had his own weapons, as well as friends in high places. *City and State* was read in the homes of hundreds of influential Philadelphians, and it carried several articles on the scandalous conditions at the school. Earlier Welsh had briefed Commissioner of Indian Affairs Jones on the Educational Home's problems, and in the summer of 1899 Brosius persuaded Jones to send a school inspector. After being thoroughly briefed on arrival by Sniffen, the inspector spent three weeks in Philadelphia. The report of his investigation upheld all that the IRA had said, and Mrs. Cox recognized that it was futile to continue the fight. In October 1899, nearly three years after Welsh first brought the matter to the attention of Dr. Hailmann, she decided not to apply for government funding for the next fiscal year.[89]

The McKinley years had not been good ones for the association in terms of its relations with the administration or its internal operations. Circumstances had forced it to lead a campaign to close a local institution which in earlier times it had fought to sustain. The change of Washington agents from Leupp to Brosius had been more disruptive than it might have been had Herbert Welsh not been so involved with other projects, particularly *City and State*. That paper's controversial stand on the Spanish-American War and imperialism, because of the phenomenon of guilt by association, damaged the standing of Herbert Welsh with some whose help was needed for the IRA's work. Despite these problems, however, the association continued to do valuable work in behalf of many tribes in the period 1897–1901.

CHAPTER FIFTEEN

A Potpourri of
Tribal Problems

Most of the tribal causes assumed by the IRA in the McKinley years related to land and natural resources. The association now found itself most frequently aiding Indians attempting to hold on to what they had. However, in at least two instances, those of the Osages of Oklahoma and the Senecas of New York, the IRA advocated allotment in severalty, which usually resulted in transfers of land from Indians to whites.

The courts were the principal arena for association efforts in behalf of the Cupeño Indians on the Warner Ranch in California. Since Charles Painter's visit with the dying Helen Hunt Jackson in 1885, the IRA had had a considerable interest in the Mission Indians, of whom the Cupeños of Warner Ranch were a part. The association had made the major financial contribution which enabled the Soboba band to win a landmark land case, and in 1891 Painter had spent most of the year as a member of a government commission trying to find homes for Mission Indians.

Throughout this period the plight of the Cupeños on Warner Ranch was unresolved. There was clear evidence that they had resided in the area throughout the period of Mexican occupation and thus should have been protected by the Treaty of Guadalupe Hidalgo, by which the United States pledged to recognize Mexican and Indian claims in California. Inexplicably, the Cupeños had not come forward to register their claims with the commission created by Congress in 1851. By the mid-1890s the Harvey Estate, which by now held title to Warner Ranch, had brought two suits in a San Diego County court to eject the Cupeños as trespassers. About 300 Indians were involved,

many of them settled around what was described as the finest mineral
spring in southern California. These Cupeños derived a living providing lodging and other services for visitors to the spring.

The ejectment suits were the beginning of a legal battle that went
on until 1901. The Harvey Estate won the first round in the San Diego
County court, presided over by a judge who rendered his verdict three
days before resigning from the bench to serve as legal counsel for the
estate. At that point the IRA was contacted for financial assistance for
an appeal to the California Supreme Court. The association was asked
specifically to provide bond which would permit the Cupeños to remain on Warner Ranch until the appeal had been adjudicated. The
bond would cover loss of income and damages the Warner Ranch
might suffer from Cupeño occupancy during the appeal period.[1]

When the matter was brought to the attention of Washington agent
Francis Leupp in April 1897, he discussed it with the attorney general,
who promised to contact federal officers in southern California to learn
what might be done.[2] However, there was no precedent for the government to provide bond in such cases. When Herbert Welsh returned
in June from a brief trip to Europe, he was told that the executive
committee already had voted to provide the $300 then thought
sufficient to get a surety company to put up a $2,000 bond. But instead
the bond was set at $6,100, and $4,000 of it was required in cash; in
Welsh's judgment, "we would not be justified in imperilling our
finances to that amount." However, he continued, "It also would seem
clear that a very grave wrong is about to be inflicted."[3] The attorney for
the Cupeños was the same one, Shirley Ward, whom the IRA had
helped pay to defend the Soboba band in 1885. Ward was confident
that this case was winnable, too, as he believed the legal principles to be
in most instances identical. The attorney also predicted that the association's loss should the appeal fail would not exceed $3,000, although it
was possible it would be liable for the entire $6,100.[4]

With only a few days left in which to file an appeal, the association
was faced with the necessity for a quick decision. At its first meeting on
the subject the executive committee could not act, having only three
members present. The following day five appeared, providing the
necessary quorum, and the committee voted the $4,000 cash required
by the surety company. W. W. Frazier, a wealthy member of the association, and Herbert Welsh each agreed to pledge $1,050 to make up the
total $6,100. It was understood that the association would promptly
launch a drive to secure donations by individuals to cover the possible
loss, but meanwhile the association, Frazier, and Welsh would be liable.[5] Within a matter of days half of the $6,100 bond had been
guaranteed by friends of the association in Boston, and the entire sum

was soon covered by cash or pledges, freeing the IRA, Frazier, and Welsh of their liability. Welsh described the decision to provide the bond as "a hard one to handle in so short a time, and I was also much occupied with other matters."[6] Nevertheless he and the executive committee were convinced that "we ought not to desert the Indians in so serious a crisis . . . even if we should be temporarily crippled thereby."[7]

Argument before the California Supreme Court did not take place until October 1898, and the decision was handed down a year later. In the interim, S. M. Brosius, who meanwhile had replaced Leupp as Washington agent, had discussed with the Justice Department the possibility of an appeal to the U.S. Supreme Court if the decision was against the Cupeños. As soon as the California court's judgment in favor of the Harvey Estate was announced, Brosius approached the Justice Department again about supporting an appeal, and it agreed to work with Attorney Ward.[8]

It was thought that a new bond would be necessary to prevent the ejection of the Cupeños from Warner Ranch while the United States Supreme Court considered the issue. This time Brosius worked with Father Stephan of the Bureau of Catholic Missions in Washington to arrange the bond. West Coast Catholics had been staunch supporters of the Mission Indians, and the Bishop of California had asked the Catholic Bureau for assistance. Mother Katharine Drexel, the Philadelphia heiress who was the founder and first Superior General of the Sisters of the Blessed Sacrament for Indians and Colored People, also took a hand and agreed to provide the bond in case the Catholic Bureau was unable to arrange it otherwise. As it developed, the court agreed to accept the old bond underwritten by the IRA, and a new one did not need to be negotiated. Nevertheless, it was an interesting example of cooperation by the association with the Catholic agency it had opposed so often.[9]

Another year and a half elapsed before the case was finally disposed of by the U.S. Supreme Court. In a decision handed down in May 1901 it ruled for the Harvey Estate. The Indians faced eviction and the IRA the loss of the bond, or at least the $5,800 the estate claimed the legal proceedings had cost it in income and damages. This sum the IRA held to be excessive, and another trial was held in San Diego, which resulted in the estate's damages being limited to $2,918.05. Meanwhile the administration had decided to assume responsibility for seeking new homes for the Cupeños and went to Congress for an appropriation of $100,000, of which $30,000 would be used to maintain the Indians during the relocation and the other $60,000 would be used to buy land. Indian Commissioner Jones also agreed to support an amendment, which early in 1903 Brosius managed to have attached to an appropriation bill, to reimburse the surety company and indirectly the IRA for the $2,918.05. Congress appropriated both for the purchase of land for the Cupeños and for reimbursement of the surety company. The association was able to return about forty percent of the sums the guarantors had provided six years earlier. The IRA had no hand in the final disposition of the Cupeños, who, until troops were brought in, resisted removal to their new homes on a 3,000-acre tract.[10]

The IRA's role in the legal problems of the Kiowas, Comanches, and Kiowa-Apaches of Oklahoma was less expensive, but of even greater significance, given the Supreme Court's decision in *Lone Wolf v. Hitchcock,* for which the association helped set the stage. As discussed in Chapter 12, the IRA had assisted in blocking early ratification of the agreement negotiated with those Indians in 1892 for the opening of their reservation. In 1898 another serious effort was underway to push the bill through the Fifty-sixth Congress. Brosius had become interested in the Kiowa, Comanche, and Kiowa-Apache Reservation because of a problem facing a Presbyterian missionary there and had prepared a circular which the association distributed to members of the Senate and others. In the publication Brosius argued for increasing the size of each allotment from 160 to 480 acres on the grounds that very little of the reservation was good for anything except grazing and that allotments of at least 480 acres were necessary to make the Indians self-sufficient.[11] In another circular, mailed out in February 1899, Brosius insisted that the agreement had not had the approval of the required three-fourths of the adult male Indians, and the 160-acre allotments were insufficient: "If the proposed legislation be enacted into law, the . . . Indians will naturally become paupers, and be thrown upon the United States for support."[12] In a covering letter to the editors Welsh referred to Cuba, the Philippines, and Puerto Rico and issued a warning:

> It is clear, also, that if upon the very verge of a colonial policy we make stronger the precedent we have established of dealing with the Indians unjustly, and so as to make vagrants and paupers of them, we shall increase the chances that our management of outside dependent peoples will be conducted in the same unhappy way.[13]

To strengthen the case against the agreement, Brosius invited a delegation from the reservation to come to Washington to lobby. he also solicited from residents of the area statements about the climate and the quality of the soil in the hope that they would convince congressmen of the need for 480-acre allotments. Early in March he was able to report to Welsh that the bill to ratify the original agreement had failed to pass.[14]

But there were powerful forces seeking to impose allotment on the Kiowas, Comanches, and Kiowa-Apaches. The Rock Island Railroad, which ran across the reservation, wanted as much land as possible opened to white settlement. As a result it resisted allotting more than 160 acres to an Indian. The deal finally struck in the Fifty-sixth Congress was the usual compromise. The allotments were limited to 160 acres, but a 480,000-acre pasture was set aside to be held in common for the three tribes, adding about another 160 acres per Indian.[15] The price the government would pay for the land declared surplus after every tribesman had been allotted was increased from $1.5 million to $2 million. In June 1900 the agreement in that form was finally ratified by both chambers, and Brosius defended it as "quite good," although it included new provisions for which Indian approval was not even sought.[16]

The battle was not over. Led by Lone Wolf, a Kiowa, a few members of the three tribes tried recourse to the courts to block the implementation of the agreement. To represent them, they employed William M. Springer, the ex-congressman who also had served as a federal judge in Indian Territory. In June 1901 Springer sought help from the IRA in delaying the opening of the surplus land to white settlement.[17] Welsh's initial reaction was to throw the association's support behind Springer's effort to get an order from the Supreme Court of the District of Columbia to prevent the secretary of the interior from opening the land to white settlement. When Sniffen turned to Francis Leupp for some publicity for the cause, the newspaperman warned the association to move slowly. Leupp suggested that Springer's word could not be depended upon and that the attorney was probably primarily motivated by the possibility of a $5,000 fee. Leupp also said that only small factions among the three tribes backed Lone Wolf, whose efforts were being subsidized by Texas cattlemen.[18] These ranchers had their own selfish reasons for wishing to delay settlement as long as possible, as it would end their access to millions of acres of cheap pasture. The agent for the Kiowas, Comanches, and Kiowa-Apaches had convinced most of the chiefs that it was not in their interest to further oppose the implementation of the agreement. All of this information served to cool the enthusiasm of Welsh and Sniffen for supporting Springer, but Brosius pressed on.

When the District of Columbia court ruled against Lone Wolf, Brosius urged the executive committee to support an appeal to the U.S. Supreme Court. He argued that, if the decision stood, very little land held by tribes would be safe from arbitrary action by Congress. The members of the executive committee were sufficiently impressed to appropriate $400 to help Attorney Springer appeal the decision. To assist Springer in presenting the case, the association also committed itself to pay for the services of a distinguished member of the Philadelphia bar, Hampton L. Carson.[19] This was the same man who had shared with Herbert Welsh the University of Pennsylvania's declamation prize for the class of '71 and had been present at the meeting in John Welsh's home which led to the founding of the IRA.

The Lone Wolf appeal was a difficult experience for the IRA. In attorney fees and court costs it drained the association of about $700 and necessitated another special fund-raising effort.[20] It also put the IRA at odds with the agent for the Kiowas, Comanches, and Kiowa-Apaches, retired Lieutenant Colonel James F. Randlett. The colonel was recognized as an able administrator who had been able to assert his authority on the reservation despite tribal factionalism and pressure from traders, ranchers, squawmen, and other special-interest groups. Lone Wolf and his supporters were lumped by Randlett with the non-progressives, who opposed his efforts to settle the Indians on their own allotments and make them self-sufficient as quickly as possible.[21]

Brosius was aware that, as he phrased it, "Lone Wolf and his followers do not represent the better element of the tribe."[22] Nevertheless, he maintained that there was a principle at stake which required the association to ally itself with dubious elements of the three tribes. Brosius even went so far as to pass on to a United States senator charges of corruption made by the Lone Wolf group against Randlett, an agent who was a model of integrity. When the senator, on the basis of these charges, demanded an investigation of agency affairs, Colonel Randlett was understandably furious. In his annual report published in late 1902 he denounced the IRA as "the allies of grafting attorneys, who seem bent upon robbing the Indians."[23] In a letter to Welsh after the Supreme Court had ruled on the case, the colonel accused Brosius of being a liar and a hypocrite and blamed the association for retarding the advancement of the Indians of his agency.[24]

The Supreme Court's decision in *Lone Wolf v. Hitchcock* was announced in January 1903. Despite what was believed to have been an excellent presentation by Hampton Carson, the justices dealt the Indians and their supporters a crushing blow. The court saw no merit in Lone Wolf's contention that the government had violated the treaty provision requiring the consent of three-fourths of the adult male Indians to land cessions. The justices held that Congress had "plenary authority over the tribal relations of the Indians" which enabled it to abrogate any treaty and exercise complete power over tribal property.[25] The association's 1903 annual report summed it up succinctly:

"It is now distinctly understood that Congress has a right to do as it pleases; that it is under no obligation to respect any treaty, for the Indians have no rights which command respect."[26] Welsh and Brosius must have had second thoughts about supporting a legal action which could produce such a sweeping declaration of government power over tribes. Writing in 1912, however, Matthew Sniffen could see merit in a decision which, "while at first startling to the friends of the red man, will probably do more toward breaking up the tribal relations and developing the Indian in his individual capacity than any other result."[27]

The Warner Ranch and Lone Wolf litigations were both defeats for the IRA, but it won with Spotted Hawk and Little Whirlwind, although it took four years. The two Northern Cheyennes were residents of the Tongue River Reservation in Montana when convicted in a Custer County court of the murder of a white sheepherder. Spotted Hawk was sentenced to be hanged and, in a separate trial, his brother Little Whirlwind received life imprisonment. A third Indian, David Stanley, testified against the other two and was sentenced to ten years in the state penitentiary.

In November 1897 George Bird Grinnell had written Welsh to ask the IRA's help in saving Spotted Hawk, who was scheduled to die the following January.[28] Grinnell knew the family well and was convinced, as was Tongue River agent Captain Stouch, that the young Cheyenne was innocent. Although "overwhelmed with all sorts of work," Welsh immediately launched the association on a campaign to save Spotted Hawk.[29] Among those whom he wrote was Secretary Bliss. Leupp, despite cool relations, also called on the secretary and discussed the problem with people in the Indian Bureau.

In what seemed to be a response totally out of character, Bliss agreed to join with the IRA in providing $500 to finance an appeal for Spotted Hawk. Welsh applauded the secretary's action as "very generous and noble"; it was one of the very few occasions the two were in harmony on an issue.[30] Having Bliss's commitment, Welsh then took the matter up with the executive committee, which voted $250 to help in the appeal.[31] With the case of the Cheyenne River policemen as a precedent, Leupp believed it would be possible for the IRA to eventually be reimbursed by Congress; to facilitate this plan he suggested that the financial side be handled by the Episcopal Bishop of Montana, Leigh Richmond Brewer. Bishop Brewer was contacted and agreed to be the local sponsor for the appeal effort, and Welsh set to work to raise the money.[32]

A stay of execution was granted the Cheyenne while the appeal process was in motion. In the summer of 1898 Brosius visited the Tongue River Reservation and obtained affividavits strengthening

Spotted Hawk's case. One of them was by Lame Woman, David Stanley's wife, who testified that her husband had admitted to her his sole guilt.[33] Unfortunately, C. H. Loud, who had presided at the original proceeding, refused to grant a new trial.

To involve the public in the appeal process the IRA published a pamphlet entitled, *A Review of the Spotted Hawk Case*.[34] Among the documents it included was a letter to Welsh from the novelist Hamlin Garland, who had witnessed what he considered the "malevolently eager" efforts of a Custer County official to incriminate as many Cheyennes as possible during the investigation.[35] When a Philadelphia lawyer protested the impropriety of the IRA's circulating the publication while the case was still under judicial scrutiny, Welsh pled the seriousness of the situation. A human life was at stake, he argued, and he informed the lawyer that Spotted Hawk had been tried in an atmosphere of "intense and unreasoning prejudice."[36]

In the weeks that followed, the association agreed to underwrite an appeal to the Montana Supreme Court for a new trial. It was granted in January 1899 and, as had been expected, the local authorities chose to drop the charges, and Spotted Hawk, after being in the shadow of the gallows, was a free man. Even before the charges had been dropped, Welsh had authorized attorneys to seek a pardon for the brother, Little Whirlwind. Informing a friend of the association of the action taken, he lamented, "We are constantly harrowed by these awful examples of injustice."[37]

Little Whirlwind's case dragged on for another year and a half. The logic that, if the Montana Supreme Court was prepared to free Spotted Hawk, Little Whirlwind—who was convicted under identical circumstances—should also go free was lost on Judge Loud, who had originally sentenced them. Brosius spoke to him in behalf of Little Whirlwind when the IRA agent visited Miles City in the spring of 1899, but the judge flatly refused to cooperate. Indeed, he maintained that both of the brothers should have been hanged.[38] Governor Robert Burns Smith was equally adamant, despite a deathbed confession by Stanley, and there appeared to be no alternative to waiting until Governor Smith left office and then hoping that his successor might prove more amenable.[39]

To intensify the pressure for a pardon, Welsh turned to old allies—the Board of Indian Commissioners, the WNIA, and the Boston friends of the Indian. All responded, and the governor who was elected in November 1900, Joseph K. Toole, received a considerable amount of mail early in his administration. Welsh's *City and State* helped keep up the flow of letters to Governor Toole by references to Little Whirlwind as "An Indian Dreyfus." *City and State* carried an editorial suggesting that the French might well accuse Americans of hypocrisy for "the hue and cry against France for the iniquity" of the conviction of the Jewish army officer, while we were inflicting an equal injustice on a Cheyenne.[40] In another issue the paper, again using the Dreyfus analogy, stated that this "monstrous miscarriage of justice" was allowed to go on so long only because the victim was an Indian, and it invited readers to write Governor Toole.[41] On June 1 the governor recommended a pardon, and Montana's board promptly complied. Little Whirlwind was finally free after an unjust imprisonment prolonged at least a year and a half by racial prejudice and local Montana politics.

In his letter to the pardon board, Governor Toole did not mention the role of the Indian Rights Association in mobilizing support for Little Whirlwind. Nevertheless, it was well known even in Montana that the IRA had been the principal mover in seeking relief for both Little Whirlwind and Spotted Hawk. George Grinnell and Captain Stouch had sounded the alarm, but it was the eastern friends of the Indian, mobilized by the association, who had saved one Cheyenne's life and drastically shortened the penitentiary term of another.

The defense of the two brothers cost the IRA more than a thousand dollars. In addition it raised nearly $150, at George Grinnell's suggestion, to help Little Whirlwind acquire a few cattle when he emerged from prison.[42] While not a large herd, the cattle probably were more useful to an ex-convict than the copies of *City and State* that Welsh had sent Spotted Hawk after his release.[43]

On a smaller scale the IRA also got involved in the legal problems of the Navajos. The association was relatively well informed about conditions on the Navajo Reservation because it received reports outside official channels. They were from the acting agent, Major Constant Williams, as well as from missionaries, a Miss Thachera (who was trying to launch a hospital), and the previously mentioned Mrs. Eldredge. The two ladies had been the beneficiaries of small sums Herbert Welsh encouraged groups and individuals to contribute.

In 1897 Francis Leupp learned from Agent Williams, who was visiting Washington, of harrassment of Navajos by Arizona's Coconino County officials. About sixteen Indian families had been permitted by agency officials to take their flocks of sheep to some public land adjoining the Navajo Reservation. Unfortunately, there were whites who wished to reserve that public land for their own stock, and they conspired with county officials to expel the Navajos. The tactic was to dispatch a sheriff's posse from Flagstaff to collect in cash a tax on the sheep of the Indians. Unable to pay, they and their flocks were stampeded out of the area by members of the posse firing their rifles and pistols. Although no Indians lost their lives, their lamb crop was wiped out and some ewes were lost when the posse chased the fleeing Indians across the Little Colorado River.[44]

Leupp took the matter up with the Justice Department, and the IRA published a pamphlet he wrote entitled, *"Civilzation's" Lesson to "Barbarism."*[45] In it Leupp proposed that the government support the Indians in a civil action to collect damages and, failing that effort, dispatch troops to escort the Navajos back to the area from which they had been driven. But nothing was done on either count, as whatever interest the federal government had had in pushing the matter evaporated when the district attorney and the governor of Arizona Territory both insisted that the Navajos had suffered no losses. Nor did the association pursue the issue further, although in 1900 it did help provide legal counsel for three Navajos indicted on charges growing out of another clash between Coconino County law officers and Navajos, in which one white man and two Indians were killed. Two of the Navajos were tried and acquitted, and the third, a man in his seventies, had the charges against him dropped after he traveled 180 miles, despite wounds and a torrid sun, to keep his trial date.[46]

Legal action also was a major factor in coping with continued efforts by whites to restrict Indian landholding. As a result of his trips into the field, S. M. Brosius had become convinced that "one of the valuable lines of our work is to secure for all Indians a home, before the ever advancing white man controls all the available lands." On his swing through the Southwest in the summer of 1900, Brosius observed firsthand the problems occasioned by "vicious Mexicans" squatting on the land of Laguna Pueblo, and "unscrupulous Mormons" crowding Navajos from portions of the public domain adjoining their reservation.[47] When he reached the Pimas in the Salt River Valley, he found a situation so serious that he interrupted his trip and hurried back to Washington to bring the matter to the attention of the Indian Bureau and the Land Office.

What Brosius had discovered was that about one hundred Pimas, who for twenty-eight years had been living on two sections of public land near their reservation, had been driven from their farms by whites who then filed homestead claims on the valuable tracts. The Pima agent was suspected of having a personal interest in seeing the Indians vacate the land; certainly he was recommending that the Pimas be forced to return to the reservation. Moreover, when Brosius arrived on the scene, the Indians were so discouraged that they were ready to comply, although it meant abandoning the homes and farms they had occupied for a quarter century. What Brosius did on his return to Washington was to present the Pimas' case to the Indian Bureau and the Land Office. He referred the land commissioner to an act of Congress of February

28, 1891, which amended the Dawes Severalty Act and permitted Indians entitled to allotments to take them on otherwise unappropriated public land.[48]

Brosius's initiative helped set in motion a train of events benefiting the Pimas. He was able to persuade the Indian division of the Interior Department to send an inspector, whose report could be used to counteract the agent's recommendation. Brosius also convinced the department of the need to nullify the settlers' claims to the disputed land, arguing that it already was legally occupied. In his 1901 annual report, Indian Commissioner Jones referred to the action he had taken to protect the Pimas after the problem had been brought to his attention. He did not credit the IRA with alerting him to the problem; however, the association, in its own annual report for that year, summarized the case and referred to a letter received from the Pimas expressing their appreciation for the association's assistance.[49]

While he was working to secure allotments from the public domain for the Pimas, Brosius also lobbied public officials in behalf of other Indians on public land. They included some Pueblos, about fifty Navajo families on the Little Colorado River, and Flatheads in Montana, of whose plight he had learned from George Bird Grinnell. As the government curtailed its issues of annuities and rations, Brosius observed, it became imperative to see that the Native Americans were located on land to which they would have a clear title. This was particularly true of the Navajos situated on a reservation "little but a dry, and sandy desert," which could not be expected to support that nations's growing population.[50]

The Delaware landholdings in Indian Territory certainly could not be classified as desert. Nevertheless, they were troubled by complicated lease relationships, as Brosius learned in 1899. Richard C. Adams, a young Delaware, had sought the help of the association on a problem involving mineral leases and the Cherokee-Delaware connection.[51] Back in 1866 the Cherokees had sold 157,600 acres of their reservation to the Delawares and, for an additional payment, had given the Delawares citizenship status and equal access to all Cherokee property and funds. In 1899 the Delawares discovered that certain Cherokees had obtained the mineral rights from the Cherokee Nation to more than 200,000 acres of land, much of it occupied by incorporated Delawares, and had then leased the rights to oil companies for $1 an acre. When Richard Adams turned to the association for help, the only recourse for the Delawares was to try to persuade the Interior Department to invalidate the leases. To prepare the way for this solution, Brosius put together a statement for release to the press, on the IRA's principle that an aroused public might generate enough heat to ensure justice for the

Delawares. *City and State* of course carried Brosius's article, but he also was able to get stories in the Philadelphia *Evening Bulletin,* the *Springfield Republican,* and the *Washington Post.* Possibly because of the publicity the association gave the issue, the secretary of the interior did refuse to approve the mineral leases.[52] However, the oil company which held the leases refused to give up the fight and employed to represent it the former chairman of the Senate Indian committee. Then this issue was submerged in the larger question of Delaware rights and privileges in the Cherokee Nation, which was undergoing dissolution by the terms of the Curtis Act of 1898. The IRA took no active role in this fight beyond expressing a general sympathy with Richard Adams and his fellow Delawares.[53]

During the same time period that the association was attempting to aid the Delawares with their land problems, Herbert Welsh helped initiate another effort to force allotment in severalty on the Senecas. It came about indirectly as a result of the role of the IRA in closing the Educational Home in Philadelphia. The demise of the Educational Home was good news to Welsh; however, it had produced one complication. Over the years the enrollment for the home had come largely from New York tribes, and Welsh was concerned that now these Indians would have difficulty finding room in other government-supported boarding schools. What began as a concern for education of New York Indians resulted in a committee report calling for the breakup of most of the reservations in the state.

In February 1900 Welsh wrote Theodore Roosevelt, now governor of New York, suggesting that the state, "being so rich and containing such tremendous forces of civilization," should assume the burden.[54] The governor replied promptly, proposing to appoint a committee to prepare a report which then would be helpful in persuading the legislature to appropriate for Indian education. Roosevelt revealed his distrust of the practicality of the eastern friends of the Indian by asking Welsh for suggestions of "thoroughly rational sensible people" who might serve on such a committee. The governor confessed to having felt ill at ease about New York's Indian population throughout his administration, "simply because it seems to me that the State has absolutely neglected its duty to them for over a century."[55]

Welsh's only initial suggestion for membership on Roosevelt's committee was Philip Garrett, the IRA's president, who during the second Cleveland administration had tried to negotiate allotment in severalty for the Senecas. Not until December 1900 did Roosevelt, who had been preoccupied by his campaign for the vice-presidency, finally get a committee together headed by Garrett. Roosevelt had asked Welsh also to serve, but the Philadelphian had obviously been reluctant to accept the appointment, and Roosevelt dropped him from consideration in December on the grounds that he needed another New Yorker on the committee.[56]

Meanwhile the thrust of the investigation had shifted from education to allotment in severalty. Shortly after he had originally written Roosevelt, Welsh had directed Brosius to discuss the problems of the New York Indians with Indian Commissioner Jones, who took the opportunity to put forth the case for allotment.[57] This aspect of the matter was communicated to Roosevelt, whose charge to the committee reflected the new emphasis. Now, as he told Welsh, he wanted a report on steps to be taken to make the Indians of New York citizens "as speedily as possible," given "the undesirability of continuing the reservation system with its attendant inevitable demoralization."[58]

As Philip Garrett would be the committee's chairman and was already committed to allotment for the Senecas, the recommendation of the committee was a foregone conclusion. *City and State* later reported that Garrett "is strongly of the opinion that these Indians are almost, if not quite, as fit for citizenship and self-support as the average white farmer around them, and many are extremely shrewd."[59] In December 1900 the committee proposed after a cursory investigation that, where possible, jurisdiction over the Indians be transferred from the State of New York to the federal government and that the Dawes Severalty Act then be applied to them "in order that they may be admitted to the full rights of American citizenship."[60] Although Roosevelt was leaving Albany to become vice-president, the committee's report would help lay the groundwork for further unsuccessful efforts to break up the reservations of the Seneca Nation. Welsh's interest in Indian education had borne unexpected fruit.

Far to the west of the Senecas, in the Grand Canyon of the Colorado, the Havasupais also were having land problems. They were confined to a very small reservation, and the association hoped to enable them to get access to public land which adjoined their own holdings. What was interesting in this case was the gap between expressions of concern and actual performance. The IRA's annual report for 1901 carried an account almost eight pages long of the problems of this people, an unusually large allotment of space for any issue before the association.[61] It is even more remarkable when it becomes apparent that the Havasupai problems generated very little association action beyond one letter by President Garrett to the secretary of the interior and some exploration of their plight by Brosius. Given the horrendous number and range of problems facing American Indians in 1901, it is not strange that the IRA was able to give much attention to only a few. What is curious is that it would devote so much space in its annual report to an issue in which it had not been deeply involved. At least that part of the report suggests that it was padded to cover up the relative inactivity of the Philadelphia office.

It was the Washington agents who did most to help the Chippewas in their never-ending troubles over their timber resources. In the late 1880s Charles Painter and J. B. Harrison both had visited Chippewa reservations, and Painter had worked to get legislation enacted to consolidate those in Minnesota. The law to accomplish this consolidation was the Nelson Act, named after its sponsor, Minnesota's Senator Knute Nelson, but known officially as "An act for the relief and civilization of the Chippewa Indians in the State of Minnesota" (25 Stat. 642). A decade after its enactment the provisions of the Nelson Act providing for the appraisal and sale of timber came under sharp attack from the association.

It took the deaths of an army officer, six soldiers, and one Indian policeman in October 1898 to focus attention on the plight of the Chippewas. The casualties resulted when members of the Pillager Band of Chippewas fired on soldiers and policemen attempting to help deputy marshals arrest Indians involved in whiskey violations. A year later Commissioner of Indian Affairs William Jones explained the attack by reference to a corrupt law enforcement system and Indian resentment of the way their timber was being stolen.[62]

Within a week of the bloodshed, eastern friends of the Indian, gathered at Lake Mohonk for their annual conference, received a full account of Chippewa conditions from J. A. Gilfillan, a missionary with twenty-five years experience among those Indians. One of his audience was Herbert Welsh, who took the occasion to blame the spoils system for the "fraud and trickery" that had driven the Pillagers to resist and who recommended getting the essential facts before the public.[63] S. M. Brosius also spoke to the issue, and in November he was dispatched by Welsh to Minnesota to learn firsthand of the Chippewa problems. While Brosius was gone, Welsh received a letter from George Davis, an educated Chippewa, who persuaded him to launch a campaign in behalf of the Chippewas even before Brosius returned.[64]

A flurry of letters on the Chippewa situation left the Philadelphia office in late November and early December 1898. Welsh wrote Secretary Bliss directly and tried to arouse others to bring pressure to bear through their representatives in Congress. *City and State* carried several stories on the Chippewas, usually in connection with its editorial policy of opposing annexation of the Philippines. In one issue the paper called upon the American people to demonstrate that they were "capable of redressing the gross wrongs which we are to-day inflicting on our own aboriginal people," citing the Chippewa example, before taking on the Filipinos.[65]

The picture that was emerging was indeed a shabby one. When the commissioners had treated with the Chippewas in 1899, they had estimated that the Indians owned timber worth up to $50 million, and that it could be managed so as to ensure all Chippewas a comfortable living.[66] Ten years later most of these Indians were living in poverty while their timber was vanishing at an alarming rate. From Minnesota, Brosius reported that he and Inspector Cyrus Beede, an elderly Quaker with much Indian Service experience, agreed that they had never seen comparable exploitation of Indians. According to Brosius these Indians, who held title to some of the best pine in the United States, had no lumber to build houses and were reduced to using old packing boxes to make coffins for their dead.[67]

The looting of the Chippewas was being accomplished by manipulation of two laws, the Nelson Act and the Dead Timber Act. The Nelson Act had provided for a three-man commission to supervise the development of Chippewa timber resources, and for the employment of appraisers to evaluate the timber tracts to be offered for sale, all at Chippewa expense. A corps of appraisers was hired by the Harrison administration, only to have them replaced by another group when the Democrats came to power in 1893. The second group contained few individuals with any competence for the job; indeed, it was said that some had never seen a pine tree before. Drinking and playing cards occupied most of their time, and their appraising had little relevance to the actual value of the pine being offered for sale. The performance of this crew was so bad that much of their work had to be redone by still another corps of appraisers, again at the expense of the Chippewas. One estimate was that the work of the first two groups of appraisers had cost the Chippewas $350,000 and was worth only about $6,000. Meanwhile, the lumber companies, among them Weyerhauser, were snapping up drastically undervalued tracts and leaving the Indians in possession of those appraised accurately or at an inflated figure.[68] Between the wasted salaries and the bargain-basement prices the lumbermen were paying for first-rate pine, the Chippewas were losing literally millions of dollars.

The way timber was being disposed of under the Dead Timber Act also was scandalous, much green timber being cut and ridiculously low prices being paid.[69] The small lumber companies were most active in this, making contracts with Indians who would put together logging crews and deliver the timber to the mill. The contracts usually went to mixed-bloods, excluding the more numerous full-bloods from one of the few avenues of employment open to Chippewas. However, even the mixed-bloods had difficulty holding their own with the mill owners, and Brosius had knowledge of some who were grossly defrauded by whites more sophisticated in business practices.[70] Moreover, all Chippewas suffered because they were supposed to share on a per capita basis in a percentage of the selling price of timber, whether green or down and dead, and it was rare indeed if the purchaser paid a fair price for Indian timber.

There was no doubt in Brosius's mind that "gigantic frauds" were being perpetrated; the question was what action the association could take to remedy the situation.[71] His strategy was to join forces with a Chippewa delegation, which arrived in Washington in January 1899, to try to repeal or at least amend the 1889 Nelson Act. It was very late in the congressional session to try to accomplish anything; however, with the aid of IRA-inspired petitions, which began to appear in senators' mail, plus impassioned testimony by Reverend Gilfillan, something was done. An amendment was added to the Indian Appropriation Act of March 1, 1899, providing for a thorough investigation of procedures for the sale of Chippewa timber and authorizing the secretary of the interior to, in the interim, suspend appraisal and sale of their pine. Brosius then prepared a petition for the Chippewa delegation to present to the secretary requesting that hereafter timber not be sold on a basis of appraised value but rather on a basis of the logs actually sent to the mill. The petition also asked that the Indians be given a large role in the logging and the manning of the sawmills.[72] Fortunately there now was a new secretary of the interior. Cornelius Bliss, who had stood by the Minnesota lumbermen, had been replaced by Ethan Allen Hitchcock, who was expected to be more concerned with protecting Indian property.

Secretary Hitchcock did put a temporary ban on the appraisal and sale of Chippewa timber, giving the investigators time to thoroughly examine the situation and Brosius an opportunity to consider a replacement for the Nelson Act. An inspector from the secretary's office and a special agent from the Indian Bureau were the investigative team, and they confirmed the charges originally made by Reverend Gilfillan. Fortunately they had arrived while the season's cut of down-and-dead timber was still in the woods. They found its value grossly underestimated and forced an additional payment of $55,000 to the tribal account.[73]

Brosius's solution to the corruption and mismanagement of the Chippewa resources was a bill which he wrote with the assistance of the Leech Lake agent, the inspector involved in the investigation, and members of the staff of the Indian Bureau and the secretary's office.[74]

The bill included most of the provisions of the petition which Brosius had prepared for the Chippewa delegation. The easy part was to draft the legislation. Brosius then had to find someone to introduce the bill. Congressman Charles Curtis of Kansas, himself an Indian, agreed to perform that chore in February 1900. However, Senator Nelson promptly let it be known that he would do what he could to see that no such bill cleared the Senate.[75] Nelson had introduced two bills of his own designed to reinstate the suspended methods of appraising and selling Chippewa timber, and to continue the commission which investigators concluded had already cost the Chippewas $266,000 in salaries. Brosius worked through Senator O. H. Pratt of Connecticut to block these bills while the Curtis proposal was bottled up in the House committee by a Minnesota congressman.[76]

An IRA circular was distributed asking editors to publicize the Chippewa situation and voters to write members of their congressional delegations, although not until June 27,1902, did new Chippewa timber legislation emerge from Congress.[77] The Morris Act, named after Representative Page Morris of Minnesota, followed the general approach Brosius had advocated. The price the Chippewas would receive for their timber would be based not on an appraisal of standing or down-and-dead timber but on an actual measurement of logs delivered to the mill. And provision was made for the secretary of the interior to have a voice in the location of new sawmills, with an eye to opening new employment opportunities for Chippewas. The Morris Act also transferred the responsibility for supervision of the operation from the commissioner of Indian affairs to the land commissioner. The result was not all that Brosius and the association had worked for, nor were the Chippewa timber resources yet completely safe from white raiders. Nevertheless, as the Leech Lake agent summed it up, "the Morris bill . . . if honestly administered will be a blessing to the Indians of this agency."[78] The association played a minimal role in the final legislative action. However, it could and did claim credit for aiding in the correction of some of the worst injustices to which the Chippewas had been subjected.

One more example will round out this effort to demonstrate the range of IRA activities in behalf of specific Indian groups in the McKinley years. This time it was the Zunis, one of the western Pueblo communities. As was so often the case, there was someone on the scene, Mary E. Dissette, who made a special effort to solicit the association's help. In about 1890 Miss Dissette had begun work among the Zunis as a Presbyterian missionary, and subsequently she had entered the Indian Service as a teacher. Over the years Miss Dissette, a prolific letter writer, had occasionally turned to the IRA for help. In 1894 the IRA had raised $250 to help her buy new looms for the Zunis.[79] Three years later she had persuaded Welsh to seek punishment of Zunis who had tortured an old woman accused of being a witch. Welsh had urged the secretary of the interior to see that action was taken to prevent the "recurrence of such shameful barbarities."[80] In January 1899 she again contacted Welsh, this time seeking help in connection with an epidemic of smallpox sweeping the Zuni Pueblo.

When the disease had struck the previous November, Miss Dissette had been employed as a teacher in the government's Indian school at Santa Fe. After several weeks of growing apprehension at what she felt was the inadequate response of the agent to the tragedy—more than 200 Zunis had died, in a population of fewer than 2,000—she decided to ignore protocol and personally contacted the commissioner of Indian affairs and also Herbert Welsh. The latter's response was to direct Brosius to see Commissioner Jones, while Welsh himself telegraphed an appeal to Jones to detach Dissette from the Santa Fe school for emergency work at the Zuni Pueblo.[81] The association's intercession apparently did help the commissioner decide to permit her to go to Zuni and to provide her with a few hundred dollars for emergency relief. The IRA also raised nearly $300 by an appeal in *City and State* and letters to members.[82]

Unfortunately, the Zuni relief work also involved the association in supporting Miss Dissette against the Pueblo agent as well as most of the other agency employers, including the physician sent to Zuni. She also had an enemy in Washington, Mrs. Matilda Coxe Stevenson, an ethnologist with the Smithsonian who had done fieldwork among the Zunis. Francis Leupp, to whom Welsh turned for advice, dismissed Mrs. Stevenson as one of the "Scientific Set" who wished to preserve Indian cultures for scholarly examination. However, Leupp thought that Miss Dissette erred as badly in wanting the Indian brought overnight into the mainstream of American society. Moreover, he thought that Miss Dissette had distinct psychological problems. He accused her of being a "sufferer from *celibacy*," preoccupied with sex and jealous of any woman who attracted male attention, while at the same time denouncing the men involved as womanizers.[83] Given the close proximity in which agency employees were forced to live, someone as vocal and driven as Miss Dissette could be a very disruptive influence, regardless of her admirable devotion to her Indian charges.

Brosius visited Zuni Pueblo in April 1899 and came down overwhelmingly on the side of Miss Dissette. In his opinion her charges that the agent and other Indian Service personnel had neglected the Zunis in their time of crisis were well founded. He proposed that Dissette be given the position of supervisor of Pueblo day schools and that the incumbent be transferred to head the boarding school at Keam's Canyon.[84] After his return to Washington he continued to work to these ends, and the association published his report on the Zuni situation. Commissioner Jones was sympathetic, and eventually the transfers were arranged as Brosius had requested.[85]

In some respects the Zuni episode illustrated the shift in IRA management which had been taking place. Prodded by Miss Dissette, Welsh had initiated the association's activity in behalf of the Zunis. However, the pressure of other commitments forced him to then turn the matter over to Brosius, even to the point of asking the agent to draft a public appeal for his signature, something he would not have been likely to do several years earlier. And Brosius, whose energy, dedication, and willingness to travel helped compensate for his lack of sophistication and literary skills, willingly had moved to fill the void.

CHAPTER SIXTEEN

Attacks on Personnel Under Roosevelt

The succession of Herbert Welsh's old ally Theodore Roosevelt to the presidency in September 1901 should have signaled a new era of influence and accomplishment for the IRA. Within three years, however, the president clearly had turned against Welsh, who in addition, was suffering from such poor health that he had to abandon even the pretense of closely supervising association business. Moreover, until his illness forced him to restrict his activities in those areas as well, Welsh obviously was giving priority to *City and State* and his crusade to expose American misconduct in the Philippines.

Beginning with the health problem in the spring of 1901, Welsh was absent from the association office more and more frequently. That year he had not returned until after his summer vacation and then for only three mornings a week. Sometimes his other projects took him out of the city for periods up to a week. Nevertheless, he managed to find time for another good cause, raising money for the Southern Training Institute, an industrial school for white girls at Camp Hill, Alabama. Welsh also kept up his interest in municipal reform. One of his many absences from executive committee meetings in the period from September 1901 to May 1904 was a result of his decision to attend instead a dinner in New York City which would bring him into contact with members of Mayor Seth Low's reform administration.

Nor was Matthew Sniffen able to take up the slack. In addition to his work on *City and State,* he was drawn by Welsh into the investigation of army activities in the Philippines. The two made several trips together to points in the East to take testimony from witnesses and to hold public meetings on the subject. On one occasion even S. M. Brosius was asked to interview a Kansas veteran about atrocities committed against Filipinos.[1]

When both Welsh and Sniffen were on the road, the Philadelphia office was managed by J. LeRoy Smith, a young man presumably on the payroll of *City and State*. He knew next to nothing about Indian affairs and could get little guidance from executive committee members on some issues. His usual solution to a problem was to pass it on to Washingon for Brosius to handle. The Washington agent was virtually unsupervised at this time and had a free hand in determining what causes to espouse and which Indian Service personnel to applaud or condemn. He continued to make extensive trips to western reservations in the summer, and the few association publications of this period were usually the result of Brosius's investigations. Nevertheless, he did find time to undertake the study of law—despite Welsh's injunction when Brosius had been hired that he must devote his full energies to the association—and in the summer of 1904 passed his bar exam.

By the spring of 1903 Welsh had decided he needed a rest and early in May headed south, with Lexington, Virginia, and Camp Hill, Alabama, on his itinerary. He never got beyond Lexington, coming down with what Sniffen described as "nervous prostration"[2] and what Welsh himself later referred to as a "typical American nervous breakdown."[3] His physician ordered him to take a complete rest, and in August the family sailed for Europe. They wintered in Sicily and were not back in Philadelphia until May 1904. In Welsh's extended absence Sniffen was saddled with trying to keep *City and State* and the IRA alive. The mere fact that the paper had to go to press every week and could not be put on the back burner meant that the association suffered further neglect. To make matters even worse, President Garrett, who had been drawn into a more active role as Welsh's attention turned elsewhere, became ill in early 1904. By the end of the year his condition had deteriorated to the point that a search was on for his successor. Garrett died late the following year. It was a real loss to the IRA, as Garrett had served the association long and well and had a reputation for knowledge in the field which Welsh respected. If Garrett was unhappy about the corresponding secretary's journalistic venture and other commitments, he did not leave record of it.

Welsh's weekly was in desperate financial straits by the spring of 1904. Its income from advertising and subscriptions could provide only about half of its operating budget.[4] And revenues were declining as advertisers, such as the proprietor of St. Luke's, a private school which catered to the children of army officers, concluded they could not afford to be associated with the paper's editorial policy.[5] No sooner was Welsh back in Philadelphia from Europe than he was faced with the question of what to do with *City and State*. Bolstered by assurances of its value by people like Schurz, who declared that "papers telling the truth without fear or favor are among the first needs of the time,"[6] Welsh determined to raise an endowment of $100,000 to sustain the crusading weekly. He argued that *City and State* performed a "particular kind of moral and intellectual instruction" and in function was comparable to an endowed university chair.[7] He pointed to his success in raising $100,000 for a professorship at Washington and Lee University and appealed to the paper's readers to come to its aid.

Given his success at other fund-raising projects, it is not unlikely that he would have been able to salvage *City and State* had his physician not intervened again. Less than a month after his return from Europe, Welsh notified President Garrett that on doctor's orders he would have to be "absolutely free during the next two years from all responsible public and philanthropic work." This meant not only shutting down *City and State*, but also that "I must hand on Indian Rights affairs into the hands of yourself, the Executive Committee, Mr. Sniffen and his assistants."[8]

In its last three years under Welsh's personal direction, if it can be so termed given his other obligations, the association had suffered further declines in efficiency and productivity. All of the indices—dues and contributions, membership, publications, addresses by association officials, and resources committed to Indian causes—indicated some slippage in performance from 1901 to 1904. Nevertheless, the work went on, and its relations with the incumbent administration were as always a key factor in IRA success or failure.

Welsh manifestly had been pleased at Roosevelt's succession to the presidency. In a fund-raising letter sent out by the association in early October 1901, Welsh spoke warmly of Roosevelt,[9] and an issue of *City and State* of the same date was lavish in its praise:

> No man in the country has a fuller practical sympathy with the Indian than President Roosevelt. The President's natural disposition is to be frank, just, and manly. This is a good beginning on the approach to Indian affairs. He first knew the Indian on the rougher, harder side, which he saw in his early experiences of frontier and cowboy life. Later he visited a number of Indian reservations and saw the governmental, educational, and philanthropic side of the question. As a member of the Civil Service Commission he took the keenest interest in all that related to ridding the Indian service of the malaria of the spoils system. One of the last efforts made by Theodore Roosevelt, when he was Governor of New York, was to inaugurate a thorough system of industrial training for the Indian tribes still living in New York

Herbert Welsh, during one of his Atlantic crossings, circa 1900
Courtesy Andrew W. Imbrie

State. . . . The facts show that any practical good thing which the President can do for the advancement of Indian civilization he will do.[10]

This praise was not simply an effort to curry favor with the new chief executive. The history of their twelve-year relationship reveals a growing respect and admiration on Welsh's part for the dynamic Theodore. No other man in public life received a Navajo rug or any other gift from Welsh as a token of his esteem, and it was a result of arrangements made by Welsh that Roosevelt had addressed a Lake Mohonk Conference and an annual meeting of the IRA. In 1897 Welsh had placed Roosevelt first on a list of four men he could recommend as commissioner of Indian affairs to the new McKinley administration, and in 1898 *City and State* had proposed Roosevelt to be appointed secretary of war.

There were hints, however, that Roosevelt was not entirely at ease with Herbert Welsh and his coterie of Christian reformers; for example, Roosevelt referred to the Mohonk meeting he attended as "an absurd, though useful, 'Indian' conference."[11] Although urged by Welsh to revisit Mohonk and to again address an IRA annual meeting, Roosevelt repeatedly declined. As civil service commissioner he was prepared to work with the reformers, and he did demonstrate the ability to alter the views of Indians he had acquired as a rancher in the Dakotas. Nevertheless, Roosevelt obviously had trouble identifying with the type of humanitarians who attended Mohonk conferences and belonged to the IRA.

Welsh's emergence as a spokesman for the anti-imperialist forces shattered any hope he might have had of maintaining a close relationship with President Roosevelt. Although they exchanged personal letters when Roosevelt was governor, during the years of his presidency any correspondence between them was conducted through Roosevelt's private secretary. Through it all, Welsh gave no visible sign of being aware of the deterioration of the relationship.

Six months before his entering the White House there was evidence of Roosevelt's exasperation with Welsh. Their mutual acquaintance Charles J. Bonaparte had passed on to Roosevelt some remark made about him by Welsh. Roosevelt's rejoinder was to describe the Philadelphian as having a "type of mind which is wholly incapable of understanding distinctions, even when the failure to understand them means complete moral and intellectual chaos."[12] Welsh's attacks on the United States army and its commander-in-chief removed any lingering doubts Roosevelt might have had about the reformer's practical intelligence.

Early in 1902 Welsh began to devote more and more time to awakening the public to the heinous crimes which American troops were being accused of committing or condoning in the Philippines.[13] A special target in these early attacks was Secretary of War Elihu Root, whom Welsh at that point was holding responsible. Indeed, Welsh was chided by a New York businessman and supporter of civil service for his relentless, detective-like pursuit of clues to discredit Secretary Root. The New Yorker warned Welsh that he might be "impairing [his] usefulness by too indiscriminate an attack and too virulent criticism."[14] But Welsh was not easily dissuaded from a crusade, and running down evidence of American excesses in the Philippines became almost an obsession with him. By April 1902, *City and State* was carrying stories about the infamous water torture in which tubes and syringes were used to force water into Filipinos until their agony made them more responsive to United States interrogators. There were also accounts of "orders of extermination, orders which have put us almost, if not quite, on a level with Turkey." *City and State* called this an "American development of Weylerism," a reference to the notorious Spanish general who had introduced concentration camps into Cuba.[15] The paper defended General Nelson A. Miles, whose own criticism of American operations in the Philippines had brought down upon his head the wrath of both Secretary Root and President Roosevelt. As was to be expected, *City and State* eventually placed the onus on President Roosevelt,

> who is the official head of the army and navy, who was himself a soldier before he became President, and who knew precisely how military responsibility runs up, directly step by step from a lower grade to the highest. With him, finally, moral and official responsibility rests inevitably.[16]

Not only did Welsh's paper attack Roosevelt and his administration, Welsh—with Charles Francis Adams, Carl Schurz, and Edwin Burritt Smith—signed letters to Roosevelt as the spokesmen for something called the Philippine Investigating Committee. These letters, which they made public, accused army personnel of kidnapping, murder, rape, and torture, and called upon the president to take action.[17] In the spring of 1903 Welsh and Sniffen arranged speaking engagements in the East, the theme being the "horrible cruelties" inflicted on the helpless Filipinos by men wearing the American uniform.[18]

It is little wonder that Roosevelt, despite *City and State's* backing when he was harshly berated by southern editors and politicians for having Booker T. Washington to dinner at the White House, should conclude that Welsh was something less than a supporter of his administration. In late 1902 the president referred, in a letter to Governor William Howard Taft of the Philippines, to "Carl Schurz, Charles Francis Adams, Herbert Welsh and the other foolish irreconcilables."[19] Seven months later he quoted approvingly Taft's denunication of the "rhetorical mouthings of Moorfield Story and Herbert Welsh," who, along with a few others, seemed to feel "that they are better than their fellow men."[20] In a letter to Lyman Abbott the worst thing that Roosevelt could say of another individual was that he was "as poor an adviser as Herbert Welsh."[21] Although their principal differences were over colonial policy, inevitably Welsh's proposals in the area of Indian affairs would be discounted as well, which perhaps helps explain an observation Roosevelt made in a speech in Arizona: "The Indians need to be protected from certain eastern philanthropy."[22] The Roosevelt correspondence for this period reveals that he was much more likely to accept advice on Indian affairs from Francis Leupp, George Bird Grinnell, Hamlin Garland, or Charles Lummis that he was from Herbert Welsh and other officers of the IRA.

Despite this situation, Welsh continued to try to influence the president, assuming that Roosevelt could accept criticism in one area if his contributions in others were recognized. Welsh himself did not enjoy censure, but, as his exchanges with Captain Pratt and Mrs. Matilda Markoe revealed, he would tolerate a great deal before letting his annoyance disrupt an otherwise useful relationship. And he was encouraged by Francis Leupp, who assured Welsh that he should be able to approach Roosevelt personally on Indian matters despite their other differences.[23] This was not the case, however, and Welsh never seems to have grasped the extent of the gulf that had opened between him and his old ally. He continued to have a high personal opinion of the president's performance in most areas, and twenty years later he applauded a proposal to name an Indian school after Theodore Roosevelt as "due the memory of that remarkable man for many services he rendered the Indian race."[24]

How Welsh hoped to gain access to the president was apparent early in Roosevelt's administration. The means was to be Francis Leupp, with whom Welsh had maintained a cordial relationship and who had not alienated Roosevelt with anti-imperialist declarations. Leupp's advice when first approached about delivering a letter to the president was to be patient. It is "a wonderful thing, seeing our old friend in the chief seat," he wrote Welsh, but "don't expect him to do everything at once, or to accomplish impossibilities." Leupp indicated that he himself was "ready to praise much that may fall a good way this side of perfection, if I am confident that he is *trying* to do right and making the best record practicable."[25] Unfortunately, moderation in anything was not one of Welsh's virtues. He would continue to denounce administration policies in one area while expecting cooperation in another, and he would continue to try to use Leupp to influence a president whom Welsh obviously had estranged.

Through the spring of 1904 the association's relations with Commissioner of Indian Affairs Jones and with Secretary of the Interior Hitchcock remained unchanged. Jones persisted in trying to please the demanding IRA leadership, and Secretary Hitchcock persisted in trying to ignore it. Indeed, relations between the secretary and the association reached a new low in 1903, when, as will be discussed in Chapter 17, Hitchcock demanded an explanation as to how a letter President Garrett addressed to him had appeared in newspapers before Hitchcock had had a chance to read it. The letter had enclosed a report by Brosius critical of administration handling of Indian Territory, a report which also was widely circulated by the IRA. The secretary, who had never made any attempt to cooperate with the association, then tried to exclude it and its Washington agent from access to sources in the Indian Bureau. Brosius got Leupp to discuss the problem with President Roosevelt and several weeks later was able to detect a relaxation of the secretary's ban.[26] As the association had to have access to Indian Service personnel both in Washington and in the field to do its job, such a ban would have been crippling in its effect.

In this three-year period the association as usual set the hiring of first-class personnel in the Indian Service as one of its principal priorities. When that task was coupled with the growing tendency of reservation employees to look to the IRA for help, the result was a growing workload which took too much of the Washington agent's time. Letters of a man whose wife was losing her position as a housekeeper at a school, of an agency farmer whose salary had been reduced, of an Indian who was an IRA member and wanted help in getting a carpenter's job were, along with many others, forwarded to S. M. Brosius for action. It was patently clear that some people joined the association in the expectation that it would improve their job situations. One woman, whom the IRA had helped get transferred from a day school to a boarding school, next requested help in getting a leave of absence. She offered $10 for the association's assistance and threatened to drop her membership if no aid was forthcoming.[27] Brosius, like Painter and Leupp before him, did not like this aspect of his job. "We are not an employment agency," he observed, "I think we weaken our work along legitimate lines when such cases are taken up and pressed."[28] Nevertheless, such requests continued to arrive at the Philadelphia office and were routinely passed on to the Washington agent for investigation.

Brosius was more prone than either of his predecessors to file with the secretary of the interior charges against Indian Service personnel, charges which frequently led to investigations of the agency involved and sometimes resulted in the dismissal of the employee. In this three-year period he asked for investigations of more than a dozen people, including agents, school superintendents, clerks, and even inspectors operating out of the secretary's office. Several of them were removed or not reappointed when their terms expired as a result of IRA intervention. The cases at the Standing Rock, Fort Berthold, Pawnee, and Osage agencies reveal the scope of the association's work in this area and the difficulties it encountered.

George H. Bingenheimer was the Standing Rock agent whose removal Brosius sought. A reservation resident, probably the missionary Thomas L. Riggs, had informed the IRA that the agent had arranged the appointment of "a notorious character" to be assistant matron at an agency boarding school and had threatened to dismiss the school's superintendent when he protested in behalf of his outraged faculty.[29] Brosius promptly filed charges against Bingenheimer based on this episode, but more serious matters were in the offing. Evidence was accumulating that the agent, at the urging of a railroad, was pressuring the Indians to lease land. That claim led to more charges and an investigation by George Bird Grinnell at the request of President Roosevelt. Bingenheimer's term expired in late 1902, and at least one North Dakota senator unsuccessfully backed his application for reappointment. As a replacement for the agent, George Bird Grinnell and the Catholic Indian Bureau supported John Carrigan, a clerk for a local trader. The IRA opposed Carrigan because of the testimony of an agency interpreter and the Standing Rock Returned Students' Association.[30] The result was that the association had helped get rid of one agent only to see him replaced by a man it felt was unqualified.

The IRA was more successful at Fort Berthold, North Dakota, where it brought charges against the agent and his chief clerk. Some of the Indians there testified that the agent not only was seen drunk on the reservation but had procured liquor for some of the tribesmen.[31] Brosius helped bring this gross violation of regulations to the attention of the Interior Department. Subsequently, on the grounds that it was a "pernicious example to set the Indians," Brosius also brought charges against the agency clerk for having a "disgraceful liaison" with a female servant in the agent's household.[32] In both cases Secretary Hitchcock sent Inspector Arthur W. Tinker to conduct an investigation, and both times Tinker exonerated the accused. Brosius maintained that Tinker had been seen drunk himself while returning from his examination of the agent, and that, when he revisited Fort Berthold to check up on the clerk, he and the accused went hunting together. The IRA did not give up and sent copies of the Indians' petition against their agent, along with a statement by Brosius on conditions at Fort Berthold, to eight newspapers. Some of them, including the Philadelphia *Ledger* and the *Washington Post*, carried stories on the situation as did, of course, *City and State*. Within a year the clerk had resigned and the agent had been replaced by a better man. The Fort Berthold Indians conveyed their thanks to the association for its assistance.[33]

Brosius had believed that a nice solution to the Fort Berthold problem would have been to abolish the agent's position and transfer the responsibilities to the superintendent of the local boarding school, who was under civil service, that presumed guarantor of honest and efficient performance. That this plan was not a panacea was apparent at the Pawnee Agency in 1903. There Brosius was confronted with the case of a dishonest and brutal school superintendent who also was the acting agent. George I. Harvey, a veteran of the Indian school service, was the subject of complaints by the Indians under his charge, complaints which led to an investigation by an inspector from Secretary Hitchcock's office. The inspector recommended Harvey's removal, but the superintendent managed to avoid that fate by a combination of support from Kansas congressmen and his own plea that the inspector had not permitted him to confront his accusers. Then Brosius visited the Pawnees, conducted his own investigation, and filed charges against Harvey. Brosius claimed that the superintendent was, among other things, using his official position to aid a bank in which he owned stock to loan money to Indians at exorbitant rates of interest. Brosius also collected evidence indicating that Harvey had leased Indian land without the owners' permission, shown favoritism in determining which of the many white applicants could lease Indian land, and held up payments to heirs of allotments which had been sold. The superintendent, who had left at least two other Indian schools in the wake of protests against his excessive punishments of students, was revealed by Brosius to have severely beaten a Pawnee girl. She was a student in his school, and Harvey had attempted a cover-up of his misconduct by transferring the girl, an orphan, to a school in Phoenix.[34]

When Brosius communicated his charges to Indian Commisioner Jones, the commisioner allowed him to select a special agent to conduct another investigation.[35] Briefed thoroughly by Brosius, this official also reported against Harvey, and Jones recommended the superintendent's dismissal. By October 1903 Brosius was confident that the overwhelming burden of evidence meant that Harvey would be ousted in short order. However, the case dragged on for months. The Pawnee superintendent had political support, particularly from Representative Charles Curtis, whom Brosius damned as "one of the worst grafters in Congress."[36] Secretary Hitchcock apparently also was permitting his bias against the IRA to influence his evaluation of Brosius's charges. The Washington agent wanted the association to put pressure on President Roosevelt, and, if he declined to act, to take the case to the public. Had Herbert Welsh been in charge, it is very likely that the IRA would have adopted this course of action. But Welsh was in Europe and, while Sniffen favored this approach, the executive committee was reluctant to push Roosevelt or go public with the case, it being rumored that Harvey's resignation was pending.[37] Meanwhile the superintendent remained in office. Not until Sniffen had gone to Washington and arranged, with Brosius's help, for a friendly senator to introduce a resolution calling for the papers in the Harvey case to be presented to the Senate was Harvey's resignation finally submitted. It is unlikely that the resignation would have been offered without the impetus the case had received from Brosius's tenacious pursuit of the facts.

While Brosius was engineering Harvey's removal, he also was moving against Osage Agent Oscar A. Mitscher, who had succeeded William J. Pollock, whom the IRA had also been instrumental in getting ousted from office, as related in Chapter 14. The Osages seemed particularly unfortunate in the men the government imposed on them as guides on the trail to civilization and full citizenship. Even as he was pushing charges against Mitscher, Brosius was congratulating himself that Asa C. Sharpe, an earlier Osage agent whom he had helped bring to account, was on his way to the penitentiary. The latest miscreant, Mitscher, had in only three years as agent demonstrated considerable ingenuity and lack of ethics in devising ways to make money out of his position of trust and responsibility. One technique was to use his power over the allotting and leasing procedures to move strategically located acreage into the hands of confederates, who could then use its nuisance value to extort money from cattlemen legitimately leasing large tracts of the Osage Reservation. Mitscher likewise was accused of diverting interest on Osage funds into his own bank account and pasturing on the reservation his own cattle without the formality of paying for the privilege. The charges against Agent Mitscher brought not only him down but one of his confederates as well, a Washington-based claims attorney who was at least temporarily disbarred from practice before the Interior Department.[38]

In the fall of 1902 Welsh decided that the IRA should give its attention to remedying the process of agent appointment. It was hardly a new concern for the association, and it is a little difficult to understand why Welsh suddenly decided to focus on this never-ending problem. But focus he did, briefly, and he had Sniffen direct Brosius to compile a list of recent appointments and dismissals. Then, in executive committee meeting, Welsh moved that President Roosevelt be asked that either there be a preliminary screening of agent appointees or they be drawn exclusively from the ranks of school superintendents.[39] The motion carried, and there was a flurry of activity. Brosius did his research in Washington and concluded that in the previous three years about half of the agents had been removed for cause. During the same time period sixteen of the fity-five agencies had been placed under school superintendents, and—these figures were gathered before the case of George Harvey at the Pawnee Agency had surfaced—Brosius believed that this arrangement was the solution. "The superintendents . . . come to the work equipped oftentimes by years of experience in the management of Indians in the school life," Brosius wrote, "and of necessity entering the work by way of the teacher's art they are intelligent and of fair moral character." In addition, as the large reservations had more than one school superintendent, it could lead to "breaking up the large reservations . . . in a measure, disintegrating tribal fealty that is so potent a factor in Indian life."[40] Commissioner Jones also backed the replacement of agents by superintendents and urged it on the president. In justice to Roosevelt, it should be said that he did try to resist the incessant pressure from office seekers and their political backers in the western states and territories. To one such politico he had stated:

> When it comes to Indian agents I want the very minimum attention paid to politics. There have been great scandals in connection with these agencies, and I do not favor putting men into them as rewards for political service. . . . The Indian agent is in a place where the chance of wrongdoing is great, where the temptation is great, and where the chances of detection are comparatively small.[41]

The outcome of the IRA's concern with the issue in late 1902 and early 1903 was a letter to the president and a call on him by Philip Garrett. In the course of that interview they discussed the possibility that the Board of Indian Commissioners, of which Garrett was a member, serve as a screening committee for presidential appointments. Roosevelt concluded, however, that frustrated congressmen would then deny the board funding. Garrett was reduced to recommending the replacement of agents by superintendents, but, as the case of George Harvey was to reveal, that solution was no panacea.[42]

In the fall of 1903 the issue came to the fore again due to the initiative of Dr. Lyman Abbott, whose *Outlook* carried a proposal that the Indian Bureau be returned to the War Department. By this time Welsh was in Europe recovering from nervous exhaustion, and it was Matthew Sniffen's responsibility to react, which he did in the columns of *City and State*. He maintained that "the War Department is organized for purposes of war and is farthest possible from an appropriate department for the constructive work of building up a nation from a state of barbarism to a state of high civilization."[43] Moreover, President Cleveland had relied heavily on army officers to act as agents, and the experiment had not been particularly successful. In this approach Sniffen was simply following the lead of Herbert Welsh, who in 1902 admitted that he had once felt that use of army officers as agents was a posible solution, only to discover that the officers too frequently revealed "personal weakness in moral character" or "inexperience in business affairs."[44]

That October, Dr. Abbott raised the issue at the Mohonk Conference. He maintained that his *Outlook* article had met with general approval, *City and State* and Herbert Welsh being mentioned by name as providing the only dissent.[45] Nevertheless, the conference failed to endorse Abbott's proposal. *City and State* stressed again the undesirability of the transfer, and Indian Commissioner Jones wrote Sniffen thanking him for the "clear manly stand that you have taken in this matter."[46] In the 1870s the idea of shifting the Indian Bureau back to the War Department had found favor in many eyes; in 1903 Abbott's proposal generated no apparent enthusiasm. The problem of getting honest and efficient Indian agents remained.

One man to whom Herbert Welsh had turned for support in improving the selection process for agents was Archbishop Ryan of Philadelphia. That he should look to Ryan for help was a manifestation of the considerably improved relations with the Roman Catholics which marked Welsh's last two years in direct control of the IRA. Despite the anti-Catholic tone of some of Welsh's rhetoric, he made an effort to recognize the contributions of Catholic educators and to assist them when possible. This aid could be as simple and direct as purchasing lace doilies from the St. Francis Mission on the Rosebud Reservation in South Dakota. Mother Leopoldine expressed the mission's appreciation for Welsh's support, but perhaps would not have been so enthusiastic had she known that Welsh had resold them to Archbishop Ryan.[47]

Welsh had become an admirer of the archbishop as a result of discussions with him over a period of several years. Closer cooperation between the Catholic Church and the IRA became a distinct possibility with the intercession of Father H. G. Ganss, formerly pastor of a church at Carlisle, where his work brought him into contact with the Indian students of Pratt's school. In January 1902 Ganss had become financial agent for the Bureau of Catholic Indian Missions, an assignment he approached with his usual enthusiasm and competence.[48] In February 1902, while in Philadelphia, he dropped Welsh a note suggesting that, with the recent death of Father Stephan, an old Welsh antagonist, "the policy of the Catholic Indian Missions and Schools, will undergo some radical changes."[49] He indicated that he would like to discuss with Welsh the possibility of greater cooperation between his church and the association. Welsh responded with an invitation to lunch at the University Club, adding that "I should rejoice in united efforts between your Church and our Association in Indian matters, on all points where without compromise to the essential principles of either your Church or our Association such union is possible."[50]

It was the beginning of a warm relationship. At the next meeting of the executive committee Welsh reported on the luncheon and praised Father Ganss's attitude and record. He also mentioned that the Catholics were interested in securing representation on the Board of Indian Commissioners. Philip Garrett noted that President Roosevelt had implied that he would like to appoint a Catholic to fill the seat vacated by the death of Bishop Whipple.[51] Any reservations Welsh might have had about Ganss evaporated when the priest subscribed to *City and State*, praised Welsh's stand on the Philippines, and promised to circulate to Catholic editors a letter by Welsh on the subject which had appeared in a local paper.[52]

Welsh and Father Ganss then collaborated in supporting Archbishop Ryan for the vacancy on the Board of Indian Commissioners. Welsh indicated to Philip Garrett that he was happy to provide such support, as he had "a very high opinion of his [Ryan's] abilities, good sense, and real desire for what is right, based on a good many years' acquaintanceship."[53] Welsh also noted that the appointment of a Philadelphian would facilitate consultation on Indian matters. Welsh wrote President Roosevelt that he "should rejoice greatly" to see Ryan, "a gentleman whose ability, noble character, and sound judgement are generally recognized and admired," get the appointment.[54] For a while it appeared that the archbishop's candidacy might be stymied by the desire of some members of the board to have a lawyer named to the vacancy. Roosevelt solved that problem by appointing both Ryan and another Catholic, the attorney Charles J. Bonaparte, a member of the IRA and someone with whom Welsh had worked for several years in civil-service reform. Shortly before his appointment was made, Bonaparte had queried Welsh about the functions of the Board of

Indian Commissioners. Welsh responded with a short history of the institution and his expression of happiness at the prospect that either the archbishop or Bonaparte would join the board.[55]

When Archbishop Ryan, Father Ganss, and Charles Bonaparte all participated in the Mohonk Conference that year, and then Ryan and Ganss joined the IRA and the latter spoke at the 1902 annual meeting, it appeared that a new era of Protestant-Catholic cooperation had arrived. Not everyone was ecstatic at the prospect. Brosius passed on to Sniffen a letter from a Protestant missionary containing a warning: "the present policy of your Association—that is, courting the favor of Roman Catholics—will make you much trouble and hurt your work."[56] Brosius himself admitted misgivings: "I have never thought that I was prejudiced against any particular religious denomination, but my experience is that it does not do to give the Catholics any leeway or they will run things to suit themselves." He concluded, "Perhaps better burn this letter."[57]

CHAPTER SEVENTEEN

The Washington Agent
Takes the Lead

As the only IRA official still devoting the bulk of his time and energy to Indian affairs in the years 1901–1904, S. M. Brosius was responsible for almost all of the association's projects. Several were carry-overs from the previous period, such as the Chippewa timber problems, the Warner Ranch case in California, and the litigation surrounding the opening of the Kiowa and Comanche Reservation, all discussed in Chapter 15. There were also significant new concerns, among them two important pieces of legislation Brosius helped draft. One of the laws related to the licensing of reservation traders and the other to safeguarding titles to allotments. The first relaxed the restrictions on the granting of licenses and went a long way toward ending the monopolies which had been so susceptible to abuse. Brosius was able to get this reform through in 1903 as an amendment to the appropriation bill for the Indian Service.[1] The second piece of legislation was much more controversial, as it pitted Brosius, Indian Commissioner Jones, and Merrill E. Gates, the secretary of the Board of Indian Commissioners, against Secretary of the Interior Hitchcock.

In September 1900 an Interior Department attorney had held that Secretary Hitchcock had the authority to cancel any allotment prior to the expiration of the twenty-five-year trust period. The ruling was asked for in connection with one Lizzie Bergen, a Chippewa whose allotment was rich in timber. Presumably it had been a typical instance of an Indian's securing an allotment solely for the purpose of disposing of it to some white operator. After the authority of the secretary in this area had been upheld by a court decision, he invalidated a number of other allotments for various reasons. Hitchcock maintained that this power was a valuable tool in preventing fraud. However, Indian Commissioner Jones, Brosius, and Merrill Gates argued that it had been done at the cost of depriving the Indians of any security for their titles during the trust period. The association distributed a pamphlet by Brosius entitled, *The Insecurity of An Allotment*, and the Washington agent inspired a number of letters backing a bill which he drafted to correct the situation.[2] He was able to get Pennsylvania's Senator Matthew M. Quay, an old political foe of Herbert Welsh, to introduce the bill, and it went through Congress with relative ease.

Secretary Hitchcock's effort to persuade President Roosevelt to veto the legislation produced a conference in which Hitchcock and two subordinates from his department confronted Commissioner Jones, Gates, and Brosius in the presence of Roosevelt. Each side made its case, Brosius presenting statistics on challenges to Indian allotments and evidence as to how the secretary's new power had resulted in severe losses to allottees who had invested years of work on their farms only to lose them.[3] The president decided that the government could better run the risk of fraud than inhibit Indian initiative by putting their titles in jeopardy, and he signed the bill.[4] In its annual report for 1904 the association proudly cited the contention of an official of the Indian Bureau that it was the most important law protecting Indian rights to pass Congress in a decade.[5]

Of the other issues the IRA took up in this period the most important also dealt with land. Leasing arrangements were in dispute at Standing Rock Agency, Rosebud Reservation Sioux faced a loss of more land, and Indian Territory was the scene of an orgy of graft and corruption involving allotments and leases.

As was the case with several Plains Indian reservations, that of the Standing Rock Sioux contained large areas of unused range land. Most of the Indian families had small herds of cattle, although only a few intermarried whites and mixed-bloods were really profiting. They had made private arrangements to pasture on the reservation the herds of neighboring white ranchers. Indian Commissioner Jones believed that the Indians would be better off if regular leases could be negotiated which would provide all of the Sioux a share of the income.

In October 1901 the government obtained the consent of the Indians to rent unoccupied areas of the reservation. Subsequently two leases were arranged, the Lemmon for nearly 800,000 acres, and the Walker for more than 450,000, totalling over half of the reservation. Only the Lemmon lease was actually implemented, because of public outcry against the arrangements—an outcry orchestrated primarily by the IRA—and even that lease was modified to meet Indian objections.

Brosius had alerted the association to the problem in late December 1901. At an executive committee meeting early in the next month Brosius stated that he already was working with the Indians to block the leases.[6] The reasons he offered were essentially those that motivated the IRA throughout the controversy and were spelled out in two pamphlets and in several articles in *City and State*.

The most fundamental objection was that the leasing agreement on which the government based its action did not contain an important provision agreed to orally by the government's negotiator. In the council which produced the agreement the Indians had held out for an all-Indian committee to make the actual determination of the area to be leased. This provision had been accepted by the government negotiator but had not appeared in the final document. The association maintained that what was at stake was the right of Native Americans to control their own land.[7]

Another IRA objection was that the introduction of large herds of cattle belonging to white ranchers would set back the civilization program. Hundreds of Indian families had already established homes in the areas to be leased and only by building miles of fence could these families shelter their homesteads and segregate their small herds from the cattle introduced. When the cattle mixed freely, as *City and State* observed, it appeared that the Indians' cows never had calves while the ranchers' cows always had twins.[8]

The burden of association opposition to the leases fell almost entirely on the shoulders of its Washington agent. Brosius's first move was to exploit IRA contacts on the reservation to secure further information as to the circumstances under which the leasing agreement was obtained and its possible impact on the Indians. Congregational missionaries Mary Collins and Thomas L. Riggs were his best sources, Riggs being employed by the association at Brosius's insistence to conduct an investigation and prepare a report.[9] Brosius also sought support from members of Congress. He was particularly successful in obtaining the cooperation of Arkansas Senator James K. Jones, who used his position on the Indian committee to elicit documents and testimony on the leases, as well as to provide a forum for a Sioux delegation from Standing Rock. Brosius worked closely with the delegation, helping arrange their appearance before the Senate committee and encouraging them to seek an injunction to restrain the government from implementing the leases. A court finally ruled against the request for an injunction, but the association's campaign, aided by the WNIA, the Boston Indian Citizenship Committee, the Board of Indian Commissioners, and individuals such as the writer Hamlin Garland, was beginning to show results.[10]

On the basis of a talk with the interpreter accompanying the Sioux delegation and a letter from Garland, President Roosevelt by the end of January was proposing to Secretary Hitchcock that he move slowly, as "I am not altogether easy about these leases."[11] Brosius later gave him additional food for thought by passing on a report of a council in which the Sioux voted unanimously against leasing.[12]

In April, Commissioner Jones, who had been charged with possible financial involvement in the leases in an article in the *Outlook* by its Washington correspondent George Kennan, went to the Standing Rock Reservation to confer with the Indians. By that time the paperwork on the Lemmon lease had been completed; however, Jones announced that the Walker lease would be cancelled. The commissioner later acknowledged that, had he known more about conditions at Standing Rock, he would not have insisted on the reservation being opened to outside cattle.[13]

The IRA tried one last maneuver to block the Standing Rock leases. Brosius and two members of the executive committee obtained an audience with President Roosevelt and persuaded him to send George Bird Grinnell, whose opinion the president valued, to check on the situation.[14] Grinnell's investigation resulted, at least, in modifications of the Lemmon lease to require that the lessee build a fence to protect some Indian holdings and that a boundary line be redrawn to secure other Sioux property.[15]

Indian Commissioner Jones's reputation had been damaged by the allegations to which George Kennan had given credence in his *Outlook* article. A large part of that piece had been reproduced and circulated in one of the IRA's pamphlets.[16] After the Senate Indian committee had cleared Jones of any personal involvement in the pasturing of cattle at Standing Rock, the commissioner suggested strongly that the association print a retraction of some sort. The IRA did so in an article appearing in *City and State* and repeated it in a pamphlet summarizing the final settlement of the Standing Rock leases.[17]

Jones also would come under some criticism from the association in connection with the agreement providing for the government purchase of 416,000 acres of the Rosebud Reservation in South Dakota. This was land left over after the Sioux of that agency had received their individual allotments. In September 1901 the Indians had consented to the sale of the "surplus" land for $2.50 per acre, and subsequently the agreement was submitted to Congress for ratification. The IRA had taken no stand when the negotiations were taking place. Its 1902 annual report observed:

> While from the standpoint of the best interests of the Indians it may not have been considered good management to dispose of so large a block of their lands, when we consider the increasing

demand from the public that large bodies of land within Indian reservations shall be thrown open to settlement, it was probably the better course to pursue.[18]

What did disturb S. M. Brosius was the position taken by the chairman of the Senate Indian committee, William M. Stewart of Nevada, during the Senate debate in April 1902 on the Burke bill to ratify the agreement. Brosius had tried to block Stewart's appointment to the committee because of his notorious anti-Indian views.[19] They were apparent in the debate when the senator argued that the Native American should not be permitted to set a "fancy price" on land, as "he has no other right but a sentimental right," to it, and had been endowed with that by the Indian Rights Association.[20] But at this point it was not that the Indians might not receive a fair price for the 416,000 acres that was bothering Brosius. He was concerned about the broader issue of Congress's power to do what it wished with Indian land, as the recent Lone Wolf decision seemed to declare.

Although during the debate on the Rosebud agreement an Idaho senator jokingly prefaced his remarks with a reference to needing protection from the IRA, given what he was about to say,[21] the association took no further action on the issue until January 1904. At that time it was approached for help by Reuben Quick Bear, head of the Rosebud tribal council. Welsh being out of the country, Matthew Sniffen passed the letter on to Brosius with a query as to what could be done to defeat the Burke bill. Quick Bear was objecting particularly to the price of $2,50 per acre. The Burke bill to ratify the agreement actually called for the price of $3 an acre for land sold during the first six months, the price then dropping to $2.50. Quick Bear, however, maintained that the land was worth much more than that; nevertheless, "we only ask $5.00 per acre."[22] Brosius was not confident that anything could be done at that late date. The bill had passed the House, had been reported favorably by the Senate Indian committee, and was on the calendar for Senate action. Brosius believed that the upper house would act quickly, and, if there was any hope for the Indians, it was in a presidential veto.[23]

Within the next three weeks the Washington agent, with the help of Rosebud missionary Aaron B. Clark, a licensed trader at the agency who provided information but did not want his name revealed, and the journalists Francis Leupp and George Kennan, gave the Rosebud agreement more publicity than it had ever received in the more than two years since it was negotiated. Reverend Clark supplied statements on the value of the land, and Kennan wrote an article for *Outlook* entitled, "Indian Lands and Fair Play," based in part on information Brosius provided. Leupp did a piece for the New York *Evening Post* for which he also was indebted to Brosius for background material.[24] The lead for Leupp's article suggested that Congress, in dealing with the Rosebud Indians, was preferring the methods of counterfeiters to those of highway robbers. For his own contribution Brosius put together some testimony on South Dakota land prices, some newspaper clippings, and Reuben Quick Bear's original letter. Then he added his own declaration that, since the Lone Wolf decision emphasizing the omnipotence of Congress, the government had an even greater moral obligation to take seriously its responsibility as guardian of the Indians. This memorial Brosius was able to get submitted as a Senate document by a friendly senator from Missouri. The association then mailed out copies accompanied by a request for letters to the president and to senators.[25]

From the beginning Brosius had recognized that a presidential veto was the best chance for stopping the Burke bill in its present form. Secretary Hitchcock and Commissioner of Indian Affairs Jones had both given the agreement their approval, although Jones had protested some of the terms.[26] After George Kennan had prepared his *Outlook* article, but before it was published, the journalist had an interview with President Roosevelt. On hearing Kennan relate the Indian side of the issue, the president had written Senator Robert Jackson Gamble of South Dakota indicating that he could not approve the bill in its present form.[27] About a week later the full South Dakota congressional delegation met with Roosevelt to discuss the issue. The assistant secretary of the interior and Commissioner Jones also were present, and Jones provided Brosius with an account of what occurred. Apparently the discussion became rather heated as Roosevelt stood his ground insisting that he would not sign the bill unless the Indians got more money.[28]

Then Kennan's article was published, and the memorial Brosius had introduced into the Senate was circulated by the association. The story by Francis Leupp appeared in the New York *Evening Post*, and Brosius was preparing an IRA pamphlet on the subject. *Another "Century of Dishonor"?* appeared in late March, and the association distributed 3,000 copies.[29] Its introduction, drafted principally by Brosius but appearing over Philip Garrett's name, concluded, "Any help rendered by the press in arousing a demand for justice will be appreciated." Included in the pamphlet were both Kennan's and Leupp's articles and the memorial by Brosius which had appeared as a Senate document. As newspapers began to give more attention to the issue and letters were written to members of Congress, Brosius and the Philadelphia office began to get pledges of support from senators. President Roosevelt now was advocating selling the land at auction, which would mean that the various tracts being offered would bring their approximate value.

Another possibility he was considering was an amendment to the Burke bill to provide a flat rate of $5 an acre. In the end Roosevelt compromised, and the bill he signed into law set the price at $4 an acre for Rosebud land purchased during the first three months, dropping to $3 for the second three months, with all land sold after that period to go at $2.50 an acre.[30] It was a better deal than the Indians had been offered under the original agreement or the first version of the Burke bill, but a far cry from the flat price of $5 an acre for which Roosevelt and the IRA had hoped. Nevertheless, in its fund-raising letters during the remainder of 1904, the IRA took credit for bringing the issue to the president's attention and enabling the Indians to receive over $600,000 more than would have been the case if the original figure of $2.50 an acre had held up.[31] This figure was an exaggeration, however, since the most that had been accomplished by the IRA's intervention was to raise the price of land sold in the first three months by $1 an acre, realizing for the Sioux of the Rosebud Reservation considerably less than the $600,000 claimed.[32]

The association was openly unhappy with the outcome of an investigation into the operations of the Dawes Commission in Indian Territory. By 1900 H. L. Dawes was in virtual retirement and the commission was really headed by Tams Bixby, who owed his appointment to his work for the Wisconsin Republican Party. Supported by a large staff, Bixby and his three colleagues were preparing official rolls for the Five Civilized Tribes and allotting land to the individual members. The commission also was supervising the leasing of Indian allotments by white entrepreneurs and the location of townsites, two activities potentially very profitable and very corrupt. In December 1900 S. M. Brosius, disturbed at reports of favoritism and conflict of interest in connection with Dawes Commission operations, advised Welsh to commit association funds to an investigation. To carry it out, Brosius had already selected a former agent for the Southern Utes who had been recommended by Francis Leupp.[33] However, it was another two and a half years before the IRA would take up the problem. Then Brosius had to do it virtually on his own, Herbert Welsh being in Europe trying to recover his health, and Matthew Sniffen laboring to keep *City and State* alive.

In the summer of 1903 Brosius visited Indian Territory and prepared a report on his findings. If anything, the situation had deteriorated badly since he had first raised the alarm about the Dawes Commission. "The air has been full of scandals," he wrote Sniffen, and expressed the hope that his findings would inspire an investigation into "yet unearthed rottenness."[34] His report was shared by the IRA with a number of newspapers. One of them was the St. Louis *Globe Democrat*, which had a reader in Fort Worth who commented in a letter to Philip Garrett, "The report is only too true and yet it does not go far enough. The Indians are in the hands of the Philistines, sharks and robbers."[35] This individual declined to sign his name for fear that, if he did so, he could not return to Indian Territory. George Bird Grinnell also read the report and was "greatly horrified" by its revelations; he congratulated Brosius on having "unearthed the most devilish conspiracy against the Indian of modern time."[36]

What Brosius had done was to detail the various ways these Native Americans were being defrauded. Conspicuous in taking advantage of the one-third of the population of the Five Civilized Tribes whom Brosius did not think competent to care for their own business interests were the many newly organized "trust companies." They were leasing land at 25¢ to 75¢ per acre from Indians who had received it as allotments and then subletting it at $1 to $2.50 per acre. The companies employed scouts to locate unallotted Indians and to bring them in to register for their homesteads under the watchful eye of company officers. Brosius claimed that Tams Bixby, the official chairman since the death of H. L. Dawes in 1903, and at least two other members of the Dawes Commission were stockholders and officers of these companies. Furthermore, a number of other present or past federal officials, including a United States district attorney, an inspector from Secretary Hitchcock's office, and the former chief law clerk for the Dawes Commission, were stockholders. Even the governor of the Chickasaw Nation was reported to have invested in one trust company. The oil and gas companies likewise were depicted as resorting to blatantly unfair tactics in the competition to secure leases. The Dawes Commission also was blamed for devising procedures which required Cherokees to travel as far as 150 miles to commission headquarters to apply for allotments and to support themselves at the site for as long as two weeks before completing the paperwork. Finally, Brosius accused more sophisticated members of the Five Civilized Tribes, who had monopolized large acreages when the land was held in common, of continuing by collusion with officials to hold excessive amounts of land.[37]

President Garrett had enclosed a copy of Brosius's charges in a letter to Secretary Hitchcock. Unfortunately, as discussed in the previous chapter, Hitchcock was away from his office for a week and did not receive it until the charges had appeared in papers all across the country. The secretary's first reaction was to demand an explanation for what he regarded as the discourtesy shown him. He was not happy with Garrett's response and indicated that he was aware of the problems in Indian Territory and indeed had taken corrective action after visiting there in the spring.[38] Just what Hitchcock had done was not clear, and the association later insisted that nothing had occurred until it aroused the public. The public was responding: *City and State* received more than twenty letters detailing additional corruption after it published Brosius's letter.

President Roosevelt may have sympathized with his secretary of the interior's outrage at the violation of proprieties; nevertheless, he moved quickly to quiet the uproar by sending an investigator to Indian Territory. Neither of the first two men he sought for this position, one of them Francis Leupp, would take on the assignment. He then turned to Charles J. Bonaparte of Baltimore, dubbed by his biographer the "Patrician Reformer."[39] A grandson of Napoleon's youngest brother and the American woman to whom he was briefly wed, he was an early advocate of civil-service reform. In 1903 Bonaparte headed the National Civil Service Reform League, and Herbert Welsh chaired its finance committee. They had fought side by side in a number of civil-service battles, and Bonaparte had been at least a dues-paying member of the Indian Rights Association for more than ten years. Welsh had happily endorsed his appointment to the Board of Indian Commissioners. Despite his reputation as a reformer, however, Bonaparte was, as Roosevelt well knew, anything but an extremist, and he was a loyal supporter of the president. Still, the IRA was very pleased with his selection to conduct the investigation. President Garrett wrote Bonaparte, "It was a great consolation to me to feel that these allegations of Mr. Brosius will be examined by one in whom I have such absolute confidence."[40] At his request Bonaparte received from Matthew Sniffen copies of letters addressed to *City and State* detailing corruption in Indian Territory.[41]

Charles Bonaparte, in his capacity as Special Inspector of the Indian Territory, did not move with the dispatch and thoroughness Brosius thought was required. Brosius wanted him to employ as an assistant a Washington lawyer suggested by Richard C. Adams, the Delaware lobbyist. Bonaparte declined to do so, apparently feeling that to employ a "detective," as Brosius once described the position, was somewhat improper. However, Bonaparte was willing to contribute to a special IRA fund to finance another trip by Brosius to the territory. This proposal in turn the Washington agent thought improper, as he would appear to be gathering evidence to support accusations he himself had made.[42]

Bonaparte's primary charge was to investigate the allegations made by Brosius, although he was given authority to broaden his search as he saw fit. Bonaparte chose to focus quite narrowly on the accusations already made, rather than trying to uncover other crimes of federal officials in Indian Territory. He himself spent less than two weeks there, although he asked for and obtained the appointment of Clinton Rogers Woodruff, a Philadelphia lawyer and civil-service reformer, as co-investigator. The two of them had then subsidized at their own expense some additional research in the area.[43] Nevertheless, Bonaparte and Woodruff disappointed Brosius by their decision not to seek depositions beyond those volunteered in response to a public invitation.[44] This less than aggressive approach was almost guaranteed to fail to uncover vital information, as people possessing it were usually reluctant to testify voluntarily, either because they themselves were involved or because they feared retribution if they testified against others. Certainly the procedure adopted by Bonaparte and Woodruff was not designed to elicit much information from the less sophisticated Indians, who were most frequently the victims.

When the Bonaparte-Woodruff report finally was made public in late February 1904, it received a mixed reception from IRA officials.[45] On the one hand it sustained most of Brosius's charges; on the other it was phrased in such away as to make it appear that the whole investigation had been a test of Brosius's credibility rather than an effort to expose corruption and inefficiency in the administration of federal policies in Indian Territory. Bonaparte and Woodruff analyzed Brosius's letter paragraph by paragraph in terms of the veracity of the charges. Examples of exaggeration in Brosius's rhetoric or the investigators' inability to document particular charges were treated as almost as significant as the conflicts of interest and misuse of authority that were documented. Nevertheless, Bonaparte and Woodruff concluded that Brosius's report "in no wise exaggerates, however (on the contrary, it rather understates), the objectionable features of the administration of public affairs in the Territory, and its specific allegations respecting Federal officers are substantially true."[46] Moreover, conditions in Indian Territory "involve imminent danger of ruin to the genuine Indian population and profound discredit to the United States. . . ."[47] Bonaparte and Woodruff recommended the abolition of the Dawes Commission and a few changes to improve the administration of tribal lands.

City and State claimed that the report of the special inspectors "more than justifies the original complaint of Mr. Brosius."[48] But what was lacking was any real follow-through. Secretary Hitchcock contented himself with directing the members of the Dawes Commission to sever any connections with companies doing business in Indian land, or to resign their positions.[49] Congress came up with a general prohibition of the same nature directed at all federal employees.[50] As the Kansas City *Journal* noted nearly two months after the publication of the report, "Barring a few insignificant exceptions, not a misdeed has been punished nor have any culprits or delinquents been ousted from office and the Territory secured from further consequences of their greed and incapacity."[51] Nor was this result surprising, given a lack of presidential leadership in the matter. Meeting with Bonaparte following his return from Indian Territory, Roosevelt had left the impression that he would ask Congress to abolish the Dawes Commission. However, Secretary Hitchcock argued that the commission could finish its work in little more than a year and that it would be better to let it continue than to try to create other machinery to complete the job. This approach appealed to Roosevelt, who had no desire, according to Clinton Rogers Woodruff, to have to publicly break with Secretary Hitchcock on the eve of a presidential campaign.[52] Roosevelt's solution was to phrase his message to Congress on the Bonaparte-Woodruff investigation in such a fashion as to suggest that it might be wise to dissolve the commission, but that he would leave it to the senators and representatives to devise an appropriate course of action. They did little.[53] Brosius reluctantly concluded that this inaction was for the best, as, surprisingly, he found himself agreeing with Secretary Hitchcock that to terminate the commission immediately could be too disruptive. Besides, Brosius believed that the publicity the commission had received should have curtailed the worst of its excesses.[54]

The Patrician Reformer showed no zeal for rooting out the corruption. In September 1904 Bonaparte wrote Matthew Sniffen that he expected the members of the commission to be fired if Roosevelt was returned to the White House.[55] However, as Congress already had specified that the commission would cease functioning in July 1905, and Bonaparte admitted that he had not spoken to Roosevelt on the subject since submitting the report, his remarks can only be dismissed as pro-Roosevelt propaganda. He made more such comments at the Mohonk Conference in October, when Albert K. Smiley honored Bonaparte by selecting him to preside. In his opening remarks, delivered on the eve of the 1904 presidential election, the chairman said that his investigation in Indian Territory "left me convinced that our President and our Secretary of the Interior are earnest and unselfish friends of the Indian, and, on the whole, I found few public servants to condemn and comparatively venial faults to lay to the charge of the most among these."[56] At that time Bonaparte was busy lending his reputation as a reformer to Roosevelt's election campaign. The grateful TR in time would reward him by first appointing him secretary of the navy and then attorney general. Tams Bixby, judged by Clinton Rogers Woodruff to be the cleverest and the most unscrupulous member of the Dawes Commission, and a special target of Brosius's charges, was appointed Commissioner of the Five Civilized Tribes to complete the commission's work. This was too much even for Bonaparte, who referred to it as "substituting for Bixby more of Bixby."[57]

As 1904 drew to a close, Brosius's evaluation of the result of the investigation was negative. "Practically nothing has been done, and it is conceded that the effort so well begun resulted in failure. . . . It is admitted on all sides that corrupt methods are more prevalent than before."[58] Herbert Welsh, now coaching from the sidelines, told Sniffen to contact Bonaparte to see if the Dawes Commission members would be prosecuted for fraud.[59] Ten years earlier a vigorous and dedicated Welsh probably would have exploited IRA contacts in Congress and the press to force the administration to reconsider the wisdom of countenancing such a whitewash of conditions in Indian Territory.

CHAPTER EIGHTEEN

The Association's Record in the Herbert Welsh Years

When in 1899 Commissioner of Indian Affairs W. A. Jones said that he knew of no one who had made a greater contribution to improving the Indian Service than had Herbert Welsh, he was not engaging in mere hyperbole. In the twenty-two years of Welsh's leadership the Indian Rights Association had compiled a remarkable record of service to the Native American population.

Commissioner Jones had coupled with his remark the observation that what made Welsh's performance even more remarkable was that it had not been inspired by "expectation of either political or financial recognition, but from a philanthropic and high minded sense of duty."[1] Again the commissioner was on target. Herbert Welsh's inherited fortune had enabled him to devote his full energies to the variety of good causes that his Christian conscience led him to espouse. He was that unusual individual who drove himself unmercifully, not to advance his own political and financial ambitions, but to aid others less fortunate. When faced with a situation of need as described in the sermon he had heard in his youth, Herbert Welsh always responded. And not with just money, which is the easiest contribution of the wealthy, but with his time and his energy, much more precious commodities. His motto, "While we live we ought to work,"[2] smacked of a Puritan ethic not unusual among members of his social class in Philadelphia. What distinguished him from his friends and acquaintances was that the drive and intelligence they applied to business and professional careers he dedicated to good causes exclusively.

Until the mid-1890s most of Herbert Welsh's drive and intelligence was devoted to Indian reform. His views on Native Americans were the accepted ones among eastern friends of the Indian. The native cultures could not endure as enclaves in the dominant white society. Indians, however, had the capacity to make the conversion to the other way of life and must in order to survive. When there was a clash among tribal members over assimilation, Welsh rarely failed to align the Indian Rights Association with the progressives, those prepared to accept the changes being thrust upon them. Even when a clear majority of a tribe decided to resist government assimilation policies, he had no reluctance to oppose them, arguing in a typical situation that the Indians were "poor ignorant people whose real welfare depends upon their being told."[3] That statement has a patronizing, even racist, ring to it in the 1980s. We should, however, refrain from the common error of ignoring history and imposing our contemporary values on the much different situation which existed a century ago.

In twenty years Welsh's views of what was good for the Indians changed little. They needed education, and he was a proponent of the reservation day and boarding schools as well as the off-reservation schools like Carlisle. Under his leadership the association waged many battles to improve the school system, both in funding and in personnel. He also believed that it was impossible for the tribes to retain title to millions of acres of relatively unused land while the nation's population burgeoned. To ensure that they were not completely stripped of land and to give them additional incentive for self-support, the Indians must be introduced to private property—allotment in severalty. They would also need a legal system compatible with that of the nation and of the state in which they resided. Last but not least, from the viewpoint of the staunch Episcopalian Herbert Welsh, the Indians to become truly civilized must give up their pagan beliefs and embrace Christianity.

To help achieve these objectives the Indian Rights Association was brought into being by Herbert Welsh and a few close associates. There was nothing particularly unusual about its organization. Like other reform groups it drew its membership from the ranks of the well-to-do. The plan to develop branches in other cities proved impractical, and the idea that it would be run by the executive committee was demonstrated to be unsound almost immediately. What was needed was a full-time director, and Welsh filled this role with the innocuous title of corresponding secretary. Clearly it was his willingness to head up a central office staff that distinguished the IRA from groups like the Boston Citizenship Committee which, without an office or a staff, functioned only when busy men were able to find time. Also of great importance was Welsh's ability to raise funds. The association could not have functioned on the dues of its members. It required additional funds, and the disagreeable task of raising them was one of Welsh's most valuable contributions.

The other thing that distinguished the IRA from other reform groups, and was its most important administrative innovation, was the decision to maintain an agent in Washington. Charles Painter proved to be a superb choice for the assignment, and Welsh, not one to deny credit where it was due, acknowledged that much of the effectiveness of the IRA was due to Painter's skills as a lobbyist. Francis Leupp and S. M. Brosius were less effective, but nevertheless indispensable.

Welsh's numerous speaking engagements were of vital importance to the success of the association. Advertising the new organization by speaking to church and parlor audiences was an obligation Welsh took very seriously in the 1880s. With some success he pressed Painter to address as many groups as possible, but he had problems with Leupp and Brosius. The first was too busy with his other jobs, and Brosius lacked the self-confidence to discharge this function.

Travel to the reservations also was something on which Welsh set a high priority, although he himself virtually ceased to do it after he launched *City and State*. Prior to that commitment he had made a number of trips, most often to the Sioux reservations because of his ties with Bishop Hare and the Episcopal missions among the Sioux. Painter saw many more reservations, being an indefatigable traveler in a period when reservations could be traversed only on horseback or in a wagon or buggy. The discomfort and time consumed were well worth it, as Painter and Welsh and the occasional other individual who made inspection trips for the IRA returned with a personal knowledge of reservation conditions which gave authority to their pronouncements. They also established valuable contacts with Indians, government employees, traders, missionaries, and army officers which could be exploited for information outside official channels. Leupp was unable to travel as frequently as Painter, but one of Brosius's strong points was his willingness to spend weeks on the road. Not even these extensive travels, though, could acquaint the IRA with more than a fraction of the over 150 reservations across the nation. Like the Indian Bureau, whose activities it monitored, the association operated on general principles which frequently did not conform to actual conditions on particular reservations, as they were located in all types of geographical settings and supported populations with widely varying cultures.

Given the great number of reservations and the horrendous range of problems the Native Americans faced, the association was never at a loss for causes to take up. Sometimes they were discovered by IRA personnel in their travels; more frequently they were brought to the association's attention by concerned missionaries, Indian Service personnel, or army officers. Increasingly in the 1890s Indians themselves were turning to the association for assistance. It was impossible for the IRA to take on all the problems referred to it, and the responsibility to determine which issues got priority was primarily Welsh's. If an outlay of funds was required, he would seek the approval of the executive committee; however, it was most unusual for it to do anything more than rubber-stamp the judgment he already had made. The Washington agent, because of his physical separation from the Philadelphia office, had some latitude even when Welsh was concentrating on association affairs. When he became distracted by other interests in the 1890s, Painter, Leupp, and Brosius were more frequently left to their own devices.

At the height of its influence in the early 1890s the IRA was a highly effective special-interest group. Welsh had always believed that bad government practices could be remedied by an aroused public—"in all these troubles our stronghold is public sentiment," as he once phrased it.[4] By writing letters to the editor and planting stories with friendly journalists, in a period when editors freely reprinted items from other papers, he was able to get the association's viewpoint before a substantial part of the American reading public. To influence selected audiences on particular topics, Welsh resorted to personal letters and mailings of the association's more than 200 publications for this period. Frequently Welsh circulated petitions and inspired letters to members of Congress and the executive branch, often seeking the cooperation of religious leaders and prominent laymen in a period when churches had considerable political clout. And he was always careful to solicit the support of other reform groups, such as the WNIA and the Boston Indian Citizenship Committee. These tactics were effective enough to make the IRA respected, even feared, by the politicos of the day. Its success varied with administrations, but overall its record for this twenty-year period and its access to public officials up to and including the president would be the envy of any special-interest group today. Not that it did not suffer many defeats. Welsh took on causes when he knew the odds were heavily against him. He rationalized that even the publicity created in a losing battle would in the long run be beneficial. And he had the true believer's assurance of ultimate victory, "confidence of a certain faith in the Spiritual Power."[5]

With the Indian the ward of the federal government, it followed that the IRA, to improve the status of Native Americans, must work through this "great machine of power."[6] This orientation explains its preoccupation with the change of administrations in Washington and the makeup of Indian committees in Congress. The substitution of a William McKinley for a Grover Cleveland in the White House could alter overnight the association's access to key officials in the conduct of Indian affairs. Each administration had its own policy for filling positions in the Indian Service, and it was of crucial interest to Welsh, believing as he did that the assimilation policies all administrations in this period concurred in were correct, and, therefore, "the solution of the whole Indian problem lies quite as much in the wise, unpartisan administration as in wise legislation."[7] As a result he involved the association in an unremitting effort to improve the quality of Indian Service personnel. He believed the Indian agent to be the "pivot of the Indian problem,"[8] but he also was concerned that clerks, assistant farmers, and teachers be competent and devoted employees. In an era when the Indian Service, with its thousands of positions, offered one of the richest prizes for the spoilsmen, it is little wonder that civil service became almost an obsession with Welsh.

As this study has attempted to demostrate, the IRA took on a staggering number of causes relating to Native Americans, ranging in importance from the picayune to the truly significant. It had to pick and choose from among the hundreds of problems called to its attention every year those few for which it would make a special effort. However, the practice of Welsh and Sniffen of forwarding to Washington for some response virtually all requests for help received in Philadelphia placed an unreasonable burden on Charles Painter and his successors. With the passage of time the workload grew, as members of the Indian Service and increasing numbers of Native Americans came to look upon the IRA as an unofficial ombudsman, their court of last resort.

In 1907 Matthew Sniffen compiled a list of the association's major accomplishments. For the period through 1904 it numbered nearly fifty, including the IRA's long campaigns in behalf of the Apache prisoners of war and the Southern Utes, the appropriation it helped win for the starving Piegans in 1885, and its battle to try to save some of the Chippewas' timber resources. There was no room to list the hundreds of other services rendered Indians, such as the scholarship to help educate William Jones, a Fox Indian and early ethnologist, or the fund raised to assist the victims of the Wounded Knee Massacre. Absent also was any reference to the IRA's long involvement in the government's efforts to reduce the Sioux holdings in the Dakotas. An indirect and unmeasurable, though significant, contribution was its well-publicized existence. From the secretary of the interior to the agent on the remotest reservation, every government official knew that there existed an institution to which any disgruntled Indian or employee could turn, and which could and would broadcast the official's misdeeds to the nation. It could only have had a very salutary effect.

By 1904 it was apparent that IRA leaders, like other eastern friends of the Indian, were being forced to modify some of their previously held views. It was becoming increasingly difficult to justify a land policy which was not producing the results which had been promised for allotment in severalty. The association, as was revealed by the case involving leases of Sioux land on Standing Rock Reservation and the Lone Wolf litigation growing out of Kiowa and Comanche problems, was by 1900 often defending the Indian's right to have the final say as to what happened to their land. Nor was the IRA pushing for the abolition of Indian agencies, which certainly would have been in line with its previously held views that no institution should be spared which contributed to the preservation of the tribe and the wardship of the Indian.

In 1904 Herbert Welsh's abdication of responsibility for the day-by-day conduct of affairs of the IRA, although he continued to be listed as corresponding secretary, did not have an immediate impact on the association. For several years he had relegated more and more responsibility to the Washington agents and Matthew Sniffen. After Welsh's illness in the spring of 1903, Sniffen had been left with both *City and State* and the association to run. Welsh did not withdraw completely from IRA affairs; indeed, he was to serve as its president for many years. But his role would never again be what it had been. In some respects, nevertheless, his relationship with Sniffen was slow to change. Although Welsh left the daily routine to Sniffen, he did not hesitate to ask his former chief clerk to perform for him a variety of chores relating to his other interests. In his new role as elder statesman Welsh continued to press his views on how the association should function. He clearly had no intention of disassociating himself from the institution to whose origin and early development he had made the greatest contribution. What Matthew Sniffen wrote at the time of Welsh's death in 1941 is still true more than one hundred years after the IRA was founded:

> In creating the Indian Rights Association, Herbert Welsh "builded better than he knew," and it stands as a monument to his foresight, his persistent and effective activity . . . for a righteous cause, to which he devoted the best years of his life.[9]

Notes to the Chapters

CHAPTER 1

1. E. Digby Baltzell, *Philadelphia Gentleman* (Chicago: Quadrangle Books, 1971).
2. For information on Herbert Welsh's early life I am deeply indebted to his grandson, Andrew W. Imbrie, who shared with me his biographical sketch of his grandfather.
3. J. Rodman Paul to Welsh, June 25, 1882, in IRAP, Reel 1.
4. Herbert Welsh, *Four Weeks Among Some of the Sioux Tribes,* p. 24, in Indian Rights Association Papers (hereafter cited as IRAP), Reel 102:A2. For the period covered by this study, the IRA published about two hundred items, ranging in length from one page to almost one hundred. Many libraries contain a scattering of these items, but only the microfilm edition cited is a source for all of them.
5. Welsh to Reverend Jas. Abercrombie, May 10, 1886, in IRAP, Reel 68.
6. Henry S. Pancoast, *Impressions of the Sioux Tribes in 1882,* p. 16, in IRAP, Reel 102:A1.
7. Ibid., p. 14.
8. Ibid., p. 19.
9. Ibid., p. 18.
10. Ibid., p. 14.
11. Ibid., p. 16.
12. Ibid., p. 17.
13. Welsh, *Four Weeks,* p. 19.
14. Ibid., p. 4.
15. Pancoast, *Impressions,* p. 17.
16. Welsh, *Four Weeks,* p. 17.
17. Ibid., p. 18.
18. Ibid., p. 15.
19. Welsh, *Four Weeks,* p. 6.
20. Ibid., p. 5.
21. Ibid., p. 23.
22. Ibid., p. 22.
23. Ibid., p. 25.
24. Pancoast, *Impressions,* p. 10.
25. Welsh, *Four Weeks,* pp. 27–28.
26. Ibid., p. 20.

CHAPTER 2

1. For the background on other reform groups in the East there are a number of works. The most recent and all-encompassing is Francis Paul Prucha, *American Indian Policy in Crisis: Christian Reformers and the Indians, 1865–1900* (Norman: University of Oklahoma Press, 1976). Others of value are Loring Benson Priest, *Uncle Sam's Stepchildren: The Reformation of United States Indian Policy, 1865–1887* (New Brunswick: Rutgers University Press, 1942); Henry E. Fritz, *The Movement for Indian Assimilation, 1860–1890* (Philadelphia: University of Pennsylvania Press, 1963); Robert Winston Mardock, *The Reformers and the American Indian* (Columbia: University of Missouri Press, 1971); and Helen Marie Bannan, "Reformers and the 'Indian Problem,' 1878–1887 and 1922–1934" (Ph.D. dissertation, Syracuse University, 1976).

2. For further information on Meacham, see Edward Steel Phinney, "Alfred B. Meacham: promoter of Indian Reform" (Ph.D. dissertation, University of Oregon, 1963).

3. Irene Joanne Westing, "Amelia Stone Quinton," in Edward T. James, Editor, *Notable American Women 1607–1950* (Cambridge: Harvard University Press, 1971), 3:108–110, and Amelia Stone Quinton, "Care of the Indian," in Annie Nathan Meyer, Editor, *Women's Work in America* (1891; reprint, New York: Arno Press, 1972), pp. 373–391.

4. *The Council Fire,* January 1878, p. 13.

5. *The Indian Rights Association,* p. 3, in IRAP, Reel 102:A17.

6. Circular No. 102, in *Circulars: Book No. 3,* Record Group 75, National Archives.

7. William T. Hagan, *Indian Police and Judges* (New Haven: Yale University Press, 1966), pp. 104–109.

8. Philadelphia *Press,* June 30, 1882, p. 8.

9. Isaiah Lightner to Welsh, August 31 and September 22, 1882, and Land Commissioner to Welsh, September 30, 1882, all in IRAP, Reel 1.

10. November 15., 1882, IRAP, Reel 1.

11. Harriet H. Outerbridge to Welsh, November 15, 1882, in IRAP, Reel 1.

12. Edwin C. Gellett to Welsh, December 17, 1882, IRAP, Reel 1.

13. Welsh to Rev. Wm. N. McVickar, December 1, 1894, in IRAP, Reel 11.

14. For an excellent account of Pratt's career, see Everett Arthur Gilcreast, "Richard Henry Pratt and American Indian Policy, 1877–1906" (Ph.D. dissertation, Yale University, 1967).

15. Pratt to Welsh, December 13, 1882, in IRAP, Reel 1.

16. Quinton to Welsh, December 19, 1882, in IRAP, Reel 1.

17. Rhoads to Welsh, December 4, 1882, in IRAP, Reel 1.

18. Minutes of the Executive Committee, December 15, 1882, in IRAP, Reel 99.

19. Philadelphia *Inquirer,* December 16, 1882, p. 8.

20. Ibid.

21. Ibid.

22. John Welsh to Herbert Welsh, December 21, 1882, in IRAP, Reel 1.

23. Constitution of the Indian Rights Association, in IRAP, Reel 99.

24. Ibid.

CHAPTER 3

1. Welsh to S. C. Armstrong, April 4, 1884, in Armstrong Papers.

2. Rhoads to Welsh, December 4, 1882, in IRAP, Reel 1.

3. Armstrong to Mrs. Astor, December 13, 1882, in IRAP, Reel 1.

4. Rhoads to Armstrong, January 13, 1883, in Armstrong Papers.
5. Rhoads to Welsh, December 4, 1882, in IRAP, Reel 1.
6. Welsh to Armstrong, January 5, 1883, in Armstrong Papers.
7. Painter to Armstrong, April 25, 1883, in Armstrong Papers.
8. Executive committee minutes, September 18, 1883, in IRAP, Reel 99.
9. Painter to Armstrong, March 7, 1884, and Welsh to Armstrong, April 4, 1884, both in Armstrong Papers; Executive committee minutes, March 21, 1884, in IRAP, Reel. 99.
10. Welsh to William N. Hailmann, January 3, 1894, in IRAP, Reel 72.
11. Executive committee minutes, March 4, 1884, in IRAP, Reel 99.
12. Welsh to Fanny Welsh, February 14, 1883, in IRAP, Reel 1.
13. Welsh to Fanny Welsh, February 18, 1883, in IRAP, Reel 1.
14. The twenty-three are listed in *The Indian Rights Association*, in IRAP, Reel 102:A17.
15. Gardiner to commissioner, February 23, 1884, in Office of Indian Affairs, Letters Received (1884–3937), Record Group 75, National Archives.
16. Lists of members and donors appeared at the end of each IRA annual report.
17. Welsh to Armstrong, June 2, 1885, in Armstrong Papers.
18. Joshua W. Davis to Welsh, May 15, 1883, in IRAP, Reel 1.
19. The trip is described in Welsh, *Report of a Visit to the Great Sioux Reserve*, in IRAP, Reel 102:A3.
20. Welsh to Fanny Welsh, June 17, 1883, in IRAP, Reel 1.
21. Ibid.
22. Welsh, *Report of a Visit to the Great Sioux Reserve*, p. 33.
23. Ibid., p. 5.
24. Ibid., p. 40.
25. Ibid., pp. 40–41.
26. This trip is described in Welsh, *Report of a Visit to the Navajo, Pueblo, and Hualapais Indians*, in IRAP, Reel 102:A25.
27. Ibid., p. 5.
28. Ibid., p. 7.
29. Ibid., p. 11.
30. Ibid., p. 7.
31. Ibid., p. 13.
32. Ibid., pp. 15–16.
33. Ibid., p. 30.
34. Ibid., p. 30
35. Ibid., p. 35.
36. Executive committee minutes, June 5, 1883, in IRAP, Reel 99.
37. Welsh, *Report of a Visit to the Navajo, Pueblo, and Hualapais Indians*, p. 45.
38. Ibid., p.20.
39. Ibid., p. 31.
40. Ibid., p. 14.
41. Ibid., p. 12.
42. Armstrong, *Report of a Trip Made in Behalf of the Indian Rights Association to Some Indian Reservations of the Southwest*, p. 4, in IRAP, Reel 102:A4.
43. Ibid., p. 26.
44. Frazer, *The Apaches of the White Mountain Reservation, Arizona*, p. 21, in IRAP, Reel 102:A36.
45. Painter to James E. Rhoads, October 28, 1884, in IRAP, Reel 1.
46. Executive committee minutes, October 30, 1883, in IRAP, Reel 99.

47. "Journal of the Fourteenth Annual Conference with Representatives of Missionary Boards and Indian Rights Associations," in *Sixteenth Annual Report of the Board of Indian Commissioners, 1884*, p. 56.

48. Executive committee minutes, May 5, 1885, in IRAP, Reel 99.

49. "Journal of the Twelfth Annual Conference with Representatives of Missionary Boards," in *Fourteenth Annual Report of the Board of Indian Commissioners, 1882*, p. 51. (Each of these January meetings was reported in the annual report of the previous year.)

50. Johnson to Welsh, December 21, 1882, in IRAP, Reel 1.

51. "Journal of the Twelfth Annual Conference," p. 51.

52. *Report of a Visit to the Great Sioux Reserve*, p. 17.

53. *Address to the Public of the Lake Mohonk Conference*, p. 15; *Second Annual Address to the Public of the Lake Mohonk Conference*, pp. 35–37.

54. Pratt to Charles C. Painter, May 22, 1884, in Pratt Papers.

55. Pratt to Welsh, July 1, 1884, in Pratt Papers.

56. Welsh to Pratt, July 4, 1884, in Pratt Papers.

57. Pratt to Welsh, July 10, 1884, in Pratt Papers.

58. *The Council Fire*, June 1883, p. 84.

59. James C. Olson, *Red Cloud and the Sioux Problem* (Lincoln: University of Nebraska Press, 1965), pp. 283–85.

60. *Springfield Republican*, August 7, 1884, p. 6.

61. *The Council Fire*, April 1885, pp. 49–50.

62. Executive committee minutes, May 5, 1885, in IRAP, Reel 99.

63. Garrett to the secretary, April 14, 1885, in Office of Indian Affairs, Letters Received (1885–1862), National Archives.

CHAPTER 4

1. The appeal is filed in IRAP, Reel 1, by the date, March 20, 1884.

2. "Responsibility for Starvation Among the Piegans," December 24, 1884, in IRAP, Reel 1.

3. *Congressional Record*, 48 Congress, 2 session, p. 862.

4. Reprinted and circulated by the IRA, January 31, 1885, in IRAP, R103:D2.

5. Burt to Welsh, November 15, 1882, in IRAP, Reel 1.

6. Hare to Welsh, October 3, 1882, in IRAP, Reel 1.

7. Martha Goddard to Dawes, February 10, 1883, in Dawes Papers.

8. Painter to S. C. Armstrong, in Armstrong Papers.

9. Welsh, *Report of a Visit to the Great Sioux Reserve*, pp. 8–10, in IRAP, Reel 102:A3.

10. "Journal of the Fourteenth Annual Conference with Representatives of Missionary Boards and Indian Rights Associations," in *Sixteenth Annual Report of the Board of Indian Commissioners, 1884*, p. 56.

11. Pratt to Charles C. Painter, March 9, 1883, in Pratt Papers.

12. Welsh, *Report of a Visit to the Great Sioux Reserve*, pp. 26ff, in IRAP, Reel 102:A3.

13. Ibid., p.6.

14. Painter to S. C. Armstrong, March 7, 1884, in Armstrong Papers.

15. Herbert Welsh, *The Sioux Bill*, p. 1, in IRAP, Reel 102:A21.

16. Ibid., p. 2.

17. Ibid., p. 2.

18. IRA *Annual Report*, 1883, p.12.

19. *Indian Land in Severalty, as Provided for by the Coke Bill*, in IRAP, Reel 102:A20.

20. Welsh, *Report of a Visit to the Great Sioux Reserve*, p. 42.

21. Pancoast, *The Indian Before the Law,* in IRAP, Reel 102:A5.
22. Executive committee minutes, January 6, 1885, in IRAP, Reel 99.
23. IRA *Annual Report,* 1885, p. 15.
24. Painter to Welsh, May 27, 1884, in IRAP, Reel 1.
25. Executive committee minutes, Dec. 31, 1883, in IRAP, Reel 99; Welsh to Teller, February 20, 1884, in Office of Indian Affairs, Letters Received (1884–3841), National Archives.
26. IRAP *Annual Report,* 1884, p. 12.
27. Whipple to Wayne MacVeagh, January 5, 1884, in IRAP, Reel 1. Whipple was seeking help for Chippewas threatened with the loss of part of their White Earth Reservation.

CHAPTER 5

1. Anna L. Dawes to Welsh, February 8, 1888, in IRAP, Reel 3.
2. Agnes L. Sulzberger to Anna L. Dawes, February 3, 1888, enclosed in Dawes to Welsh, February 8, 1888, in IRAP, Reel 3.
3. Lists of donors appeared at the end of each IRA *Annual Report.*
4. Welsh to Henry J. Winser, February 28, 1889, in IRAP, Reel 69.
5. Welsh to Bishop Hare, May 12, 1886, in IRAP, Reel 68.
6. Welsh to Mrs. MacIntosh, April 23, 1887, in IRAP, Reel 68.
7. Welsh to Anna L. Dawes, January 22, 1888, in Dawes Papers; Welsh to Painter, December 23, 1887, in IRAP, Reel 68.
8. Harriet Outerbridge to Welsh, September 18, 1886, in IRAP, Reel 2.
9. Welsh to S. C. Armstrong, January 8, 1887, in IRAP, Reel 68.
10. Harrison to Welsh, October 4, 1888, in IRAP, Reel 3.
11. Welsh to S. C. Armstrong, November 19, 1888, in IRAP, Reel 69.
12. *The Condition of Affairs in Indian Territory and California,* p. 39, in IRAP, Reel 102:A96.
13. Ibid., p. 41.
14. Ibid., p. 3.
15. Painter to Welsh, May 9, 1887, in IRAP, Reel 2.
16. Painter, Memoranda for January 1889, in IRAP, Reel 101.
17. Howard Roberts Lamar, *Dakota Territory in 1861–1889* (New Haven: Yale University Press, 1956), p. 246.
18. Executive committee minutes, March 3, 1885, in IRAP, Reel 99.
19. *Crow Creek Reservation, Dakota. Action of the Indian Rights Association, and Opinions of the Press, West and East. . . . ,* pp.14ff, in IRAP, Reel 102:A40.
20. Pancoast to Dawes, March 8, 1885, in Dawes Papers.
21. Copy of Gasmann to Welsh, March 18, 1885, in Dawes Papers.
22. Executive committee minutes, April 7, 1885, in IRAP, Reel 99.
23. Executive committee minutes, May 5, 1885, in IRAP, Reel 99.
24. Reprinted in *Crow Creek Reservation, Dakota,* p. 13, in IRAP, Reel 102:A40.
25. Ibid., p. 43
26. Ibid., pp. 24–25.
27. Ibid., p. 35.
28. Ibid., pp. 36–38.
29. Ibid., p. 23.
30. Ibid., p. 28.
31. Welsh to Dawes, June 20, 1885, in Dawes Papers; IRA to the President, June 24, 1885, in IRAP, Reel 1.

32. Painter to Welsh, November 8, 1888, in IRAP, Reel 4; report of Agent W. W. Anderson, August 25, 1888, in *Annual Report of the Commissioner of Indian Affairs of 1888,* p. 33.
33. Untitled circular authored by Welsh and dated February 23, 1886, p. 6, in IRAP, Reel 102:A47.
34. Executive committee minutes, November 3, 1885, in IRAP, Reel 99.
35. Quinton to Welsh, May 4, 1886, in IRAP, Reel 1.
36. Quinton to Welsh, June 4, 1886, in IRAP, Reel 1.
37. Welsh to Kinney, May 4, 1886, in IRAP, Reel 68.
38. Welsh to Dr. James E. Rhoads, March 12, 1886, in IRAP, Reel 68.
39. Welsh to Dr. James E. Rhoads, June 12, 1886, in IRAP, Reel 68.
40. Welsh to P. F. McClure, June 17, 1886, in IRAP, Reel 68.
41. Welsh, *The Indian Problem,* pp. 6-7, in IRAP, Reel 102:A70.
42. Welsh to McClure, March 29, 1886, in IRAP, Reel 68.
43. Welsh to Bishop Hare, May 12, 1886, in IRAP, Reel 68.
44. Welsh to Philip Deloria, May 14, 1886, in IRAP, Reel 68.
45. Sniffen to McClure, May 7, 1886, in IRAP, Reel 68; McClure to Welsh, May 11, 1886, in IRAP, Reel 1.
46. Cleveland to Welsh, May 31, 1886, in IRAP, Reel 1.
47. Welsh to McClure, June 17, 1886, in IRAP, Reel 68.
48. McClure to Welsh, February 25 and March 4, 1887, both in IRAP, Reel 2.
49. Painter to Welsh, January 18, 1888, and Smedley Darlington to Welsh, February 9, 1888, both in IRAP, Reel 3.
50. Welsh to Painter, February 6, 1888, in IRAP, Reel 69.
51. Welsh to Samuel J. Randall, February 7, 1888, in IRAP, Reel 69.
52. Dawes to Welsh, February 19, 1888, in IRAP, Reel 3.
53. Painter to Welsh, March 5 and March 8, 1888, both in IRAP, Reel 3.
54. Welsh to Alexander Kent, March 10, 1888, in IRAP, Reel 69.
55. Welsh to Reverend Amos Ross, March 15, 1886, in IRAP, Reel 68.
56. Welsh to Deloria, May 14, 1886, in IRAP, Reel 68.
57. Joseph Fast Horse to Welsh, February 25, 1888, and Asa Kills-A-Hundred to Welsh, April 24, 1888, both in IRAP, Reel 3; Welsh to High Eagle, July 7, 1888, in IRAP, Reel 69.
58. Welsh to Francis P. Chardon, June 22, 1888, in IRAP, Reel 69.
59. Vilas to Welsh, June 22, 1888, in IRAP, Reel 3.
60. Vilas to Welsh, May 31, 1888, in IRAP, Reel 3.
61. McGillycuddy to Welsh, April 16, 1888, in IRAP, Reel 3.
62. McChesney to J. B. Harrison, April 16, 1888, in IRAP, Reel 3.
63. Robinson to J. B. Harrison, April 23, 1888, in IRAP, Reel 3.
64. Robinson to J. B. Harrison, June 6, 1888, in IRAP, Reel 3.
65. Robinson to Harrison, June 9, 1888, in IRAP, Reel 3.
66. Vilas to Welsh, July 11, 1888, in IRAP, Reel 3.
67. McLaughlin to Welsh, July 16, 1888, in IRAP, Reel 3.
68. Cleveland to Welsh, July 29, 1888, in IRAP, Reel 3.
69. Cook to Welsh, July 16, 1888, in IRAP, Reel 3.
70. Vilas to Pratt, August 21, 1888, in Indian Division Letterbook No. 56, National Archives.
71. Welsh to Mrs. N. N. Stokes, December 18, 1888, in IRAP, Reel 69.
72. Hare to Welsh, December 28, 1888, in IRAP, Reel 4.
73. Welsh to Painter, Feb. 5, 1889, in IRAP, Reel 69.
74. Welsh to Asa Kills-A-Hundred, May 11, 1889, in IRAP, Reel 69.

75. Crook to Welsh, December 16, 1889, in IRAP, Reel 5; Welsh to Crook, December 19, 1889, in IRAP, Reel 70.
76. Hare to Welsh, January 19, 1890, in IRAP, Reel 5; Welsh to Painter, January 21, 1890, in IRAP, Reel 70.
77. Welsh to Pettigrew, January 22, 1890, in IRAP, Reel 5.
78. Welsh to R. T. Woods, February 3, 1890, in IRAP, Reel 70.

CHAPTER 6

1. Painter to Welsh, June 8, 1886, in IRAP, Reel 1.
2. Lamar to Commissioner of Indian Affairs, August 24, 1888, in Indian Division Letterbook No. 46, National Archives.
3. Painter to Welsh, December 15, 1886, in IRAP, Reel 2.
4. Charles H. Allen to Welsh, December 18, 1886, in IRAP, Reel 2.
5. Welsh to editor of the Boston *Herald,* December 29, 1886, in IRAP, Reel 68.
6. *The Dawes Land in Severalty Bill and Indian Emancipation,* p. 1, in IRAP, Reel 102:A77.
7. IRA *Annual Report,* 1886, pp. 9–10.
8. Welsh to editor of *The Catholic Columbian,* April 9, 1887, in IRAP, Reel 68.
9. IRA *Annual Report,* 1886, p. 9.
10. "Journal of the Sixteenth Annual Conference with Representatives of Missionary Boards and Indian Rights Associations," in *Eighteenth Report of the Board of Indian Commissioners, 1886,* p. 131.
11. IRA *Annual Report,* 1886, p. 14.
12. Painter to Welsh, August 18, 1888, in IRAP, Reel 2.
13. Welsh to Childs, March 1, 1889, in IRAP, Reel 69.
14. IRA *Annual Report,* 1889, p. 18.
15. IRA *Annual Report,* 1888, p. 45.
16. Secretary Vilas to Secretary of War, September 10, 1888, in Indian Division Letterbook No. 57, National Archives.
17. Welsh to Waldo M. Higginson, December 27, 1888, in IRAP, Reel 69.
18. Copy of Painter to J. W. Davis, June 30, 1887, in IRAP, Reel 2.
19. The background on the case is to be found in *The Case of the Mission Indians in Southern California. . . .,* in IRAP, Reel 102:A49.
20. Executive committee minutes, December 22, 1885, in IRAP, Reel 99.
21. *The Case of the Mission Indian in Southern California. . . .,* pp. 14–15, in IRAP, Reel 102:A49.
22. Ward to Welsh, March 11, 1886, in IRAP, Reel 1.
23. *Proceedings of the Fourth Annual Lake Mohonk Conference,* 1886, p. 39.
24. Executive committee minutes, September 1 and November 9, 1886, both in IRAP, Reel 99.
25. Painter to Welsh, February 28, 1887, in IRAP, Reel 2.
26. "Proceedings of the Fifth Annual Meeting of the Lake Mohonk Conference," in *Twentieth Report of the Board of Indian Commissioners, 1888,* p. 92.
27. "Journal of the Seventeenth Annual Conference With Representatives of Missionary Boards and Indian Rights Associations," in *Nineteenth Report of the Board of Indian Commissioners,* 1887, p. 131.
28. Dawes to Welsh, February 24 and March 2, 1888; Painter to Welsh, March 8 and March 20, 1888, all in IRAP, Reel 3.
29. Report of Agent Edwin Eells, August 20, 1885, in *Annual Report of the Commissioner of Indian Affairs for 1885,* p. 193.
30. Executive committee minutes, December 22, 1885, in IRAP, Reel 99.
31. IRA *Annual Report,* 1886, p. 12.

32. Painter to Welsh, March 5, 1888, in IRAP, Reel 3.
33. Painter to Welsh, March 20, 1888, in IRAP, Reel 3.
34. Painter to Welsh, April 18, 1888, in IRAP, Reel 3.
35. United States v. Cook, 19 Wall. 591 (1873).
36. Annual Report of the Secretary of the Interior for 1888, p. 46.
37. Welsh to Vilas, December 21, 1888, in IRAP, Reel 69.
38. Vilas to Welsh, December 22, 1888, in IRAP, Reel 4.
39. Welsh to Dawes, December 24, 1888; Welsh to Chace, December 24, 1888, both in IRAP, Reel 69.
40. Painter to Welsh, January 8 and February 8, 1889, both in IRAP, Reel 4; Painter's Report for January, 1889, and Painter's Report for February, 1889, both in IRAP, Reel 101.
41. *Annual Report of the Commissioner of Indian Affairs for 1889*, p. 89.
42. Report of La Pointe Agent T. J. Gregory, August 20, 1888, in *Annual Report of the Commissioner of Indian Affairs for 1888*, p. 256.
43. Report of La Pointe Agent M. A. Leahy, September 16, 1889, in *Annual Report of the Commissioner of Indian Affairs for 1889*, p. 303.
44. IRA *Annual Report*, 1886, p. 13.
45. C. H. Beaulieu to Welsh, June 10, 1888, in IRAP, Reel 3.
46. Painter to Welsh, April 2, 1888, in IRAP, Reel 3.
47. Painter to Welsh, March 5, 1888, in IRAP, Reel 3; Welsh to Painter, March 6, 1888, in IRAP, Reel 69.
48. Painter to Welsh, April 2, 1888, in IRAP, Reel 3.
49. *The Proposed Removal of Indians to Oklahoma,* in IRAP, Reel 102;A91.
50. *Harper's Weekly,* March 31, 1888, p. 223.
51. Harrison to Executive Committee, April 3, 1888; Ryerson Ritchie to Welsh, June 19, 1888, both in IRAP, Reel 3.
52. Painter to Harrison, April 24, 1888, in IRAP, Reel 3.
53. Welsh to Mrs. Brinton Coxe, January 14, 1889, in IRAP, Reel 69.
54. Welsh to Painter, February 21, 1889, in IRAP, Reel 69.
55. Welsh to Painter, January 20, 1889, in IRAP, Reel 69; Painter to Welsh, February 1, 1889, in IRAP, Reel 4.

CHAPTER 7

1. Welsh to Cleveland, January 29, 1885, in Office of Indian Affairs, Letters Received (1885–6690), Record Group 75, National Archives.
2. "Proceedings of the Third Annual Lake Mohonk Conference, 1885," in *Seventeenth Annual Report of the Board of Indian Commissioners, 1885,* p. 70.
3. Welsh to S.C.Armstrong, August 6, 1885, in Armstrong Papers.
4. *Proceedings of the Fourth Annual Lake Mohonk Conference, 1886,* p. 1.
5. Executive committee minutes, February 2, 1886, in IRAP, Reel 99.
6. Executive committee minutes, January 6, 1887, in IRAP, Reel 99.
7. Welsh to Henry W. Farnum, November 2, 1887, in IRAP, Reel 68.
8. Welsh to Ward, November 14, 1887; Welsh to Curtis, December 8, 1887, both in IRAP, Reel 68.
9. Painter to Welsh, November 11, 1886, in IRAP, Reel 2.
10. Welsh to Benjamin Harrison, November 17, 1886, in IRAP, Reel 68.
11. Milroy to Welsh, May 9, 1885, in IRAP, Reel 1.
12. Circular No. 153, June 22, 1885, in Record Group 75, National Archives.

13. Extract of McLaughlin to Welsh, June 15, 1886, in IRAP, Reel 1.
14. Welsh to George William Curtis, November 29, 1886, in IRAP, Reel 68.
15. Welsh to Painter, September 27, 1886, in IRAP, Reel 68.
16. Welsh to Lamar, April 5, 1886, in IRAP, Reel 68.
17. Welsh to Dana, March 15, 1886, in IRAP, Reel 68.
18. IRA *Annual Report,* 1888, p.32.
19. Ibid.
20. Welsh to E. L. Godkin, February 28, 1888, in IRAP, Reel 69.
21. Welsh to Eaton, June 26, 1886, in IRAP, Reel 68.
22. Welsh to Curtis, June 14, 1886, in IRAP, Reel 68.
23. Welsh to Mrs. Sara T. Kinney, May 26, 1886, in IRAP, Reel 68.
24. IRA *Annual Report,* 1886, pp. 7—8.
25. *Address of Herbert Welsh ... Delivered Before the Mohonk Indian Conference, October 14, 1886,* in IRAP, Reel 102:A60.
26. Welsh to George William Curtis, November 30, 1886, in IRAP, Reel 68.
27. Sniffen to S. C. Armstrong, December 1, 1886, in IRAP, Reel 68.
28. New York *Daily Tribune,* September 28, 1888, p. 6.
29. Welsh to Thomas V. Keam, November 10, 1888; Welsh to George William Curtis, January 19, 1889, both in IRAP, Reel 69.
30. Armstrong, *The Indian Question* (Hampton: Normal School Steam Press, 1883), p. 11.
31. Welsh to Joseph Howard, June 21, 1886, in IRAP, Reel 68.
32. Welsh to E. L. Godkin, March 23, 1888, in IRAP, Reel 69.
33. Welsh to Vilas, July 3, 1888; Welsh to V. T. McGillycuddy, July 3, 1888, both in IRAP, Reel 69.
34. IRA to Cleveland, May 11, 1888, in IRAP, Reel 69.
35. *Harper's Weekly,* May 27, 1888, p. 371; New York *Daily Tribune,* June 17, 1888, p. 4.
36. Welsh to E. L. Godkin, June 22, 1888, in IRAP, Reel 69.
37. Welsh to Dana, November 1, 1888, in IRAP, Reel 69.
38. Everett Arthur Gilcreast, "Richard Henry Pratt and American Indian Policy, 1877—1906" (Ph.D. dissertation, Yale University, 1967), p. 70.
39. Cutcheon to Welsh, March 31, 1886; Dawes to Welsh, April 1, 1886, both in IRAP, Reel 1.
40. In IRAP, Reel 102.
41. *The Senator and the Schoolhouse,* in IRAP, Reel 102:A51.
42. *Are the Eastern Industrial Training Schools for Indian Children A Failure?,* in IRAP, Reel 102:A52.
43. Form letter, April 6, 1886, in IRAP, Reel 68.
44. Welsh to Byron M. Cutcheon, March 26, 1886, in IRAP, Reel 6.
45. Pratt to Alice Fletcher, November 26, 1887, in Pratt Papers.
46. Welsh to Armstrong, February 2, 1888, in IRAP, Reel 69.
47. Welsh to Dawes, February 25, 1888, in IRAP, Reel 69; Cox to Welsh, February 25, 1888, in IRAP, Reel 3.
48. Painter to Welsh, December 11, 1885, in IRAP, Reel 1.
49. *A Visit to the Mission Indians of Southern California and Other Western Tribes,* p. 18, in IRAP, Reel 102:A50.
50. Painter to Welsh, March 5, 1888, in IRAP, Reel 3.
51. Copy of Peabody to Alice L. Darlington, March 24, 1888, in IRAP, Reel 3.
52. Atkins to secretary of the interior, December 28, 1887, in Education Volume No. 11, pp. 74—75, National Archives.

53. "Proceedings of the Fifth Annual Meeting of the Lake Mohonk Conference," in *Nineteenth Annual Report of the Board of Indian Commissioners, 1887,* p. 111.
54. Welsh to Joshua W. Davis, September 30, 1887, in IRAP, Reel 2.
55. *The Independent,* October 6, 1887, p. 10, and December 22, 1887, p. 14.
56. *Springfield Republican,* February 28, 1888, p. 4.
57. Welsh to F. F. Ellinwood, February 2, 1888, in IRAP, Reel 69.
58. Cook to Welsh, February 3, 1888; Ward to Welsh, February 22, 1888, both in IRAP, Reel 3.
59. Welsh to William Hayes Ward, February 23, 1888, in IRAP, Reel 69.
60. *Springfield Republican,* March 2, 1888, p. 3.
61. Welsh to Ward, December 5, 1887, in IRAP, Reel 68.
62. Ellinwood to Eliphalet Whittlesey, October 23, 1886, in Board of Indian Commissioners Papers, National Archives.
63. "Proceedings of the Fifth Annual Meeting of the Lake Mohonk Conference," in *Nineteenth Annual Report of the Board of Indian Commissioners, 1887,* p. 71.
64. Welsh to Painter, June 11, 1886; Welsh to Harrison, June 21, 1886, both in IRAP, Reel 68.
65. Painter to Welsh, October 12, 1887, in IRAP, Reel 2.
66. Armstrong to Welsh, October 15, 1887, in IRAP, Reel 2.
67. Welsh to Dawes, October 19, 1887, in IRAP, Reel 68.
68. *The Independent,* February 9, 1888, p. 10.
69. *The Independent,* June 21, 1888, p. 12.
70. *The Apaches In Fort Marion, St. Augustine, Florida,* pp. 12–13, in IRAP, Reel 102:A78.
71. Welsh to William Hayes Ward, October 29, 1887, in IRAP, Reel 68.
72. Welsh to Harrison, September 11, 1888, in IRAP, Reel 3.
73. Pratt to B. M. Cutcheon, December 26, 1888, Pratt Papers.
74. Electa Dawes to H. L. Dawes, September 30, 1888, Dawes Papers.
75. Painter to Welsh, October 2, 1888, in IRAP, Reel 3.
76. "Proceedings of the Lake Mohonk Conference," in *Twentieth Annual Report of the Board of Indian Commissioners, 1888,* p. 97.
77. Lamar to Childs, October 20, 1887, in Indian Division Letterbook No. 52, National Archives.
78. Welsh to Vilas, July 9, 1888, in IRAP, Reel 69.
79. Vilas to Welsh, July 20, 1888, in IRAP, Reel 3.
80. Hare to Welsh, November 15, 1888, in IRAP, Reel 4.
81. Welsh to Painter, February 4, 1888, in IRAP, Reel 68.
82. Schurz to Welsh, February 15, 1887; Dawes to Welsh, February 24, 1887, both in IRAP, Reel 2.
83. Wood to Dawes, March 10, 1887, in Dawes Papers. See also Wood to Welsh, March 10, 1887, in IRAP, Reel 2.
84. Welsh to H. L. Dawes, April 26, 1887, in IRAP, Reel 68; Executive committee minutes, May 2, 1887, in IRAP, Reel 99.
85. Kinney to Welsh, March 22, 1886, in IRAP, Reel 3.
86. Boston *Evening Transcript,* May 15, 1888, p. 1.
87. Dawes to Electa Dawes, September 28, 1888, in Dawes Papers.
88. For a thorough treatment of the Apache experience, see David Michael Goodman, "Apaches as Prisoners of War, 1886–1894" (Ph.D. dissertation, Texas Christian University, 1969).
89. Welsh to H. L. Dawes, May 3, 1886; Welsh to J. R. Coolidge, Jr., May 5, 1886, both in IRAP, Reel 68.
90. Goodman, "Apaches as Prisoners of War," p. 43.
91. Bourke to Welsh, September 22, 1886, in IRAP, Reel 2.

92. Welsh to Painter, February 3, 1887; Welsh to Coolidge, January 6, 1887, both in IRAP, Reel 68.
93. *The Apache Prisoners in Fort Marion, St. Augustine, Florida,* p. 9, in IRAP, R102:A78.
94. Langdon to Welsh, March 31, 1887, in IRAP, Reel 2.
95 *The Apache Prisoners in Fort Marion, St. Augustine, Florida,* in IRAP, Reel 102:A78.
96. Painter to Welsh, March 28, 1887, and April 1, 1887, both in IRAP, Reel 2.
97. Executive committee minutes, April 5, 1887, in IRAP, Reel 99; Welsh to Brown, April 9, 1887, in IRAP, Reel 68; Joshua W. Dawes to Welsh, April 12, 1887, in IRAP, Reel 2.
98. Bourke to Welsh, April 23, 1887, in IRAP, Reel 2.
99. Sam Bowman to Welsh, July 26, 1887; Bourke to Welsh, October 3, 1887, both in IRAP, Reel 2.
100. R. H. Pratt to Welsh, December 1, 1887, in IRAP, Reel 3.
101. *The Apache Prisoners in Fort Marion, St. Augustine, Florida,* p. 4.
102. Welsh to Nelson D. Miles, May 14, 1887, in IRAP, Reel 68.
103. Pratt to S. C. Armstrong, January 19, 1888, in Pratt Papers; Painter to Welsh, May 10, 1888, in IRAP, Reel 3.
104. Welsh to Waldo Higginson, July 7, 1888, in IRAP, Reel 69.
105. Welsh to J. B. Harrison, August 2, 1888, in IRAP, Reel 3.
106. Welsh to S. C. Armstrong, January 9, 1889, in IRAP, Reel 69.

CHAPTER 8

1. These estimates are drawn from the statistics provided at the end of each annual report.
2. Welsh to Rhoads, January 21, 1891, in IRAP, Reel 70; Rhoads to Welsh, January 22, 1891, in IRAP, Reel 6.
3. Garrett to Welsh, January 17, 1893, in IRAP, Reel 9.
4. For example, see Welsh to Edwin D. Means, March 24, 1892; Welsh to Theodore S. Rummey, March 25, 1892, both in IRAP, Reel 71.
5. *New York Times,* September 8, 1890, p. 1; Welsh to Thomas W. Beaver, September 16, 1890. in IRAP, Reel 70.
6. Welsh to Roosevelt, November 24, 1891, in IRAP, Reel 71.
7. Welsh to Roosevelt, November 11, 1892; Welsh to David Scull, November 12, 1892, both in IRAP, Reel 71.
8. Welsh to Mrs. William B. Buckingham, November 29, 1892, in IRAP, Reel 72.
9. Welsh to Lyman Abbott, January 11, 1889, in IRAP, Reel 69.
10. Welsh to Oberly, November 16, 1888, in IRAP, Reel 69.
11. Welsh to Painter, January 26, 1889, in IRAP, Reel 69.
12. The pamphlet was *The Question of Indian Commissioner Oberly's Retention,* in IRAP, Reel 102:A110.
13. J. Rodman Paul to Welsh, February 17, 1889, in IRAP, Reel 4.
14. J. Y. Stowitts to Welsh, October 17, 1892, in IRAP, Reel 9; Welsh to Stowitts, October 24, 1892, in Reel 71.
15. Morgan to Welsh, April 17, 1891, in IRAP, Reel 7; Welsh to Ward, April 18, 1891, in Reel 71.
16. M. Emma Register to Roosevelt, October 22, 1892, in IRAP, Reel 71.
17. Welsh to Painter, February 4 and February 27, 1889, in IRAP, Reel 69.
18. Quinton to Welsh, February 15, 1889, in IRAP, Reel 4.
19. Teller to Welsh, March 2, 1889; Plumb to Welsh, March 8, 1889, both in IRAP, Reel 4.

20. Ingalls to Welsh, March 13, 1889, in IRAP, Reel 4.
21. Welsh to James E. Rhoads, November 28, 1888, in IRAP, Reel 69.
22. Rhoads to Welsh, February 20, 1889, in IRAP, Reel 4.
23. H. D. Houghton to Welsh, February 23, 1889, in IRAP, Reel 4.
24. Painter to Welsh, May 23, 1889, in IRAP, Reel 4.
25. Welsh to Curtis, May 25, 1889, in IRAP, Reel 69.
26. Dawes to Welsh, February 9, 1889, in IRAP, Reel 4.
27. Welsh to Bowditch, March 2, 1889, in IRAP, Reel 69.
28. Dawes to Welsh, March 9, 1889, in IRAP, Reel 4.
29. *Springfield Republican,* March 19, 1889, in a scrapbook in IRAP, Reel 104.
30. Welsh to editor of Boston *Post,* March 22, 1889, in IRAP, Reel 4.
31. Welsh to S. C. Armstrong, November 19, 1888, in IRAP, Reel 69.
32. Welsh to Harrison, December 4, 1888, in IRAP, Reel 69.
33. Welsh to Painter, June 7, 1889, in IRAP, Reel 69.
34. Welsh to George William Curtis, June 8, 1889, in IRAP, Reel 70.
35. Welsh to Morgan, June 8 and June 14, 1889, in IRAP, Reel 70.
36. Morgan to Welsh, June 11, 1889, in IRAP, Reel 4.
37. For the best discussion of the Catholic attitude toward Morgan and Dorchester, see Francis Paul Prucha, *The Churches and the Indian Schools 1888–1912* (Lincoln: University of Nebraska Press, 1979), pp. 12ff.
38. *Annual Report of the Commissioner of Indian Affairs for 1890,* p. xvii.
39. Prucha, *The Churches and the Indian Schools,* pp. 12ff.
40. Executive committee minutes, December 3, 1889, in IRAP, Reel 99.
41. Doane to Welsh, December 2, 1889, in IRAP, Reel 5.
42. Mallalieu to Welsh, December 5, 1889, Reel 5.
43. Quinton to Welsh, December 8, 1889; Kinney to Welsh, December 14, 1889, both in IRAP, Reel 5.
44. Welsh to Reverend W. Henry Green, December 11, 1889, in IRAP, Reel 70.
45. Gorman to Welsh, December 15, 1889, in IRAP, Reel 5.
46. Welsh to Gorman, December 16, 1889; Welsh to J. W. Harding, December 21, 1889, both in IRAP, Reel 70.
47. Pratt to Senator John Coit Spooner, February 12, 1890, in Pratt Papers.
48. Pratt to Caroline S. Morgan, January 18, 1890; Pratt to Secretary John W. Noble, January 21, 1890, both in Pratt Papers.
49. Morgan to Welsh, December 30, 1889, in IRAP, Reel 5.
50. Welsh to George William Curtis, January 2, 1889, in IRAP, Reel 70.
51. Welsh to Bishop Doane, February 21, 1890, in IRAP, Reel 70.
52. Welsh to Cardinal Gibbons, July 9, 1889, in IRAP, Reel 70; Lucy B. Arnold to Welsh, July 20, 1889, in IRAP, Reel 133.
53. Morgan to Welsh, August 19, 1889, in IRAP, Reel 133.
54. J. George Wright to Welsh, August 30, 1890, in IRAP, Reel 133.
55. Welsh to T. J. Morgan, November 15, 1889, in IRAP, Reel 70.
56. Welsh to Foy, December 16, 1889, in IRAP, Reel 70.
57. Dawes to Electa Dawes, September 8, 1890, in Dawes Papers.
58. Welsh to Morgan, July 8, 1891, in IRAP, Reel 71.
59. Welsh to Charles Collins, April 18, 1891, in IRAP, Reel 71.
60. McLaughlin to Welsh, June 12, 1891, in IRAP, Reel 7.
61. Morgan to Welsh, January 30, 1891, in IRAP, Reel 6.
62. Pratt to McCutcheon, February 19, 1891; Pratt to Alice C. Fletcher, August 7, 1891, both in Pratt Papers.
63. Painter to Welsh, June 29, 1892, in IRAP, Reel 9.

64. Gibbons to Welsh, January 23, 1892, in IRAP, Reel 8.
65. Marty to Welsh, February 17, 1892, in IRAP, Reel 8.
66. Welsh to Painter, January 25, 1892, in IRAP, Reel 71.
67. Pratt to President Cleveland, March 20, 1893, in Pratt Papers.
68. Welsh to William E. Dodge, November 16, 1892, in IRAP, Reel 71.
69. Morgan to Welsh, June 20, 1892, in IRAP, Reel 9; Welsh to Morgan, June 22, 1892, in Reel 71.
70. Welsh to Roosevelt, June 22, 1892, in IRAP, Reel 71.
71. S. M. McCowan to Welsh, March 16, 1891, in IRAP, Reel 7.
72. Welsh to Roosevelt, August 25, 1892, in IRAP, Reel 71.
73. Painter to Welsh, July 1, 1892, in IRAP, Reel 9; Welsh to Painter, July 2, 1892, in Reel 71; Morgan to Welsh, August 5, 1892, in Reel 9.
74. Welsh to Senator Redfield Proctor, October 25, 1892, in IRAP, Reel 71.
75. Welsh to T. J. Morgan, October 26, 1892, in IRAP, Reel 71.
76. Roosevelt to Welsh, September 30, 1892, in IRAP, Reel 9.
77. Goodale to Welsh, December 28, 1890, in IRAP, Reel 6.
78. Welsh to W. A. Linn, November 30, 1892, in IRAP, Reel 72.
79. Hare to Welsh, December 19, 1892, in IRAP, Reel 9.
80. Elaine Eastman to Welsh, December 24, 1892, in IRAP, Reel 9.
81. Wood to Welsh, undated but filed January 25, 1893, in IRAP, Reel 9.
82. Welsh to Roosevelt, February 11, 1893, in IRAP, Reel 72.
83. Welsh to Mrs. W. W. Crannell, February 15, 1893, in IRAP, Reel 72.
84. The committee of about a dozen included, besides Welsh, Charles Painter, Bishop Hare, General S. C. Armstrong, Whittlesey of the Board of Indian Commissioners, Mrs. Amelia Quinton, and representatives of missionary groups. See the clipping from *The Springfield Republican,* March 16, 1889, in scrapbook in IRAP, Reel 104.
85. Noble to Welsh, June 11, 1889, in IRAP, Reel 4.
86. Welsh to Noble, June 25, 1889, in IRAP, Reel 70.
87. Noble to Welsh, July 1, 1889, in IRAP, Reel 4.
88. Welsh to Morgan, July 2, 1889, in IRAP, Reel 7.
89. Noble to Commissioner Morgan, March 10, 1891, in IRAP, Reel 7.
90. Welsh to Nelson A. Miles, November 14, 1891, in IRAP, Reel 71.
91. Welsh to John Hemsley Johnson, January 31, 1890, in IRAP, Reel 70; IRA *Annual Report,* 1889, p. 42.
92. Welsh to John Addison Potter, April 15, 1889, in IRAP, Reel 69.
93. Welsh to Roosevelt, July 11, 1889, in IRAP, Reel 70.
94. Roosevelt to Welsh, July 12, 1889, in IRAP, Reel 4.

CHAPTER 9

1. For a good background on the Ghost Dance and its impact on the Sioux, see Robert M. Utley, *The Last Days of the Sioux Nation* (New Haven: Yale University Press, 1963).
2. Noble to Welsh, July 1, 1890, in IRAP, Reel 6.
3. Utley, *Last Days,* pp. 109ff.
4. Stewart to Welsh, November 11, 1890, in IRAP, Reel 6.
5. These letters went out November 19, 1890. See IRAP, Reel 70.
6. McLaughlin to Welsh, November 25, 1890; Miles to Welsh, December 1, 1890; Cook to Welsh, December 2, 1890; Hare to Welsh, December 12, 1890, all in IRAP, Reel 6. Welsh to editor of the *Springfield Republican,* November 25, 1890, in Reel 70.
7. Welsh to V. T. McGillycuddy, December 12, 1890, in IRAP, Reel 70.

8. Elaine Goodale was one of those who proposed the replacement of Royer by McGillycuddy; see Goodale to Welsh, December 12, 1890, in IRAP, Reel 6.
9. Welsh to Talcott Williams, December 4, 1890, in IRAP, Reel 70.
10. Copy of Morgan to secretary of interior, December 23, 1890, in IRAP, Reel 6; Welsh to Morgan, December 27, 1890, in Reel 70.
11. Caroline Morgan to Welsh, December 16, 1890, in IRAP, Reel 6.
12. Welsh to Cleveland, December 22, 1890, in IRAP, Reel 70; Hare to Welsh, December 30, 1890, in Reel 6.
13. Stewart to Welsh, December 15, 1890, in IRAP, Reel 6.
14. Welsh to Roosevelt, December 31, 1890, in IRAP, Reel 70.
15. Welsh to the editor of *The Civil Service Record,* December 31, 1890, in IRAP, Reel 70.
16. Ibid.
17. Hare to Welsh, January 6, 1891, in IRAP, Reel 6.
18. Welsh to Laura E. Tileston, January 22, 1891, in IRAP, Reel 70.
19. Eastman to Wood, January 3, 1891, published in the Boston *Transcript,* January 7. This version, with accompanying editorial comment, was circulated by the IRA under the date January 9. See IRAP, Reel 102.
20. Welsh to Talcott Williams, January 9, 1891; Welsh to Bourke, January 19, 1891, both in IRAP, Reel 70.
21. Welsh to Edward M. Bacon, January 23, 1891, in IRAP, Reel 70.
22. Welsh to the editor of the *Washington Post,* January 10, 1891, in IRAP, Reel 70.
23. Welsh to the editor of the Philadelphia *Press,* March 16, 1891, in IRAP, Reel 71.
24. Utley, *Last Days,* pp. 257–58, 265–66.
25. Ibid., pp. 261–65.
26. Welsh to Noble, February 4, 1891, in IRAP, Reel 70.
27. *To the Public Press,* in IRAP, Reel 102:A138.
28. Roosevelt to Welsh, February 13, 1891, in IRAP, Reel 7.
29. Burns to Welsh, March 28, 1891; Sumner to Welsh, March 29, 1891, both in IRAP, Reel 7.
30. Welsh to T. J. Morgan, April 3, 1891; Welsh to Edwin M. Bacon, April 7, 1891, both in IRAP, Reel 71.
31. Law committee report, April 6, 1891, in IRAP, Reel 7.
32. Charles E. Pancoast to Welsh, May 8, 1891, in IRAP, Reel 7.
33. Welsh to F. L. Stevens, May 11, 1891, in IRAP, Reel 71.
34. Welsh to Miller, April 3, 1891, in IRAP, Reel 71; Miller to Welsh, April 6, 1891, in IRAP, Reel 7.
35. Welsh to Charles Collins, April 29, 1891, in IRAP, Reel 71.
36. Welsh to editor of the Philadelphia *Press,* April 28, 1891, in IRAP, Reel 71.
37. Miller to Welsh, May 11, 1891, in IRAP, Reel 7; Welsh to Miller, May 12, 1891, in IRAP, Reel 71.
38. Welsh to Elizabeth Gilman, May 19, 1891, in IRAP, Reel 71.
39. Welsh to Jennings, July 13, 1891, in IRAP, Reel 71.
40. IRA *Annual Report,* 1891, p. 7.
41. Morgan to Welsh, January 15, 1891, in IRAP, Reel 6.
42. Welsh to Mary Fuller, February 14, 1891, in IRAP, Reel 70.
43. Copy of H. L. Dawes to Frank Wood, enclosed in M. E. Strieby to E. Whittlesey, November 24, 1891, in Board of Indian Commissioners Papers.
44. IRA *Annual Report,* 1891, p. 4.
45. Welsh to Cleveland, January 15, 1891; Sniffen to Cleveland, February 14, 1891; both in IRAP, Reel 70.
46. Welsh to Cleveland, February 16, 1891, in IRAP, Reel 70.

47. Cleveland to Welsh, February 24, 1891, in IRAP, Reel 7.
48. IRA *Annual Report*, 1891, p. 28.

CHAPTER 10

1. Harrison's annual message to Congress, December 19, 1891, in Benjamin Harrison, *Public Papers and Addresses of Benjamin Harrison* (New York: Kraus Reprints Company, 1979), p. 116.
2. The man was H. W. Spray, who had been in charge of a Quaker school for seven years. This time Welsh found himself at odds with the Quakers, not with the Indian office. The woman was a Mrs. Gause, an employee of a school in Albuquerque. Welsh sided with Mrs. Gause, but Commissioner Morgan supported the superintendent of the school with whom she had exchanged charges.
3. *Protest of the Indian Rights Association Against the Proposed Removal of the Southern Ute Indians,* p.2, in IRAP, Reel 102:A117.
4. Circular by Welsh, dated February 25, 1890, in IRAP, Reel 102:A116.
5. Welsh to Gibbons, February 23, 1892, in IRAP, Reel 71.
6. Painter to Welsh, March 7, 1892, in IRAP, Reel 8.
7. Painter to Welsh, November 4, 1889, in IRAP, Reel 5.
8. *Removal of the Southern Utes,* p. 6, in IRAP, Reel 102:A114.
9. Their report, *A Further Report to the Indian Rights Association on the Proposed Removal of the Southern Utes,* can be found in IRAP, Reel 102:A145.
10. Each IRA annual report listed the association's publications for that year and the number printed of each. However, letters that were duplicated and sent out by the hundreds of copies were not included in these listings.
11. Denver *Times*, April 5, 1890, in scrapbook in IRAP, Reel 104.
12. *Colorado Sun*, January 25, 1892, in IRAP, Reel 102:A142.
13. Painter to Welsh, August 16, 1889, in IRAP, Reel 133.
14. Dunn to Welsh, January 25, 1890, in IRAP, Reel 5.
15. *Removal of the Southern Utes,* p. 7, in IRAP, Reel 102:A114.
16. The list is dated December 23, 1892, and is to be found in IRAP, Reel 133.
17. Quinton to Welsh, February 21, 1892, in IRAP, Reel 8.
18. Lake Mohonk, *Proceedings*, 1889, p. 9; Lake Mohonk, *Proceedings*, 1891, p. 114.
19. Morgan to Noble, March 1, 1890, in IRAP, Reel 5.
20. *Annual Report of the Commissioner of Indian Affairs for 1890,* p. xliii.
21. Dawes to Welsh, March 9, 1890, in IRAP, Reel 5.
22. Dawes to Welsh, March 22, 1890, in IRAP, Reel 5.
23. Welsh to Quinton, March 28, 1890, in IRAP, Reel 70.
24. Samuel Bowles to Dawes, March 29, 1890, in Dawes Papers.
25. Anna L. Dawes to Welsh, April 14, 1890, in IRAP, Reel 5.
26. *Congressional Record* 23:2641.
27. Welsh to Dawes, March 30, 1892, in Dawes Papers.
28. Painter to Welsh, January 29, 1890, in IRAP, Reel 5.
29. Welsh to Morgan, April 29, 1891, in IRAP, Reel 71.
30. Copy of Morgan to Noble, December 30, 1891, in IRAP, Reel 8.
31. Welsh to Painter, March 1, 1892, in IRAP, Reel 71.
32. Roosevelt to Welsh, March 22, 1892, in IRAP, Reel 9.
33. Painter to Welsh, May 10, 1892, in IRAP, Reel 9.
34. Painter to Welsh, May 11, 1892, in IRAP, Reel 9.

35. Painter's report, filed "May, 1892" in IRAP, Reel 101; Painter to Welsh, August 3, 1892, in Reel 9.

36. Painter to Welsh, January 9, 1893, in IRAP, Reel 9.

37. Walker to Welsh, June 22, 1891, in IRAP, Reel 7.

38. Welsh to Abbott, June 26, 1891, in IRAP, Reel 71.

39. Welsh to Quick Bear, November 23, 1892, in IRAP, Reel 71.

40. George W. Nellis to Welsh, November 25, 1892, in IRAP, Reel 9; IRA *Annual Report*, 1892, pp. 45–46.

41. Painter to Welsh, January 23, 1893, in IRAP, Reel 9.

42. Copy of Williamson to Joshua W. Davis, February 18, 1893, in IRAP, Reel 10.

43. Painter to Welsh, February 15, 1893, in IRAP, Reel 9.

44. Welsh to Roosevelt, February 15, 1893, in IRAP, Reel 72.

45. *Protest by the Executive Committee of the Indian Rights Association. . . .*, in IRAP, Reel 102:B5.

46. Welsh to Bishop Hare, March 6, 1893, in IRAP, Reel 72; IRA *Annual Report*, 1893, p. 52.

47. *Annual Report of the Commissioner of Indian Affairs for 1874*, p. 26; Thomas Jennings to the commissioner of Indian Affairs, August 24, 1889, in *Annual Report of the Commissioner of Indian Affairs for 1889*, p. 300.

48. IRA *Annual Report*, 1886, p. 15.

49. Painter to Welsh, March 1, 1889, in IRAP, Reel 4.

50. Painter to Welsh, March 2, 1893, in IRAP, Reel 10.

51. Painter to Welsh, February 25, 1893, in IRAP, Reel 10.

52. IRA *Annual Report*, 1893, p. 40.

53. Painter to Welsh, January 30, 1891, in IRAP, Reel 6; Welsh to Painter, February 14, 1891, in Reel 70.

54. Painter to Welsh, April 3, 1891, in IRAP, Reel 7.

55. "Journal of the Twenty-First Annual Conference of the United States Board of Indian Commissioners With Representatives of Missionary Boards and Indian Rights Association," in *Twenty-Third Annual Report of the Board of Indian Commissioners, 1891*, p. 141.

56. Painter to Welsh, December 15, 1891, in IRAP, Reel 8.

57. IRA *Annual Report*, 1891, p. 17.

58. Painter, *How We Punish Our Allies*, pp. 2–4, in IRAP, Reel 102:A103.

59. Ibid.

60. Painter to Welsh, March 11, 1890, in IRAP, Reel 5.

61. Painter to Welsh, January 1, 1891, in IRAP, Reel 6.

62. *The Sisseton Indians*, in IRAP, Reel 102:A136.

63. IRA *Annual Report*, pp. 18–20. Even Senator Pettigrew, notorious for his own efforts to fleece the Indians, thought Sanborn's actions "a swindle in every particular." See Pettigrew to E. Whittlesey, February 24, 1892, in Board of Indian Commissioners Papers.

64. Painter to Welsh, July 1, 1892, in IRAP, Reel 9.

65. Painter to Welsh, March 18, 1892, in IRAP, Reel 9.

66. Painter to Welsh, July 1, 1892, in IRAP, Reel 9.

67. Painter to Welsh, March 10, 1892, in IRAP, Reel 8.

68. Painter to Welsh, March 29, 1892, in IRAP, Reel 9.

69. Painter to Welsh, May 11, 1892, in IRAP, Reel 9.

70. Miles to Welsh, July 12, 1892, in IRAP, Reel 9.

71. *Cheyennes and Arapahoes Revisited*, in IRAP, Reel 102:B3.

72. *Proceedings of the Tenth Annual Meeting of the Lake Mohonk Conference of Friends of the Indian 1892*, p. 121.

73. IRA *Annual Report,* 1892, p. 18.
74. Painter to Welsh, May 27, 1889, in IRAP, Reel 4.
75. Painter to Welsh, June 7, and September 9, 1889, both in IRAP, Reel 4.
76. *New York Times,* September 30, 1889, in scrapbook in IRAP, Reel 104.
77. Painter to Welsh, December 13, 1889, in IRAP, Reel 6.
78. Welsh to Secretary Proctor, June 13 and June 24, 1889, both in IRAP, Reel 6; IRA *Annual Report,* 1890, pp. 13–15.
79. Welsh to T. J. Morgan, March 11, 1891, in IRAP, Reel 71.
80. Copy of Morgan to Senator Charles F. Manderson, March 2, 1891, in IRAP, Reel 7.
81. Welsh to M. N. Gilbert, March 26, 1891, in IRAP, Reel 71.
82. Welsh to J. B. Thayer, April 4, 1891, in IRAP, Reel 71.
83. Copy of Salsbury to Welsh, May 18, 1891, enclosed in Welsh to Whittlesey, May 18, 1891, in Board of Indian Commissioners Papers.
84. Copy of Salsbury to Captain Charles G. Penney, in IRAP, Reel 8.
85. Sniffen to Commissioner of Indian Affairs, August 11, 1891, in IRAP, Reel 8; Acting Commissioner R. V. Belt to Welsh, August 17, 1891, and G. W. Lillie to Sniffen, August 17, 1891, both in IRAP, Reel 8.
86. Copy of G. W. Lillie to Welsh, August 13, 1891; Sniffen to Welsh, August 14, 1891, both in IRAP, Reel 8.
87. Painter to Welsh, April 20, 1892; circular dated April 29, 1892, both in IRAP, Reel 9.
88. A copy of Noble's circular, dated May 2, 1892, is to be found in IRAP, Reel 9.
89. Welsh to Morgan, May 11, 1892, in IRAP, Reel 71; Caroline Morgan to Welsh, May 14, 1892, in IRAP, Reel 9.
90. Riggs to Welsh, May 28, 1892, in IRAP, Reel 9.
91. Welsh to William J. Cleveland, November 29, 1892, in IRAP, Reel 72.
92. Welsh to William E. Dodge, November 10, 1892, in IRAP, Reel 71.
93. Painter to Welsh, November 5, 1892, in IRAP, Reel 9.
94. Welsh to William E. Dodge, November 10, 1892, in IRAP, Reel 71.

CHAPTER 11

1. Despite the key role played by these three women in sustaining the IRA, I have uncovered nothing to explain their generosity.
2. Welsh to Edward H. Magill, May 2, 1894, in IRAP, Reel 73.
3. Welsh to Mrs. Samuel Colt, March 6, 1894, in IRAP, Reel 72.
4. Welsh to William N. Hailmann, January 3, 1894, in IRAP, Reel 72.
5. Welsh to Painter, December 19, 1893, in IRAP, Reel 72.
6. The committee backed ex-Governor Robert E. Patteson, whose election Welsh judged to be "of the most vital importance to the moral welfare of the city." See Welsh to Miss Sarah Newlin, February 12, 1895, in IRAP, Reel 73.
7. Welsh to Francis E. Leupp, February 22, 1895, in IRAP, Reel 73.
8. Welsh to Mrs. Brinton Coxe, September 28, 1895, in IRAP, Reel 73.
9. Copy of Joseph May to Welsh, January 6, 1896, in IRAP, Reel 12.
10. Welsh to Bishop Hare, April 15, 1895, in IRAP, Reel 73.
11. Welsh to Mrs. John Markoe, April 19, 1895, in IRAP, Reel 73.
12. Welsh to F. F. Kane, April 16, 1895; Welsh to Mrs. John Markoe, April 19, 1895; Welsh to Arthur B. Emmons, April 20, 1895, all in IRAP, Reel 73.
13. Welsh to Mrs. M. E. Baxter, April 20, 1895, in IRAP, Reel 73.
14. Welsh to Ernest Russell, May 2, 1895, in IRAP, Reel 73.
15. Welsh to Carl Schurz, June 7, 1895, in IRAP, Reel 73.

16. Welsh to Leupp, April 27, 1895, in IRAP, Reel 73.
17. Welsh to Mrs. Winthrop Cowdin, April 19, 1895, in IRAP, Reel 73.
18. Welsh to Henry W. Farnam, January 18, 1894; Welsh to Reverend J. Max Hark, March 19, 1894, both in IRAP, Reel 72.
19. Welsh to R. Fulton Cutting, March 2, 1895, in IRAP, Reel 73.
20. Welsh to Reuben Quick Bear, May 25, 1895, in IRAP, Reel 73.
21. F. F. Kane to Welsh, December 30, 1895, in IRAP, Reel 12; Executive committee minutes, January 8, 1896, in Reel 99.
22. It also proved a financial burden as the IRA paid Painter's widow his salary for three months after learning of her straitened financial situation.
23. Welsh to Whittlesey, January 15, 1895, in IRAP, Reel 73.
24. Welsh to executive committee members, April 14, 1894, in IRAP, Reel 72.
25. Welsh to Meserve, January 19, 1895, in IRAP, Reel 73.
26. Roosevelt to Welsh, January 23, 1895; Leupp to Roosevelt, February 6, 1895, both in IRAP, Reel 12.
27. Welsh to Smith, January 17, 1894, in IRAP, Reel 72.
28. Schurz to Welsh, November 21, 1892, in IRAP, Reel 9.
29. Executive committee minutes, January 3, 1893, in IRAP, Reel 99.
30. Painter to Welsh, December 28, 1892, in IRAP, Reel 9.
31. Hare to Welsh, December 28, 1892, in IRAP, Reel 9.
32. Welsh to Philip Garrett, January 11, 1893, in IRAP, Reel 72.
33. Charles Wood to Welsh, January 16, 1893, in IRAP, Reel 9; Welsh to Cleveland, January 17, 1893, in Reel 72; Executive committee minutes, February 7, 1893, in Reel 99.
34. Cleveland to Welsh, March 13, 1893, in IRAP, Reel 10; Welsh to Cleveland, March 15, 1893, in Reel 72.
35. Pratt to Cleveland, March 20, 1893, in Pratt Papers.
36. Welsh to Philip G. Garrett, April 14, 1893, in IRAP, Reel 72.
37. Welsh to Captain G. L. Brown, in IRAP, Reel 72.
38. Welsh to Painter, June 10, 1893, in IRAP, Reel 72.
39. Ibid.
40. Welsh to Roosevelt, December 4, 1893, in IRAP, Reel 72.
41. Smith to Welsh, April 11, 1894, in IRAP, Reel 11.
42. Smith to Welsh, November 21, 1894, in IRAP, Reel 11.
43. Welsh to Smith, January 15, 1895, in IRAP, Reel 73.
44. Dorchester to Welsh, June 9, 1893, in IRAP, Reel 10; Welsh to Dorchester, June 14, 1893, in Reel 72. The circular is dated June 22, 1893 for filing purposes and can be found in Reel 10.
45. Welsh to Painter, November 27, 1893, in IRAP, Reel 72.
46. Roosevelt to Welsh, November 28, 1893, in IRAP, Reel 10; Welsh to Roosevelt, December 1, 1893, in Reel 72.
47. Welsh to Roosevelt, December 12, 1893, in IRAP, Reel 72.
48. *The Secretary of the Interior and the Indian Educational Problem—A Rift in the Cloud*, in IRAP, Reel 102:B12.
49. Welsh to Philip Garrett, January 11, 1893; Welsh to Captain G. L. Brown, May 5, 1893, both in IRAP, Reel 72.
50. *Annual Report of the Commissioner of Indian Affairs for 1893*, p. 6.
51. The circular, dated March 20, 1894, appears in IRAP, Reel 11; Welsh to J. George Wright, April 2, 1894, in Reel 72.
52. Welsh to Gilman, November 1, 1893, in IRAP, Reel 72. Welsh also sought help from a Georgia minister to bring pressure to bear on Georgian Hoke Smith, see Welsh to Reverend F. F. Dripps, November 2, 1893, in Reel 72.

53. C. W. Crouse to Welsh, July 10, 1893, in IRAP, Reel 10.
54. Erasmus Van Deerlin to Welsh, April 20, 1894, in IRAP, Reel 11.
55. Roosevelt to Welsh, June 28, 1893, in IRAP, Reel 10.
56. Roosevelt to Welsh, July 1, 1893, in IRAP, Reel 10.
57. Pratt to Dr. Carlos Montezuma, April 1, 1893, in Pratt Papers.
58. Welsh to Pratt, February 13, 1894, in IRAP, Reel 72.
59. Welsh to Painter, February 16, 1894, in IRAP, Reel 72.
60. Leupp to Welsh, November 9, 1896, in IRAP, Reel 13.
61. Pratt to Quay, February 13, 1897, in Pratt Papers.
62. Leupp to Welsh, February 8, 1897. in IRAP, Reel 13.
63. "Monthly Report of Washington Agency," January 31, 1897, in IRAP, Reel 133.
64. Pratt to Mrs. Charles Russell, January 29, 1897, in Pratt Papers.
65. Welsh to Charles L. Davis, February 9, 1897, in IRAP, Reel 74.
66. *City and State,* March 4, 1897, p. 2.
67. Welsh to Daniel C. Gilman, November 1, 1893, in IRAP, Reel 72.
68. Roosevelt to Welsh, November 10, 1893, in IRAP, Reel 10.
69. The circular is to be found in IRAP, Reel 102:B9.
70. IRA *Annual Report,* 1893, p. 16.
71. Reprint of an article in *Good Government,* dated February 15, 1895, in IRAP, Reel 102:B21; *Civil Service Reform Essential to a Successful Indian Administration,* dated April, 1895, in Reel 102:B23.
72. IRA *Annual Report,* 1896, p. 4.
73. *The Teller Bill,* in IRAP, Reel 102:B28.
74. Welsh to Leupp, December 18, 1896, in IRAP, Reel 74.
75. "Monthly Report of Washington Agency," January 31, 1897, in IRAP, Reel 133.

CHAPTER 12

1. *The Latest Phase of the Southern Ute Question,* p. 18, in IRAP, Reel 102:B25.
2. Ibid., pp. 21–22.
3. Sniffen to Leupp, July 8, 1896, in IRAP, Reel 73.
4. Welsh to Leupp, January 18, 1897, in IRAP, Reel 74.
5. Much of this correspondence related to rival Lower Brulé delegations wishing to visit Washington. Leupp attributed some of this to the Indians' nomadic instinct. See Leupp to Welsh, March 27, 1897, in IRAP, Reel 13.
6. Welsh to the editor of the Philadelphia *Press,* March 16, 1891, in IRAP, Reel 71.
7. Welsh to Secretary David R. Francis, February 4, 1897; Welsh to Leupp, February 10, 1897, both in IRAP, Reel 74.
8. IRA *Annual Report,* 1893, pp. 43ff.
9. Sniffen to Painter, March 19, 1894, in IRAP, Reel 72; Painter to Welsh, March 22, 1894, in Reel 11.
10. IRA *Annual Report,* p. 25.
11. *City and State,* March 5, 1896, p. 6.
12. For the interest of the State of New York in this issue, see Helen M. Upton, *The Everett Report in Historical Perspective* (Albany: New York State American Revolution Bicentennial Commission, 1980), 53ff.
13. Mooney to Welsh, October 17, 1893, in IRAP, Reel 10.
14. Lee to Welsh, November 3, 1893, in IRAP, Reel 10.
15. Painter's report for January 1894 and March 1894, both in IRAP, Reel 101.

16. For a fuller discussion, see William T. Hagan, *United States-Comanche Relations* (New Haven: Yale University Press, 1976), pp. 250ff.

17. Quoted in Roy Gittinger, *The Formation of the State of Oklahoma 1803 – 1906* (Norman: University of Oklahoma Press, 1939), p. 223.

18. Welsh to Painter, December 29, 1894, in IRAP, Reel 73.

19. *Annual Report of the Board of Indian Commissioners for 1895,* pp. 6 – 7.

20. Garrett to Charles F. Meserve, July 8, 1896, in IRAP, Reel 73; Leupp to Welsh, June 19, 1896, in Reel 13.

21. Welsh to Leupp, June 22, 1896, in IRAP, Reel 73.

22. *The Dawes Commission and the Five Civilized Tribes of Indian Territory,* p. 11, in IRAP, Reel 102:B33.

23. "A Definite Step Toward Municipal Reform," in *The Forum,* XVII (April, 1894), 184.

24. Sniffen to Susan P. Wharton, May 2, 1894, in IRAP, Reel 73.

25. Executive committee minutes, June 2, 1896, in IRAP, Reel 99.

26. 29 Stat. 321.

27. Copy of Thayer to Markoe, June 3, 1896, in IRAP, Reel 13.

28. Coxe to Welsh, September 12, 1896, in IRAP, Reel 13; Welsh to Coxe, September 17, 1896, in Reel 73.

29. Leupp to Welsh, June 19, 1896, in IRAP, Reel 13.

30. Kane to Welsh, June 23, 1896, in IRAP, Reel 13.

31. Meserve to Welsh, June 29, 1896, in IRAP, Reel 13.

32. Welsh to F. F. Kane, June 25, 1896, in IRAP, Reel 73.

33. *The Dawes Commission and the Five Civilized Tribes of Indian Territory,* in IRAP, Reel 102:B33.

34. Coxe to Welsh, September 12, 1896, in IRAP, Reel 13.

35. Welsh to Coxe, September 17, 1896, in IRAP, Reel 73.

36. Coxe to Welsh, January 20, 1897, in IRAP, Reel 13.

37. Welsh to Leupp, October 8, 1896, in IRAP, Reel 74.

38. *Proceedings of the Fourteenth Annual Meeting of the Lake Mohonk Conference of Friends of the Indian,* 1896, pp. 112 – 13.

39. "Journal of the Twenty-Eighth Annual Meeting of Board of Indian Commissioners and Secretaries of the Religious Missionary Societies," in *Twenty-eighth Annual Report of the Board of Indian Commissioners, 1896,* p. 130.

40. Welsh to Lieutenant Plummer, April 14, 1893, in IRAP, Reel 72.

41. Welsh to acting secretary of the interior, June 14, 1893, in IRAP, Reel 72.

42. IRA *Annual Report,* 1893, p. 18. This amount included a donation from the association of $129.

43. Roosevelt to Welsh, October 17, 1893; Lodge to Welsh, October 17, 1893, both in IRAP, Reel 10.

44. As quoted in IRA circular dated February 2, 1894, in IRAP, Reel 11.

45. Welsh to Plummer, June 19, 1893, in IRAP, Reel 72; Plummer to Welsh, July 1, 1893, in Reel 10.

46. Welsh to Hoke Smith, January 29, 1894; Welsh to Plummer, April 16, 1894, both in IRAP, Reel 72.

47. Plummer to Welsh, September 19, 1893, in IRAP, Reel 10; Welsh to Philip Garrett, September 25, 1892, in Reel 72.

48. Welsh to Charles F. Meserve, October 5, 1895, in IRAP, Reel 73; Meserve to Welsh, October 8, 1895, in Reel 10; Leupp to Welsh, June 4, 1895, in Reel 12.

49. Williams to Welsh, December 5, 1894, in IRAP, Reel 12.

50. Welsh to Smith, January 4, 1895, in IRAP, Reel 73; Smith to Welsh, January 12, 1895, in Reel 12; Welsh to Smith, January 15, 1895, in Reel 73.

51. Welsh to Williams (telegram), January 21, 1895, in IRAP, Reel 73.

52. Welsh to Roosevelt, January 26, 1895; Welsh to Commissioner Browning, January 26, 1895, both in IRAP, Reel 73; Executive committee minutes, February 7, 1895, in Reel 99.
53. Welsh to David Scull, February 24, 1895; Welsh to Mrs. O. J. Hiles, February 27, 1895; Welsh to R. Fulton Cutting, March 2, 1895, all in IRAP, Reel 73.
54. IRA *Annual Report,* 1895, pp. 32–35, 63.
55. Welsh to Leupp, June 7 and June 11, 1895; Welsh to Mrs. Bigelow Lawrence, June 14, 1895, all in IRAP, Reel 73.
56. Welsh to Mrs. Alfred Hardy, January 8, 1896, in IRAP, Reel 73; Leupp to Welsh, February 10, 1896, in IRAP, Reel 12.
57. Welsh to Fannie Schuyler, March 29, 1895, in IRAP, Reel 12.
58. IRA *Annual Report,* 1895, pp. 14ff.
59. *City and State,* August 1, 1895, p. 2.
60. Executive committee minutes, August 8, 1895, in IRAP, Reel 99.
61. Leupp to Welsh, September 21, 1895, in IRAP, Reel 12; Leupp's report for October, 1895, in Reel 101.
62. *Annual Report of the Commissioner of Indian Affairs for 1896,* pp. 59–60.
63. F. G. Irwin, Jr., to commissioner of Indian affairs, August 25, 1897, in *Annual Report of the Commissioner of Indian Affairs for 1897,* p. 128.
64. The case is summarized in an IRA pamphlet, *The Attorney-General and Seven Indian Policemen of Cheyenne River Agency–A Case where to Serve Faithfully Came Near Meaning the Gallows,* in IRAP, Reel 102:B22.
65. Welsh to Leupp, March 7, 1895, in IRAP, Reel 73.
66. "IRA Office Report - June 6th to Oct. 3, 1895," in IRAP, Reel 100.
67. Welsh to Leupp, March 30, 1895, in IRAP, Reel 73.
68. Welsh to John Cadwallader, April 9, 1895, in IRAP, Reel 73.
69. The circular is to be found in IRAP, Reel 102:B22.
70. *Civil Service Reform Essential to a Successful Indian Administration,* in IRAP, Reel 102:B23.
71. Browning to Welsh, April 13, 1895, in IRAP, Reel 12.
72. Welsh to F. F. Kane, April 16, 1895, in IRAP, Reel 73.
73. Leupp to Welsh, November 30, 1895, in IRAP, Reel 12.
74. Painter to Welsh, March 17, 1893, in IRAP, Reel 10; Welsh to Painter, March 20, 1893, in Reel 72.
75. Painter to Welsh, June 5, 1893, in IRAP, Reel 10.
76. IRA *Annual Report,* 1893, p. 34.
77. Ibid., p. 36.
78. Welsh to Painter, March 6, 1894, in IRAP, Reel 72.
79. Welsh to Leupp, February 21, 1896, in IRAP, Reel 73; "Summary Report of Washington Agent for February, 1896, " in Reel 101.

CHAPTER 13

1. Welsh to Theodore Roosevelt, October 14, 1893; Welsh to Painter, October 14, 1893, both in IRAP, Reel 72.
2. Welsh to Abbott, October 16, 1893, in IRAP, Reel 72.
3. Welsh to Roosevelt, October 14, 1893; Welsh to Painter, October 14, 1893, both in IRAP, Reel 72.
4. Painter to Welsh, November 16, 1893, in IRAP, Reel 10.
5. Painter to Welsh, March 11, 1893, in IRAP, Reel 10.

6. John Higham, *Strangers in the Land* (New York: Atheneum, 1963), p. 60.
7. Welsh to King, November 4, 1893, in IRAP, Reel 72.
8. King to Welsh, November 25, 1893, in IRAP, Reel 10.
9. Welsh to Gibbons, November 7, 1893, in IRAP, Reel 72.
10. Welsh sent the cardinal's letter to Reverend Lyman Abbott to read, and Abbott promptly published it in *The Outlook,* to Welsh's embarrassment. See Welsh to Abbott, December 2, 1893, in IRAP, Reel 72; Abbott to Welsh, December 4, 1893, in Reel 10.
11. Welsh to William N. Hailmann, November 24, 1894, in IRAP, Reel 73.
12. Welsh to Edward Carey, May 29, 1894, in IRAP, Reel 73.
13. Welsh to Schurz, May 24, 1894, in IRAP, Reel 73.
14. Welsh to Charles Collins, June 5, 1894, in IRAP, Reel 73.
15. Welsh to Francis E. Leupp, March 2, 1896, in IRAP, Reel 73.
16. Welsh to Mrs. S. D. Wharton, May 24, 1894, in IRAP, Reel 73.
17. Welsh to Smith, April 12, 1894, in IRAP, Reel 72.
18. *Indian School Welfare,* in IRAP, Reel 102:B16.
19. Roosevelt to Welsh, May 28, 1894, in IRAP, Reel 11.
20. Welsh to Edward Carey, May 29, 1894; Welsh to Silas McBee, June 15, 1894, both in IRAP, Reel 73.
21. 29 Stat. 345.
22. Welsh to Evans Woolen, October 20, 1896, in IRAP, Reel 74.
23. IRA *Annual Report,* 1894, p. 11.
24. Welsh to Secretary Smith, January 17, 1894, in IRAP, Reel 72.
25. Leupp to Welsh, January 9, 1896, in IRAP, Reel 73.
26. IRA *Annual Report,* 1894, p. 11.
27. Welsh to Browning, January 11, 1894, in IRAP, Reel 72; Browning to Welsh, January 12, 1894, in Reel 10.
28. Welsh to Holman, January 23, 1894, in IRAP, Reel 72.
29. Leupp to Welsh, January 29, 1897, in IRAP, Reel 13.
30. Red Cloud et al. to Welsh, February 17, 1897, in IRAP, Reel 13.
31. The pamphlet appears in IRAP, Reel 102:B37.
32. IRA *Annual Report,* 1897, p. 29.
33. IRA *Annual Report,* 1896, p. 23.
34. The pamphlet appears in IRAP, Reel 102:B30.
35. IRA *Annual Report,* 1897, p. 24.
36. See IRA Office Report, October 3, 1893, in IRAP, Reel 100.
37. Circular dated December 21, 1893, and signed by Welsh, in IRAP, Reel 72.
38. Painter to Welsh, February 27, 1894, in IRAP, Reel 73.
39. It was finally determined that it would cost more to ship the eagle east than it was worth. The novel was by Frances C. Sparhawk, founder of Indian Industries League, on whose board Welsh sat. The IRA purchased 500 copies of the novel for resale and finally had to give away the last 100.

CHAPTER 14

1. Welsh to Brosius, January 13, 1899, in IRAP, Reel 74.
2. Welsh to Philip C. Garrett, December 17, 1898, in IRAP, Reel 74.
3. Welsh to Q. W. Kelsey, March 30, 1900, in IRAP, Reel 75.
4. Welsh to Fanny Welsh, November 27, 1896, in IRAP, Reel 74.
5. Welsh to Reverend B. S. Lasseter, April 3, 1897, in IRAP, Reel 74.

6. *City and State,* June 23, 1898, p. 671.

7. *City and State,* June 30, 1898, p. 689.

8. *City and State,* July 28, 1898, p. 55.

9. Welsh to Henry W. Farnam, November 28, 1898, in IRAP, Reel 74.

10. *City and State,* December 1, 1898, p. 340.

11. Welsh to Samuel Morris, August 9, 1899, in the Quaker Collection.

12. Welsh to Mrs. E. Stuart Patterson, January 17, 1900, in IRAP, Reel 75.

13. "Memorandum Concerning the Relations of the Indian Rights Association and City and State," April 17, 1901, in IRAP, Reel 15.

14. Welsh to Henry C. Lea, December 1, 1898, in IRAP, Reel 74.

15. Welsh to Samuel Morris, Quaker Collection.

16. Welsh to Miss E. F. Mason, May 1, 1900, in IRAP, Reel 75.

17. *City and State,* June 21, 1900, p. 394.

18. Welsh to Bishop Whipple, May 1, 1900, in IRAP, Reel 75.

19. Ibid.

20. "Impressions of a Southern College," in *City and State,* April 19, 1900, p. 250; Welsh to Miss E. F. Mason, May 1, 1900, in IRAP, Reel 75.

21. Sniffen to Reverend H. Burt, April 14, 1901, in IRAP, Reel 75.

22. Sniffen to F. F. Avery, May 5, 1901, in IRAP, Reel 75.

23. Sniffen to Brosius, March 13, 1901, in IRAP, Reel 75.

24. Leupp to Welsh, December 29, 1897, in IRAP, Reel 24.

25. Leupp had earlier recommended him for an inspectorship in the Indian Service. See Leupp to Welsh, March 27, 1897, in IRAP, Reel 13.

26. Leupp to Welsh, January 24, 1898, in IRAP, Reel 13.

27. Executive committee minutes, April 6, 1898, in IRAP, Reel 99.

28. Welsh to Leupp, February 11, 1898, in IRAP, Reel 74.

29. Welsh to Bliss, March 4, 1897, in IRAP, Reel 74.

30. Leupp to Welsh, March 27, 1897, in IRAP, Reel 13.

31. Bliss to Welsh, June 24, 1897, in IRAP, Reel 13.

32. Leupp to Welsh, June 14, 1897, in IRAP, Reel 13.

33. "Monthly Report of Washington Agency," February 28, 1898, in IRAP, Reel 133.

34. Brosius to Welsh, December 14, 1898, in IRAP, Reel 14.

35. Brosius to Welsh, January 27, 1899, in IRAP, Reel 14.

36. Welsh to Brosius, December 23, 1898, in IRAP, Reel 14.

37. Welsh to Brosius, April 10, 1899, in IRAP, Reel 74.

38. Hitchcock to Welsh, May 4, 1899, in IRAP, Reel 14.

39. Jones to Welsh, October 26, 1897, in IRAP, Reel 13.

40. Welsh to George McAneny, December 21, 1898, in IRAP, Reel 74.

41. Jones to Welsh, January 11, 1899, in IRAP, Reel 14.

42. Jones to Welsh, January 3, 1899, in IRAP, Reel 14.

43. Jones to all agents, May 5, 1899, in IRAP, Reel 14.

44. Brosius to Welsh, January 27, 1899; Jones to Welsh, January 30, 1899, both in IRAP, Reel 14.

45. Welsh to William McKinley, February 27, 1897; Welsh to Secretary Bliss, March 10, 1897, both in IRAP, Reel 74.

46. Welsh to Leupp, February 12, 1897, in IRAP, Reel 74.

47. *City and State,* April 15, 1897, p. 2.

48. IRA *Annual Report,* 1896, p. 6.

49. *City and State,* February 4, 1897, p. 2.

50. The pamphlet appears in IRAP, Reel 102:B38.

51. Welsh to Roosevelt, April 8, 1897, in IRAP, Reel 74.
52. Roosevelt to Leupp, January 29, 1898, in Roosevelt Papers, Reel 315.
53. Welsh to Mrs. Wm. H. Schieffelin, in IRAP, Reel 74.
54. Welsh to Cardinal Gibbons, February 5, 1898, in IRAP, Reel 74.
55. Cardinal Gibbons to Welsh, February 7, 1898, in IRAP, Reel 133; Welsh to Leupp, February 11, 1898, in IRAP, Reel 74.
56. The petition for Hailmann appears in *City and State,* February 10, 1898, p. 315.
57. Welsh to Bishop O. W. Whitaker, May 27, 1898, in IRAP, Reel 74.
58. The pamphlet appears in IRAP, Reel 102:B46.
59. Welsh to Reel, June 8, 1898, in IRAP, Reel 74.
60. *City and State,* June 9, 1898, p. 636.
61. Reel to Welsh, May 22, 1898, in IRAP, Reel 133.
62. Welsh to Brosius, December 23, 1898, in IRAP, Reel 74.
63. Welsh to Brosius, December 28, 1900, in IRAP, Reel 75.
64. Welsh to Bliss, January 5, 1898, in IRAP, Reel 74; Bliss to Welsh, January 10, 1898, in Reel 13.
65. Brosius to Welsh, November 23, 1899, in IRAP, Reel 14.
66. "Monthly Report of the Washington Agency," February 28, 1899, in IRAP, Reel 133.
67. Executive committee minutes, March 7, 1900, in IRAP, Reel 99.
68. IRA *Annual Report,* 1900, p. 16.
69. Brosius to Welsh, August 11, 1899, in IRAP, Reel 14.
70. Brosius to Welsh, November 22, 1900, in IRAP, Reel 15.
71. "Monthly Report of the Washington Agency," May 1, 1901, in IRAP, Reel 134.
72. "IRA Office Report, May 2, to June 5, 1901," in IRAP, Reel 100.
73. Welsh to Reverend Joshua Kimber, February 1, 1899, in IRAP, Reel 74.
74. Welsh to Jones, January 3, 1899, in IRAP, Reel 74.
75. Clark to Welsh, August 28, 1899, in IRAP, Reel 14.
76. Gates to Welsh, December 4, 1899, in IRAP, Reel 14.
77. IRA *Annual Report,* 1899, p. 29.
78. Brosius to Welsh, May 18, 1898, in IRAP, Reel 13.
79. Welsh to Commissioner Jones, Novemberr 21, 1899, in IRAP, Reel 75.
80. The priest was Father Degmann; see his letter to Sniffen, in IRAP, Reel 134.
81. Brosius to Welsh, October 5, 1900, and February 15, 1901, both in IRAP, Reel 15; Brosius to Commissioner Jones, March 22, 1901, in Reel 134.
82. Welsh to John V. Farwell, Jr., February 11, 1901, in IRAP, Reel 75.
83. Jones to Welsh, February 18, 1901, in IRAP, Reel 15.
84. Sniffen to Leupp, January 18, 1897, in IRAP, Reel 74.
85. Welsh to Mrs. James C. Fisk, March 23, 1899. On another occasion, Welsh described Mrs. Cox as "a woman of coarse fibre, little education, tremendous will power, and by nature not veracious, and not scrupulous in her methods of doing things." See Welsh to Leupp, December 3, 1897, in IRAP, Reel 74.
86. Welsh to Henry Cabot Lodge, February 23, 1899, in IRAP, Reel 74.
87. Brosius to Welsh, February 20, 1899, in IRAP, Reel 14.
88. Welsh to Miss Catherine Meredith, February 21, 1899, in IRAP, Reel 74.
89. Brosius to Sniffen, July 25, 1899, in IRAP, Reel 14; Sniffen to Brosius, August 21, 1899, in Reel 74; Sniffen to Brosius, September 11, 1899, in Reel 75; *City and State,* November 23, 1899, p. 329.

CHAPTER 15

1. For background on the case, see Brosius to Welsh, July 25, 1901, in IRAP, Reel 15, and IRA *Annual Report,* 1899, p. 4–5, 81–82.

2. "Monthly Report of Washington Agency," April 30, 1897, in IRAP, Reel 133.

3. Welsh to Leupp, June 18, 1897, in IRAP, Reel 74.

4. Welsh to Mrs. Sara Palfrey, June 22, 1897, in IRAP, Reel 74.

5. Welsh said of his pledge: "I cannot afford to lose the one thousand dollars, in justice to my family, but I took this step because I saw at a critical juncture that it was necessary in order to push the matter through and encourage others." Welsh to Mrs. Eckley B. Coxe, June 25, 1897, in IRAP, Reel 74.

6. Welsh to Joshua W. Davis, June 24, 1897, in IRAP, Reel 74.

7. Welsh to Shirley Ward, June 24, 1897, in IRAP, Reel 74.

8. Brosius to Welsh, January 13, 1899, in IRAP, Reel 14; IRA Office Report, October 1 to November 1, 1899, in Reel 100.

9. Brosius to Welsh, October 16, 21, and 28, 1899, all in IRAP, Reel 14. In 1897 Mother Katharine Drexel also had agreed to support the IRA bond if necessary; see Leupp to Welsh, June 26, 1897, in Reel 13.

10. For the last stages of this complicated case, see Brosius to Welsh, February 20, 1902, in IRAP, Reel 16; Welsh to Rev. Dr. Henry G. Ganss, March 11, 1902, in Reel 75; IRA *Annual Report*, 1903, pp. 30–31.

11. The pamphlet can be found in IRAP, Reel 102:B47.

12. *An Appeal on Behalf of the Apaches, Kiowas, and Comanches*, in IRAP, Reel 102:B51.

13. The letter can be found in IRAP, Reel 102:B50A.

14. "Monthly Report of the Washington Agency," February 28, 1899, in IRAP, Reel 133; Brosius to Welsh, March 6, 1899, in Reel 14. In the House, Brosius had had the assistance of a cousin who was in the Pennsylvania delegation; in the Senate he had worked through Oliver H. Platt of Connecticut.

15. The large pasture was later used to provide allotments for Indians born after the agreement was ratified.

16. Brosius to Welsh, June 13, 1900, in IRAP, Reel 15.

17. IRA Office Report, June 6, to October 1, 1901, in IRAP, Reel 100.

18. Leupp to Sniffen, June 25, 1901, in IRAP, Reel 134; Leupp to Welsh, June 26, 1901, in Reel 15.

19. Executive committee minutes, March 5, 1902, in IRAP, Reel 99; "Report of the Washington agency, March 4, 1902," in Reel 16; Welsh to Brosius, March 11, 1902, in Reel 16.

20. IRA *Annual Report*, 1902, p. 71.

21. Hagan, *United States-Comanche Relations*, pp. 262ff.

22. Brosius to Welsh, July 30, 1902, in IRAP, Reel 16.

23. Randlett's report, September 1, 1902, in *Annual Report of the Commissioner of Indian Affairs for 1888*, p. 289.

24. Randlett to Welsh, January 8, 1903, in IRAP, Reel 134.

25. 187 U.S. Supreme Court 553.

26. IRA *Annual Report*, 1903, p. 24.

27. *The Record of Thirty Years*, p. 8, in IRAP, Reel 102:B87.

28. Grinnell to Indian Rights Association, November 20, 1897, in IRAP, Reel 13.

29. Welsh to Mrs. Eckley B. Coxe, November 22, 1897, in IRAP, Reel 74.

30. Welsh to Leupp, November 24, 1897, in IRAP, Reel 74.

31. Executive committee minutes, December 1, 1897, in IRAP, Reel 99.

32. Leupp to Welsh, November 23, 1897, in IRAP, Reel 13; Sniffen to Bishop Brewer, January 18, 1898, in Reel 74.

33. Brosius to Sniffen, July 18, 1898, in IRAP, Reel 133.

34. The pamphlet may be found in IRAP, Reel 102:B48.

35. Ibid., p. 14.

36. Welsh to Charles Wetherill, September 24, 1898, in IRAP, Reel 74.

37. Welsh to Henry W. Farnam, November 28, 1898, in IRAP, Reel 74.

38. Brosius to Welsh, June 6, 1899, in IRAP, Reel 14.
39. Sniffen to Reverend I. Newton Ritner, in IRAP, Reel 14.
40. *City and State,* September 21, 1899, p. 182.
41. *City and State,* May 16, 1901, p. 314.
42. Sniffen to Grinnell, July 22, 1901, in IRAP, Reel 75.
43. Welsh to Spotted Hawk, March 23, 1899, in IRAP, Reel 74.
44. "Monthly Report of Washington Agency," May 31, 1897, in IRAP, Reel 133.
45. The pamphlet may be found in IRAP, Reel 102:B42.
46. IRA *Annual Report,* 1900, pp. 38–40.
47. Brosius to Welsh, August 14, 1900, in IRAP, Reel 15.
48. Brosius to Welsh, August 29, and September 5, 1900, both in IRAP, Reel 15.
49. *Annual Report of the Commissioner of Indian Affairs for 1901,* p. 114; IRA *Annual Report,* 1901, p. 34.
50. "Monthly Report of the Washington Agency," May 1, 1901, in IRAP, Reel 134.
51. IRA Office Report, June 15 to October 3, 1899, in IRAP, Reel 100.
52. Brosius to Welsh, July 25, 1899, in IRAP, Reel 14.
53. IRA *Annual Report,* 1899, pp. 69–72; IRA *Annual Report,* 1900, pp. 63–64; IRA *Annual Report,* 1901, pp. 67–70.
54. Welsh to Roosevelt, February 8, 1900, in IRAP, Reel 133.
55. Roosevelt to Welsh, February 10, 1900, in IRAP, Reel 133.
56. Roosevelt to Welsh, June 13, 1900, in IRAP, Reel 133; Welsh to Roosevelt, June 15, 1900, in Reel 75; Roosevelt to Garrett, Dec. 4, 1900, in Theodore Roosevelt Manuscripts, Reel 319. I am indebted to Laurence M. Hauptman for providing me with the last citation.
57. Brosius to Welsh, February 20, 1900, in IRAP, Reel 15; Sniffen to Roosevelt, February 21, 1900, in Reel 133.
58. Roosevelt to Welsh, June 13, 1900, in IRAP, Reel 133.
59. *City and State,* July 25, 1901, p. 51.
60. *Thirty-second Annual Report of the Board of Indian Commissioners, 1900,* p. 22.
61. IRA *Annual Report,* 1901, pp. 21–29.
62. *Annual Report of the Commissioner of Indian Affairs for 1899,* pp. 135–36.
63. *Proceedings of the Sixteenth Annual Meeting of the Lake Mohonk Conference of Friends of the Indian 1898,* p. 27.
64. Welsh to Frank Wood, November 26, 1898, in IRAP, Reel 74.
65. *City and State,* December 1, 1898, p. 340.
66. Brosius to Welsh, January 8, 1900, in IRAP, Reel 15.
67. Brosius to Welsh, November 17, 1898, in IRAP, Reel 14.
68. *Proceedings of the Sixteenth Annual Meeting of the Lake Mohonk Conference of Friends of the Indian 1898,* p. 21.
69. Ibid., p. 22.
70. Brosius to Welsh, November 26, 1898, in IRAP, Reel 14.
71. Brosius to Welsh, December 19, 1898, in IRAP, Reel 14.
72. "Report of Washington Agency, January, 1899," in IRAP, Reel 133; IRA *Annual Report,* 1899, pp. 51ff.
73. IRA *Annual Report,* 1899, p. 54.
74. Brosius to Welsh, February 13, 1900, in IRAP, Reel 15.
75. Brosius to Welsh, February 16, 1900, in IRAP, Reel 15.
76. Brosius to Welsh, January 9, 1900, in IRAP, Reel 15.
77. *The Urgent Need of New Legislation to Protect the Timber Interests of the Chippewa Indians in Minnesota,* in IRAP, Reel 102:B53.
78. Report of Agent G. L. Scott, June 27, 1902, in *Annual Report of the Commissioner of Indian Affairs for 1902,* p. 221.

79. Sniffen to Dissette, December 5, 1894, in IRAP, Reel 73.
80. Welsh to Secretary Bliss, April 6, 1897, in IRAP, Reel 74.
81. Brosius to Welsh, January 4, 1899, in IRAP, Reel 14; IRA Office Report, January 5, 1899 to February 1, 1899, in Reel 100.
82. IRA Office Report, February 1, 1899 to March 1, 1899, in IRAP, Reel 100. About $60 was sent to the field matron of the Hopis, who also were suffering from smallpox.
83. Leupp to Welsh, March 20, 1899, in IRAP, Reel 14.
84. Brosius to Welsh, April 29, 1899, in IRAP, Reel 14.
85. Brosius to Welsh, July 29, 1899, in IRAP, Reel 14.

CHAPTER 16

1. J. LeRoy Smith to Brosius, July 12, 1902, in IRAP, Reel 75.
2. Sniffen to Brosius, June 1, 1903, in IRAP, Reel 75.
3. *City and State,* May 12, 1904, p. 289.
4. Ibid.
5. Charles Henry Strout to Welsh, May 10, 1904, in IRAP, Reel 17.
6. Schurz to Welsh, May 12, 1904, in IRAP, Reel 17.
7. *City and State,* May 12, 1904, p. 290.
8. Welsh to Garrett, May 21, 1904, in IRAP, Reel 76.
9. Welsh to George H. Earle, October 3, 1901, in IRAP, Reel 15.
10. *City and State,* October 3, 1901, p. 214.
11. Roosevelt to Henry Cabot Lodge, October 16, 1892, in Elting E. Morison et al., eds., *The Letters of Theodore Roosevelt,* 8 vols. (Cambridge: Harvard University Press, 1951—1954), I, 293.
12. Roosevelt to Bonaparte, March 30, 1901, in Morison, *Letters of Theodore Roosevelt,* III, 36.
13. For a general discussion of the movement of which Herbert Welsh was a part, see Richard E. Welch, Jr., *Response to Imperialism* (Chapel Hill: The University of North Carolina Press, 1979), particularly pp. 134ff.
14. George R. Bishop to Welsh, March 17, 1902, in IRAP, Reel 16.
15. *City and State,* April 24, 1902, p. 263.
16. Ibid.
17. *City and State,* September 25, 1902, p. 199.
18. *The Albany Argus,* quoted in *City and State,* May 7, 1903, p. 367.
19. Roosevelt to Taft, December 26, 1902, in Morison, *Letters of Theodore Roosevelt,* III, 2536.
20. Roosevelt to Elihu Root, July 17, 1903, in Morison, *Letters of Theodore Roosevelt,* III, 519.
21. Roosevelt to Abbott, September 5, 1903, in Morison, *Letters of Theodore Roosevelt,* III, 590.
22. Executive committee minutes, June 3, 1903, in IRAP, Reel 99.
23. Leupp to Welsh, October 12, 1904, in IRAP, Reel 17.
24. Welsh to Brosius, September 25, 1922, in IRAP, Reel 134.
25. Leupp to Welsh, October 7, 1901, in IRAP, Reel 15.
26. Brosius to Sniffen, November 3 and December 4, 1903, both in IRAP, Reel 16; Brosius to Sniffen, March 22, 1904, in Reel 17.
27. Sniffen to Brosius, January 23, 1902, in IRAP, Reel 75.
28. Brosius to Welsh, January 27, 1902, in IRAP, Reel 16.

29. "Report of the Washington Agency," September 30, 1901, in IRAP, Reel 134.
30. Executive committee minutes, February 4, 1903, in IRAP, Reel 99; Brosius to Sniffen, February 10, 1903, in Reel 16; Brosius to President Roosevelt, March 10, 1903, in Reel 134.
31. "Report of the Washington Agency," September 30, 1901, in IRAP, Reel 134.
32. Brosius to Welsh, October 15, 1901, in IRAP, Reel 134.
33. IRA *Annual Report,* 1902, p. 16.
34. IRA *Annual Report,* 1903, pp. 50ff.; Brosius to Sniffen, November 3 and November 20, 1903, both in IRAP, Reel 16.
35. Executive committee minutes, October 7, 1903, in IRAP, Reel 99.
36. Brosius to Sniffen, December 1, 1903, in IRAP, Reel 16.
37. Executive committee minutes, December 2, 1903, in IRAP, Reel 99; Sniffen to Brosius, December 5, 1903, in Reel 76.
38. Executive committee minutes, October 7 and November 4, 1903, both in IRAP, Reel 99; Sniffen to Secretary Hitchcock, November 11, 1903, in Reel 76; Brosius to Sniffen, May 31, 1904, in Reel 17; IRA *Annual Report,* 1904, pp. 62–63.
39. Sniffen to Brosius, October 28, 1902, in IRAP, Reel 75; Executive committee minutes, November 5, 1902, in Reel 99.
40. Brosius to Welsh, November 22, 1902, in IRAP, Reel 134.
41. Roosevelt to E. L. Bonner, in Morison, *Letters of Theodore Roosevelt,* III, 254.
42. Executive committee minutes, February 4, 1903, in IRAP, Reel 99; Garrett to Roosevelt, February 25, 1903, in Reel 134.
43. *City and State,* September 24, 1903, p. 200.
44. Welsh to Mrs. Edith A. Talbot, October 21, 1902, in IRAP, Reel 75.
45. *Proceedings of the Twenty-first Annual Meeting of the Lake Mohonk Conference of Friends of the Indians,* 1903, pp, 40–44.
46. *City and State,* November 5, 1903, p. 302; Jones to Sniffen, November 6, 1903, in IRAP, Reel 16.
47. J. LeRoy Smith to Archbishop Ryan, November 4 and November 13, 1901, both in IRAP, Reel 75; Mother Leopoldine to Welsh, December 3, 1901, in Reel 15.
48. For background on Father Ganss, see Prucha, *The Churches and the Indian Schools,* pp. 50–51.
49. Ganss to Welsh, February 28, 1902, in IRAP, Reel 16.
50. Welsh to Ganss, March 1, 1902, in IRAP, Reel 75.
51. Executive committee minutes, March 5, 1902, in IRAP, Reel 99.
52. Ganss to Welsh, March 18, 1902, in IRAP, Reel 16.
53. Welsh to Garrett, March 18, 1902, in IRAP, Reel 75.
54. Welsh to Roosevelt, March 20, 1902, in IRAP, Reel 75.
55. Welsh to Bonaparte, April 5, 1902, in IRAP, Reel 72.
56. W. R. Johnson to Brosius, January 27, 1903, in IRAP, Reel 16.
57. Brosius to Sniffen, February 10, 1903, in IRAP, Reel 16.

CHAPTER 17

1. 32 Stat. 1009. For Brosius's account of this legislation, see IRA *Annual Report,* 1903, pp. 42–43.
2. The pamphlet appears in IRAP, Reel 102:B67.
3. Brosius to Sniffen, May 3, 1904, in IRAP, Reel 17.
4. 33 Stat. 254.
5. IRA *Annual Report,* 1904, pp. 54–55.
6. Executive committee minutes, January 8, 1902, in IRAP, Reel 99.

7. "Report of the Washington Agency," January 9, 1902, in IRAP, Reel 134.

8. *City and State*, February 6, 1902, p. 85.

9. The report, dated March 17, 1902, can be found in IRAP, Reel 16.

10. Executive committee minutes, February 5, 1902, in IRAP, Reel 99; Philadelphia *Ledger*, quoted in *City and State*, January 30, 1902, pp. 74–75.

11. Roosevelt to Hitchcock, January 30, 1902, in Morison, *Letters of Theodore Roosevelt*, III, 223.

12. Brosius to Welsh, April 21, 1902, in IRAP, Reel 16.

13. *City and State*, June 5, 1902, p. 356.

14. Sniffen to Mrs. Theo. F. Randolph, June 10, 1902, in IRAP, Reel 75.

15. *City and State*, June 19, 1902, p. 389.

16. *The Action of the Interior Department in Forcing the Standing Rock Indians to Lease Their Lands to Cattle Syndicates*, in IRAP, Reel 102:B61.

17. *City and State*, June 19, 1902, pp. 389–90. *The Standing Rock Indians and the Grazing Leases*, in IRAP, Reel 102:B63.

18. IRA *Annual Report*, 1902, pp. 33–34.

19. Among other tactics, Brosius supplied Francis Leupp with material for an anti-Stewart article which appeared in the New York *Evening Post;* see Brosius to Welsh, December 16, 1901, in IRAP, Reel 15.

20. *Congressional Record*, 35:4805.

21. Ibid., p. 4860.

22. Quick Bear to Welsh or Sniffen, January 1904, in IRAP, Reel 16.

23. Brosius to Sniffen, February 8, 1904, in IRAP, Reel 16.

24. Both the Leupp and Kennan articles are reprinted in *Another "Century of Dishonor"?*, in IRAP, Reel 102:B68.

25. The memorial also appears in *Another "Century of Dishonor"?*

26. Brosius to Sniffen, February 25, 1904, in IRAP, Reel 16.

27. Roosevelt to Gamble, February 15, 1904, in Morison, *Letters of Theodore Roosevelt*, IV, 729.

28. Brosius to Sniffen, February 23, 1904, in IRAP, Reel 16.

29. The pamphlet appears in IRAP, Reel 102:B68.

30. 33 Stat. 254.

31. For example, see Sniffen to Miss Ida M. Mason, October 8, 1904, in IRAP, Reel 76.

32. In the first month, which would have seen the greatest surge of activity, only 938 claims were filed by settlers; see *Annual Report of the Commissioner of Indian Affairs for 1904*, p. 4.

33. Brosius to Welsh, January 2 and January 9, 1904, both in IRAP, Reel 15.

34. Brosius to Sniffen, August 16, 1903, in IRAP, Reel 134.

35. The letter is dated August 15, 1903, and is in IRAP, Reel 134.

36. Grinnell to Brosius, August 17, 1903, in IRAP, Reel 16.

37. The report was reprinted in IRA *Annual Report*, 1903, pp. 4–11.

38. Hitchcock to Garrett, August 20 and August 29, 1903, both in IRAP, Reel 134.

39. Eric F. Goldman, *Charles J. Bonaparte* (Baltimore: The Johns Hopkins Press, 1943).

40. Garrett to Bonaparte, September 17, 1903, in IRAP, Reel 76.

41. Sniffen to Bonaparte, September 18, 1903; Sniffen to Brosius, September 19, 1903, both in IRAP, Reel 76.

42. Executive committee minutes, October 7 and October 26, 1903, both in IRAP, Reel 99; Garrett to Bonaparte, October 28, 1903, in Reel 76.

43. Goldman, *Charles J. Bonaparte*, p. 70.

44. Bonaparte to Sniffen, January 1, 1904, in IRAP, Reel 134.

45. The report appeared as Senate Document 189, 58th Congress, 2 session, "Report of Charles J. Bonaparte and Clinton Rogers Woodruff, Special Inspectors."

46. Ibid., p. 39.
47. Ibid., p. 40.
48. *City and State,* March 10, 1904, p. 149.
49. Goldman, *Charles J. Bonaparte,* p. 72.
50. 33 Stat. 205.
51. Quoted in Sniffen to Brosius, April 22, 1904, in IRAP, Reel 76.
52. Sniffen to Brosius, April 10, 1904, in IRAP, Reel 76.
53. Goldman, *Charles J. Bonaparte,* p. 75.
54. Executive committee minutes, April 6, 1904, in IRAP, Reel 99.
55. Bonaparte to Sniffen, September 9, 1904, in IRAP, Reel 134.
56. *Proceedings of the Twenty-second Annual Meeting of the Lake Mohonk Conference of Friends of the Indian and Other Dependent Peoples 1904,* p. 15.
57. Goldman, *Charles J. Bonaparte,* p. 78.
58. IRA *Annual Report,* 1904, p. 65.
59. Welsh to Sniffen, November 13, 1904, in IRAP, Reel 17.

CHAPTER 18

1. Jones to all agents, May 5, 1899, in IRAP, Reel 14.
2. Welsh to Q. W. Kelsey, March 30, 1900, in IRAP, Reel 75.
3. Welsh to Roosevelt, February 15, 1893, in IRAP, Reel 72.
4. Welsh to F. F. Ellinwood, February 2, 1888, in IRAP, Reel 69.
5. Welsh to Samuel Morris, Quaker Collection.
6. Welsh to Edward H. Magill, May 2, 1894, in IRAP, Reel 73.
7. Welsh to Benjamin Harrison, November 7, 1886, in IRAP, Reel 68.
8. Welsh, *Report of A Visit to the Great Sioux Reserve,* p. 42, in IRAP, Reel 102:A3.
9. *Indian Truth,* September 1941, p. 1.

Bibliography

Manuscripts

Historical Society of Pennsylvania
    Indian Rights Association Papers (microfilm edition by Microfilming Corporation of America, Glen Rock, New Jersey, 1975, 136 reels)
National Archives
    Letters Received by the Office of Indian Affairs
    Letter Books of the Office of Indian Affairs
    Letter Books of the Indian Division, Office of the Secretary of the Interior
    Letters Received by the Indian Division, Office of the Secretary of the Interior
    Records of the Board of Indian Commissioners
Library of Congress
    Theodore Roosevelt Papers
    Henry L. Dawes Papers
Haverford College Library
    Quaker Collection
Beinecke Library, Yale University
    Richard H. Pratt Papers
Harvard Law School Library
    James Bradley Thayer Papers
Collis P. Huntington Memorial Library, Hampton Institute
    General Samuel Chapman Armstrong Papers

Annual Reports

Commissioner of Indian Affairs
Secretary of the Interior

Annual Reports *(continued)*
    Board of Indian Commissioners
    Proceedings of the Annual Meeting of the Lake Mohonk Conference

Secondary Sources

Anderson, Grant K. "Samuel D. Hinman and the Opening of the Black Hills." *Nebraska History* 60 (Winter 1979), 520–42.

Armstrong, S. C. *The Indian Question*. Hampton: Normal School Steam Press, 1883.

Baltzell, E. Digby. *Puritan Boston and Quaker Philadelphia*. New York: The Free Press, 1979.

———. *Philadelphia Gentlemen*. Chicago: Quandrangle Books, 1971.

Bannan, Helen Marie. "Reformers and the 'Indian Problem,' 1878–1887 and 1922–1934. Ph.D. dissertation; Syracuse University, 1976.

Burgess, Larry E. "The Lake Mohonk Conference on the Indian, 1883–1916." Ph.D. dissertation; Claremont Graduate School, 1972.

DeMallie, Raymond J. "The Lakota Ghost Dance: An Ethnohistorical Account." *Pacific Historical Review* 51 (November 1982), 385–405.

Fritz, Henry E. *The Movement for Indian Assimilation, 1860–1890*. Philadelphia: University of Pennsylvania Press, 1963.

Gilcreast, Everett Arthur. "Richard Henry Pratt and American Indian Policy." Ph.D. dissertation; Yale University, 1967.

Gittinger, Roy. *The Formation of the State of Oklahoma 1803–1906*. Norman: University of Oklahoma Press, 1939.

Goldman, Eric F. *Charles J. Bonaparte*. Baltimore: The Johns Hopkins Press, 1943.

Goodman, David Michael. "Apaches as Prisoners of War, 1886–1894." Ph.D. dissertation; Texas Christian University, 1969.

Grantham, Dewey W. *Hoke Smith and the Politics of the New South*. Baton Rouge: Louisiana State University Press, 1958.

Hagan, William T. "Civil Service Commissioner Theodore Roosevelt and the Indian Rights Association." *Pacific Historical Review* 44 (May 1975), 187–200.

———. *Indian Police and Judges*. New Haven: Yale University Press, 1966.

———. *United States–Comanche Relations*. New Haven: Yale University Press, 1976.

Harrison, Benjamin. *Public Papers and Addresses of Benjamin Harrison*. New York: Kraus Reprint Company, 1969.

Hauptman, Laurence M. "Governor Theodore Roosevelt and Indians of New York State." *Proceedings of the American Philosophical Society* 112 (February 1975), 1–7.

―――. "Senecas and Subdividers: Resistance to Allotment of Indian Lands in New York, 1875–1906." *Prologue* 9 (Summer 1977), 105–16.

Higham, John. *Strangers in the Land.* New York: Atheneum, 1963.

Holm, Tom. "Indians and Progressives, From Vanishing Policy to the Indian New Deal." Ph.D. dissertation, University of Oklahoma, 1978.

Howe, M. A. DeWolfe. *The Life and Labors of Bishop Hare.* New York: Sturgis & Walton, 1911.

Hoxie, Frederick E. "The End of the Savage: Indian Policy in the United States Senate, 1880–1900." *Chronicles of Oklahoma* 45 (Summer 1977), 157–79.

Kvasnicka, Robert M., and Herman J. Viola, editors. *The Commissioners of Indian Affairs, 1824–1977.* Lincoln: University of Nebraska Press, 1979.

Lamar, Howard Roberts. *Dakota Territory, 1861–1889.* New Haven: Yale University Press, 1956.

Lukacs, John. *Philadelphia Patricians and Philistines, 1900–1950.* New York: Farrar, Straus, Giroux, 1981.

Marchand, C. Roland. *The American Peace Movement and Social Reform, 1898–1918.* Princeton: Princeton University Press, 1972.

Mardock, Robert Winston. *The Reformers and the American Indian.* Columbia: University of Missouri Press, 1971.

Morison, Elting E., et al., editors. *The Letters of Theodore Roosevelt,* 8 volumes. Cambridge: Harvard University Press, 1951–54.

Murphy, James B. *L. Q. C. Lamar: Pragmatic Patriot.* Baton Rouge: Louisiana State University Press, 1973.

Olson, James C. *Red Cloud and the Sioux Problem.* Lincoln: University of Nebraska Press, 1965.

Phinney, Edward Steel. "Alfred B. Meacham: Promoter of Indian Reform." Ph.D. dissertation; University of Oregon, 1963.

Priest, Loring Benson. *Uncle Sam's Stepchildren: The Reformation of United States Indian Policy, 1865–1887.* New Brunswick: Rutgers University Press, 1942.

Prucha, Francis Paul. *American Indian Policy in Crisis: Reformers and the Indian, 1865–1900.* Norman: University of Oklahoma Press, 1976.

―――. *The Churches and the Indian Schools, 1888–1912.* Lincoln: University of Nebraska Press, 1979.

Quinton, Amelia Stone. "Care of the Indian." In Annie Nathan Meyer, editor, *Woman's Work in America.* 1891. Reprint. New York: Arno Press, 1972, pp. 373–391.

Schirmer, Daniel B. *Republic or Empire: American Resistance to the Philippine War.* Cambridge: Schenckman Publishing Company, 1972.

Upton, Helen M. *The Everett Report in Historical Perspective.* Albany: New York State American Revolution Bicentennial Commission, 1980.

Utley, Robert M. *The Last Days of the Sioux Nation.* New Haven: Yale University Press, 1963.

Welch, Richard E., Jr. *Response to Imperialism.* Chapel Hill: University of North Carolina Press, 1979.

Welsh, Herbert. "A Definite Step Toward Municipal Reform." *The Forum* 17 (April 1894), 184.

———. *The Other Man's Country: An Appeal to Conscience.* Philadelphia: J. B. Lippincott Company, 1900.

———. "Samuel Chapman Armstrong." *Educational Review* (September 1893), 105–25.

Westing, Irene Joanne. "Amelia Stone Quinton." In Edward T. James, editor, *Notable American Women, 1607–1950.* Cambridge: Harvard University Press, 1971, vol. 3, pp. 108–10.

Index

Page numbers for illustrations are in italics